Sharon Macdonald (ed.)
Doing Diversity in Museums and Heritage

Cultural Heritage Studies | Volume 1

Sharon Macdonald is Alexander von Humboldt Professor of Social Anthropology at Humboldt-Universität zu Berlin, where she directs the Hermann von Helmholtz-Zentrum für Kulturtechnik and CARMAH (the Centre for Anthropological Research on Museums and Heritage).

Sharon Macdonald (ed.)

Doing Diversity in Museums and Heritage

A Berlin Ethnography

[transcript]

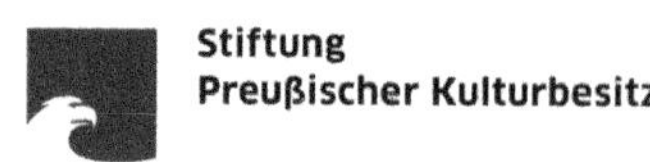

Bibliographic information published by the Deutsche Nationalbibliothek
The Deutsche Nationalbibliothek lists this publication in the Deutsche Nationalbibliografie; detailed bibliographic data are available in the Internet at http://dnb.d-nb.de

First published in 2023 by transcript Verlag, Bielefeld

https://www.transcript-verlag.de/

Cover layout: Maria Arndt, Bielefeld
Cover illustration: Opposition to the Humboldt Forum, August 2020. Photograph by Andrei Zavadsky.

https://doi.org/10.14361/9783839464090
Print-ISBN 978-3-8376-6409-6
PDF-ISBN 978-3-8394-6409-0
ISSN of series: 2752-1516
eISSN of series: 2752-1524

Contents

Acknowledgements

This book is a product of the research project *Making Differences in Berlin. Transforming Museums and Heritage in the Twenty-First Century* (a title that we later came to use in shortened versions). The project was generously funded primarily by the Alexander von Humboldt Foundation in the form of a Professorship to myself, Sharon Macdonald. This was an extraordinary privilege and allowed me to work with an amazing group of researchers, many of whom contribute to this book. Unlike so many funders, the Alexander von Humboldt Foundation gives an unusual degree of freedom, for which I am grateful not only as it helped to reduce administrative burdens but also because it meant that it was possible to reshape the research as it developed, responding to issues and concerns that emerged in this dynamic field. Alongside the positions funded by the Alexander von Humboldt Foundation, further much appreciated posts were financed by the Humboldt-Universität zu Berlin, the Museum für Naturkunde, and the Prussian Cultural Heritage Foundation.

The funding was also used to establish the Centre for Anthropological Research on Museums and Heritage – CARMAH – which was located within the Institute of European Ethnology, within the Philosophical Faculty of the Humboldt-Universität zu Berlin. As such, this book and the research more generally, also benefited from discussions with members of other research projects at and visitors to CARMAH, as well as colleagues within the Institute, Faculty and wider University. There are too many people to name here individually but we are grateful to all. Likewise, to many productive discussions elsewhere. In particular, however, a panel that we held at the *Heritage Futures* conference of the Association of Critical Heritage Studies, hosted (online) by University College London, in 2020 was an opportunity to collectively present work on the topic of this book and receive valuable feedback.

Many of those whose work is included in this book were part of an earlier reading group and read earlier drafts of chapters of some of the others, though as the project and book were produced over several years, some joined later or left earlier than others. Many thanks to all for the various and always valuable input. Gratitude also extends to others who participated in discussions and gave helpful feedback or other support: Tal Adler, Alice von Bieberstein, Hannes Hacke, Irene Hilden and Anna Szöke. Andrei Zavadsky additionally provided the photograph for the cover as well as for within the introduction. Extra appreciation is due to Christine Gerbich for helping with mobilizing and managing submissions at an important stage, and to the student assistants, especially Dominik Biewer and Sarah Felix but also Clara Dröll, Emma Jelinski and Harriet Merrow, for extensive and vital work of chasing picture rights, formatting and bibliographies, liaising with authors and more. We were fortunate to have been able to enlist the skillful language editor, Dominic Bonofiglio, to improve all of our texts. The Humboldt-Universität covered the costs to make this book open access. Jakob Horstmann at transcript has been wonderfully responsive and enthusiastic throughout. He is the only person I know who says 'swell' but it is a good description of working with him. I have been accompanied in my Berlin adventure by my husband, Mike Beaney, and I thank him for being there alongside during the long making of this book too.

Conducting a Berlin ethnography has meant that we have interacted with and learned from many different individuals and groups, even beyond those with whom we more formally worked. Thanks to all for being part of such a stimulating conversation.

Sharon Macdonald, Berlin, June 2022

List of Images

Doing Diversity, Making Differences
Multi-Researcher Ethnography in Museums and Heritage in Berlin

Sharon Macdonald

'Diversity' is undoubtedly a key word in contemporary museum and heritage debates and practice. Numerous initiatives and developments to promote, celebrate, identify, manage, preserve and, sometimes, to contest, diversity are underway. Yet what is meant by 'diversity' in these many instances—and what it is hoped it will achieve—is itself varied. So too for terms with which it is entangled or that operate as apparent or near synonyms, such as 'variety', 'plurality' and 'difference', and the German 'Vielfalt', 'Diversität', 'Verschiedenheit', 'Mannigfaltigkeit', 'Pluralität' and 'Differenz'.

This book brings together studies of the lives and workings of such terms within recent and ongoing museum and heritage contexts in Berlin. While the question of which terms are used is important to this study, the primary interest of those of us writing here is in practice, including both discursive and non-discursive practice. That is, we are concerned both with how and where those terms are used and to what effects; as well as how diversity and difference may be implicated and produced even beyond the explicit use of such language. Indeed, our central proposition is that 'diversity' is something that is *done*: that is, it is assembled through specific uses.

To examine *doing* requires ethnographic research. In essence, it means getting up close and personal to what we aim to understand (Shore and Trnka 2013). Accordingly, we have looked in depth and at close range at what actually happens in practice. The studies presented here are part of a large multi-researcher ethnographic research project conducted primarily within Berlin: *Making Differences: Transforming Museums and Heritage.*[1] Our ethnographic approach, which is explained further below, has allowed us to examine processes as they unfold over time. By doing so, we have been able to show how intentions and ambitions may shift or not be met, how particular infrastructures or formats may exert certain shaping effects, and how unexamined assumptions or entangled processes can lead to unanticipated outcomes. This, indeed, can be seen as a central finding of our research. Beyond that general finding, however, we seek to identify some of the more specific forms that diversity and difference take and the ways in which the associated processes work. By doing so, we not only provide in-depth analyses of certain cases but also point out the implications of certain ways of thinking and doing diversity and difference more widely.

In this introduction, the *Making Differences* project is first briefly outlined. This is followed by a discussion of why and how museums and heritage are especially significant in relation to questions of diversity and difference (a distinction that is explained below), and, correlatively, why such questions are of importance for museums and heritage. This entails charting the rise of the emphasis on diversity and difference, both internationally and more specifically in Germany, together with questions that this raises, especially, though not only, for the museum and heritage field. The introduction then turns to some of the events and developments with major implications for difference and diversity that have occurred or markedly intensified since 2015, when the *Making Differences* project began. Prominent among these are 'the refugee crisis' and the wider debates about migration, cultural diversity, Islam and 'German values' that this has raised; and calls and moves for the decolonisation of Western institutions, refracted and given added impetus especially by restitution debates and the Black Lives Matter campaign. As experienced in our research, these developments implicated museums and heritage in various, sometimes far-reaching ways—though with more effects surely still to come. A sketch of some ways that they did so is followed by further discussion of the project, including its methodological approach, before introducing the individual contributions to this book. The chapter concludes by commenting on some of the directions of transformation evident in the collective work, together with considerations raised by the chapters for doing diversity in both theory and practice.

Making Differences in Berlin

In a project spanning more than six years—though consisting of a number of mostly shorter studies—*Making Differences* has ethnographically examined heritage-making and its implications for difference and diversity in a wide range of locations and groups within Berlin. In keeping with the project's focus on transformation in museums and heritage, all of the cases explore relatively new developments and initiatives, including some that are still in process. This has enabled researchers to explore not simply how difference and diversity are being done in contemporary museum and heritage settings but how such processes themselves may be in transformation.

The scope of organisations, groups and practices researched has been broad, encompassing established museums, national heritage organisations and national monuments, as well as more local, quotidian or (self-avowedly) alternative venues and practices. The locations have included, among others, the Humboldt Forum, the Ethnological Museum, the Museum of Natural History, the Museum of Islamic Art, the Museum of European Cultures, the Bode Museum, the German Historical Museum, Neukölln Museum, the Memorial to the Murdered Jews of Europe (colloquially known as the Holocaust Memorial), SAVVY Contemporary, Galerie Wedding and the IfA (Institut für Auslandsbeziehungen) Gallery. As well as with curators and publics, the research has been conducted with postcolonial and LGBTI+ activists, with a Muslim slam poetry group, representatives of Muslim communities, artist collectives, refugee initiatives and citizen scientists. Research interlocutors have included individuals who hold or do not hold German citizenship, who speak a variety of first languages, who have varying life experiences, and who are connected in many different ways within the city and beyond. This breadth—along with a degree of heady eclecticism—has enabled the project to gain insight into the possible variety of practices, as well as communalities and exchange, in play.

Altogether, around twenty researchers have been employed over the years to undertake this work. They have done so primarily in what were also stand-alone studies, partly organised into themes. Two of topics, Representing Islam and Transforming the Ethnographic, are concerned with areas of the museum and heritage field that are often seen as particularly challenging for questions of difference and diversity. They are also areas in which there have been significant recent developments and increasing moves towards creative practice. The other two themes, Media and Mediation and Science and Citizenship, are more broadly conceived, relating to wider, intersecting areas of transformation. Media and Mediation includes consideration of the role of various media, with a particular emphasis on social media, in transforming museums and heritage, including how certain media may help afford particular forms of diversification. Examining how the relationship between science and citizenship might be in transformation, and its implications for diversity, is the remit of Science and Citizenship, though this is refracted particularly through attention to 'biodiversity' and citizen science. It is important to note that not all of the studies have been situated within this framework and not all have worked directly with 'diversity', or theorised it as is done in this introduction. Furthermore, there has been considerable conversation between, and often a degree of blurring of, the themes.

All of the research has taken place within a shared working environment, namely the Centre for Anthropological Research on Museums and Heritage—CARMAH—which has allowed for considerable and ongoing exchange. The Centre has welcomed many guests to present their research or otherwise work with us, which has been especially valuable in helping us to consider how far what we are seeing in Berlin is happening elsewhere. The exchange has made clear that while what we have seen in Berlin is unique in its detail, it is also part of wider transformations in museums and heritage—and in the doing of diversity—underway elsewhere too. As we explain below, these transformations build on the inherent capacity of museums and heritage to make differences.

Museums, heritage and making difference

As Daniel J. Sherman points out in the introduction to the classic volume *Museums and Difference* (2008), the performance of classification, which has been a key activity of modern museums, can be seen as inherently concerned with the marking of differences. At one level, this is primarily between kinds of objects, classified into various categories and taxonomies. Such classifying is in part about trying to represent what have come to be thought of as 'objective' facts about the world. Indeed, it has been argued that museum processes of presenting knowledge through objects helps substantiate historically and culturally specific ideas of 'objectivity' (Bennett et al. 2017; Geismar 2018; Macdonald

2006; Mitchell 1988). At the same time, however, museum and heritage classifications are entangled with other kinds of differences, such as those between nations, peoples or forms of life. While this is widely understood, including by many of those working in museums or other heritage or research institutions, as a matter of the mere *identification* of differences that exist in the world, post-structural scholarship has emphasised such acts of 'differencing' as selective and performative; that is, as involving the *making*, producing or at least *negotiating* of differences rather than simply depicting or displaying them (e.g. Bal 1996; Bennett 2018; Rottenburg 2006). This positions representation and display as significant parts of the inevitably selective 'making' process—acting as 'mediators' rather than 'intermediaries', to use Bruno Latour's (2014) distinction—and, thus, all the more deserving of analytical attention. Given the role of display in making differences evident in legitimised and substantiated form to wider constituencies or publics, this is all the more important. As Sherman emphasises, 'As public institutions assigned both to safeguard and to define culture, museums have always been sites for the negotiation of difference' (2008: 2).

This has been extensively documented in relation to the making and maintaining of nations (e.g. Knell et al. 2011; Levitt 2015; Mason 2013). While the building of a national heritage, including in museums, can be seen as part of the construction of national identity, this simultaneously and inextricably entails marking and making differences from others. '[D]ifference always shadows and doubles identity, always entails a relationship between self and other' says Sherman (2008: 1). In some cases, such difference is made by explicit commentary and contrast. More often, however, it is more implicitly enacted, through what is included and what is not, as well as through how classifications are made, and the explicit or implied hierarchies between them.

The division between 'self' and 'other', mentioned by Sherman, has been a particular focus for investigation of such processes. Inspired especially by Edward Said's *Orientalism* (1978), research has investigated how certain formulations of 'self'—such as that of one's own nation—are constructed through binary contrasts with others or a specific other. Capitalisation is often used here—for both Self and Other—to indicate these as specific categories of analysis. The term Othering is also used to describe the process whereby an Other is formed as part of the making of the Self. In relation to museums and heritage, such processes have been most extensively explored in relation to those museums called ethnographic or ethnological (e.g. Lidchi 1997; Shelton 2006). Here, the focus has been on how peoples outside Europe have served as an Other to the Self-projection of Europe, supposedly embodying contrasting characteristics. It is not, however, only with reference to outside of Europe that these processes can take place. The modern metropolis might, for example, be defined in part through contrast with the rural peripheries within Europe. Here, museums that in some countries may also be called ethnographic or ethnological, as well as other rural museums, may act as the locus for such rustic Others (e.g. de Cesari 2017; Pieterse 1997; Macdonald 2016)

Beyond binaries

While such analyses highlight relevant processes and effects, they can easily overlook complications and contradictions that may be involved. The Other is not necessarily projected as just the repository for all that the Self does not wish to be. On the contrary, it may be seen as the locus of much that is desired and even sometimes aspired to, such as ways of living perceived as more authentic or sustainable. Moreover, specific local histories and the biographies of particular objects may well speak to alternative possibilities that disrupt simple and simplistic binaries, as well as relating to alternative concerns, emphases and ontologies. This can disrupt the very assumption of a Self and Other binary, as well as complicating the question of to what these designations may refer. Those who act as Other for national selves, may well be engaged in their own projects of Self-definition, which may involve other acts of Othering. There has been considerable debate over many years, some even preceding Said, about such processes and their implications. W.E.B. Du Bois's notion of 'double consciousness' posits that those who are marginalised may be aware of both mainstream perspectives and also their own alternative reality (1903/1994). Gayatri Spivak, however, has posed the question of whether the subaltern—those Othered by the mainstream—can even speak, in the sense of give voice to their experience (Spivak 1988). Much debated by others, her reply is only equivocally affirmative (e.g. Morris 2010). Classical as well as more recent anthropology is replete with accounts of self-definition involving what we might call 'other Othering' (e.g. Barth 1969; Cohen 1985; see also Appadurai 2013; Appiah 2005, 2018; Hall 1992; Minh-Ha 1989). That might include, say, the non-Western Othering of the West, or groups marginal to the national centre differentiating themselves from that centre or from their other neighbours. It has also highlighted the layering of identities, in which, say, it may be entirely compatible to be a member of a neighbourhood, a city, a nation and a continent; and it has demonstrated how self- and other-ascriptions can shift 'situationally' (e.g. Rogers and Vertovec 1995; Jenkins 2014). Notions of 'intersectionality' further complicate simple binaries by highlighting how certain differences may become compounded or 'plaited together' (Pollock 2019: 268; see also, Crenshaw 2017; Hill Collins 2004; McCall 2005). As Patricia Hill Collins and Sirma Bilge explain, intersectionality's 'core insight' is that 'power relations of race, class, and gender, for example, are not discrete and mutually exclusive entities but rather build on each other and work together' (Hill Collins and Bilge 2020: 5; see also Goel 2020 for the implications for ethnographic research). This results in distinct positionalities, and a need for research to recognise that the position of, say, a working-class woman of colour would not be identical with that of a working-class white woman, and that the effects of marginalisation can interact to produce distinct positionalities.

Employed in museums and heritage, practices can be investigated empirically. What differences are produced through the various classifications and displays, their inclusions and exclusions? For whom, or as who, do museums and heritage speak? In terms of the models of differentiation performed, do they posit binaries or other possibilities? And in doing so, do they give recognition to different positionalities in terms of their content coverage, as well as whom they seek to invite as interlocutors? It is also possible to investigate how those who are not part of established heritage institutions relate to these—for example, by visiting or not, and through their interpretations of what is on display (or missing). Moreover, beyond this, the ways in which those who find themselves Othered (possibly in multiple ways) construct their own senses of collectivity and difference, perhaps mobilising certain notions of heritage in the process, can also be explored. In this book, as in the *Making Differences* project more widely, we engage in just such empirical investigation. Before introducing this more concretely, however, more needs to be said about the term 'diversity' and its relationship to 'difference', as well as about the wider context in which notions of diversity have come to be regarded as so important in museum and heritage practice.

Difference, differencing, diversity

So far in this introduction, the emphasis has been on 'difference' as that which results from processes of differentiation. This may potentially indicate differences of many kinds, even referring, for example, to the difference between life and death—a difference which, Sherman notes, has been suggested to be fundamental to museums (2008: 1). Most often, however, discussion centres on cultural differences. Examples of cultural differentiation that we will encounter in the chapters that follow include those made between European, African and Islamic—categories that can all potentially overlap but that readily come to be depicted as mutually exclusive alternatives. Whether and how such cultural difference maps onto lived experience and the social differences that are part of the latter are questions to be explored. But this still does not exhaust the possibility for investigating the work of difference-making. How nature is differentiated from culture, and how not only culture but also nature is then further differentiated (though a whole panoply of notions of genus, species, family, etc), are all (mutually entangled) realms of differencing in which museums and heritage play significant roles. This is the case too for any other kinds of differences that might be drawn, such as those of race, religion, gender, sexuality, ableness/disability, age or class.

Differencing

Here, it is also worth noting that the term 'differencing' has also come to be used to indicate active attempts to give attention to and promote differences that have previously been overlooked or underplayed. Art historian and theorist, Griselda Pollock's germinal call for 'differencing the canon' was directed to art history, making a feminist case not simply for adding women into the existing pantheon of great art but for seeing the canon itself as 'a discursive strategy in the production and reproduction of sexual difference and its complex configurations with gender and power' (1999: 26). Regarding the canon in this way is to deconstruct it by undermining its claim to be based on pure artistic prowess. While gender was the focus of this original argument, the same moves can also be made, and have been made, with refence to other differences, such as those of sexuality or race.

Museums, as key sites for proclaiming the canon—especially, though not only, of art—are of considerable importance for such moves. Over the twenty years since Pollock's important text, not only has more scholarship been directed towards disciplinary differencing; it has also been taken up by some museums and heritage institutions, albeit more often through strategies of trying to increase the space given to difference rather than more extensive revision of approach and practice (Bayer, Kazeem-Kaminski and Sternfeld 2017; Modest 2020; Reilly 2019). Tony Bennett, a long-time commentator on museums and power, uses the term 'differencing machines' (2006) to refer to this increased tendency of at least some museums to 'refashion' themselves in this way, doing so particularly with reference to 'the promotion of cross-cultural understanding, especially across divisions that have been racialized' (2006: 46). Such developments can also be seen as significant precursors and accompaniments to more recent moves to diversify, queer and decolonise museums and heritage (e.g. Lonetree 2012; Ndikung 2017; Sullivan and Middleton 2020).

Diversity

The related term that we use in our title here, and that is often used with reference to differencing museums and heritage, is 'diversity'. While it is often pointed out, rightly, that the term is used—perhaps appropriately enough—in multiple ways and can be hard to define (e.g. Vertovec 2012, 2021; Blum et al. 2016), a basic characterisation is that it denotes the co-existence of many acknowledged differences. This means that it is, in effect, a particular model of how 'difference' might exist or be arranged. Alternative models of organising difference include the dualistic or binary, as in the Self-Other distinction discussed above. Unlike 'diversity', these involve a limited number of differences—only two. The elements in such binaries may be either in equal or in hierarchical relationship with each other, and sometimes fluctuating, perhaps officially presented as equal but experienced, especially by one side, as hierarchical. In the case of diversity, the various elements—the differences—involved may well also be in unequal relationships. It is often said, for example, that modern cities are characterised by increasing diversity, to refer to the (not always or entirely correct) fact of there being more people from many parts of the globe, subscribing to a greater range of religions and undertaking more diverse cultural practices, living in them. Clearly, there are many inequalities between such groups, including in terms such as income and work opportunities, as well as presence in official heritage institutions. Despite this, however, the language of 'diversity' tends to imply a non-hierarchical organisation of difference. Christian Reus-Smit refers to this as the 'billiard ball model' (2018)—to capture the sense of neat, separate units of difference all of equal size and on one surface. This idea of diversity as entailing equal differences is also belied by a contradictory tendency for 'diversity' to be used as a contrast to an implied background of 'non-diversity'. An imagined 'non-diverse' mainstream is thus reinforced as a norm from which the diverse departs.

In an insightful discussion of ethnographic museums, especially the Musée du Quai Branly, in France, historian Nélia Dias shows well how a distinction between (cultural) difference and (cultural) diversity may operate in museum and heritage contexts. The former, she argues, always involves a 'comparative perspective' that is 'absent in the notion of cultural diversity, which presupposes cultural variability' (Dias 2008: 124). As she explains, in France, the idea of cultural diversity 'is shaped by concerns about "'l'égalité des cultures", a concept translated as "equivalence of cultures"' (2008: 128; see also Debary and Roustan 2017: 5), which is particularly associated with ideas linked to an official 'denial of religious distinctions and respect for all beliefs' (2008: 143) that go along with a strong affirmation of the State as purely secular. The Musée du Quai Branly's stated and performed emphasis on cultural diversity—reinforced by its display of natural diversity in the plants that adorn and surround the building—acts, she argues, to uphold this State position, and with it, a vision of diversity (and equivalence) without difference (and hierarchy). As she puts it:

> At stake...is the desire to solve sensitive political and social issues through culture—the conviction that art and culture can bring together peoples, ethnic groups, and nations, and become the new magical bond. Through objects, museums attempt to palliate government policies and social exclusions. The claim that 'there is no hierarchy among the arts, and no hierarchy among peoples' obscures the relationships between France and non-European peoples. Thus the role ascribed to museums: to exonerate society for its failings to deal with peoples and cultures whose objects are in museums devoted to cultural diversity (Dias 2008: 149).

While the strong emphasis on the secular State is characteristic of France, deployment of notions of 'diversity' that obscure or flatten difference by making all differences appear equal are widespread in other countries too. In a study of higher education diversity practitioners in Australia, for example, Sara Ahmed makes this point, arguing that the tendency for diversity to be implicitly assumed as a set of equal relations is what makes it feel 'secure' rather than 'threatening' (Ahmed 2007: 238). For the U.S., Walter Benn Michaels, in *The Trouble with Diversity: How We Learned to Love Identity and Ignore Inequality* (Michaels 2006), argues that the emphasis on identity, culture and race—and the celebration of cultural difference and even events such as Black History Month—supports a vision of 'different but equal [that] is one of our strategies for managing inequality rather than minimising or eliminating it' (2006: 10; see also Partridge and Chin 2019). It also means that the problem becomes one of addressing discrimination rather than tackling inequality.

Other potentials?

Yet, to see an emphasis on diversity as inherently or only negative would be to underrate the perniciousness of discrimination and its interplay with inequality. As Michael Rothberg (2009) has argued, one does not have to work with a zero-sum logic here (which he sees as itself neoliberal in its modelling as competition): acknowledging or celebrating diversity does not need to be an alternative to addressing inequality. Instead, the attempt could be to realise what Steven Vertovec calls diversity's 'optimistic orientation' (2012: 302). By this he means its normative aspirations—namely, that there should be equivalence and lack of hierarchy. Moreover, he suggests that the 'pervasiveness' of the notion of diversity in many areas of contemporary life has the potential to 'transform the social imaginary' (2012: 305) and thus help bring this very change about. He draws here on the theorising of Charles Taylor (2007), who defines the social imaginary as 'the ways that people imagine their social existence, how they fit together with others, how things go on between them and their fellows, the expectations that are normally met, and the deeper normative notions and images that underlie these expectations' (2007: 23; and quoted by Vertovec on p.305). If the spread and uptake of the notion of 'diversity' does indeed have the potential to transform the social imaginary, what this would mean, according to Vertovec, is acting according to 'the basic social and moral code that everyone manifests "difference" in some way, indeed multiple ways, and that this fact should be integral to the way that everyone treats each other in society' (2012: 306). Potentially, one might argue, it could also be harnessed to an agenda of reducing inequality. Yet whether it does indeed prompt such transformations remains an open question. If it is to do so, however, museums and heritage will necessarily need to be on board, precisely because they have operated as institutions of difference, in Dias's sense, in their establishing hierarchies of value. The question, in other words, is whether museums and heritage can really act as 'differencing machines' in Bennett's terms. That is, can they help change the social imaginary—and actual social practice—by doing difference in other ways?

This question leaves open whether 'diversity' is indeed the best model for the conceptualisation or organisation of difference. Can its tendency to overlook inequalities be addressed? Multiculturalism can be seen as a specific version and cultural-political implementation of the diversity model—one that encourages and even celebrates (certain) differences (Ang 2018; Modood 2013; Song 2020). It is not, therefore, surprising that it too has also been accused of ignoring inequality. Moreover, by imagining diversity in terms of a 'zoological' (Hage 1998) constellation of differences or a set of billiard balls (Reus-Smit 2018), multiculturalism has been accused of failing to acknowledge the relations between the parts and instead reifying into distinct and non-overlapping or non-mixing kinds of difference. Amartya Sen insightfully calls it 'plural monoculturalism' (2006). Furthermore, the difference given attention within multiculturalism is almost always relatively uncontroversial or 'safe' dimensions of difference. Indeed, it might be suggested that one reason for the rise of cultural heritage initiatives is that these are often thought to offer relatively anodyne and apolitical modes for performing diversity. Yet, cultural heritage only sometimes operates in this way (Macdonald 2013). The now large and constantly expanding field of critical heritage studies increasingly recognises not only that heritage is frequently highly political and often fraught but also that it is not merely instrumentalised from above (e.g. ibid.; Harrison 2013; Robertson 2012). That heritage is so entangled in senses of self and others, and regarded as an expression of important values, makes potentials to work otherwise integral to it.

Some commentators have recently suggested that multiculturalism can be rethought (perhaps again, Parekh 2007)—and implemented—in ways that avoid the problems identified (Joppke 2017; Modood 2018). Indeed, Modood (2017) regards critiques of multiculturalism as often relying on rather stereotypical accounts; and Chin (2017) argues that there have in fact been very few thoroughgoing State attempts to implement multiculturalism, and that even these have been criticised from their inception and before their results were known. Declaring multiculturalism a failure has been a prelude for various politicians in Europe, especially on the political Right, to argue for more integrationist and even nationalistic policies. In the 2010s this led to a flurry of proposals for new national museums, in which it was imagined that strong national narratives would help instil national values (Macdonald 2016). Interestingly, most of these did not get beyond the proposal stage—suggesting, perhaps, that the task was just too difficult to achieve. The question that remains, then, is whether there are other models of thinking difference and diversity—and even multiculturalism—that can overcome the problems identified thus far.

Diversity in action

It is useful at this point to probe into the question of just how 'diversity' is imagined and done in practice—especially in initiatives to address or increase it. As Sara Ahmed puts it: 'What does diversity "do" when it is "put into action"?' (2007: 237). Any thorough investigation needs to address explicit formulations of 'diversity' and the expectations of the initiatives that are supposed to implement it, as well as the more implicit ways in which it is expressed and instantiated. Do statements follow through into practice? And how does what is produced play through into wider social imaginaries or specific lived experiences? In effect, this pursuit of how 'diversity' is done is to shift the analytical focus from being on certain categories as given to instead 'making categorizing itself the object of investigation' (Hirschauer 2021: 65).

This does not, however, mean to ignore the forms that particular ideas or models of diversity take, for these are part of what might be called the conceptual infrastructure of thinking and doing difference and diversity. This is not unchanging – far from it – but is shaped by certain conventions and concepts that may be in popular and professional, as well as academic, use to varying extents. Among others, these include notions such as 'identity', 'ethnicity', 'race', 'gender', 'belonging' and 'home', as well as terms including 'intersectionality', 'inclusion', 'solidarity', and 'difference' and 'diversity' themselves. One longstanding debate that has seen the waxing and waning of some of these terms and that re-emerges at various times and places in somewhat altered ways is that over the extent to which the focus should be on sameness (and identity) or difference (and diversity). This is a political as much as an analytical question and, indeed, the two are intertwined. The act of giving main emphasis to identifying either commonalities or features that differentiate – and just how this is done (e.g. with heed to the repercussions and contra-indications or not) – itself supports certain understandings and has socio-political ramifications. In general, the move during the last decades within social and cultural disciplines, as well as in many areas of cultural life, such as those explored in this book, has been towards greater emphasis on difference (e.g. van Meijl 2010; Gaupp 2021), accompanied by some significant critique of notions of 'identity' (e.g. Jackson 2022). There have, however, also been significant attempts to reclaim 'sameness' as well as to 'dissolve' or blur the distinction, including through notions such as 'hybridity' and 'transculturality' (e.g. Williams 1991; Hirschauer 2021; Pellilo-Hestermeyer 2021).

While, so far, this introduction has predominantly looked at models of 'diversity' that claim an 'equivalence of difference', in practice this may well exist alongside ideas of some being 'more diverse' or 'more different' than others. What this establishes are certain 'diversity regimes' – that is, 'principles underlying the arrangement of diverse populations, their configuration...[which] entail moral orders, sets of beliefs and values that provide guidelines (or imperatives) for right and proper conduct within or between diverse populations' (Grillo 2010: 3) – which result in being exclusionary in certain ways. Also relevant for exploration is how far various models of difference can persist alongside each other, or whether they come into conflict. So, for example, might binary models of difference—of othering and alterity—persist alongside, or even be produced by, certain diversity practices?

Important too is the question of what further possible models of thinking and doing difference there might be. Notions such as those mentioned above which consider partial difference and blurring – others of which include 'translocality' (Puzon 2018) and 'creolization' and 'syncretism' (Stewart 2011); though all of these begin from a stance in which there are entities to be transcended or mixed rather than regarding the blurry, messy, impure states as the baseline. Rosi Braidotti has also written of the need for a written of the need for a 'dislocation of difference from binaries to rhizomatics' (2013: 96) in order to achieve what she sees as a necessary 'affirmation of the positivity of difference' (2013: 11). For our purposes here, all of these are helpful ideas to sensitise us to possible assumptions within our own analytical frames, as well as to those of our interlocutors in our museum and heritage fieldsites – frames that may well overlap. Moreover, they also point to possible alternatives for both analysis and practice, a point that recurs during the contents to follow.

While in this book we offer reflection on a range of possible ways of thinking about diversity and other models for organising difference, we do so primarily through considering how they are 'done' in actual museum and heritage—and related—practice. This is to take them as 'ethnographic objects' that can be observed, described and interacted with. Doing so does not mean that our approach is just to give empirical accounts of specific cases—though that is important. Rather, as we set out further below, we are concerned with how the *doing* that we describe intersects with existing theoretical ideas in the academy and opens up possibilities for future theorising. Before further explaining our approach, however, I offer some comments on the rise of diversity discourses, as well as on the German context.

The flourishing of *Diversität*, etc

The German term *Diversität* is generally agreed to have become more widely used in the later 20th century, though with significant earlier uses, especially in relation to *Biodiversität* (biodiversity) (see Garbellotto and Nadim, below; Blum et al 2016; Kirschhoff & Köchy 2016; Toepfer 2017). Its flourishing is argued to have been influenced by international developments, which are reflected in a parallel (though not necessarily identical or coterminous) expansion of diversity discourse in other languages, especially English and French (Salzbrunn 2014). Three semi-linked inflections of *Diversität*, each with partly distinct trajectories, can be discerned.

Cultural diversity, Kulturelle Vielfalt

One of these is associated with the English term 'cultural diversity' and the French '*diversité culturelle*', which, as various commentators note, have come to be used more widely especially since the 1990s. UNESCO (the United Nations Educational, Scientific and Cultural Organisation) was a key player in their international spread, prompted especially by French members during the Presidency of Jacques Chirac. That the Musée du Quai Branly was founded and opened under his enthusiastic watch is no coincidence, for the same idea of cultural equivalence, as described by Dias above, was involved here too.

Indeed, he was a leading proponent in successfully introducing 'cultural diversity' as an alternative to the notion of 'cultural exception' that was previously used in international trade agreements (Musitelli 2006). This position in effect made culture and diversity the baseline—rather than singling out cultural exceptions against a backdrop of economic sameness—and, as such, stood against 'an Anglo-Saxon model of globalisation as free-trade' (Smiers 2016: 213). It took until 2001 for the UNESCO's Universal Declaration on Cultural Diversity to be formally adopted—unanimously, shortly after the attacks of September 11th, which, as the Director-General wrote in its preface, made it all the more relevant, emphasising, he said, 'that intercultural dialogue is the best guarantee of peace'. Significantly, 'heritage' was another key word of the Declaration. Cultural diversity itself was proclaimed as 'the common heritage of humanity' and said to be 'as necessary for humankind as biodiversity is for nature' (UNESCO 2001). This supported a wider democratisation of heritage that was already underway, and in which the heritage of numerous diverse groups and interests was accorded greater recognition, including from national and international organisations, such as World Heritage lists (Brumann 2021; Meskell 2018; Salemink 2021). Casting cultural diversity and its manifestation as heritage as analogous to biodiversity also further embedded an idea of cultural diversity and heritage as being 'at risk' and thus as in need of initiatives to 'save' or 'preserve' it (Harrison 2013; Harrison et al. 2020).

These developments intersected with the rise of what has been called the politics of identity or the politics of recognition in many parts of the world (e.g. Taylor 1994; Heyes 2020; Noury and Roland 2020). Gathering momentum in the later 20th century, this has seen groups of citizens calling for their differences from the mainstream to be recognised and accommodated by the State, and increasingly States have done so, though to widely varying extents, ranging from mere toleration to active support and funding. Culture has often been the focus of such developments, with calls for recognition of religious and linguistic difference to the forefront. That this has often been presented as 'heritage' is indicative of the legitimating capacity of that term, ensuring that whatever is so designated is understood as something that stretches back in time and that deserves preservation. The heritage, memory and museum boom of the later 20th century and since is also significantly linked to the rise of identity and recognition politics—or what is sometimes also called the politics of difference—as diverse groups seek to explore and perform their distinctiveness through museum and heritage formats.

As Müller and Schmieder (2017) observe, while *Diversität* is sometimes used as a translation for 'diversity' in cultural contexts, more often it is the term '*Vielfalt*', particularly in the formulation '*kulturelle Vielfalt*', which appears in the German version of the UNESCO Declaration.[2] While *Diversität* and *Vielfalt* are generally listed as synonyms, and used fairly interchangeably, they carry subtly different connotations. *Vielfalt*, which might be translated as 'variety', has a less politicised tone, putting its emphasis particularly on the multiplicity of kinds, whereas the differences between the elements seem more central in *Diversität*. With its Old Germanic (rather than Latin) roots and sense of multiple enfolding, *Vielfalt* is part of the everyday vernacular and according to figures provided by the *Digitales Wörterbuch der deutschen Sprache* has been in longer use in Germany.[3] In the 20th century, *Vielfalt* sees a major upswing in use—perhaps paralleling a wider expansion of publishing—and then levels off in the latter quarter. *Diversität*, by contrast, has relatively negligible use before the 21st century. Its use has proliferated since then, though its level is considerably below that of *Vielfalt*.

Social diversity, Soziale Diversität and different but equal

While many commentators note the use of *Diversität* in biology starting in the 1960s, most agree that a more recent political use of the English-language term 'diversity' in the US has been particularly influential to *Diversität's* use in Germany. This brings us to its second inflection. Here, 'diversity' primarily designates social diversity, having been promoted by social movements and attempts to bring about socio-political change, especially within institutions and with respect to antidiscrimination and affirmative action policies. A legal case at the University of California in 1978, in which affirmative action was approved for the first time, is often pinpointed as a significant origin (Salzbrunn 2014: 28; Partridge and Chin 2019: 197). Steven Vertovec, who heads up the Max Planck Institute for the Study of Religious and Ethnic Diversity in Göttingen and has written widely on contemporary diversity, including in Germany, sees such developments in the US, especially in relation to affirmative action, as particularly influential in the uptake of discourse about *Diversität* in Germany (Vertovec 2012). Here, rather than cultural or natural diversity, the emphasis is on social diversity—especially that of race and ethnicity (two terms with shifting positions, whose histories are closely entangled, and both of which are sometimes articulated as 'cultural'), though also embracing gender, sexuality, physical abledness, class and age, among others. Moreover, where the former variety or *Vielfalt* conception emphasised equivalence, this notion of diversity/*Diversität* is premised on the existence of inequality that needs to be addressed.

To do so, initiatives employing notions such as 'access', 'accessibility' and 'social inclusion' may be devised (Sandell 1998; 2003). Inherent in this discourse is the idea that some are excluded from full citizenship by not being able to play a full role in society. Diversity, in other words, is also linked to unequal political presence and representation. These terms are not only used in theorising but also with respect to policy and practice initiatives, including in the museum and heritage field. They acknowledge that citizenship is unequally distributed and that effort needs to be made to 'include' more but they have been criticised for seeming to invite to join an already given 'offer' rather than to more fundamentally change the system itself. While some argue that 'access' and 'inclusion' should not be regarded in that way, they have tended to lose ground in the museum and heritage field to the term 'participation', which tends to be considered as indicating a greater degree of activity—though it too is also sometimes criticised as operating from a premise of encouraging joining in, rather than changing the foundations. In the migration field, the term 'integration' is similarly contested, with some arguing that, especially by contrast with 'assimilation', it allows for the maintenance of difference, whereas others regard it as putting too much emphasis on changing those immigrating rather than changing society itself (Schinkel 2017). Likewise, the notion of 'citizenship' has been ambiguously evaluated. On the one hand, the mobilization of the idea of citizenship – and its use in initiatives such as 'citizen science' (see Garbellotto and Nadim, this volume) – is part of a democratizing impulse, seeking to involve a wide range of members of society. On the other hand, however, it can also serve to exclude those who are not recognized as full citizens and, moreover, risks imposing a narrow set of criteria for what constitutes appropriate citizenly behaviour and, thus, being exclusionary in this way too.

The more social and change-oriented conceptions of diversity – recognized through the use of the term *Diversität* – were, according to Vertovec, brought to Germany through calls for U.S.-style 'diversity mainstreaming', which were incorporated into various EU policies, together with the actual presence of the U.S. corporate sector (2012: 292). He notes that it is sometimes employed rather instrumentally in these corporate renditions, either to head off possible accusations of discrimination or as part of managerialist ideas about the creative potential of diversity (2012: 291).

This brings us to what might be listed as the third inflection of *Diversität.* In this, an emphasis on social as well as cultural, perhaps including religious, diversity is coupled with ideas of institutional, as well as broader social, change. But rather than being anchored in ideas of inequality, diversity in this sense is considered more like in the first inflection described above, namely, as 'different but equal'. Monika Salzbrunn, reflecting on *Diversität,* the Anglo term 'diversity' and the French *diversité,* sees all of the terms moving in this direction (2014). Like, and indeed largely influenced by, Walter Benn Michaels, she sees diversity—and its German and French equivalents—as having largely lost the political edge and emphasis on inequality of its earlier association with social movements. Instead, she too suggests that it is more often instrumentalised in ways that allow inequality to be ignored or marginalised.

Differences in diversity debate and practice

Perhaps, however, this diagnosis is too broad-brush. As suggested above, it is not necessarily the case that different approaches supplant one another: they may co-exist and even in some contexts supplement each other. Migration debates and policies are undoubtedly one of the areas in which diversity discourse most often occurs but as literature in the field shows, this cannot be reduced just to one of these senses of the term (Römhild 2014). Indeed, what may happen in practice—as we will see in the volume that follows—is that blurring or shifts between senses can themselves be significant. Differences between countries also deserve careful handling. Michaels (2008) has emphasised that his analysis is primarily about the U.S., noting that the levels of difference between rich and poor—the wealth gap—is significantly greater in the U.S. than in France and Germany, and that U.S. higher education is considerably more hierarchical, which both mean, in his analysis, that diversity is more likely to operate as an alibi for inequality.[4] This same remains the case today.[5] Moreover, as noted above, the French tendency 'to promote the principle of equality as a way of dealing with cultural diversity', and to do so within 'a universalist approach to cultural differences, races, and religions' (Debary and Roustan 2017: 5) is significantly different from the emphasis on the 'recognition of differences' that has developed in 'Anglo-Saxon countries' (ibid.).

Which histories and differences are given emphasis and how also varies internationally. Questions of race and slavery, for example, have been at the forefront in the U.S. longer than in Europe. But the situation is changing. For example, in 2014, Salzbrunn, describing the role that French museums have played in disseminating certain ideas of diversity, noted that 'the German debate about memory cultures is...scarcely shaped by colonial history' (2014: 51). Today, less than a decade later, this is no longer the case. On the contrary, the colonial past and colonial continuities have considerable—and even pre-eminent—presence in current German diversity and memory debates, as is abundantly evident in this volume (see especially Förster, Merrow and Jethro). While Michael Rothberg's argument (2009) that promoting any one particular memory does not necessarily diminish the visibility or effectiveness of any other, precisely what a new presence or emphasis may lead to in practice needs to be investigated. Perhaps, as his 'multidirectional memory' formulation proposes, it will indeed lead to each community's memory—and sense of recognition—being substantiated. But this is not inevitably so. Equally, as his arguments also emphasise, memories do not necessarily stack up cumulatively, each just adding another instance to the library of diversities along the shelf. They might instead change existing modes of engagement by bringing new considerations into play or doing difference in other ways.

This sketch of the rise of a discourse of *Diversität* and some of its entanglements and inflections is not intended to be comprehensive. Nevertheless, it provides some shared background and highlights considerations and questions for the studies that follow. All of the research presented here has been undertaken within this broader context of expanded and pervasive diversity discourse. But that does not mean that the term is necessarily in direct use within them. Rather, all of the cases that we present are concerned in some way or another with how people and institutions handle difference, and the ways in which they do so speak directly or indirectly to concerns about diversity in some of the senses above. At the same time, however, they map out and explore more specific realisations and terminologies, some of which may operate rather differently from organising difference as diversity in the ways introduced above. That, indeed, is precisely our interest: how is difference being done in (or in relation to) museums and heritage within this wider flourishing of concern with *Diversität*?

Ethnographic timing

While this flourishing of variously inflected diversity discourse has provided the broad context for the *Making Differences* project, and thus of the studies we present, it has also taken place amidst more specific events and developments with ramifications for difference and diversity. Indeed, the period from 2015 (when the project officially began) to 2020 (the time when most of the contents here were drafted, though the project continues and many articles have been redrafted since) has often felt like one of seismic change, though how far this is the case will only be fully possible to assess over a longer time span. Nevertheless, with our focus on ongoing transformation, we were well positioned to look at them. This was exciting—and challenging.

'Refugee Crisis'

The project officially began in October 2015 following months of planning. At this time, what came to be widely referred to as the 'refugee crisis' or 'the migration crisis' was newly underway. Hundreds of thousands of people, the majority of whom were fleeing from the conflict-battered countries of Syria, Afghanistan and Iraq, were arriving in Europe. Germany took in more of these refugees (to use the term in its broad rather than formal legal sense) than did any other country (Bock and Macdonald 2019). The coverage in German media was intense and featured debates about what the influx of refugees might mean for social integration and the diversity of German society in the future. On the one hand were those who saw it as a moral imperative that Germany welcome those fleeing persecution—especially given the country's Holocaust history—and who often maintained that diversity would enrich German society. On the other hand were those who warned that accepting so many 'foreigners' would damage core German values (which they generally considered to be coterminous with Christianity) and lead to social fragmentation and unrest. In effect, these were debates about how much difference and diversity Germany, and Europe more generally, wanted or could accept. They were also about the relative desirability of particular kinds of difference and how to manage the differences that the new arrivals were seen to bring with them.

In the *Making Differences* project, it felt important to understand the significance and implications of the 'crisis'. To do so, we brought together researchers to provide insight into the longer historical, political and legal frameworks pertinent to difference and diversity in Germany, as well as into the representations and experiences of particular groups.[6] A workshop in April 2016 became the basis for an edited book (Bock and Macdonald 2019). The workshop and book did not focus specifically on museums and heritage—our aim was to assess the developments more broadly—though these topics appeared intermittently throughout, including in the book's conclusion, which discussed some of the many museum and heritage initiatives that had sprung up to address 'the crisis' (Macdonald 2019). The efforts of these cultural institutions showed them to be active sites not only for reflecting on the plight of refugees but also for engaging with them and with wider publics in often innovative ways. Investigating some of these initiatives in more depth became an unanticipated dimension of our research (see Gram, this volume; Puzon 2019; Macdonald, Gerbich, Gram, Puzon & Shatanawi 2021).

In public debates about the influx of refugees, the difference that was often depicted as the cause for most concern, particularly by those who were opposed to permitting so many to stay, was Islam. While not all refugees were practicing Muslims, the majority were from countries in which Islam was the state religion. This gave fuel to opponents of immigration, especially to the AfD (*Alternative für Deutschland*, Alternatives for Germany) and the anti-Islamist Pegida (*Patriotische Europäer gegen die Islamisierung des Abendlandes*, Patriotic Europeans against the Islamicisation of the Occident) movement, whose negative depiction of refugees included painting them as harbingers of a dangerous 'Islamicisation of the West'. Due to Islam's long history of complex and contested entanglements in definitions of Europe, as well as it being the subject of high-profile new galleries or museum refurbishments in various countries—including that underway in the Museum of Islamic Art in Berlin (see Gerbich, this volume)—it was already planned that Islam would be a research topic in the *Making Differences* project. It is represented, among other things, by Christine Gerbich's longstanding research at the Museum of Islamic Art, which includes a project called Tamam, which works with Imams, and the making of the exhibition *The Heritage of the Old Kings*, as well as Museum Diwan, which is the focus of her chapter for this volume. A separate edited collection, *Islam and Heritage in Europe. Pasts, Presents and Future Possibilities* (2021), edited by Katarzyna Puzon, Sharon Macdonald and Mirjam Shatnawi, provides further exploration of these themes. The refugee arrivals of 2015 and since have, however, made the issue all the more pressing. Though this context has informed all the work presented in this volume, it is most prominent in the contribution by Rikke Gram, who looks at the award-winning Multaka project, a 'tours by refugees for refugees' programme initiated by various Berlin museums. It is also notable in Katarzyna Puzon's chapter on the *i,Slam* initiative, as well as in her fieldwork with KUNSTASYL, a project with asylum seekers to create an exhibition at the Museum of European Cultures in Berlin on the subject of being a refugee, on which she has published elsewhere (Puzon 2019; see also Tietmeyer 2017).

Colonialism and Decolonisation

As Christine Gerbich's research shows, 'Islamic' heritage in Europe needs to be considered in terms of colonialism. While research on the colonial histories of museums and collections has been underway for several decades now (Förster 2019), the years since the launch of the *Making Differences* project have seen a major escalation of debate and activism. This has been felt in many parts of the world, especially those that had colonies or were colonised. With Germany's colonial history coming into the spotlight only recently, the debates of the past several years have been particularly intense. Much of the attention has been on Berlin, where most of pivotal events and decision-making took place. First and foremost among them was the conference of 1884–1885, at which European powers divided up Africa. The 2016 exhibition *Deutscher Kolonialismus* at the German Historical Museum can be seen as a landmark moment in Germany's acknowledgment of its past colonial atrocities. That the exhibition led to such a mix of praise and criticism—reflected not least in the contributions to its visitor books, discussed here by Harriet Merrow—highlights just how sensitive this history remains. One reason for the subject's contentiousness is the concern that focus on Germany's colonial past might draw attention away from the Holocaust. For others, however, the fact that the first German concentration camp was in colonial Namibia is only further evidence of Germany's longstanding problem with Otherness and race—a problem that predates the rise of National Socialism in the 20th century (e.g. Kössler 2015).

A key site for the playing out of debates about Germany's difficult colonial heritage has been, and is, the Humboldt Forum. Constructed to look like the former imperial palace on whose site it stands, the Forum has widely been seen as a statement about Germany's relationship to its past (von Bose 2016, 2017; Bach 2021; Tinius and von Zinnenburg Carroll 2020; Macdonald 2016, forthcoming). Initially, it was the relationship to the history of the German Democratic Republic that was at the forefront of public debate. The reconstruction of the palace had required the destruction of the GDR's parliamentary building, the Palace of the Republic, which seemed like an effort to erase Germany's divided past from public memory. The past that was being 'returned to' lay further back. This was brought more fully under the spotlight when a decision was made to display exhibitions from the Ethnological Museum and Museum of Asian Art in the Humboldt Forum. Statements maintaining that such a move would be appropriate because some of the first collections from beyond Europe had been housed in the palace inadvertently served to highlight the fact that some of this collecting had taken place as part of the colonial ambitions of those in power at the time (Bose 2016: 127). Already, ethnological collecting, which took place not only by colonising powers in lands they had claimed but also within broader structures of coloniality between Europe and other parts of the world, was under criticism, with growing calls for repatriation and restitution.

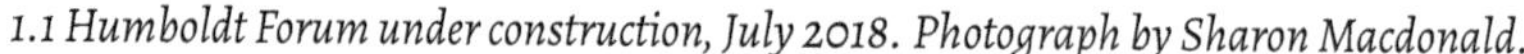

1.1 Humboldt Forum under construction, July 2018. Photograph by Sharon Macdonald.

The Humboldt Forum was a central case for the *Making Differences* project. *Berlin Global*, which is the focus of Sharon Macdonald's fieldwork, is one of the permanent galleries of the Humboldt Forum. Margareta von Oswald conducted fieldwork in the Ethnological Museum as it prepared for its move to the Humboldt Forum and she writes here of how that context impacted on work within the museum, and elsewhere of how curatorial activity inevitably took place, to some extent at least, within existing, and often colonial, infrastructures and assumptions (von Oswald 2020). Nnenna Onuoha likewise explores an aspect of what we might see as part of the preparatory infrastructure for the Humboldt Forum, in this case an exhibition called *Beyond Compare: Art from Africa in the Bode Museum* that was billed as 'on the way to the Humboldt Forum'. Her analysis too highlights the persistence of past models, despite this exhibition's forward-looking ambition. The activities of the curators and artists with whom Jonas Tinius worked, as well as the activists in Duane Jethro's research, were also mobilised in no small part by what they saw as the colonial wrongs coalescing around the Humboldt Forum. Beyond the contents of this book – and forming a subproject in a final phase of *Making Differences*

– Irene Hilden and Andrei Zavadsky have conducted research on the reception of the Humboldt Forum by the press and visitors (Hilden, Merrow and Zavadski 2021; Zavadsky and Hilden 2022). In addition, and also part of *Making Differences*, artist-researcher Tal Adler has created an exhibit for the University's exhibiting space, the Humboldt Labor, within the Humboldt Forum.[7] Designed to reflect critically upon collecting and exhibiting practices themselves, this exhibit is also intended not only to reflect upon what is currently done but also to generate debate and contribute to changing practice (Macdonald 2023).

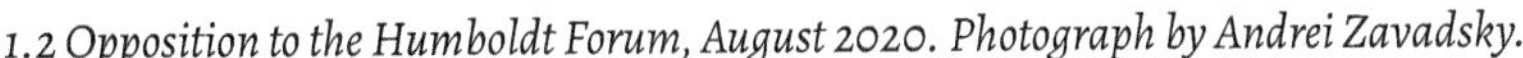

1.2 Opposition to the Humboldt Forum, August 2020. Photograph by Andrei Zavadsky.

The making and contesting of the Humboldt Forum underway by 2015 were, along with the wider debates about colonial histories and continuities, followed by further twists and turns locally and further afield. The widely reported 2017 statement by French President Emmanuel Macron that 'conditions should be created for the… restitution of African patrimony to Africa' (Rea 2017), was highly significant, especially as it came to be developed in a report that he commissioned (Sarr and Savoy 2018; see also von Oswald 2018), in proposing that instead of the burden of proof for the return of objects resting on proof that they had been misappropriated, the onus should be on proving that there had been 'free consent' by those from whom the objects came if they were to be retained. One of the authors of a report that he commissioned to help make the case was art historian Bénédicte Savoy, who, in 2017, resigned from the Humboldt Forum's advisory board, citing among other reasons the failure of its organisers to sufficiently address questions of provenance (Haentschel 2017; Förster 2019: 79). Since then, several permanent provenance research posts have been created to work with the collections of the Ethnological Museum and Museum of Asian Art.[8] One of our team members, Larissa Förster, has worked for many years on the provenance of objects from colonial contexts. She helped create the 2018 provenance guidelines for the German Museums Association, published an edited collection and other contributions dedicated to questions of provenance in ethnological museums (Förster, Edenheiser, Fründt and Hartmann 2018; Förster and Bose 2018; Förster 2018a, 2018b, 2019) and co-edited an introduction to museum ethnology (Edenheiser and Förster 2019) that aimed, among other things, to improve provenance education. In addition, she has undertaken innovative provenance research herself (Förster and Stoecker 2016). Her chapter here draws on some of her experience—in effect treating it as a form of fieldwork—to look at the way that particular terms came to be adopted and the consequences of these within the ongoing debates.

While questions of ethnological museums and colonialism were already on our agenda when we began the *Making Differences* project, particularly for the research area Transforming the Ethnographic, other edited volumes that we produced (Lidchi, Macdonald and Oswald 2017; Oswald and Tinius 2020) reflected more recent events and debates. These works contribute not only to documenting and analysing transformations but also to the transformational aim of decolonising museums and heritage. They bring often overlooked but nevertheless ramifying forms of coloniality within certain heritage and institutions to light, and explore and propose modes of addressing them.

Giving further momentum to decolonisation efforts was the widespread global mobilisation in support of the Black Lives Matter movement, following the brutal killing of George Floyd by U.S. police in 2020. Among other forms of protest, statues of slave owners were toppled not only in the U.S. but also in Europe (see, for example, Atuire 2020; Buchczyk and Jethro 2020; Jethro 2021). Duane Jethro's research on colonial street renaming shows that attempts to decolonise had some success in past years but that the events of 2020 have helped accelerate the process. One example is Berlin's decision to change the name of the street in which our Institute and Research Centre is located—a decision for which postcolonial activists and various others had long campaigned (Azaryahu 2009; Engler 2013; Jethro and Macdonald forthcoming).

These were certainly not the only significant developments during our research. Nazli Cabadağ discusses new developments in the LGBTI+ Pride movements in Istanbul as well as in Berlin, further demonstrating how what happens in Germany may be part of a specific transnational dynamic (see also Cabadağ and Ediger 2020). A political move to the right in Turkey is part of the worrying context of these events. A rightwards move, characterised by growing neo-nationalism and intolerance of diversity, has also been evident in various other parts of the world during these years, with museums and heritage frequently being enlisted in service of promoting such positions (Eckersley 2020; Macdonald 2016, 2021). This is recognised by some museums as a particular problem for how they present 'culture', as shown in Magdalena Buchczyk's discussion of attempts to diversify the collections of the Museum of European Cultures (this volume). Increasingly, social media is being deployed to extend the reach of intolerance (though as research by Nazli Cabadağ and Christoph Bareither, this volume, shows, social media is also being used to work against such views).[9]

Notable in recent years is the growth of public concern over the climate, as evidenced by the Fridays for Future protests, which have taken place all around the world. While this recent intensification of public concern was predated by citizen science initiatives, it is nevertheless part of their wider context, and, indeed, of the wider context of all such work.

The 'busyness' of the past years is testament to the prominence in public discourse of museums, heritage and questions of diversity. As evident from the persistence and even the resurgence of efforts to deploy museums and heritage against diversity and in service of conservative and exclusionary ends, the 'direction' of this activity is clearly not one-way. Nevertheless, certain lines of travel and emphases can be detected amidst the plethora of developments. In order to set out the ways that the *Making Differences* project has approached these tendencies, more needs to be said about our methodology.

Methodology

As noted above, most of the ethnographic research in *Making Differences: Transforming Museums and Heritage* took place in Berlin—hence, the subtitle of this online book: *A Berlin Ethnography.* In the classic tradition of ethnography, our work speaks not only to what is happening in each case but also to wider developments. This includes those outlined above, which the chapters that follow expand on, as well as others that the various authors identify. What we present here, in essence, are particular struggles over, and realisations of, how to do difference and diversity in the present. All of these struggles and realisations, in one way or another, implicate heritage, be it in the form of museums and collections or in notions of belonging, history and culture. And all involve innovation—attempts to craft new ways of doing things or new concepts or new alliances, often against a backdrop of established and even limiting infrastructures, practices and ways of thinking. As such, they highlight the potential of museums and heritage to transform how difference and diversity are done more widely.

'An Ethnography'

That all of the studies were conducted in Berlin within the same time frame enables an in-depth understanding of a particular setting and moment. It is what allows us to describe our approach as 'an ethnography', even though it was conducted by multiple researchers, each bringing a particular kind of expertise, fieldwork experience and set of perspectives to the project. It is a *multi-researcher ethnography* not just in the sense that many ethnographers have all worked on one topic but also in that it preserves their distinct inputs. Rather than begin from the idea of a known or potential 'whole', we leave open how different organisations, groups and other components or elements—to use the language of assemblage theory—interrelate or form particular constellations (DeLanda 2016).

Our ethnography does, nevertheless, attempt to include a broad range of museum and heritage organisations and settings. And it does so without purporting to be comprehensive or imagining its selections to be representative of parts within a system. Given that the city's official tourism organisation, *Visit Berlin*, lists 170 museums alone, and that there are many more heritage sites, and an incalculable number of the heritage-related practices, exhaustive coverage would have been not only exhausting but impossible. Instead, our approach has been to select contexts and venues that tap into questions of diversity and difference from a range of positions and perspectives. How these might relate to each other—whether through similar language or other practices—was a matter for investigation rather than presumption. At the same time, however, we did work on the assumption that there *would* be many interrelationships, not least due to geographical proximity and the potential for shared discourse, as sketched above. Moreover, some of the groups and organisations that we worked with are part of overarching governmental structures—for example, the Museum of Islamic Art, the Ethnological Museum and the Museum of European Cultures, among others, are all part of the Staatliche Museen zu Berlin (SMB) and the Stiftung Preussischer Kulturbesitz (SPK, Prussian Cultural Heritage Foundation). They thus operate under various shared organisational conditions, and sometimes are spoken of as a collective. In addition, some of these museums, as well as others, engage in common endeavours, most notably, the Humboldt Forum. By giving recognition to links and interrelationships, we aimed to avoid what—in an article for which Christine Gerbich came up with the apt title, 'No Museum is an Island'—we have called 'ethnographic containerism' (Macdonald, Gerbich and Oswald 2018). Modelled on critiques of the widespread tendency in social science research to regard the nation as a taken-for-granted analytical 'container' ('methodological nationalism'), our collective ethnographic approach avoided taking each component ethnographic study as representing an isolated island of operation.

Here it is also important to note that although a good deal of our research was 'real time'—that is, looking at what was ongoing—we did not see it as disconnected from the past. On the contrary, we were centrally concerned with how the past articulates with the present, be it through consciously addressing history or through the persistence of earlier discourse or infrastructure.

Approaching difference and diversity

The methodological approach adopted was also important in order to break with conventional framings of difference and diversity. By not limiting ourselves to one kind of organisation and by not working with predefined notions of 'communities' or 'differences', we were able to bring together heterogeneous elements (any of which alone might risk becoming a 'container') and to disrupt the ways in which they could be taken for granted. Mixing things up in this heterogeneous fashion allowed for the methodological 'messiness' that John Law (2004) advocates to avoid replicating existing analytical frameworks and, thus, to help open up new perspectives.

A characteristic of ethnographic methodology, especially that rooted in social anthropology, is to give close attention to the framings, categories and practices deployed by those we are trying to understand. How do they see and do difference and diversity? Who is included and how in their grouping of subjects? Accordingly, our research often followed our interlocutors in their networks, groups and communities. In looking at participatory projects at the Museum of Islamic Art, the Museum of Natural History, the

Museum of European Cultures or *Berlin Global*, we examined the ways in which participants were defined and enlisted. Likewise, we explored the affiliations made in Berlin Pride, in *i,Slam*, in the visitor books of the German colonialism exhibition or by visitors posting online about the Holocaust Memorial. And we followed attempts to come up with new and different classifications of difference, as in Jonas Tinius's study of SAVVY Contemporary's 'Dis-Othering' project, conducted with the Belgian Centre for Fine Arts and Austria's *Kulturen in Bewegung*. Centrally, then, our ethnographic work gives attention to the kinds of sameness and difference, the categories and relationships, that our participants invoke through the terms that they use (e.g. 'Berliners', 'Europe', 'Africa', 'community', 'race'), as well as to how they put these into practice (e.g. who they label or define by such terms, whom they invite to participate in certain events, who turns up). Doing so opens up the potential gap between terms and their use. Sometimes the gap is between expectations and results, ambitions and reality. Sometimes it signals interesting possibilities beyond those contemplated at the outset. And sometimes—in processes of recursivity (Tinius and Macdonald 2020)—it can be refracted back into both practice and academic theorising, to show alternatives to the terminologies currently in use.

Our research methodology adopts a particular take on difference and diversity. Rather than following the equivalent of a multicultural model, which would have identified particular groups or venues, or particular kinds of diversity, as offering an equivalent set of distinctive positions, we developed a multi-scalar, multifocal approach that was responsive to the heterogeneous context and approaches of our researchers. If not exactly rhizomatic (in Braidotti's sense, above), it is nevertheless a model that does not presuppose a single 'whole picture'; rather, it allows for degrees of sharing, partial connections, mutual reverberations and traffic between them. As such, it leaves the possibilities for what is going on more open than they would be otherwise.

Ethnographic engagement

The researchers in the *Making Differences* project have spent time in their various fieldwork settings and engaged with those who participate in them. None of the studies rely on post-hoc documentation by others or recollections by interviewees, though many use these as part of an overall raft of approaches. A mix of techniques is usual in ethnography, though it always includes some degree of 'being there' (Geertz 1988), of being in the presence of interlocutors, even when 'there' can also mean online (see especially Bareither, this volume). A characteristic of much ethnography is the direct observation of objects, images, movements, bodies, spaces, animals and other other-than-human participants. All of the ethnographic contributions in this volume pay close attention to detail: particular words or tones of voice; the placing of objects in relation to one another or to texts; facial expressions in photographs or looks exchanged during a meeting; the mounting disquiet when events are not quite working out or the ebullience of participating in a successful effort. Such details are not 'mere' or 'incidental'. Rather, they are often where struggles or contradictions coalesce or plans get tripped up.

While all of the ethnographic research undertaken in *Making Differences* has involved some in situ presence, the forms that this has taken, and the emphasis given to particular techniques, has varied. In some cases, researchers have been deeply embedded in their fieldsites over years, even prior to their joining the project. This is particularly the case for Nazli Cabadağ, Larissa Förster, Christine Gerbich, Tahani Nadim and Margareta von Oswald, though depending on how one defines 'fieldsite' includes others as well. Their position can be described as observant-participation — a term used here by Margareta von Oswald, who co-curated an exhibition in the Ethnological Museum. Inverting the classical term 'participant-observation', which advocates understanding through involvement, observant-participation implies a more active role, even a leading one.

Many of our other researchers have also taken active roles that had the potential to change what they were investigating. Duane Jethro has spoken in public in favour of changing colonial street names in Berlin and describes his position as one of 'occupying a space of solidarity' with activists; Jonas Tinius organised activities for some of the galleries that he worked with and acted as a 'sparring partner' (Tinius 2021; Tinius and Macdonald 2020); I was a member of *Berlin Global's* advisory board and made input in other capacities too; Chiara Garbellotto's innovative approach collaborates with participants, and sometimes also with the visual anthropologist in our team, Nnenna Onuoha, to devise workshops (Garbellotto and Onuoha 2019). In addition, beyond the scope of this volume, the project has entailed further engagements, including, as mentioned above, artist-researcher Tal Adler's exhibit *Who is ID8470?* which is shown in the Humboldt Labor in the Humboldt Forum. We do not see such roles as contaminating the research process but, rather, as opportunities to learn more and open up spaces for reflection, and to engage deeply by directly experiencing the details, complexities and affective dimensions of practice. Occupying various roles allows a 'multifaceted granularity' of understanding, as Larissa Förster puts it below; and it is perhaps inevitable in contexts in which, as Jonas Tinius has written elsewhere, the 'membranes' between organizations are 'porous' (Tinius 2020). Active participation helps us get a better handle on how those we are working with are likely to see and feel the activities in which they are involved. Hence, it gives us a stronger grasp of how and why things turn out as they do, and, by extension, positions us to make a difference to ongoing practice.

Making a difference in the sense of changing museum and heritage practice for the better is part of the project's objective. Through careful observation and analysis, researchers identified concepts and practices that can help or hinder the improvement of how things are customarily done. Likewise, highlighting seeming self-evident assumptions or overlooked influences can lead to ways of thinking—and doing—otherwise (CARMAH 2018). Working closely with fieldwork interlocutors helps ensure that our insights and the results of our analysis flow into future practice. So too does the use of multiple formats, ranging from informal discussions to more formal meetings, reports, workshops, films, conferences and various kinds of publications (blogs, co-written experimental pieces, academic articles, etc.). Making as much of our work as possible open access—as with this volume—has also been important in this regard. Other, direct forms of *making a difference* to which the project has contributed include exhibition-making, activism and devising new pedagogical programmes and guidelines.

Team work

All ethnographic research requires reflexivity—that is, attention to one's own role. This is all the more so when research involves as much active participation as the *Making Differences* project has. Work in a multi-researcher team has been invaluable in promoting reflexivity, for it provides an environment of alert colleagues, with complementary experience and expertise, who can ask questions and prompt (sometimes uncomfortable) interrogations of each other's roles, assumptions, actions and findings.

Our team work was aided by the fact that members of the *Making Differences* project were all based in a shared research space—that of the Centre for Anthropological Research on Museums and Heritage (CARMAH). Regular meetings, presentations, co-organised events and co-written publications all helped bring the studies together by detecting connections and disparities, and by highlighting further lines of enquiry. Our ethnography was 'more-than-individual' in that we worked within a constant buzz of information relevant to our research, with news articles being sent around on email and clusters of researchers gathering in the kitchen to discuss them. Attending talks and conferences fostered an ongoing conversation across and beyond specific fieldsites. Not infrequently, the fieldsite of one researcher would be visited by others in the team. For example, many team members collectively visited the *German Colonialism* exhibition, *DaHEIM* at the Museum of European Cultures, *Beyond Compare* at the Bode Museum and the *Heritage of the Old Kings* at the Museum of Islamic Art. Many also participated in events connected with the renaming of our institute's street. Some of us also visited exhibitions and events elsewhere and analysed them together (e.g. Merrow, Gerbich and Jethro 2020).

The composition of the *Making Differences* team was fluid in that it was made up of various members at different times over a wide range of positions and levels of commitment: some came later than others or left earlier, some were full-time, others were affiliated. We also drew on input from visiting researchers who came either specifically for *Making Differences* or for other projects as well as from external associates of CARMAH and beyond. Nevertheless, this particular volume was the result of a core conversation over a dedicated series of meetings and drafts.

This volume

The chapters in this volume address questions of how difference and diversity are being done in museums and heritage today. Rather than presenting summaries of the overall findings from each study, they explore particular dimensions of the wider research. Collectively, they offer many more insights and deploy many more theoretical resources than I have covered here. The articles in this volume, emanating as they do from the same research project, are linked in a multitude of ways, and need not be read in any specific order. Nevertheless, the following offers one possible approach by means of a meta-narrative about doing diversity in museums and heritage.

Colonial provenance, persistence and decolonisation

Debates about colonial provenance and restitution are a major strand of contemporary diversity discourse in German public culture, which asks how Germany—and Europe more generally—position themselves with regard to other parts of the world, especially former colonies in Africa. Larissa Förster, in her chapter for this volume, discusses the unique forms that growing concerns about colonial provenance, restitution, human remains and cultural artefacts in various parts of the world take in Germany. She gives particular attention to German colonial history and its relationship to other histories such as that of National Socialism, as well as to certain political and cultural structures and developments. From her own close involvement, she highlights changes over time as debates have increasingly come to be framed in moral rather than in exclusively legal terms. This shift also encompasses an emphasis on decolonising museums and heritage more widely.

Margareta von Oswald's fieldwork in the Ethnological Museum in Berlin was carried out as these debates became particularly acute, intensified by the fact that the Ethnological Museum was preparing exhibitions for the Humboldt Forum. As she describes, this led to tense atmospheres within the museum as curators – including herself – sought to negotiate certain resulting tensions. Evident here is also how museums' earlier work of 'making differences' continues into the present, making current attempts by museum staff to work in new ways more challenging (see also von Oswald 2020, 2022; Phillips 2011; Lidchi, Macdonald and von Oswald 2017). Co-curating an exhibition that was intended to address questions of colonial provenance and 'looted art', von Oswald directly experienced the challenges involved, emanating variously from the conditions and assumptions of the organizational context, as well as from issues that only became more evident during the making process (see also Oswald and Rodatus 2017). On the one hand, the resulting exhibition, *Object Biographies,* was an attempt to bring a more critical approach to conventional modes of collecting and exhibiting African objects within ethnological museums – and, thus, to be a form of decolonising – but at the same time, as she herself makes clear, it was compromised in various ways.

Object Biographies was created as part of the process of developing ideas for the future Forum. Another notable exhibition that was developed as part of this process and that also involved objects from the collections of the Ethnological Museum was *Beyond Compare: Art from Africa,* which Nnenna Onuoha discusses in this volume (see also Loeseke 2019). The exhibition placed items from the Africa collections alongside those already on display in the Bode Museum, which is devoted to Byzantine, Gothic, Renaissance and Baroque art. The juxtaposition of Africa and Europe posed the question of comparability alluded to in the title. While this inclusion of African objects in a museum of European art was intended, as Onuoha explains, to 'transcend...stereotypical, Eurocentric perceptions of African Art', she argues that it 'ends up reinforcing' them. Her argument rests on a historically informed analysis that includes detailed attention to the particular juxtapositions of objects with one another and with the accompanying texts and gallery space. Instead of 'difference' being 'enunciated' in ways that open up questions, it is instead, she maintains, 'flattened' into familiar binaries, performing in effect a simple form of 'cultural diversity' in which difference is neatly contained.

1.3 German Colonialism exhibition at the German Historical Museum. Photograph by Wolfgang Siesing reproduced courtesy of the German Historical Museum.

German Colonialism, an exhibition that opened at the German Historical Museum in 2016, was, as noted above, widely seen as part of a turn towards a more direct and open confrontation with Germany's colonial past—in contrast, as some would claim, to the Humboldt Forum. As Harriet Merrow explains, though some saw it as a welcome sign of Germany at long last coming clean about its past, it also received a good deal of criticism from politicians, activists, members of the public and even those who had been involved in its making. Putting it crudely, some believed it was too critical of Germany, whereas for others it did not go nearly far enough. Drawing on analysis of media coverage, thousands of entries in visitor books, participant-observation in the exhibition and interviews, Merrow identifies the variety of statements, the key issues on which disagreement tended to fall and the features of the exhibition that led to particular, sometimes problematic, interpretations and limitations. A better understanding of these responses can help create exhibitions that are effective in tackling the contentious topic of German colonialism and in spreading awareness of its continuities amidst broader decolonisation efforts.

Duane Jethro addresses issues of decolonisation in his examination of campaigns to rename streets with colonial histories and/or connotations in Berlin. He compares the situation with that of post-apartheid South Africa, where he has also conducted research (see especially Jethro 2020). The very efficiency and speed of street-renaming in South Africa meant that a public debate scarcely took place there. The struggles that accompany such debates, he argues, are worthwhile because they raise awareness not only about the past but also about how race is articulated in relation to national identity. Moreover, they show that the term 'decolonisation' itself is variously understood and can indicate a range of different processes, some more unsettling and probing than others.

Diversity initiatives

Scholarship and activism have increasingly shown colonialism to have had much more extensive and lasting consequences than previously recognised (e.g. Azoulay 2019; Stoler 2016), highlighting the need for more extensive decolonisation. This requires thoroughgoing examination of taken-for-granted structures of thought and action, as well as the challenging of problematic conceptions of difference such as Otherness, and the addressing of diversity and white privilege. Initiatives to begin this work of decolonising and diversifying have begun to flourish in cultural organisations, including museums and heritage (see, for example, Dilger and Warstat 2021; Insaf 2020; Knudsen et al. 2021; Sieg 2021).

One such initiative is the Dis-Othering project, discussed by Jonas Tinius, which sought to look at how various cultural organisations themselves imagine Africa, including as part of their own attempts to diversify. The project was a collaboration between two non-mainstream organisations that had strong reputations for their critical engagement with questions of diversity and difference, and a public cultural and exhibition venue that acted as project manager and, eventually, the subject of curators' criticism. One part of the project entailed creating a survey to map diversity within a wide range of arts organisations, both mainstream and more avant-garde, in Austria, Belgium and Germany. As Tinius' engaged ethnography shows, this turned out to be highly problematic, with contention over which diversities to include, as well as over the format and approach of the questionnaire, and the constituency to address. What became evident, he argues, was that the very attempts to map diversity themselves frequently ended up replicating the categories and formats of which they were critical. While this might seem a depressing conclusion—and it is surely a cautionary one—he points out that the struggle and reflection that resulted were themselves valuable and can be seen as a positive outcome of the project.

Trying to actively diversify was also the aim of a number of our other fieldsites, including the exhibition *Berlin Global* in the Humboldt Forum, discussed by me, and the Museum of European Cultures, analysed by Magdalena Buchczyk. *Berlin Global* attempted to embrace many forms of diversity and diversification while critiquing Othering and exoticisation. As I show, attempting to do the latter—as with *Beyond Compare* and the Dis-Othering project—often risked reproducing stereotypes or dualisms in the very process of attempting to make visitors aware of them. Here again, it was in the practice of realisation that the difficulty often lay. Much debate and careful consideration of the 'visual metaphors' of the exhibition sought to find ways around the perceived problems. This was also the case in relation to the dilemmas of categorisation in the Dis-Othering project, and to the possible endless proliferation of diversities—dilemmas with which political theory also struggles.

Berlin Global is not based on a particular collection: the objects that it includes have been selected primarily to illustrate the story and 'message' (*Botschaft*) that the curators devised. In this, it differs from the Ethnological Museum's presence in the Humboldt Forum, as discussed by Oswald and Onuoha, as well as from the Museum of European Cultures example, presented by Buchczyk. Which objects are present in the collections—and what information is available about them—is inevitably shaped by previous historical circumstances, chance and the predilections of previous curatorial ideas and ambitions—factors that can limit current curatorial aims, as Buchczyk shows particularly clearly. The desire of curators at the Museum of European Culture to be 'socially responsive', which they see as being 'more diverse', is often made more difficult due to the coverage of the current collections. During Buchczyk's fieldwork, the curators devised new ways to try to do what they refer to as 'diversifying the collections' and 'addressing gaps'. This includes writing a new collecting policy, which will diversify not only what is collected in the future but also who is involved. But as the curators' thoughtful discussions show, operationalising the policy and deciding which specific objects to collect face thorny problems that are inherent to many diversification projects, particularly those that, like museums, carry the weight of the past and stand to shape the future.

Expanding the remit of who is involved in museum work is a major motivation of citizen science initiatives. These have been developed especially by museums of natural history, where an emphasis on biodiversity is variously entangled with ideas of social diversity, as Chiara Garbellotto and Tahani Nadim show here in examples from their fieldwork in the Berlin Museum of Natural History. Initiatives that enlist 'citizens' in mapping biodiversity, such as the Nightingale Project on which they focus, tend to do so within empiricist approaches that understand diversity as 'there' to be discovered and documented. By contrast, Garbellotto and Nadim emphasise that diversity is 'co-produced by the material-semiotic devices used to record it' and, therefore, they explore the practices and infrastructures of producing diversity data (see also Nadim 2021). As with various other *Making Differences* studies, especially those of Tinius and Buchczyk, this brings attention to issues of the classifications used, as well as to the other ways in which certain data-making practices afford particular kinds of engagement (or not) and particular kinds of connections (or not). They show how, on the one hand, citizen science biodiversity initiatives attempt to articulate social diversity by involving 'more diverse' sections of the population, including 'new Berliners' who are not formally citizens. On the other, however, they also stress that the link between a loss of biodiversity and a loss of social diversity—as when urban gentrification results in a loss of both—tends to be overlooked by views that see citizen science as lying outside the sphere of civic participation.

Forging new belonging and relations

Garbellotto and Nadim argue that citizen science initiatives can be seen not simply as involving citizens but as producing them (or what they call 'sensing' them). If citizenship is seen as not just about formal legal status—and not as something that one has or does not—but as a more graded and multifaceted matter including feelings of belonging and of being able to participate in public culture, then cultural organisations and initiatives have an important role to play in enabling it. Indeed, their major motivation for trying to diversify collections, exhibitions and the like is to give recognition—and thus some sense of connection—to the diversity of Germany's population. Enabling the active participation of 'citizens' in this broader sense takes that recognition to another level. As we have already seen, however, opportunities for active participation face certain difficulties, though various innovative solutions have been and are being developed.

One of the established museums in Berlin that has embraced the goal of inclusivity is the Museum of Islamic Art. The goal has been particularly valuable in light of the fact that Islam is often popularly regarded to be, as Katarzyna Puzon writes, 'not German'. Both Christine Gerbich and Rikke Gram present examples of significant participatory initiatives that the Museum of Islamic Art was instrumental in establishing. For example, *Museum Diwan*, a project that Gerbich played a major role in designing and running, brought together people from a range of backgrounds to help rethink the museum's approaches. This included what was called 'revisiting the collections', in which participants explored the potential of the existing collections for connecting with contemporary inhabitants of Berlin and for telling other stories than those of academic art history. As Gerbich shows, understanding these processes merely as 'adding on' to what was already underway was not enough: it also requires from curators and other museum workers a questioning of current accepted practice, undertaking what Gerbich refers to as 'organisational unlearning'.

Multaka was another important initiative of the Museum of Islamic Art, which it undertook together with three other Museums in Berlin (the German Historical Museum, the Bode Museum and the Museum of the Ancient Near East). It began in 2015 in response to the refugee crisis, and it came to win various awards for its efforts to 'integrate' new arrivals. Central to its novelty was the use of Arabic-speaking refugees and other newcomers to the city as museum guides. On the basis of her fieldwork and interviews, Gram shows how the question of 'difference' was variously negotiated in the initiative. On the one hand, the label 'refugee' and the fact that the tours were not only 'by' but also 'for' refugees (though in practice many others also attended) highlighted the 'difference' of the newcomers, something that was also reinforced by certain structural work conditions due to bureaucratic status. On the other, however, the project succeeded in helping newcomers share their expertise through meaningful work that would otherwise have been hard to attain, and it allowed them to bring their own perspectives into these major cultural institutions.

While *Museum Diwan* and *Multaka* were organised by established museums, the developments discussed by Puzon and Cabadağ were realised by individuals and groups. The initiators can be seen as belonging to specific 'communities', though it needs bearing in mind that this term can be problematic because it implies that people can be neatly divided into different but equivalent and internally homogeneous groups. This is often seen, for example, in relation to migration, which is often depicted as resulting in distinct 'communities' with shared 'cultures' and shared sets of ties to their 'homelands'. *Museum Diwan* was designed precisely to avoid such an assumption. The chapters by Puzon and Cabadağ also show how a shared 'migration background' (*Migrationshintergrund*)—a term commonly used by Germans for immigrants and for those whose parents or grandparents are immigrants—does not necessarily lead to shared interests or senses of collectivity. In the case of the poetry slam group, *i,Slam*, discussed by Puzon, individuals from various such backgrounds come together not to express an already fixed identity but, rather, to negotiate what it means to be both Muslim and German. The cultural form that this takes is, likewise, not fixed as 'traditional'; rather, it draws on Islamic heritage in creative ways, sometimes reaching translocally to other parts of the world as well.

The LGBTI+ event *Berlin Walks with Istanbul Pride*, analysed by Cabadağ, can also be seen as a newly crafted translocal 'heritage'. In particular, the activists running it—including Cabadağ herself—sought to express solidarity with Istanbul Pride, which had not taken place since 2015 after being banned by Turkey's right-wing government. But Istanbul-based LGBTI+ activists saw *Berlin Walks with Istanbul Pride* differently, arguing that it highlighted difference and inequality by performing Western privilege and promulgating the idea that Europe was an emancipatory destination for migrants. While Cabadağ accepts the critique in part, she also points out that to see members of the Berlin-based Turkish-speaking LGBTI+ 'community' (or of the Istanbul one, for that matter) as all alike is problematic: here, too, there is difference when it comes to degrees of privilege and freedom, especially between generations. Nevertheless, the possibility of 'community without commonality' enables 'multiple attachments of queer migrants to multiple locations and temporalities'. This means that while an event such as *Berlin Walks with Istanbul Pride* might be rejected by some, it will also be embraced, perhaps ambivalently, by others. Indeed, the very differences of opinion about it can be welcomed as part of a wider reflection on 'making differences queerly'—that is, on finding alternative modes of making not only differences but also connections of various kinds.

As Christoph Bareither shows in his analysis of posts by visitors to the Memorial to the Murdered Jews of Europe in Berlin, an important means for connecting translocally is digital media. Bareither gives careful attention to visitors' practices of photography—especially taking selfies—along with their posting of the images online and their comments about the site's 'difficult heritage'. As he argues, even in cases of what might initially seem like 'emotionally indifferent' or even 'disrespectful' engagements with the site—such as smiling for a photograph—visitors often express more complicated emotions and reflections. In addition, rather than connecting with the site from positions of fixed identity categories, visitors' posts and their responses to Bareither's questions show multiple and varied forms of engagement. These indicate less an atomisation of relationships to heritage, he maintains, than their *personalisation*, one in which visitors forge their own particular mix of connections, both with the site and with others in the online sphere.

Final comments

The chapters in this volume make many more important points than is possible to cover here, and provide rich ethnographic illustration regarding questions of diversity and difference in museums and heritage. To boil them down to one overall set of findings would be reductive. Nevertheless, there are certain core themes and directions that emerge. One of the most notable of these is the struggle against established classifications and other rigid 'containers'. Despite the wide variety of cases that we have taken, models of diversity that rely on mono-dimensional and fixed categories are shown time and again to miss the complexities of contemporary relationships and senses of self. Concepts such as 'community' and 'identity' are increasingly viewed as, if not inoperable and redundant, at least requiring revision and reconceptualisation to allow for more fluidity and less communality, as Cabadağ puts it. When terms such as 'Berliners' or 'Germans' are used, they are often put in quotation marks, or their problematic status is indicated by changing our tone of voice or by prefixing with 'so-called' (*sogenannte*). Online, users may (and usually do) tag their posts with many hashtags simultaneously, or, as shown in Bareither's study, they may deploy hashtags such as #jewish to signal a sense of connection or to indicate that they have visited the Holocaust Memorial, rather than making a strong identity claim (such as 'being Jewish'). Numerous initiatives—started by local or translocal groups, individuals, alternative venues and more mainstream organisations—have begun the search for new connections and relationships, for new ways of belonging, of being 'German' and of doing diversity. As we discuss in this volume, these new practices are already being forged and realised.

Our cases also show, however, that abandoning or reworking existing categories is difficult and usually impossible. This is perhaps especially true for museums, which in many ways rely on classificatory activity. The classification of collections cannot easily be changed, as the case of the Museum of European Cultures shows. But even classifications that are not materialised in collections can be hard to avoid, as shown in the case of the *Berlin Global*. Figuring out strategies to diversify and engage with those who are not usually involved necessarily involves some kind of naming and labelling, even if it is more or less self-aware, cautious and innovative. Furthermore, the gathering of data can deploy categories that the researchers themselves find dubious, as in the Dis-Othering project, or that do not attend critically to the data assemblages that result, as in the Nightingale Project. At issue here are not simply categories and labels but also the patterns into which they are organised, which may imply hierarchies or deny inequalities. In this way, associations and positions such as where particular exhibitions or museums are located also establish certain 'constellations of difference' to convey meaning and hierarchy (Macdonald 2016).

An aim of our research is to address problematic modes of differencing—an aim we share with some of the organisations and practices that we have explored. In some cases, organisations examined their own practices, as was the intention of the survey conducted for the Dis-Othering project, of the meetings leading up to the new collecting policy of the Museum of European Cultures and of the Museum Diwan workshops. In other cases, the aim has been to make the public aware of past practices by calling attention to them in exhibitions, as the *German Colonialism* exhibition and *Berlin Global* did for colonial practices of display. Activism has also sought to highlight problematic differencing, as in the case of colonial street names, as well as to bring activist-desired difference into the public domain, as in Berlin Pride.

In some ways what activism does is to change the people who get to make differences. Instead of leaving city and cultural management to established institutions, activists rely on more ad hoc arrangements, though these may develop into more structured organizations (such as Berlin Postkolonial). In some cases, activism begins with a focus on a specific issue, though as we see in the case of Berlin, it can gain traction by gathering various causes together and focusing on specific issues such as street names, restitution and the Humboldt Forum. In other cases, activism is based on identity or difference, as in the case of *i,Slam* and LGBTI initiatives, though here too these tend to reinforce themselves through translocal networking and online media. While activism is generally regarded as an 'outsider' movement (Pettinicchio 2012) challenging the status quo, what is also clear in our Berlin ethnography is that the boundaries between inside and outside may be traversed and indistinct, as surprised Margareta von Oswald when she began working in the Ethnological Museum. Organisations such as SAVVY Contemporary and Galerie Wedding blur the boundaries more explicitly. They are semi-established in that they are relatively longstanding organisations with physical premises that have received various types of state funding but they often take oppositional stances and try to change the status quo, sometimes allying themselves with, or even instigating, activist campaigns. In addition, there is what has been called 'institutional activism', in which attempts to bring about major changes to established norms emerge 'from within organisations and institutions' (Pettinicchio 2012: 501). While there is a risk here of stretching the term 'activism' too far, some mainstream organisations have embraced causes that have been promoted primarily by activists and have worked together with the activists themselves. An example of a move towards greater institutionalisation is the establishment in 2018 of an office of the German Lost Art Foundation to deal with objects from colonial contexts. The office is headed by Larissa Förster, whose work falls under both scholarship and activism. Such fluidity is, indeed, another feature of the situations that we have analysed. Duane Jethro's work is also both scholarly and activist—his scholarship provides further substance for his causes, and his activist participation enriches his scholarly contemplation. The same is true for Christine Gerbich, who works within an established museum and is thus to some degree an 'institutional insider'. More generally, those identifying as activists as well as scholars participated in events organised by our research centre, and are thus an important part of the overall conversation. Indeed, operating as a locus for such boundary-crossing interaction was a role that CARMAH came to play.

Changing—diversifying—who is involved in heritage-making is something that almost all of the museums that we have looked at have undertaken. This is part of a wider development that often falls under the heading of 'participation' and that is often cast as part of a 'democratisation' of such institutions. Examples in our volume include the Museum of Islamic Art (both *Museum Diwan* and *Multaka*), *Berlin Global*, the Museum of European Cultures and the Museum of Natural History. In another publication, we have discussed these and other examples in more depth (Macdonald, Gerbich, Gram, Puzon & Shatanawi 2021). Our ethnographic research has made clear that the term 'participation' is used in various ways and that the participatory measures go from minor and temporary to more substantial and enduring. Changes to how collecting is undertaken, as in the case of the Museum of European Cultures, are likely to have a deeper impact on the future than, say, a temporary exhibition. But even developments that started out temporary, such as *Multaka*, can have unanticipated effects in the long term by making curators better understand the value of diverse perspectives.

Efforts to increase participation raise the general issue of categorisation and coverage: who ends up being included and how? While participation measures are sometimes less transformational than hoped, they remain worthwhile. The accompanying struggles are part of understanding what the difficulties are—the points at which conversation tends to stop or categories tend to solidify—and can themselves be an important dimension of learning and civic participation. As Garbellotto and Nadim argue when writing about participative data-gathering in citizen science projects, what is needed is not just more understanding 'of nature' but also more 'critical data consciousness', that is, more awareness of how knowledge itself is constructed. As public organisations of knowledge-making, museums are especially well placed to undertake that task — a task that, I suggest, might be considered as fostering 'co-criticality'.

It is worth noting that members of the public may be eager to participate in museums and heritage. (Trans)local heritage marches, musical events, activist campaigns, writing in visitor books, taking photographs at heritage sites and posting comments online are all intellectually and emotionally engaged activities. Sometimes, as with the *German Colonialism* exhibition, engagement is visible and significant. But even in cases in which active participation may not be immediately evident, it may be occurring elsewhere or taking non-conventional forms, as Bareither's work on the Holocaust Memorial suggests. The question for established organisations is how to engage with public forms of interest and how to do so in ways that broaden involvement rather than making space for only certain voices.

The issue of voice takes us to one of the most important questions of diversification: does it simply create *more* inputs or does it aim specifically at those who are usually left out? This struggle is especially evident in the case of *Berlin Global*, where the question was also raised whether the participative offer should extend to members of right-wing organisations such as the Alternative for Germany party. Is it perhaps especially important to target those less likely to be convinced of the case for diversity? Or should those who seek to exclude others from public debate be denied platform? Just what kind of diversity should be promoted? These are questions that are faced not only by museums and heritage but are of relevance to many cultural organizations.

The fact that we have mostly undertaken ethnographic fieldwork, often over long time periods of months or even years, means that we have directly witnessed debating and struggling with questions such as these, and have, thus, been able to gain an appreciation of the many issues and steps taken or not taken, as well as the assumptions that have been involved. In many cases, this has highlighted the role of a greater range of actors, such as objects and non-human creatures, atmospheres and feelings, in addition to people, along with their specific histories and entanglements. All of this, we hope, will help us offer a deeper understanding of what goes into making heritage and of what heritage produces.

As this introduction has hopefully made clear, and as will become still more evident in the chapters that follow, much of what we present is of relevance to significant questions concerning diversity and difference in museums and heritage in general. At the same time, however, our ethnography of Berlin in the early 21st century paints a vivid portrait of concerns and developments in Germany's capital. While we certainly do not cover all of what has been going on in Berlin's museums and heritage, we focus on some of the most significant developments and transformations underway. In particular, we track how a new emphasis on colonialism, on new arrivals to the city from beyond Europe and on participation have reshaped debates not only about what diversity might mean and how it might be done but also about the very nature of Germany and German-ness.

The *Making Differences* project is not yet finished: there is work still to complete and publications to come. The conversation between us and our many interlocutors – now including readers of this book – goes on.

Acknowledgments

This chapter was written as part of my Alexander von Humboldt Professorship. I am grateful to the Alexander von Humboldt Foundation, as well as to the Humboldt-Universität zu Berlin, the Museum für Naturkunde and the Prussian Cultural Heritage Foundation for the support. I thank all members of CARMAH (the Centre for Anthropological Research on Museums and Heritage) and especially the members of the *Making Differences* project for sharing reading suggestions and discussing ideas over these last years. The following deserve particular thanks for comments on this text: Christoph Bareither, Larissa Förster, Christine Gerbich, Duane Jethro, Margareta von Oswald, Katarzyna Puzon, Jonas Tinius and Andrei Zavadsky.

Notes

1 Further information about the project is available here: http://www.carmah.berlin/making-differences-in-berlin/ (accessed 1 June 2022).
2 https://www.unesco.de/kultur-und-natur/kulturelle-vielfalt (accessed 1 June 2022).
3 https://www.dwds.de/wb/Vielfalt; https://www.dwds.de/wb/Diversität (accessed 1 June 2022).
4 This remains the case today, as the OECD figures show. See https://data.oecd.org/inequality/income-inequality.htm (accessed 1 June 2022).
5 https://data.oecd.org/inequality/income-inequality.htm) (accessed 1 June 2022).
6 This workshop was a collaboration with the Woolf Institute, Cambridge, UK, and was primarily organised by Jan-Jonathan Bock, a visiting researcher at CARMAH.
7 https://www.humboldt-labor.de/en/projects/other-research-projects/who-is-id-8470 (accessed 1 June 2022).
8 https://www.smb.museum/en/research/provenance-research/ (accessed 1 June 2022).
9 We are further exploring the capacities of online media in relation to questions of 'post truth' in another project. See http://www.carmah.berlin/chapter/ (accessed 1 June 2022).

References

Ahmed, S. 2007. 'The language of diversity', *Ethnic and Racial Studies*, 30(2): 235–56.

Ang, I. 2018. 'Museums and cultural diversity: a persistent challenge', in K. Drohter, V. Dziekan, R. Parry, and K. C. Schrøder (eds), *The Routledge Handbook of Museums, Media and Communication*, 315–329. London: Routledge.

Appadurai, A. 2013. 'Diversity and disciplinarity as cultural artifacts', in C. McCarthy, W. Crichlow, G. Dimitriadis, and N. Dolby (eds), *Race, Identity, and Representation in Education*, 2nd ed., 427–437. London, New York: Taylor and Francis.

Appiah, K. A. 2005. *The Ethics of Identity*. New Jersey: Princeton University Press.

Appiah, K. A. 2018. *The Lies That Bind: Rethinking Identity.* New York: W. W. Norton.

Atuire, C.A. 2020 'Black Lives Matter and the removal of racist statues. Perspectives of an African', *Inquiries into Art, History and the Visual*, 21: 449–67.

Azaryahu, M. 2009. 'Naming the past: The significance of commemorative street names', in L. D. Berg, and J. Vuolteenaho (eds), *Critical Toponymies: the Contested Politics of Place Naming*, 53–70. London: Ashgate.

Azoulay, A.A. 2019. *Potential History. Unlearning Imperialism.* London: Verso.

Bach, J. 2021. 'Brand of Brothers? The Humboldt Forum and the Myths of Innocence', *German Politics and Society*, 39 (1): 100–111.

Bal, M. 1996. *Double Exposures. The Subject of Cultural Analysis.* London: Routledge.

Barth, F. (ed.). 1969. *Ethnic Groups and Boundaries. The Social Organization of Cultural Difference.* Copenhagen: Universitetsforlaget.

Bayer, N., B. Kazeem-Kaminiski, and N. Sternfeld (eds). 2017. *Kuratieren als antirassistische Praxis. Kritiken, Praxen, Aneignungen*. Berlin: de Gruyter.

Bennett, T. 2006. 'Exhibition, difference, and the logic of culture', in I. Karp, C. A. Kratz, L. Szwaja, and T. Ybarra-Frausto (eds), *Museum Frictions. Public Cultures/Global Transformations*, 46–69. Durham NC: Duke University Press.

Bennett, T. 2018. *Museums, Power, Knowledge.* London: Routledge.

Bennett, T., F. Cameron, N. Dias, B. Dibley, R. Harrison, I. Jacknis, and C. McCarthy. 2017. *Collecting, Ordering, Governing.* Durham NC: Duke University Press.

Blum, A., N. Schocke, H.-J. Rheinberger, and Vincent Barras (eds). 2016. *Diversität. Geschichte eines Konzepts*, Würzburg: Könighausen & Neumann.

Blum, André, N. Schocke, H.-J. Rheinberger, and V. Barras. 2016. 'Vorwort', in A. Blum, N. Schocke, H.-J. Rheinberger, and V. Barras (eds), *Diversität. Geschichte eines Konzepts*, 9–19. Würzburg: Könighausen & Neumann.

Bock, J.-J., and Sharon Macdonald (eds). 2019. *Refugees Welcome? Difference and Diversity in a Changing Germany.* Oxford: Berghahn.

Bose, F. von 2016. *Das Humboldt-Forum. Eine Ethnographie seiner Planung*. Berlin: Kulturverlag Kadmos.

Bose, F. von 2017. 'Strategische Reflexivität. Das Berliner Humboldt Forum und die postkoloniale Kritik', *Historische Anthropologie*, 3: 409–417.

Braidotti, R. 2013. *The Posthuman.* Cambridge: Polity.

Brumann, C. 2021. *The Best We Share. Nation, Culture and World-Making in the UNESCO World Heritage Arena.* Oxford: Berghahn.

Buchczyk, M., and D. Jethro. 2020. 'Statues can't swim: Heritage forms washed away in decolonial currents'. *CARMAH Reflection.* https://www.carmah.berlin/reflections/statues-cant-swim/ (accessed 23 May 2022).

Cabadağ, N. and G. Ediger 2020. 'We disperse to Berlin: transnational entanglements of LGBTI+ movements in Turkey', in M. do Maro Castro Varela and B. Ülker (eds), *Doing Tolerance. Urban Interventions and Forms of Participation*, 194–210. Berlin: Verlag Barbara Budrich.

CARMAH. 2018. *Otherwise. Rethinking Museums and Heritage.* Berlin: Centre for Anthropological Research on Museums and Heritage. https://www.carmah.berlin/wp-content/uploads/2018/07/CARMAH-2018-Otherwise-Rethinking-Museums-and-Heritage.pdf (accessed 1 June 2022).

Cesari, C. de 2017. 'Museums of Europe. Tangles of memory, borders and race', *Museum Anthropology* 40(1): 18–35.

Chin, R. 2017. *The Crisis of Multiculturalism in Europe. A History.* Cambridge, Mass.: Princeton University Press.

Cohen, A. 1985. *The Symbolic Construction of Community.* London: Routledge.

Crenshaw, K. 2017. *On Intersectionality. Essential Writings.* New York: Columbia University Press.

Dias, N. 2008. 'Cultural difference and cultural diversity: the case of the Musée du Quai Branly', in D. J. Sherman (ed.), *Museums and Difference,* 124–154. Bloomington: Indiana University Press.

Debary, O., and M. Roustan. 2017. 'A journey to the Musée du quai Branly. The anthropology of a visit', *Museum Anthropology* 40(1): 4–17.

DeLanda, M. 2016 *Assemblage Theory.* Edinburgh: Edinburgh University Press.

Dilger, H. and M. Warstat (eds). 2021 *Unkämpfte Vielfalt. Affektive Dynamiken institutioneller Diversifizierung.* Frankfurt: Campus.

Du Bois, W.E.B. 1994 [1903]. *The Souls of Black Folk.* New York: Gramercy Books.

Eckersley, S. 2020. 'Between appropriation and appropriateness. Instrumentalizing dark heritage in populism and memory?', in C.DeCesari and A.Kaya (eds), *European Memory in Populism. Representations of Self and Other.*

Edenheiser, I., and L. Förster (eds). 2019. *Museumsethnologie: Eine Einführung.* Berlin: Dietrich Reimer.

Engler, J. 2013. 'Renaming streets, inverting perspectives: Acts of postcolonial memory citizenship in Berlin', *Focus on German Studies,* 20: 41–62.

Förster, L. 2018a. 'Whoever's Right. Remarks about the Debate on Provenance and Return from the Perspective of Social and Cultural Anthropology', *Boasblog—How to Move on with Humboldt's Legacy?.* https://boasblogs.org/dcntr/whoevers-right/ (accessed 23 May 2022).

Förster, L. 2018b. 'Provenance' in *Otherwise: Rethinking Museums and Heritage.* Berlin: Centre for Anthropological Research on Museums and Heritage. https://www.carmah.berlin/wp-content/uploads/2018/07/CARMAH-2018-Otherwise-Rethinking-Museums-and-Heritage.pdf (accessed 1 June 2022).

Förster, L. 2019. 'Der Umgang mit der Kolonialzeit. Provenienz und Rückgabe', in I. Edenheiser and L. Förster (eds), *Museumsethnologie: Eine Einführung,* 78–103. Berlin: Dietrich Reimer.

Förster, L. and H. Stoecker 2016. *Haut, Haar und Knochen. Koloniale Spuren in naturkundlichen Sammlungen der Universität Jena.* Weimar: Verlag und Datenbank für Geisteswissenschaften.

Förster, L., and F. von Bose. 2018. 'Discussing ethnological museums. The epistemology of postcolonial debates', in P. Schorch, and C. McCarthy (eds), *Curatopia. Museums and the Future of Curatorship,* 95–122. Manchester: Manchester University Press.

Förster, L., I. Edenheiser, S. Fründt, and H. Hartmann (eds). 2018. *Provenienzforschung zu ethnografischen Sammlungen der Kolonialzeit. Positionen in der aktuellen Debatte.* https://edoc.hu-berlin.de/handle/18452/19814 (accessed 1 June 2022).

Garbellotto, C., and D. Onuoha. 2019. 'Taxidermic cinema. Reflections on a workshop at Berlin's Naturkundemuseum'. *CARMAH Reflection.* https://www.carmah.berlin/reflections/taxidermic_cinema/ (accessed 1 June 2022).

Gaupp, L. 2021. 'Epistemologies of diversity and otherness', in L.Gaupp and G.Pellilo-Hestermeyer (eds) *Diversity and Otherness. Transcultural Insights into Norms, Practices, Negotiations,* 13–61. Berlin: De Gruyter.

Geertz, C. 1988. *Works and Lives: The Anthropologist as Author.* Stanford: Stanford University Press.

Geismar, H. 2018. *Museum Object Lessons for the Digital Age.* London: UCL Press.

Goel, U. 2020. 'Intersektional forschen – kontextspezifisch, offen, selbst-reflexiv', in A. Biele Mefubue, A. Bührmann and S. Grenz (eds) *Handbuch Intersektionalitäts Forschung,* 1–13. Wiesbaden: Springer.

Grillo, R. 2010. *Contesting Diversity in Europe. Alternative Regimes and Moral Orders.* MMG Working Paper 10–02.

Haentschel, J. 2017. '"The Humboldt Forum is like Chernobyl". Interview mit Bénédicte Savoy'. *Süddeutsche Zeitung,* 7 July.

Hage, G. 1998. *White Nation. Fantasies of White Supremacy in a Multicultural Society,* Annandale: Pluto Press.

Hall, S. 1992. 'The West and the Rest: Discourse and Power', in B. Gieben, and S. Hall (eds), Formations of Modernity, 185–225. Cambridge: Polity Press.

Harrison, R. 2013. *Heritage: Critical Approaches.* London: Routledge.

Harrison, R., C. DeSilvey, C. Holtorf, S. Macdonald, N. Bartolini, E. Breithoff, H. Fredheim, A. Lyons, S. May, J. Morgan, and S. Penrose. 2020. *Heritage Futures. Comparative Approaches to Natural and Cultural Heritage Practices.* London: UCL Press.

Heyes, C. 2020 [2002]. 'Identity Politics', *The Stanford Encyclopedia of Philosophy,* E. N. Zalta (ed.) https://plato.stanford.edu/entries/identity-politics/ (accessed 31 March 2022).

Hilden, I., H. Merrow and A. Zavadsky 2021. 'Present imperfect, future tense: the opening of the Humboldt Forum'. *CARMAH Reflection* https://www.carmah.berlin/reflections/present-imperfect-future-intense/ (accessed 1 June 2022)

Hill Collins, P. 2004. *Black Sexual Politics: African-Americans, Gender and the New Racism.* New York: Routledge.

Hill Collins, P., and S. Bilge. 2020. *Intersectionality.* New York: Wiley.

Hirschauer, S. 2021. 'Un/doing differences. The contingency of social affiliations', in L. Gaupp and G. Pellilo-Hestermeyer (eds), *Diversity and Otherness. Transcultural Insights into Norms, Practices, Negotiations,* 62–95. Berlin: De Gruyter.

Insaf, H. 2020. 'The complexities of addressing the past while decolonizing museums'. *The Caravan.* https://caravanmagazine.in/culture/the-complexities-of-addressing-past-while-decolonising-museums (accessed 1 June 2022).

Jackson, M. 2022 *Critique of Identity Thinking.* Oxford: Berghahn.

Jenkins, R. 2014. *Social Identity.* London: Routledge.

Jethro, D. 2020. *Heritage Formation and the Senses in Post-Apartheid South Africa: Aesthetics of Power.* London: Routledge.

Jethro, D. 2021. 'Monuments', in H. Callan and S. Coleman (eds) *International Encyclopaedia of Anthropology* (online).

Jethro, D. and S. Macdonald forthcoming. 'Difficult heritage at the door. Doing heritage research in precarious times', in N. Shepherd (ed.), *Rethinking Heritage in Precarious Times*. London: Routledge.

Joppke, C. 2017. *Is Multiculturalism Dead? Crisis and Persistence in the Constitutional State.* Cambridge: Polity.

Kirschhoff, T., and K. Köchy (eds). 2016. *Wünschenswerte Vielheit. Diversität als Kategorie, Befund und Norm.* Munich: Verlag Karl Alber Freiburg.

Knell, S. J., P. Aronsson, A. Bugge Amundsen, A. J. Barnes, S. Burch, J. Carter, V. Gosselin, S. A. Hughes, and A. Kirwan (eds). 2011. *National Museums: New Studies from Around the World.* London: Routledge.

Knudsen, B., J. Oldfield, E. Buettner and E. Zabunyan (eds). 2021. *Decolonizing Colonial Heritage. New Agendas, Actors and Practices in and Beyond Europe.* London: Routledge.

Kössler, R. 2015 *Namibia and Germany. Negotiating the Past.* Windhoek: University of Namibia Press.

Latour, B. 2014. *Reassembling the Social. An Introduction to Network Theory.* Oxford: Oxford University Press.

Law, J. 2004. *After Method: Mess in Social Science Research*. London: Routledge.

Levitt, P. 2015. *Artefacts and Allegiances. How Museums put the Nation and the World on Display.* Berkeley: University of California Press.

Lidchi, H. 1997. 'The poetics and politics of exhibiting other cultures', in S. Hall (ed.), *Representation: Cultural Representation and Signifying Practices*, 153–208. London: Sage Publications.

Lidchi, H., S. Macdonald, and M. von Oswald (eds). 2017. *Engaging Anthropological Legacies toward Cosmo-optimistic Futures?*, special section, *Museum Worlds* 5(1): 95–107.

Loeseke, A. 2019. 'Beyond Compare – Art from Africa in the Bode Museum, Berlin', *Museum and Society* 17(3): 533–35.

Lonetree, A. 2012. *Decolonizing Museums. Representing Native America in National and Tribal Museums*. Chapel Hill: University of North Carolina Press.

Macdonald, S. 2006. 'Collecting practices', in S. Macdonald (ed.), *Companion to Museum Studies*, 81–97. Oxford: Blackwell.

Macdonald, S. 2013. *Memorylands: Heritage and Identity in Europe Today*. London: Routledge.

Macdonald, S. 2016. 'New constellations of difference in Europe's 21st Century Museumscape', *Museum Anthropology*, 39(1): 4–19.

Macdonald, S. 2019. 'Refugee futures and the politics of difference', in J.-J. Bock, and S. Macdonald (eds), *Refugees Welcome? Difference and Diversity in a Changing Germany*, 312–331. Oxford: Berghahn.

Macdonald, S. 2023. 'Perspectives in and on heritage-making. Anthropological engagements with the Humboldt Forum, Berlin', in E.Gilberthorpe and F. de Jong (eds), *Anthropological Perspectives on Global Challenges.* London: Routledge.

Macdonald, S., C. Gerbich, R. Gram, K. Puzon, and M. Shatanawi. 2021. 'Reframing Islam? Potentials and challenges of participatory initiatives in museums and heritage', in K. Puzon, S. Macdonald, and M. Shatanawi (eds), *Heritage and Islam in Europe*, 212–230. Abingdon: Routledge.

Macdonald, S., C. Gerbich, and M. von Oswald. 2018. 'No museum is an island: ethnography beyond ethnographic containerism', *Museum and Society* 16(2): 138–156.

Mason, R. 2013. 'National museums, globalization and postnationalism. Imagining a cosmopolitan museology', *Museum Worlds* 1(1): 40–64.

McCall, L. 2005. 'The complexity of intersectionality', *Signs* 30(3): 1771–1800.

Meijl, T. van 2010. 'Anthropological perspectives on identity: from sameness to difference', in M. Wetherell and C. T. Mohanty (eds), *The Sage Handbook of Identities*, 63–81. London: Sage.

Merrow, H., C. Gerbich and D. Jethro 2020. 'Decolonising museum practices? Connecting "Afro Futures" at Berlin's Kunstgewerbemuseum'. *CARMAH Reflection*. https://www.carmah.berlin/reflections/reflections-on-the-making-of/ (accessed 1 June 2022).

Meskell, L. 2018. *A Future in Ruins. UNESCO, World Heritage, and the Dream of Peace*. Oxford: Oxford University Press.

Michaels, W. B. 2006. *The Trouble with Diversity: How We Learned to Love Identity and Ignore Inequality*. New York: Macmillan.

Michaels, W. B. 2008. 'Against diversity', *New Left Review* 52: 33–36.

Morris, R. C. 2010. *Can the Subaltern Speak? Reflections on the History of an Idea*. New York: Columbia University Press.

Müller, E., and F. Schmieder 2017. 'Diversität, begriffsgeschichtlich', ZfL BLOG. https://www.zflprojekte.de/zfl-blog/2017/04/01/ernst-muellerfalko-schmieder-diversitaet-begriffsgeschichtlich/ (accessed 1 June 2022).

Minh Ha, T. T. 1989. *Woman, Native, Other: Writing Postcoloniality and Feminism*. Bloomington: Indiana University Press.

Mitchell, T. 1988. *Colonizing Egypt*. Berkeley: University of California Press.

Modest, W. 2020. 'Museums are investments in critical discomfort', in M. v. Oswald, and J. Tinius (eds), *Across Anthropology. Troubling colonial legacies, museums, and the curational*, 65–76. Leuven: Leuven University Press.

Modood, T. 2013. *Multiculturalism. A Civic Idea*, 2nd ed. Cambridge: Polity.

Modood, T. 2017. 'Must interculturalists misrepresent multiculturalism?', *Comparative Migration Studies*, 5(15).

Modood, T. 2018. 'The continuing relevance of a concept of multiculturalism', in Bertelsmann Stiftung (ed.), *Living Diversity – Shaping Society. The Opportunities and Challenges Posed by Cultural Difference in Germany*. Gütersloh : Bertelsmann Stiftung Verlag.

Musitelli, J. 2006. 'La convention sur la diversité Culturelle : anatomie d'un succès', *Revue internationale et stratégique*, 62(2) : 11–22.

Nadim, T. 2021. 'The datafication of nature: data formations and new scales in natural history', *Journal of the Royal Anthropological Institute* 27(S1): 62–75.

Ndikung, B. S. B. 2017. 'The globalized museum? Decanonisation as method: A reflection in three acts', Mousee Magazine. www.moussemagazine.it/the-globalized-museum-bonaventure-soh-bejeng-ndikung-documenta-14-2017/ (accessed 1 June 2022).

Noury, A., and G. Roland. 2020. 'Identity politics and populism in Europe', *Annual Review of Political Science* 23: 421–39.

Oswald, M. von 2018. 'The "Restitution Report": First reactions in academic, museums and politics'. https://boasblogs.org/dcntr/the-restitution-report/ (accessed 1 June 2022).

Oswald, M. von 2020. 'Troubling colonial epistemologies in Berlin's Ethnologisches Museum: Provenance research and the Humboldt Forum', 106–130, in: M. von Oswald and J. Tinius (eds), *Across Anthropology. Troubling Colonial Legacies, Museums, and the Curatorial*. Leuven: Leuven University Press.

Oswald, M. von. 2022. *Working through Colonial Collections. An Ethnography of the Ethnological Museum in Berlin*. Leuven: Leuven University Press.

Oswald, M. von, and V. Rodatus. 2017. 'Decolonizing research, cosmo-optimistic collaboration? Making *Object Biographies*', *Museum Worlds*, 5(1): 211–23.

Oswald, M. von, and J. Tinius (eds). 2020. *Across Anthropology. Troubling Colonial Legacies, Museums, and the Curatorial*. Leuven: Leuven University Press.

Partridge, D. J., and M. Chin. 2019. 'Interrogating the histories and futures of "diversity": Transnational perspectives', special issue of *Public Culture* 31(2): 197–214.

Pellilo–Hestermeyer, G. 2021. 'Rethinking diversity and transculturality: introduction', in L. Gaupp and G. Pellilo-Hestermeyer (eds), *Diversity and Otherness. Transcultural Insights into Norms, Practices, Negotiations*, 1–12. Berlin: De Gruyter.

Pettinicchio, D. 2012. 'Institutional activism: reconsidering the inside/outsider dichotomy', *Sociology Compass* 6/6 (2012): 499–510.

Parekh, B. 2007. *Rethinking Multuculturalism*, 2nd ed. Cambridge, Mass.: Harvard University Press.

Phillips, R. 2011. *Museum Pieces. Towards the Indigenization of Canadian Museums*, Montreal: McGill University Press.

Pieterse, J. N. 1997. 'Multiculturalism and museums: discourse about Others in the Age of Globalization', *Theory, Culture and Society*, 14(4): 123–46.

Pollock, G. 1999. *Differencing the Canon: Feminist Desire and the Writing of Art's Histories*. London: Routledge.

Pollock, G. 2019. 'Feminism and language', in H. Robinson, and M. E. Buszek (eds), *A Feminist Companion to Art*, 261–281. New York: Wiley.

Puzon, K. 2018. 'Translocality', in *Otherwise: Rethinking Museums and Heritage*. Berlin: Centre for Anthropological Research on Museums and Heritage. https://www.carmah.berlin/wp-content/uploads/2018/07/CARMAH-2018-Otherwise-Rethinking-Museums-and-Heritage.pdf (accessed 1 June 2022).

Puzon, K. 2019. 'Participatory matters: Access, migration and heritage in Berlin museums', in H. Oevermann, and E. Gantner (eds), *Securing Urban Heritage: Agents, Access, and Securitization*, 31–46. Abingdon and New York: Routledge.

Puzon, K. 2021. 'Germans without footnotes: Islam, belonging and poetry slam', in K. Puzon, S. Macdonald, and M. Shatanawi (eds). 2021. *Islam and Heritage in Europe*, 68–82. Abingdon: Routledge.

Puzon, K., S. Macdonald, and M. Shatanawi (eds). 2021. *Islam and Heritage in Europe*. Abingdon: Routledge.

Rea, N. 2017. 'Will French museums return African objects? Emmanuel Macron says restitution is a "priority"'. *Artnet News*. 28, November.

Reilly, M. 2019. *Curatorial activism. Towards an Ethics of Curating.* London: Thames & Hudson.

Reus-Smit, C. 2018. *On Cultural Diversity. International Theory in a World of Difference.* Cambridge: Cambridge University Press.

Robertson, I. J.M. 2012. *Heritage from Below.* London: Routledge.

Rogers, A., and S. Vertovec. 1995. *The Urban Context. Ethnicity, Social Networks and Situational Analysis.* Oxford: Berg.

Römhild, R. 2014. 'Diversität?! Postethnische Perspektiven für eine reflexive Migrationsforschung', pp.255–70, in B. Nieswand and H. Drotbohm (eds), *Kultur, Gesellschaft und Migration. Studien zur Migrations- und Integrationspolitik.* Wiesbaden: Springer.

Rothberg, M. 2009. *Multidirectional Memory. Remembering the Holocaust in the Age of Decolonization.* Stanford University Press.

Rottenburg, R. 2006. *The Making and Unmaking of Differences. Anthropological, Sociological and Philosophical Perspectives.* Bielefeld: transcript.

Said, E. 1978. *Orientalism.* New York: Pantheon Books.

Sarr, F., and B. Savoy. 2018. *The Restitution of African Cultural Heritage. Toward a New Relational Ethics.* http://restitutionreport2018.com *(accessed 1 June 2022).*

Salemink, O. 2021. 'Anthropologies of cultural heritage', in L. Pedersen, and L. Cliggitt (eds), *The Sage Handbook of Cultural Anthropology,* 423–441. Thousand Oaks: Sage.

Salzbrunn, M. 2014. *Vielfalt/Diversität.* Bielefeld: transcript.

Sandell, R. 1998. 'Museums as agents of social inclusion', *Museum Management and Curatorship,* 17(4): 401–418.

Sandell, R. 2003. 'Social inclusion, the museum and the dynamics of sectoral change', *museum and society* 1(1): 45–62.

Sarr, F. and B. Savoy 2018. *The Restitution of African Cultural Heritage. Towards a New Relational Ethics.* http://restitutionreport2018.com/sarr_savoy_en.pdf (accessed 1 June 2022).

Schinkel, W. 2017 *Imagined Societies. A Critique of Immigrant Integration in Western Europe.* Cambridge: Cambridge University Press.

Sen, A. 2006. *Identity and Violence. The Illusion of Destiny.* New York: W.W. Norton.

Shelton, A. A. 2006. 'Museums and anthropologies. Practices and narratives', in S. Macdonald (ed.) *A Companion to Museum Studies,* 64–80. New York: Wiley-Blackwell.

Sherman, D. J. 2008. *Museums and Difference,* Bloomington: Indiana University Press.

Sherman, D. J. 2008. 'Introduction', in D. J. Sherman (ed.), *Museums and Difference,* 1–24. Bloomington: Indiana University Press.

Sieg, K. 2021. *Decolonizing German and European History at the Museum.* Ann Arbor: University of Michigan Press.

Shore, C. and S. Trnka (eds). *Up Close and Personal. On Peripheral Perspectives and the Production of Anthropological Knowledge.* Oxford: Berghahn.

Smiers, J. 2016. 'Kulturelle Diversität: Ein vielschichtiges Konzept in den Mühlen der Realität', in A. Blum, N. Schocke, H.-J. Rheinberger, and V. Barras (eds), *Diversität. Geschichte eines Konzepts,* 203–220. Würzburg: Könighausen & Neumann.

Song, S. 2020 [2010]. 'Multiculturalism', *The Stanford Encyclopedia of Philosophy,* E. N. Zalta (ed.) https://plato.stanford.edu/entries/multiculturalism/ (accessed 1 June 2022).

Spivak, G. C. 1988. 'Can the Subaltern speak?', in C. Nelson, and L. Grossberg (eds), *Marxism and the Interpretation of Culture*, 271–313. Basingstoke: Macmillan.

Stewart, C. 2011. 'Creolization, hybridity, syncretism, mixture', *Portuguese Studies* 27(1): 43–55.

Stoler, A.L. 2016. *Durress. Imperial Durabilities in our Times.* Durham NC: Duke University Press.

Sullivan, N., and C. Middleton. 2020. *Queering the Museum.* London: Routledge.

Taylor, C. 1994. *The Politics of Recognition.* Cambridge, Mass.: Princeton University Press.

Taylor, C. 2007. *Modern Social Imaginaries.* Durham NC: Duke University Press.

Tietmeyer, E. 2017. *Glances into Fugitive Lives.* Heidelberg: arthistoricum.

Tinius, J. 2020. 'Porous membranes. Alterity, hospitality and anthropology in a Berlin district gallery', 254–77, in M. von Oswald, M. and J. Tinius (eds), *Across Anthropology: Troubling Colonial Legacies, Museums, and the Curatorial.* Leuven: Leuven University Press.

Tinius, J. 2021. 'The Anthropologist as sparring partner: Instigative public fieldwork, curatorial collaboration, and German colonial heritage', *Berliner Blätter.* 83: 65–85.

Tinius, J., and S. Macdonald. 2020. 'The recursivity of the curatorial', in R. Sansi (ed.), *The Anthropologist as Curator*, 35–58. London: Bloomsbury.

Tinius, J. and K. von Zinnenburg Carroll 2020 'Phantom palaces: Prussian centralities and Humboldtian spectres', in J. Bach and M. Murawski (eds) *Re-Centring the City*, 90–103. London: UCL Press.

Toepfer, G. 2017. 'Biodiversität', ZfL Blog. https://www.zflprojekte.de/zfl-blog/2017/05/05/georg-toepfer-biodiversitaet/ (accessed 1 June 2022).

UNESCO Universal Declaration on Cultural Diversity. 2001. Adopted by the 31st Session of the General Conference of UNESCO, Paris, 2 November 2001. http://www.unesco.org/new/fileadmin/MULTIMEDIA/HQ/CLT/pdf/5_Cultural_Diversity_EN.pdf (accessed 1 June 2022).

Vertovec, S. 2012. '"Diversity" and the social imaginary', *European Journal of Sociology* LIII (3): 287–312.

Vertovec, S. 2021. 'The social organization of difference', *Ethnic and Racial Studies*, 44(8): 1273–1295.

Williams, J.C. 1991. 'Dissolving the sameness/difference debate: a post-modern path beyond essentialism in Feminism and Critical Race Theory', *Duke LJ*, Vol.296: 296–323.

Zavadsky, A. and I. Hilden 2022. 'Participatory countermonuments of colonial violence'. *CARMAH Reflection* https://www.carmah.berlin/reflections/participatory-countermonuments-of-colonial-violence/ (accessed 1 June 2022).

Talking and Going about Things Differently

On Changing Vocabularies and Practices in the Postcolonial Provenance and Restitution Debates

Larissa Förster

In early 2017, the South African museum scholar Ciraj Rassool characterised the situation of German museums as a 'difficult mixture of outdated debates and new opportunities' (Rassool 2017: 149). Since then, the situation has changed dramatically. Germany has seen the eruption of heated and at times acrimonious debates on colonialism and on colonial legacies in German museums. Moreover, the focus of ethnographic museums in Germany has shifted decisively towards issues pertaining to decolonisation.

Before looking at that transformation more closely, it is helpful to recall the events leading up to the colonialism debates in Germany. For a long time, working through the legacies of colonialism in museums had been a concern only of a small cadre of activists, scholars and museum practitioners. The majority of academics, museum directors, institutions and politicians gave it little attention. However, starting in 2004, the cadre's work began to pay off, and slowly but surely decolonisation appeared on the agenda of institutional actors. Several pivotal events including the return of human remains from Berlin to Windhoek in 2011 and the resignation of art historian Bénédicte Savoy from the advisory board of the Humboldt Forum in Berlin helped crystallise the debate. Last but not least, position statements such as the German Museum Association's Recommendations for the Care of Human Remains in Museums and Collections (DMB 2013), its Guidelines for the Care of Collections from Colonial Contexts (DMB 2018, 2019, 2021), and the very influential Report on the Restitution of African Cultural Heritage (Sarr and Savoy 2018) put pressure on administration bodies, especially museum funders. As a consequence, regional and national political actors began to address colonialism, provided political backing and funding for the project of working through the provenances of collections from colonial contexts[1] and created long-term structures for decolonialisation, including the Department for Cultural Goods and Collections from Colonial Contexts at the German Lost Art Foundation, four permanent positions for provenance research at the Prussian Cultural Heritage Foundation as well as a Contact Point for Collections from Colonial Contexts at the Cultural Foundation of the German Federal States. Cultural institutions and their governing bodies made public pledges such as the pivotal 'Framework Principles for Dealing with Collections from Colonial Contexts' (Federal Government Commissioner for Culture and Media et al. 2019) and the 'Heidelberg Statement' (Annual Conference of the Directors of Ethnographic Museums in the German Speaking Countries 2019) and started a variety of initiatives aimed at increasing access to their collections and shedding critical light on their history.

The changes long demanded by activists and scholars, implemented step by step by museum practitioners and eventually codified by politicians are an effort to distance German institutions from past, outdated and 'contaminated' practices perpetuating colonial power imbalances, colonial stereotypes and knowledge orders. They testify to a fundamental unease with established ways and a desire of 'doing things differently than before'. The work of doing things differently has gone hand in hand with speaking about things differently. New vocabulary has emerged and become crucial for talking about the history of collections. This includes *sensible Objekte/Sammlungen* (sensitive objects/collections), *koloniale Kontexte* (colonial contexts), *Erwerbungskontexte* (contexts of acquisition), *Unrechtskontext* (context of injustice) and *Zusammenarbeit mit Herkunftsgesellschaften* (cooperation with societies of origin). Over the past years, these and other terms have become critical for re-assessing museum objects and collections and making decisions about their future.

I would like to take language as a point of departure for approaching the broader dynamics of decolonialisation. Literary scholars Susan Arndt and Nadja Ofuatey-Alazard (2011) have pointed to the crucial role that language and terminology play not only in the formation and reproduction of colonial and racist stereotypes but also in their eradication. Initiatives for renaming streets (see the essay by Duane Jethro in this volume) have shown how interventions in existing vocabularies can be an important lever and symbol for decolonisation. In the museum sector, the debate on discriminatory language and the revision of racist titles for artwork have pointed in the same direction (Modest and Lelijveld 2018). The arguments about denominations, definitions and categorisations are evidence of a broader struggle of museum professionals and culture workers to 'reform' museums and turn them into 'differencing machines' of a more sensitive kind (see the Introduction of this volume). The rampant production of guidelines and programmatic texts in the museum sector and by government agencies is part of an ongoing search for new, more appropriate and self-reflexive ways of speaking, thinking and approaching museums and their colonial legacies.

However, change in the world of institutions is rarely brought about by independent invention or internal insight alone. Rather, it fundamentally owes its impetus to external criticism and inspiration, i.e. ideas and arguments that cross institutional, disciplinary and geographical boundaries (Macdonald, Gerbich and Oswald 2018). Even though in a different context – the analysis of practices of conflict resolution – Andrea Behrend has coined the term 'travelling model' (Behrends et al. 2014) that appears to be useful here as well. With Germany being a relative newcomer to the postcolonial restitution and repatriation debate (Fründt 2011), the question arises as to how far its recent debates and changes have been shaped by earlier discussions and experiences elsewhere, in fact by 'traveling models' or 'traveling concepts' (Bal 2002).

To that end, I focus on two concepts that have influenced the German debate in fundamental ways: *human remains* and *Unrechtskontext*. I identify the previous debates and practices that gave rise to them, and ask why and how they came to be mobilised today. Their trajectories do not follow a linear or circular pathway originating from a single centre. Rather, they have entered the current German debate by way of multi-polar, non-simultaneous and meandering routes of proliferation. Their wide-scale adoption in the German museum world indicates a major shift in the conceptualisation of museum collections and museum work both by professionals and the broader public.

Methodologically, my analysis draws on various sources: fieldwork conducted on the repatriation of human remains from German institutions to Namibia, Australia and New Zealand between 2008 and 2018 (Förster 2013, 2020, Fründt and Förster 2021), on provenance research in institutions in Berlin and Jena (Förster and Stoecker 2016, Förster and Henrichsen, Stoecker and #Eichab 2018) and on the German provenance and restitution debate itself (Förster 2017a,b, Förster 2018a,b, Förster and von Bose 2018, Förster and Fründt 2017). In addition, my analysis is based on observations made as a speaker of the Working Group on Museums of the German Anthropological Association, where I co-convened the 2017 conference "Provenienzforschung in ethnologischen Sammlungen der Kolonialzeit" (Förster, Edenheiser, Fründt and Hartmann 2018a), as a member of the German Museum Association's working group for the "Guidelines on the Care of Collections from Colonial Contexts" (see (DMB 2021) and as a member of its working group for the second edition of the "Recommendations for the Care of Human Remains in Museums and Collections" (first edition: DMB 2013).[2] My involvement in the working groups requires carefully navigating the roles of observer, critic, initiator and occasional co-author. However, I believe that the insights gained from moving fluidly between these roles provide the analysis with a multifaceted granularity and a keen awareness of the major actors in the discussion.

'Human remains': catching up with the global repatriation movement

I have argued elsewhere that the repatriation of human remains from German institutions to their countries and communities of origin has played a vital role in decolonising museum language and practice (Förster 2018a: 16). When, in 2011, the Charité university hospital embarked on a series of returns to Namibia, Paraguay, Australia and Tasmania (Förster 2020: 120–112), resistance to restitution claims began to crack. A number of ethnographic museums and university collections followed Charite's example and returned human remains to Australia, Brazil, Japan, Hawai'i, Namibia, New Zealand and Peru; one private owner returned human remains to Tanzania (Fründt and Förster 2021, Winkelmann 2020). Thanks to the German Museum Association's 'Recommendations for the Care of Human Remains in Museums and Collections' (German Museums Association 2013), which emerged in response to–amongs others–the 2011 Namibia repatriations, a kind of consensus was reached in the German museum world: human remains from people of non-European descent that had been acquired as 'specimens' in former colonial territories needed to be returned.

When the subject of repatriating skeletal remains from former colonial territories entered the German debate, 'human remains' became the preferred term, despite the existence of *menschliche Überreste*, its literal German translation. In the following I explore why the English term has become so widely used in German debates.

As the number of postcolonial nation states submitting repatriation claims to German institutions began to mount, museum practitioners and critics looked to the anglophone world for orientation. They considered the UK's 'Guidance on the Care of Human Remains' (Department for Culture, Media and Sports 2005)[3] and the US legislation under the Native Graves Protection and Repatriation Act of 1990 (DMB 2013: 6, Bouteloup and Colin 2011: 4). Moreover, when planning handover ceremonies, German institutions familiarised themselves with the experiences, routines and protocols of former settler colonies such as Australia and New Zealand. In those encounters, German institutions learned not only good practices (Förster 2020: 116–118) but a new vocabulary for talking about repatriation.

'Human remains' figures prominently not only in anglophone repatriation discussions but also in contemporary anglophone museum practice and theory in general. One reason why the phrase took off in Germany is certainly that many German practitioners came to regard anglophone museums as more professional and progressive than their own. Another is that the foreign term has allowed German speakers to distance themselves from earlier institutional discourses and practices and signal postcolonial empathy with claimants. In their working paper 'Human Remains in deutschen Sammlungen' written for the Humboldt Law Clinic Grund- und Menschenrechte (Constitutional and Human Rights), Florence Stürmer and Julian Schramm explain why they prefer 'human remains' over 'menschliche Überreste':

> Jedoch wird unserer Meinung nach der deutsche Begriff der menschlichen 'Überreste' dem Andenken der verstorbenen Menschen nicht gerecht. So impliziert er, ausgehend vom allgemeinen Sprachgebrauch, lediglich das Übrigbleiben materieller 'Reste'. Bei der Diskussion um Human Remains geht es jedoch um mehr. Es geht um das Andenken von Menschen, die (Re-)Individualisierung von verstorbenen oder getöteten, in der Regel zu Forschungsobjekten degradierten Personen. Der Begriff Human Remains lässt hingegen eine breitere Begriffsdeutung zu und kann so neben physischen Überresten auch immateriell Verbleibendes umfassen. Die vorliegende Arbeit verwendet daher bewusst den englischen Ausdruck Human Remains (Stürmer and Schramm 2019: 8).
>
> However, in our opinion the German term *menschliche 'Überreste'* does not do justice to the memory of deceased people. Based on everyday language use it describes only the left-over of material 'remnants'. But in the discussion of *human remains* more is at stake. It is about the memory of people, the (re-)individualisation of deceased or killed people that were degraded to objects of study. The term *human remains* allows for a broader interpretation and can, in addition to physical remains, also comprise immaterial remains. Therefore, this article consciously uses the English term *human remains*. (Unless otherwise indicated, all translations are my own.)

Stürmer and Schramm's ascription of a broader moral and spiritual meaning to 'human remains' is indicative of an understanding that has become widely held in German museum practice and debate. Of course, the literal meaning of 'human remains' is no more moral or spiritual than 'menschliche Überreste'. Nevertheless, the English term provides Germans more room for imaginative reinterpretation. It has become a marker of cosmopolitan thinking and for a less demeaning, more sensitive stance to the human remains of formerly colonised people.

Two notable attempts were made early on in German discussions to introduce alternatives to 'human remains'. The working group of the German Museums Association, which drafted the 'Empfehlungen für den Umgang mit menschlichen Überresten in Museen und Sammlungen' (DMB 2013), made the case for the German term:

> Bewusst wird in den Empfehlungen der Ausdruck 'menschliche Überreste' anstelle des inzwischen eher gebräuchlichen englischen Begriffs 'human remains' verwendet. Der deutsche Ausdruck, der uns aus der Formulierung 'sterbliche Überreste' vertraut ist, führt uns deutlich vor Augen, wovon hier in der Regel die Rede ist: von verstorbenen Menschen. Anders als der Distanz schaffende englische Begriff berührt uns der Ausdruck 'menschliche Überreste' emotional. Das ist auch beabsichtigt, denn dies trägt zu einer Sensibilisierung bei (DMB 2013: 6–7).

> A conscious decision has been made to use the German term 'menschliche Überreste' in the German version of the recommendations instead of the common English term 'human remains'. The German term, which is familiar as it calls to mind the expression 'sterbliche Überreste' ['mortal remains'], clearly brings home to the reader what is generally being talked about here: deceased human beings. Unlike the English term, which, being in a foreign language, is more remote for the German reader, the term 'menschliche Überreste' has an emotional resonance, which was indeed our intention because it contributes to making people more sensitive to the issue.

The working group seemed to prefer 'menschliche Überreste' to 'sterbliche Überreste' because it signifies the human being behind the skeletal remains. But it could also be argued the other way round: the term 'menschliche Überreste' originates in practices of comparing human and animal remains and thus exemplifies rather than transcends scientific classification.

The other effort came in 2013 when the Charité Berlin used the term *menschliche Gebeine* in the title of its edited volume on the human remains and repatriation debate (Stoecker, Schnalke and Winkelmann 2013).[4] *Gebeine* is a somewhat old-fashioned synonym for the more mundane *Knochen* (bones). But it is also respectful, almost pious—consider the related term *Beinhaus*, or ossuary. Remarkably, by using *menschliche Gebeine*, Charité, one of Germany's most prestigious institutions for the life sciences, opted for a religiously inflected word over that of the more scientific-sounding *menschliche Überreste*. Nevertheless, *Gebeine* did not catch on, and *menschliche Überreste* remained fairly common (e.g. Fuchs et al. 2020), albeit less prominent than *human remains*.

Another term that has had a remarkable career, especially in the media, is *Schädel* (skull). *Schädel* appeared frequently in German discussions,[5] and the term *skulls* was used extensively by Namibian descendant communities and Namibian media when referring to the human remains returned from the Charité in 2011.[6] There is a number of reasons why it gained traction. For one, a great majority of human remains from the colonial era held in German institutions *are* indeed skulls. Around 1900, skulls were 'collected' in Namibia and in other colonies not only because of their physical longevity, but also because they provided more data than other parts of the skeleton. For another, and perhaps more surprisingly, skulls provided graphic documentary value. After the Charité returned its human remains to Namibia, the skulls were exhibited in public and their photographs were widely circulated. From a Namibian perspective, an international public long ignorant of the 1904–1908 genocide needed to be confronted with and educated about the skulls' acquisition context. During the war against the Ovaherero, officials from the German Empire abducted bodies of Africans who died in concentration camps and sent the remains to Berlin as anatomical specimens. In the long struggle of Namibian activists for the international recognition of the genocide of the Ovaherero and Nama,[7] the skulls were a stand-in for the individuals who had been killed and positive proof of German savagery (Förster 2020). The more visible the proof, the more awareness it could raise. At first glance, the approach may seem to contradict international standards in repatriation, which urge that images of human remains not be put in circulation. But Namibia's efforts should not be misunderstood as sensationalistic or as ethically insensitive towards the individuals whose skulls were on display. Rather, they were a practice of naming and shaming colonial perpetrators and of paying tribute to their victims.

The term *Schädel* has nevertheless not become predominant in German discussions about repatriation; instead, it tends to be subsumed under *human remains*. One likely reason is that not all human remains are crania alone—pieces of hair and skin have been found in collections as well (Förster and Stoecker 2016). Another may be that *Schädel* has a somewhat informal, casual sound to it that may seem insufficiently sensitive. Also in an anglophone context, *skull* can be perceived as too scientific and too in thrall to the language of past eras.[8]

Finally, another term closely related to 'human remains' that continues to appear is 'ancestral remains' (Fforde, Keeler and McKeown 2020). Most common in Australian, New Zealandic and Hawaian contexts, the term 'ancestral remains' or 'ancestors' reflects indigenous practices of creating a more intimate link between the repatriated and the repatriating, between the living and the dead, between subjects and objects.[9] In line with general calls to re-humanise and re-individualise human skeletons (Rassool 2015), 'ancestral remains' is also a critical revision of 'human remains' and the scientific distinction between human and animal remains. In the report of the 2020 conference held in Tanzania titled 'Beyond Collecting: New Ethics for Museums in Transition', the event's organisers—Goethe-Institut Tanzania, the National Museum of Tanzania, the Museum am Rothenbaum and Berlin Postkolonial—make this explicit:

> The scientific notion of 'human remains' was discussed among the participants. Out of respect, African experts suggested the term 'ancestors' instead. Therefore, this conference report uses hereinafter the notion 'ancestors'. This distinction is especially relevant in Tanzania, where the return of ancestors is a major subject in public discussions. [...] From an African perspective, 'human remains' should no longer be called in this Eurocentric way, as it degrades them to scientific objects or museum exhibits. Instead, they should be treated as human individuals, family members and community leaders, whose absence is in some cases deplored until this very day. It is therefore

> more appropriate to talk about this theft as dehumanisation of the ancestors rather than of their objectification, so that we remain in the human's logic. (Goethe-Institut Tanzania et al. 2020: 11)

The equivalents to 'ancestral remains' or 'ancestors' have not yet taken hold in the German debate, however. For those who tend to regard themselves as the descendants of colonial perpetrators, talk of 'ancestors' does not come easily. Nevertheless, the Grassi Museum für Völkerkunde zu Leipzig has made a first attempt to replace 'human remains' and *menschliche Überreste* with *Ahnen* and *Vorfahren* (ancestors).[10] As its director stated in an interview:

> Wir möchten den Begriff 'menschliche Überreste' nicht mehr benutzen. Wir benutzen lieber 'Vorfahren' oder 'Menschen', weil die Überreste wieder zu Menschen gemacht und zurückgegeben werden.[11]

> We do not wish to use the term 'human remains' any longer. We prefer 'ancestors' or 'human beings', because the remains are remade into human beings and returned.

It remains to be seen whether *human remains* will continue to be the most popular term in the German debate, or whether that spot will eventually go to *ancestors*. At any rate, the use of *human remains* can be read as an attempt on the part of German speakers to distance themselves not only from earlier, colonial scientific discourse, but also from uncritical talk of 'specimens' and 'collection materials' in today's discussions. Its use has encouraged Germans to see the German repatriation debate as part of the wider efforts of indigenous communities around the world to reclaim the mortal remains of their ancestors from museum storages, to access cultural heritage and to achieve self-determination.[12] As the trajectory of *human remains* and its alternative terms demonstrate, the questions of who speaks, to whom and about whom one speaks, and in which language and with which words one speaks, have become key issues in decolonisation debates.

Unrechtskontext: coming to terms with Germany's violent past

While the career of 'human remains' is an example of how terminology in Germany was shaped by international debates, I now want to consider a word in colonialism discussions that arose from German memory culture: *Unrechtskontext*. Its use shows how working through the legacy of German colonialism draws on earlier experiences of working through and coming to terms with Germany's other 'difficult heritages' (Macdonald 2009).

The operative word in *Unrechtskontext* is *Unrecht*, which translates into 'unlawfulness' or 'injustice'.[13] The term *Unrechtskontext*—literally, the context of unlawfulness or injustice—is used widely in the German museum world to refer to the acquisition of an object under improper circumstances. In 2019, directors from ethnographic museums across Germany, Switzerland and Austria agreed that acquisitions that implied *Unrecht* should be returned:

> Es versteht sich von selbst, dass aufgrund von Unrecht im Moment des Herstellens oder Sammelns in die Museen gelangte Objekte—wenn dies von Vertreter/innen der

> Urhebergesellschaften gewünscht wird—zurückgegeben werden sollten (Jahreskonferenz der Direktor/innen der Ethnologischen Museen im deutschsprachigen Raum 2019).
>
> It is a matter of course that objects that were brought into the museums through unlawful circumstances at the moment of their creation or of collecting should be repatriated if desired by representatives of the originator communities.

The directors made clear that the determination of an *Unrechtskontext* is tantamount to an ethical obligation.

In contrast to *human remains*, *Unrechtskontext* is specific to the German-language debate. For example, Sarr and Savoy, writing in French, speak of 'dispossession' without mentioning 'historical injustices'. The two key documents in the Dutch debate—Return of Cultural Objects: Principle and Processes (National Museum for World Cultures 2019) and Guidance for the Way Forward for Colonial Collections (Council for Culture 2021)—use 'involuntary disposal and separation' and 'involuntary loss of possession' as criteria for return. Interestingly, the idea of 'involuntary loss' reflects the perspective of the deprived person or community rather than a general judgement on circumstances at the time.[14]

Unrechtskontext first appeared in the German colonialism debate on account of the recommendations that the German Museums Association published in 2013. Though the recommendations apply to a broad range of human remains from prehistorical times to today, they were written against the backdrop of the repatriation debate (4–5). The museum association defines *Unrechtskontext* as a 'particularly problematic' acquisition in which 'the person from whom the human remains originate was a victim of injustice' (DMB 2013: 10). For an acquisition to be unjust or unlawful, the death of the person must have been caused by an act of violence or the extraction of his or her body parts or their placement in a collection must have been made without proper consent (DMB 2013: 10–11). In such instances, the German Museums Association recommends that the remains be returned if requested.

The recommendations were published at a time when the legality of museum collections in Germany were not yet in question. For many years, museums emphasised that they had acquired their objects legally from donors or sellers and that no local or international law had been in place at the time of the object's acquisition on whose basis it could be reclaimed (DMB 2019: 65–74).[15] Of course, these arguments ignored the possibility of donors' acquiring objects violently from previous owners and the violation of any customary laws. The purpose of the term *Unrechtskontext* was, therefore, to shift the debate from the legal field, where little could be gained, to a moral arena. It claimed that the non-justiciability of violent acts of acquisition under colonial rule did not mean an end to the debate on provenance and return but its starting point.

In 2018 the German Museums Association issued 'Guidelines. The Care of Collections from Colonial Contexts' (Deutscher Museumsbund 2018, 2019, 2021). Though focused on artefacts, the guidelines address the topic of colonialism more fundamentally. The second and third edition recommends that 'zu Unrecht entzogenes Kulturgut' ('cultural objects removed unlawfully') be returned. As in the Dutch policy papers, other criteria also apply:

> Rückgaben von Sammlungsgut aus kolonialen Kontexten sollten also sowohl dann in Erwägung gezogen werden, wenn die Erwerbungsumstände aus heutiger Sicht als Unrecht erscheinen, also auch dann, wenn es sich um Sammlungsgut handelt, das zum Zeitpunkt, als es aus der Herkunftsgesellschaft entfernt wurde, für diese von besonderer religiöser oder kultureller Bedeutung war und diese Bedeutung bis heute behalten oder auch wiedererlangt hat (DMB 2021: 84).
>
> The return of collection objects from colonial contexts should be considered when the circumstances of acquisition appear wrong from today's point of view, and when the object at the time of its removal from the community of origin was of special religious or cultural significance and it has maintained or regained this significance today.

The notion of *Unrecht* recurs in Germany's key policy document on the subject: the 'Framework Principles for Dealing with Collections from Colonial Contexts', which was issued in March 2019 by the ministers of the German federal government, the federal states, and the national associations of local municipalities. Here, *Unrecht* encompasses both a wider meaning ('the injustices committed during the colonial era' [p. 1]) and a narrower sense ('acquired in a way that is no longer legally or ethically defensible' [p. 2]).

Despite the ubiquity of the terms *Unrecht* and *Unrechtskontext*, their use has encountered pushback.[16] Some critics complained about its lack of a broader ethical framework (Förster et al. 2017: 15), while others argued that singling out specific contexts of injustice skirted around the issue of whether – or rather the fact that – colonialism as such was historical injustice (Eckstein et al. 2017: 2). At the GMA conference in 2015, the German historian and public intellectual Jürgen Zimmerer argued against differentiating legitimate and illegitimate acquisitions under colonial rule. Instead, he maintained, we should consider all colonial objects to be unethically acquired unless proven otherwise:

> Entgegen der häufig zu findenden Praxis, dass ein Erwerb als rechtmäßig angesehen wurde und wird, bis der Unrechtscharakter erwiesen wird, gilt eigentlich das Gegenteil: Koloniale Objekte stehen unter dem Verdacht, unrechtmäßig erworben zu sein, bis das Gegenteil bewiesen ist (Zimmerer 2015: 24).
>
> Contrary to the usual practice of regarding an acquisition as lawful until its unlawfulness is proved, the following is actually valid: colonial objects are under the suspicion of having been acquired unlawfully until the opposite has been proved.

Zimmerer raises the crucial question of where the burden of proof in provenance research lies. Though this question merits further discussion, it lies beyond the scope of my work here.[17] At any rate, Zimmerer's call to reverse the burden of proof is reminiscent of the presumption rule in National Socialist-era provenance research, which generally considers 'losses of property of persons persecuted under National Socialism during the persecution period' as 'unlawful seizures'—unless evidence to the contrary can be presented (German Lost Art Foundation et al. 2019: 21–22, 97–98).

The similarity is not coincidental. In fact, I would like to argue that the debate on *Unrecht* committed or experienced under National Socialist rule underlies the use of *Unrechtskontexte* in Germany's postcolonial discussions, though the connection is rarely mentioned today. One exception is Wiebke Ahrndt of the Übersee-Museum Bremen, speaker of the working group that issued the 2013 recommendations. In her summary of the latter she describes how the understanding of human remains acquired between 1933 and 1945 became a point of departure for defining *Unrechtskontexte* in the 2013 recommendations:

> Bei unseren Überlegungen sind wir zunächst von dem Unrecht ausgegangen, das Deutsche anderen Menschen in der Vergangenheit zugefügt haben. Einigkeit herrschte [in der Arbeitsgruppe; L.F.] darüber, dass ein Mensch, der im 'Dritten Reich' in einem Konzentrationslager ermordet wurde und dessen sterbliche Überreste anschließend in eine Sammlung verbracht wurden, schweres und nicht wieder gut zu machendes Unrecht erlitten hat. Kein noch so großes wissenschaftliches Interesse kann es rechtfertigen, dass diese menschlichen Überreste in der Sammlung verbleiben und eventuell sogar Forschungszwecken dienen. Nur die Rückgabe an die Hinterbliebenen oder—falls dies nicht möglich ist—eine würdevolle Beisetzung sind hier geboten. Wenn Konsens über diesen Sachverhalt besteht, muss dann Gleiches nicht auch für die Opfer anderer Genozide gelten (Ahrndt 2013: 316)?
>
> In our reasoning we departed from the injustice that Germans have inflicted on others in the past. We [the working group; L.F.] agreed that a person who was murdered in a concentration camp in the 'Third Reich' and whose mortal remains were subsequently placed in a collection, suffered a grave and irreparable injustice. No research interest, however large, can justify human remains being kept in the collection and serving scientific purposes. The return to the bereaved—or if not possible, a dignified burial—is imperative. Must not the same consensus apply to the victims of other genocides?

Ahrndt's remarks built on the work of the 'Arbeitskreis Menschliche Überreste', a working group of anatomists, lawyers, historians and ethicists that had convened ten years earlier to assess anatomy and pathology collections. In 2003, the group issued the 'Stuttgart recommendations'[18] for collections 'die nach früheren Grundsätzen bzw. nach Grundsätzen anderer Rechtsordnungen rechtmäßig, nach unserer gegenwärtigen Bewertung aber unrechtmäßig hergestellt wurden' ('that have been produced lawfully according to earlier principles or principles of other legal systems, but unlawfully according to our current validation') (Jütte 2011: 43).[19] A paragraph under the heading 'Ethical viewpoints' in the Stuttgart recommendations concludes:

> Ergibt sich, dass der Verstorbene aufgrund seiner Abstammung, Weltanschauung oder wegen politischer Gründe durch staatlich organisierte und gelenkte Gewaltmaßnahmen sein Leben verloren hat oder besteht die durch Tatsachen begründete Wahrscheinlichkeit dieses Schicksals, ist dies eine schwere Verletzung seiner individuellen Würde. Wurde ein solcher *Unrechtskontext* festgestellt, sind die Präparate aus den einschlägigen Sammlungen herauszunehmen und würdig zu bestatten oder

> es ist in vergleichbar würdiger Weise damit zu verfahren (Arbeitskreis 'Menschliche Präparate in Sammlungen' 2003; highlights are my own).
>
> If it turns out that the deceased person has lost his/her life as a consequence of state-induced violence because of his/her descent, world view or for political reasons, or if the latter is considered likely, this is a grave violation of individual human dignity. If *circumstances of injustice* have been diagnosed, it is imperative to remove the specimens from the collection, bury them in a dignified manner or proceed with them in a similarly dignified way.

Another paragraph specifies the specimens whose provenance bothered curators most at the time: 'Präparate aus der NS-Zeit' ('specimens from the National Socialist era'). The anatomist and historian Sabine Hildebrandt has noted that the study of anatomical collections from the National Socialist era started in the 1990s and eventually resulted in a 2004 initiative by the Kultusministerkonferenz (Standing Conference of the Ministers of Culture in the German States) to study specimens from victims of National Socialism in German university collections (Hildebrandt 2016: 14). The 2003 Stuttgart recommendations grew out of these developments and laid the groundwork for a heightened sensitivity to acquisition practices and mechanisms for human remains; it was to human specimens acquired during the National Socialist rule what the Washington Principles on Nazi-Confiscated Art of 1998 was to artefacts acquired during National Socialist rule.

Consciously or not, the term *Unrechtskontext* in the Stuttgart recommendations invokes the National Socialist regime, which is referred to as an *Unrechtsstaat, Unrechtsregime* or *Unrechtssystem* in German public discourse and memory culture.[20] The genealogy of *Unrecht* in this context starts with a 1946 essay by the legal scholar Gustav Radbruch titled 'Gesetzliches Unrecht und übergesetzliches Recht'[21] (Hackmack and Kaleck 2021: 390) and the ground-breaking plea by Hessen's Attorney General Fritz Bauer in 1952 that National Socialist Germany be seen as an *Unrechtsstaat* (Claer 2003). Since then, legal scholars and academics have debated the proper definition of *Unrechtsstaat*. Some voices in the public sphere have also associated the term with the former GDR, which prompted others to ask whether the National Socialist regime and the East German state can be compared (ibid.). At any rate, *Unrechtskontext* references debates that lie at the heart of recent political discourse. Indeed, the German government's coalition agreement from 2018 states that working through the legacies of the National Socialist terror regime, the dictatorship of the Socialist Unity Party of [East] Germany and German colonial history is part of Germany's 'democratic consensus' (CDU, CSU and SPD 2018: 7994–7997).

In sum, the term *Unrechtskontext* draws significantly on debates about Germany's National Socialist past. First formulated in the Stuttgart recommendations from 2003 and then operationalised in the German Museum Association's 2013 recommendations, it provides criteria for museum professionals in the handling of human remains across separate historical and museological debates. Its moral appeal has created momentum for postcolonial repatriation and restitution and has made professionals as well as a broader public more aware of problematic acquisition practices and mechanisms.

Conclusion and outlook

The two terms examined above represent two different frames of reference for the German debate on postcolonial provenance research and restitution: global discussions of the history and the future of museum collections and German memory culture. Both suggest that the debate about human remains can be a motor for decolonising efforts in and around museums and that 'traveling models', concepts and practices are fundamental for achieving change.

The repatriation debates in the USA, the UK and in former settler nations have considerably shaped discussions in German museums, not only with regard to issues of human remains, but also to cultural heritage and the decolonisation of museums. Museum practices in Australia and New Zealand have inspired German anthropologists, curators and scholars, and provide good-practice examples of how to care for sensitive objects, how to cooperate with countries and societies of origin in provenance research and how to work towards the return of museum artefacts and human remains. More recently, the Black Lives Matter Movement has given the debate another important twist by focusing attention on antiracism and pointing towards discriminatory language and practices in museums. Perspectives and objections of societies of origin and diasporic communities continue to be instrumental in challenging German institutional practices and instigating their change.

At the same time, the memory culture and memory politics that have evolved in Germany since the Second World War provide a productive resonance chamber for the debate on colonialism. Working through the pasts of the National Socialist and East German regimes has helped forge a language for addressing historical injustices in Germany. Mobilising the notion of *Unrecht* has, if indirectly, helped create a lever for postcolonial restitution. In particular, the on-going institutionalisation of National Socialist-era provenance research and the increasing number of Jewish property restitutions have become points of reference that postcolonial provenance researchers and restitution advocates can look to and work towards, dock on to, borrow from or distinguish their work from if needed. Nevertheless, the relationship between decolonising efforts and efforts to come to terms with the National Socialist past remains in negotiation. A vivid example is the controversy that erupted surrounding the invitation of Achille Mbembe to hold the keynote address at the Ruhrtriennale.[22]

The terms *human remains* and *Unrechtkontexte* have demonstrated that a substantial part of the work of decolonisation is epistemic, that is to say, it depends on a revision of (museum) concepts, categories and classifications, many of which were established more than a century ago, and the creation of new language for decolonial approaches to museum objects and practices. Searching for new ways of talking about old collections is part of a growing desire to break with the past and to reform the museum as an institution and an attempt to overcome what has been so aptly called 'colonial aphasia' by Anne Stoler (Stoler 2016; see also Habermas 2019).

The trajectory of the two terms I traced here remains incomplete, of course. In a watershed moment like ours, when after decades of activist and scholarly engagement wider swaths of society are finally ready to confront Germany's colonial past, future disputes about appropriate terminology are likely to emerge anywhere that contestations over the postcolonial consensus arise.

Acknowledgements

This research was completed with funding from Sharon Macdonald's Alexander von Humboldt Professorship as part of the project *Making Differences: Transforming Museums and Heritage in the Twenty-First Century*. I would like to thank the CARMAH team, Stefanie Michels, Anne Brandstetter and Jonathan Bach for their critical comments. Special thanks go to Sharon Macdonald for her unwavering support of my work through turbulent times and for her encouragement to keep theorising while going practical.

Notes

1 Cf. in the coalition treaty of 2018: 'Die Aufarbeitung der Provenienzen von Kulturgut aus kolonialem Erbe in Museen und Sammlungen wollen wir [...] mit einem besonderen Schwerpunkt fördern' (CDU, CSU and SPD 2018: 8048–49).

2 Though I finished parts of this article after assuming the position of Head of the Department for Cultural Goods and Collections from Colonial Contexts at the German Lost Art Foundation, I completed the fieldwork beforehand. Most recent developments like the second edition of the 'Guidelines. Care of Human Remains in Museums and Collections' issued in June 2021 could not be considered in this article.

3 The Guidance on the Care of Human Remains was based on provisions from the UK's Human Tissues Act of 2004. Interestingly, the Human Tissue Act was created in response to a scandal involving the unauthorised removal of organs from corpses in a Liverpool hospital in the 1980s—not in response to the colonialism debate.

4 The volume was published as part of the Charité's Human Remains Project, which investigated the provenance of Namibian, Australian and Tasmanian human remains between 2010 and 2014.

5 This has been well-documented here: https://www.freiburg-postkolonial.de/Seiten/anthropologische-schaedelsammlungen.htm. In 2016, an artwork created by the German theatre company Flinn Works used the term in the play 'Schädel X': https://flinnworks.de/de/projekt/sch%C3%A4del-x

6 See the front pages and headlines in *The Namibian* and *Republikein* and other Namibian daily newspapers on 4 and 5 October 2011.

7 For a more detailed history of this struggle, see Kößler 2015.

8 For example, a member of the Charité reported that the Australian repatriation team of 2013 was irritated to hear Charité staff speak about 'skulls' that they had returned to Namibia in 2011. See Andreas Winkelmann, personal communication to author, 26 April 2013.

9 Indigenous communities often use their own specific terms. These include 'Old People' (Australia), *iwi kupuna* (Hawai'i) or *koiwi tangata* (New Zealand).

10 See the museum's website: https://grassi-voelkerkunde.skd.museum/forschung/dekolonisierung-restitution-und-repatriierung/

11 See 'Sächsische Museen starten Website zur Dekolonisierung'. Interview mit Léontine Meijer van Mensch, *mdr*, 20 March 2021. https://www.mdr.de/kultur/ausstellungen/grassi-museum-voelkerkunde-plattform-dekolonisierung-100.html und https://grassi-voelkerkunde.skd.museum/forschung/dekolonisierung-restitution-und-repatriierung/anfragen/

12 Claimants frequently cite article 12 of the United Nations Declaration on the Rights of Indigenous People of 2007.

13 Depending on the context, the term *Unrecht* is translated differently. Vice versa, the English term 'injustice' can be translated into *Unrecht* or *Ungerechtichkeit*. Although the various dimensions of *Unrecht* merit further discussion, their discussion lies beyond the scope of this essay.

14 Involuntary loss is one out of three criteria put forward in these documents. The other two are 'illegal acquisition' and 'heritage value'.

15 See Förster 2018b. For more details, see Hackmack and Kaleck 2021 and Theurer and Kaleck 2020.

16 Criticism of the term was the reason why an explicit definition of *Unrechtskontexte* was not provided in in the German Museum Association's 2018 guidelines. *Unrecht* itself, however, remained a criterion in the guidelines.

17 Broadly speaking, the 'Restitution Report' by Sarr and Savoy also advocates a reversal of the burden of proof, which is one reason why it has been so controversial.

18 The full name of the recommendations is the 'Empfehlungen zum Umgang mit Präparaten aus menschlichem Gewebe in Sammlungen, Museen und öffentlichen Räumen'.

19 One of the reasons for the establishment of the working group was the controversial exhibition 'Body Worlds' by Gunther von Hagens. The exhibition had stirred heated debates about body donation, informed consent and the question of whether and how to exhibit human tissue (Jütte 2011: 1).

20 *NS-Unrecht* (National Socialist injustice) has become a common term in Germany's official compensation politics. See: https://www.auswaertiges-amt.de/de/aussenpolitik/themen/internationales-recht/Historische_Verantwortung/entschaedigung-ns-unrecht/203834; in English: https://www.auswaertiges-amt.de/en/aussenpolitik/themen/internatrecht/compensation-for-national-socialist-injustice/228224

21 This can be translated as 'legal injustice and supralegal justice' or as 'statutory lawlessness and superstatutory law'.

22 For a list of articles about the debate, see https://serdargunes.wordpress.com/2020/05/18/wer-zuerst-x-sagt-hat-gewonnen-die-achille-mbembe-debatte-eine-artikelliste/

References

Ahrndt, W. 2013. 'Zum Umgang mit menschlichen Überresten in deutschen Museen und Sammlungen—Die Empfehlungen des Deutschen Museumsbundes', in H. Stoecker,

T. Schnalke, and A. Winkelmann (eds), *Sammeln, Erforschen, Zurückgeben—Menschliche Gebeine aus der Kolonialzeit in akademischen und musealen Sammlungen*, 314–322. Berlin: Ch. Links Verlag.

Annual Conference of the Directors of Ethnographic Museums in the German Speaking Countries. 2019: *Decolonising requires dialogue, expertise, and support. The Heidelberg Statement.* https://boasblogs.org/dcntr/decolonising-requires-dialogue-expertise-and-support/ (accessed 21 February 2022).

Arbeitskreis 'Menschliche Präparate in Sammlungen.' 2003. 'Empfehlungen zum Umgang mit Präparaten aus menschlichem Gewebe in Sammlungen, Museen und öffentlichen Räumen', *Deutsches Ärzteblatt* Heft 8: 378–383. https://www.aerzteblatt.de/archiv/38021/Mitteilungen-Empfehlungen-zum-Umgang-mit-Praeparaten-aus-menschlichem-Gewebe-in-Sammlungen-Museen-und-oeffentlichen-Raeumen (accessed 21 February 2022).

Arndt, S., and N. Ofuatey-Alazard (eds). 2011. *Wie Rassismus aus Wörtern spricht. (K)Erben des Kolonialismus im Wissensarchiv deutsche Sprache. Ein kritisches Nachschlagewerk.* Münster: Unrast Verlag.

Bal, M. 2002. *Travelling Concepts in the Humanities: A Rough Guide.* Toronto: University of Toronto Press.

Behrends, A., S.-J. Park, and R. Rottenburg (eds). 2014. *Travelling Models in African Conflict Management. Translating Technologies of Social Ordering*. Leiden: Brill.

Bouteloup, M., and A. Colin. 2011. Une légende en cache une autre. *Journal de Bétonsalon*, 12. Paris : Bétonsalon—Centre d'art et de recherche.

CDU, CSU and SPD. 2018. *Ein neuer Aufbruch für Europa. Eine neue Dynamik für Deutschland. Ein neuer Zusammenhalt für unser Land. Koalitionsvertrag zwischen CDU, CSU und SPD. 19. Legislaturperiode.* Berlin. https://www.bundesregierung.de/resource/blob/975226/847984/5b8bc23590d4cb2892b31c987ad672b7/2018-03-14-koalitionsvertrag-data.pdf?download=1 (accessed 21 February 2022).

Claer, T. 2003. *Negative Staatlichkeit: von der 'Räuberbande' zum 'Unrechtsstatt.'* (Schriftenreihe Schriften zur Rechts- und Staatsphilosophie; 1). Hamburg: Kovac.

Council for Culture. 2021. *Guidance for the way forward for colonial collections. Colonial collection—a recognition of injustice.* https://www.raadvoorcultuur.nl/documenten/adviezen/2021/01/22/colonial-collection-and-a-recognition-of-injustice [English translation of a document issued in Dutch already in 2020] (accessed 21 February 2022).

Department for Culture, Media and Sports. 2005. *Guidance on the Care of Human Remains in Museums*. London. https://www.britishmuseum.org/sites/default/files/2019-11/DCMS-Guidance-for-the-care-of-human-remains-in-museum.pdf (accessed 21 February 2022).

Deutscher Museumsbund. 2013. *Empfehlungen zum Umgang mit menschlichen Überresten in Museen und Sammlungen*. Berlin: Deutscher Museumsbund. https://www.museumsbund.de/wp-content/uploads/2017/04/2013-empfehlungen-zum-umgang-mit-menschl-ueberresten.pdf (accessed 21 February 2022).

Deutscher Museumsbund. 2021 (2018, 2019). *Leitfaden—Umgang mit Sammlungsgut aus kolonialen Kontexten. 3. Fassung*. Berlin: Deutscher Museumsbund. https://www.museumsbund.de/wp-content/uploads/2021/03/mb-leitfanden-web-210228-02.pdf (accessed 21 February 2022).

Deutsches Zentrum Kulturgutverluste in Zusammenarbeit mit Arbeitskreis Provenienzforschung, Arbeitskreis Provenienzforschung und Restitution—Bibliotheken, Deutscher Bibliotheksverband, Deutscher Museumsbund, ICOM Deutschland. 2019. *Leitfaden Provenienzforschung zur Identifizierung von Kulturgut, das während der nationalsozialistischen Herrschaft verfolgunsbedingt entzogen wurde*. Berlin. https://www.kulturgutverluste.de/Webs/DE/Recherche/Leitfaden/Index.html (accessed 21 February 2022).

Eckstein, L., D. Wiemann, N. Waller, and A. Bartels. 2017. *Postcolonial Justice—An Introduction*. Potsdam: Institutional Repository of the Potsdam University. https://publishup.uni-potsdam.de/opus4-ubp/frontdoor/deliver/index/docId/10322/file/eckstein_postcolonial_justice.pdf (accessed 21 February 2022).

Federal Government Commissioner for Culture and Media et al. 2019. *Framework Principles for Dealing with Collections from Colonial Contexts*. https://www.cp3c.org/ (accessed 21 February 2022). [English translation of Staatsministerin des Bundes für Kultur und Medien 2019]

Fforde, C., H. Keeler, and T. McKeown (eds). 2020. *The Routledge Companion to Indigenous Repatriation: Return, Reconcile, Renew*. London: Routledge.

Förster, L. 2013. "You are giving us the skulls—where is the flesh?" Die Rückkehr der namibischen Human Remains', in H. Stoecker, T. Schnalke, and A. Winkelmann (eds), *Sammeln, Erforschen, Zurückgeben—Menschliche Gebeine aus der Kolonialzeit in akademischen und musealen Sammlungen*, 419–446. Berlin: Ch. Links Verlag.

Förster, L. 2017a. 'Es geht um mehr als Raubkunst—Ethnologische Provenienzforschung zwischen Erstcheck und Sysiphusarbeit', in *CARMAH Reflections*. http://www.carmah.berlin/reflections/ethnologische-provenienzforschung-zwischen-erstcheck-und/ (accessed 21 February 2022).

Förster, L. 2017b. 'The Long Way Home. Zur Biografie zurückgegebener Objekte/Subjekte', in T. Greub, and M. Roussel (eds), *Figurationen des Porträts*, 637–656. Paderborn: Wilhelm Fink.

Förster, L. 2018a. 'Provenance—An essay based on a panel with Ciraj Rassool, Paul Basu and Britta Lange', *CARMAH Paper 1, Otherwise: Rethinking Museums and Heritage*: 16–26. www.carmah.berlin/wp-content/uploads/2017/10/Carmah_Paper-1.pdf (accessed 21 February 2022).

Förster, L. 2018b. 'Whoever's Right. Remarks about the Debate on Provenance and Return from the Perspective of Social and Cultural Anthropology', *Boasblog—How to Move on with Humboldt's Legacy?*. https://boasblogs.org/dcntr/whoevers-right/ (accessed 21 February 2022).

Förster, L. 2020. '"The Face of Genocide": Returning human remains from German institutions to Namibia', in C. Fforde, H. Keele, and T. McKeown (eds), *The Routledge Companion to Indigenous Repatriation: Return, Reconcile, Renew*, 101–127. London: Routledge.

Förster, L. and H. Stoecker (eds). 2016. *Haut, Haar und Knochen. Koloniale Spuren in naturkundlichen Sammlungen der Universität Jena*. Band 9, Laborberichte. Weimar: VDG Verlag.

Förster, L. and F. von Bose. 2018. 'Discussing Ethnological Museums: The Epistemology of Postcolonial Debates', in P. Schorch, and C. McCarthy (eds), *Curatopia. Museums and the Future of Curatorship*, 95–122. Manchester: Manchester University Press.

Förster, L., I. Edenheiser, S. Fründt, and H. Hartmann (eds). 2018a. *Provenienzforschung zu ethnografischen Sammlungen der Kolonialzeit. Positionen in der aktuellen Debatte. Berlin.* https://edoc.hu-berlin.de/handle/18452/19768 (last accessed 21 February 2022).

Förster, L., I. Edenheiser, and S. Fründt. 2018b. 'Eine Tagung zu postkolonialer Provenienzforschung. Zur Einführung', in L. Förster, I. Edenheiser, S. Fründt, and H. Hartmann (eds), *Provenienzforschung zu ethnografischen Sammlungen der Kolonialzeit. Positionen in der aktuellen Debatte*, 13–37. https://edoc.hu-berlin.de/handle/18452/19814 (accessed 21 Feburary 2022).

Förster, L., D. Henrichsen, H. Stoecker, and H. A. Eichab. 2018. 'Re-individualising human remains from Namibia—Colonialism, grave robbery and intellectual history', *Human Remains and Violence: An Interdisciplinary Journal*, 4(2): 45–66.

Förster, L., S. Fründt, D. Preuß, K. Schramm, H. Stoecker, and A. Winkelmann (eds). 2017. 'A Good Starting Point? Critical Perspectives from Various Disciplines', in L. Förster, and S. Fründt (eds), *Historisches Forum no. 21 »Human Remains in Museums and Collections. A Critical Engagement with the ›Recommendations‹ of the German Museums Association*. https://edoc.hu-berlin.de/handle/18452/20147 (accessed 21 February 2022).

Fründt, S. 2011. *Die Menschen-Sammler. Über den Umgang mit menschlichen Überresten im Übersee-Museum Bremen.* Marburg: Tectum.

Fründt, S., and L. Förster. 2021. 'Menschliche Überreste aus ehemals kolonisierten Gebieten in deutschen Sammlungen. Historische Entwicklungen und zukünftige Perspektiven', in M. Bechhaus-Gerst, and J. Zeller (eds), *Deutschland postkolonial? Die Gegenwart der imperialen Vergangenheit*, 2nd ed., 527–556. Berlin: Metropol.

Fuchs, J., D. Gabler, C. Herm, M. Markert, and S. Mühlenberend. 2020. *Menschliche Überreste im Depot. Empfehlungen für Betreuung und Nutzung*. Dresden: Hochschule für bildende Künste. https://wissenschaftliche-sammlungen.de/de/nachrichten/aktuelles/menschliche-ueberreste-im-depot-empfehlungen-fuer-betreuung-und-nutzung-2020 (accessed 21 February 2022).

German Lost Art Foundation in cooperation with Arbeitskreis Provenienzforschung, Arbeitskreis Provenienzforschung und Restitution—Bibliotheken, Deutscher Bibliotheksverband, Deutscher Museumsbund, ICOM Deutschland. 2019. *Provenance Research Manual to Identify Cultural Property Seized due to Persecution during the National Socialist Era*. Berlin. https://www.kulturgutverluste.de/Webs/EN/Research/Manual/Index.html (accessed 21 February 2022).

German Museums Association (GMA). 2013. *Recommendations for the Care of Human Remains in Museums and Collections.* Berlin: German Museums Association.

German Museums Association (GMA). 2021 (2018, 2019). *Guidelines for German Museums—Care of Collections from Colonial Contexts*, 3rd ed. Berlin: German Museums Association.

Goethe-Institut Tanzania, National Museum of Tanzania, Museum am Rothenbaum, Berlin Postkolonial e.V. and the German Federal Foreign Office. 2020. *Beyond Collecting: New Ethics for Museums in Transition*. https://www.goethe.de/ins/ts/de/kul/sup/beyond-collecting.html (accessed 21 February 2022).

Habermas, R. 2019. 'Restitutionsdebatten, koloniale Aphasie und die Frage, was Europa ausmacht', *Aus Politik und Zeitgeschichte* 40–42: 17–22.

Hackmack, J., and W. Kaleck. 2021. 'Warum restituieren? Eine rechtliche Begründung', in T. Sandkühler, A. Epple, and J. Zimmerer (eds), *Geschichtskultur durch Restitution? Ein Historikerstreit*, 385–410. Köln: Böhlau.

Hildebrandt, S. 2016. *The Anatomy of a Murder. Ethical Transgressions and anatomical science during the Third Reich*. New York: Berghahn Books.

Jahreskonferenz der Direktor/innen der Ethnologischen Museen im deutschsprachigen Raum in Heidelberg 2019: *Dekolonisierung erfordert Dialog, Expertise und Unterstützung—Heidelberger Stellungnahme.* https://www.rem-mannheim.de/museen-in-mannheim/museum-weltkulturen/die-sammlungen/kulturen-der-welt/heidelberger-erklaerung/ (accessed 21 February 2022).

Jütte, R. 2011. 'Die Stuttgarter Empfehlungen zum Umgang mit Präparaten aus menschlichem Gewebe in Sammlungen, Museen und öffentlichen Räumen', in C. Weber, and K. Mauersberger (eds), *Universitätsmuseen und -sammlungen im Hochschulalltag—Aufgaben, Konzepte, Perspektiven; Beiträge zum Symposium vom 18.–20. Februar 2010 an der Humboldt-Universität zu Berlin*, 43–48.

Kößler, R. 2015. *Namibia and Germany. Negotiating the Past.* Windhoek: University of Namibia Press.

Macdonald, S. 2009. *Difficult Heritage. Negotiating the Nazi Past in Nuremberg and Beyond.* Oxford/New York: Routledge.

Macdonald, S., C. Gerbich, and M. von Oswald. 2018. 'No Museum is an Island: Ethnography beyond Methodological Containerism', *Museum and Society*, 16 (2): 138–156.

Modest, W., and R. Lelijveld. 2018. *Words Matter—An Unfinished Guide to Word Choices in the Cultural Sector*. Leiden: Research Center for Material Culture. https://www.materialculture.nl/en/publications/words-matter (accessed 21 February 2022).

National Museum for World Cultures. 2019. *Return of Cultural Objects: Principles and Process*. Amsterdam: Nationaal Museum van Wereldculturen. https://www.volkenkunde.nl/sites/default/files/2019-05/Claims%20for%20Return%20of%20Cultural%20Objects%20NMVW%20Principles%20and%20Process.pdf (accessed 21 February 2022).

Rassool, C. 2015. 'Re-storing the skeletons of empire: return, reburial and rehumanisation in Southern Africa', *Journal of Southern African Studies*, 41 (3): 653–670.

Rassool, C. 2017. 'Rückführung in das "Neue Museum". Ein Interview mit Ciraj Rassool', in AfricAvenir e. V. (ed.), *No Humboldt21! Dekoloniale Einwände gegen das Humboldt-Forum*. Berlin.

Sarr, F., and B. Savoy. 2018. *The Restitution of African Cultural Heritage. Toward a New Relational Ethics.* http://restitutionreport2018.com *(accessed 21 February 2022)*.

Staatsministerin des Bundes für Kultur und Medien. 2019. *Erste Eckpunkte zum Umgang mit Sammlungsgut aus kolonialen Kontexten*. https://www.kmk.org/aktuelles/artikelansicht/eckpunkte-zum-umgang-mit-sammlungsgut-aus-kolonialen-kontexten.html (accessed 21 February 2022).

Stoecker, H., T. Schnalke, and A. Winkelmann (eds). 2013. *Sammeln, Erforschen, Zurückgeben—Menschliche Gebeine aus der Kolonialzeit in akademischen und musealen Sammlungen*. Berlin: Ch. Links Verlag.

Stoler, A. L. 2016. 'Colonial aphasia: disabled history and race in France', in A. Stoler, *Duress. Imperial Durabilities in Our Times*. Durham, 122–170. Durham: Duke University Press.

Stürmer, F., and J. Schramm. 2019. 'Human Remains in deutschen Sammlungen—Rechtspflichten zur Rückgabe'. *Humboldt Law Clinic Grund- und Menschenrechte Working Paper*, 18. Berlin: Humboldt-Universität zu Berlin.

Theurer, K., and W. Kaleck (eds). 2020. *Dekoloniale Rechtskritik und Rechtspraxis*. Baden-Baden: Nomos.

Winkelmann, A. 2020. 'Repatriations of human remains from Germany–1911 to 2019', *Museum and Society*, 18(1): 40–51.

Zimmerer, J. 2015. 'Kulturgut aus der Kolonialzeit—ein schwieriges Erbe', *Museumskunde*, 80(2): 22–25.

Being Affected
Shifting Positions at the Ethnological Museum of Berlin

Margareta von Oswald

On 22 October 2013 approximately 200 people gathered at the Werkstatt der Kulturen to hear talks about the Humboldt Forum, a new cultural centre to be built on Berlin's museum island.[1] In the event's introduction Arnim Massing and Kien Nghi Ha called the plans for the museum 'particularly uninspired and unimaginative', 'revisionist' and 'lacking any kind of sensibility when it comes to dealing responsibly with one's own colonial history'.[2] Frequent ironic laughter from the audience accompanied the discussion, and people murmured when the moderator introduced Peter Junge, a curator at the Ethnological Museum of Berlin, which along with the Museum of Asian Art would become part of the Humboldt Forum in the reconstructed Berlin City Palace when it opened. Junge was the only representative from the planned Humboldt Forum—he was responsible for the Africa department's exhibition as well as managing the liaison between the Ethnological Museum and the Humboldt Forum—to accept an invitation from the Werkstatt der Kulturen. Visibly nervous, Junge tried to explain his position. He expressed his gratitude for being invited and highlighted the need for dialogue. He foregrounded the work done in the Africa department at the Ethnological Museum and mentioned his practical work on exhibitions for the Humboldt Forum. He emphasised the discrepancy between how the Humboldt Forum was publicly perceived and what it would actually do, which he described as 'breaking with the colonial past'. A day before the event, during lunch at the Museum canteen, Peter Junge had reassured himself: 'We have everything they want: collection history, contemporary art, visible storage'. But at the event the anthropologist Larissa Förster asked him why the museum had not been more outspoken in recent discussions of colonialism:

> You know the collections and its histories best, the problematic as well as the unproblematic parts. Where is your expert's voice correcting the cultural politics you are criticising? Why don't you take the chance to position yourself in the debate, taking the controversies as an opportunity?

Junge responded diplomatically. He stressed his work at the Museum while refusing to take a critical stance.

The next day, in the Museum canteen, staff said to Junge that he had been 'skewered' (*aufgespießt*) by the critics. He vehemently denied it: 'I would never let myself be skewered!' Nevertheless, for the audience members at the Werkstatt der Kulturen event, he was the face of the Prussian Cultural Heritage Foundation (*Stiftung Preußischer Kulturbesitz*, henceforth: SPK), which was the owner of the Ethnological Museum's collections and represented the Humboldt Forum. 'This event was about exposing me, not about dialogue. It's like in 1968, but', he sighed and then continued: '[s]till, it is important not to dial in (*abhaken*) these kinds of events. Even if they are only a minority, and even if this kind of event dampens our mood'—the others seated at the table laughed again and seemed to agree—'we have to remain in dialogue with them. These are the only people who are interested in the Forum, apart from the conservatives who want to rebuild the Palace! Ten years ago, no one questioned the origin of the objects. Today you are asked about it at every guided tour. That's why these people are important.'

In this chapter, I examine what it means to work in an organisation mired in anti-colonial controversy, between 2013 and 2015. In doing so, I use Jeanne Favret-Saada's notion of 'being affected' to support the study of these contested collections and to contribute to the understanding of the curatorial struggles that were underway at that time.

My thinking about Favret-Saada's reflections on affect began when I co-curated the exhibition *Object Biographies*, which explicitly dealt with the colonial provenance of the Ethnological Museum's Africa collection.[3]

Monitoring my own affects allowed me to pay particular attention to the emotional dimension of curatorial work, which is only rarely considered in museological literature. From my earliest work in the field, I described the general mood and emotions in my notes with observations such as 'is enraged', 'feels desperate', 'describes as draining' and 'feels accused of colonial crime'. Also, I myself was confronted with recurring feelings of unease, discomfort and malaise. Taking these emotions as analytical clues, below I discuss the curatorial responsibility to 'appropriately' address Germany's colonial history in a polarised climate while considering signs of colonial violence in the Ethnological Museum's past. Part of that responsibility is to make knowledge and information accessible, to respond to the politics of representation and exclusion and to avoid reproducing the mechanisms inherent to colonial collections and governance.

The Humboldt Forum, anti-Humboldt activism and German colonialism

In June 2013, Berlin city officials held a foundation stone ceremony for the Berlin Palace. Described as a 'little act of state' by the press, the ceremony included federal ministers and members of parliament who were joined via video by the British Museum's director, Neil MacGregor, and the former US Foreign Minister Henry Kissinger (Haubrich 2013). Under beautiful skies, shouts of 'bravo' for the Palace's most prominent initiators were accompanied by encomiums praising the Humboldt Forum as 'an opportunity for the whole of Europe' (MacGregor). A journalist wrote that '...a new phase begins' and 'the time of ideological struggles is over'. 'Construction is finally underway' (Schaper 2013). For some, more than two decades of dissent seemed to end with the beginning of construction work.

While the joyful event was taking place, however, members of a newly formed coalition known as No Humboldt 21! had gathered in protest. The purpose of the coalition was to stop the construction of the Humboldt Forum, which they considered 'Eurocentric' and 'restorative', 'a direct contradiction to the aim of promoting equality in a society of immigrants' (No Humboldt 21! 2013, 21). Whereas the journalist had pronounced the end of 'ideological struggles', No Humboldt 21! refocussed the discussion from debates about Germany's socialist past—triggered by the demolition of the GDR-era Palace of the Republic—to Germany's colonial history.

The physical separation between the festive foundation stone ceremony and the activists demonstrating outside the construction perimeters created a set of seemingly insurmountable binary oppositions: between an organisation that perpetuated colonial modes of conceiving the world and one that opposed such worldviews, between 'inside' and 'outside' the Museum, between 'good' and 'bad', between the Humboldt Forum and the activists.

No Humboldt 21! and the anti-Humboldt Forum campaign

The coalition's resolution was signed by 82 organisations, most of them located in Berlin and elsewhere in Germany. Their specific objectives differed, but most were engaged in de-colonial, anti-racist and feminist missions and some represented diaspora groups and their interests.

The logo for the No Humboldt 21! campaign merges the image of the Humboldt Forum Foundation in the Berlin Palace (*Stiftung Humboldt Forum im Berliner Schloss*) and that of the SPK. The difference is the eagle, which is crying and whose tears seem to morph into blood. The point was to signal which objects belonged to its critique—the building, its content, its name—and which did not (the Humboldt-Universität zu Berlin and the Berlin State Library).

3.1 Logo of the 'No Humboldt 21!' initiative. Reproduced courtesy of No Humboldt 21!
3.2 Logo of the Stiftung Preußischer Kulturbesitz. Reproduced courtesy of the Stiftung Preußischer Kulturbesitz.
3.3 Logo of the Stiftung Berliner Schloss. Reproduced courtesy of the Stiftung Berliner Schloß.

The activists focused their criticism on the publication 'The Humboldt Forum: "To Be in Touch with as Much of the World as Possible": The Goal and Significance of Germany's Most Important Cultural Project at the Beginning of the Twenty-First Century'. Authored by the SPK's president Hermann Parzinger in 2011, the brochure was considered its *de facto* 'concept'.[4] The No Humboldt 21! campaign drew on international museum practice and recent scholarship as they identified five particular points of critique. First, the activists challenged the idea that museums were 'the legitimate owners of their holdings'. In view of the colonial origins of the museum's collection, they called for the 'disclosure of the ownership history', adherence to a UN resolution in favour of repatriation and 'dialogue' with the 'descendants of the artists and the legal owners of the exhibits'. Second, they accused the Humboldt Forum of 'redeeming Berlin's colonial past', and demanded that no objects acquired during colonial times be exhibited in the Berlin Palace. Third, they denounced a politics of representation in which 'the cultures of the world are discriminated against, marked as "strangers" and "other"'. They pointed to the Forum's particular position on the Museum Island, and noted the separation between the 'classical collections' (*Altes Museum, Bodemuseum, Museum für Islamische Kunst, Alte Nationalgalerie*) and the 'Non-European' ones. Fourth, they criticised forms of knowledge production from the 'era of discovery'. In their opinion, Alexander von Humboldt, the German naturalist and one of the Forum's eponyms, embodied 'colonial dominance' and was thus not 'an appropriate person to name an intercultural centre after'. Fifth, they focused on the politics of access, criticising the way in which cultural goods remain unequally available to populations around the globe. They demanded that cultural goods in the Global North be permanently returned to their countries of origin in the Global South.

Neither the SPK, the Ethnological Museum nor the Humboldt Forum had released an official statement or position paper on German colonialism. But the statements they did publish didn't allay and even added to the activists' criticisms. SPK representatives relativised the impact of German colonialism on the collections by comparing it with those of other European colonial powers. Official representatives stated in 2001 that '([i])n contrast to the typical colonial countries Great Britain, France, the Netherlands, Spain, etc. where selected objects reached the European motherlands as spoil, German collectors and scientists developed systematic and—astonishingly modern—databases in Humboldt's tradition' (quoted in König 2013: 33). Hermann Parzinger offered a similar argument in 2010, stating that 'concerning the collection's genesis, Germany has...a colonial past, but it is not like other European powers' (Hermann Parzinger [2010]; quoted in V. König 2012: 56). The SPK focused on the accuracy and scientific rigour of collecting and research practices, and downplayed the role of German colonialism in the museum's collections (Parzinger 2011: 31–32). Another argument put forward was that only a small portion of the collections was shaped by colonialism; most of it, like Berlin's Royal Cabinet of Curiosities, was of a 'precolonial' provenance. This argument overlooks that era's contested politics of acquisition and representation (von Bose 2016, 128–29).

These statements reflected a then-common understanding of Germany's colonial history and national politics. Since the early 2000s, German diplomacy had neglected or circumvented its colonial past and the crimes related to it (Lutz and Gawarecki 2005; Eckert 2007; Eckert and Wirz 2013; Zimmerer 2013). At the same time, the statements of the SPK ignored the latest academic research on the relationship between anthropological museums and colonialism in general[5] and Berlin's collections and German colonialism in particular. [6]

The activists' campaign received a boost from the German Green Party *Bündnis 90/ Die Grünen*[7] and the left-wing party *Die Linke*,[8] who in local governments and in the Bundestag vowed to investigate the colonial origins of the Museum's collections, in particular the human remains they contain. Support for the critique of the Humboldt Forum, therefore, had become entrenched among activists, politicians and academics, at the grassroots level and in local and national political arenas.

Inside the Ethnological Museum—complicating the picture

I started my research at the Ethnological Museum of Berlin in October 2013. I focused on the past, present and future of selected objects from the Africa collection as part of a larger ethnographic study of processes of transformations underway in ethnological museums in Europe. My archival and field research concentrated on practices related to the planned new permanent exhibition, which was to include the museum's Africa collections for the Humboldt Forum.

When I started my work, I sympathised with many of the arguments of the No Humboldt 21! activists. At that time, it was difficult not to. After the Forum's foundation stone ceremony, activists organised a variety of public events, such as the travelling exhibition 'Anti-Humboldt Box'[9]. They coordinated conferences,[10] published articles and edited volumes.[11] Meanwhile, the SPK, the SMB and the Ethnological Museum remained silent about the collection's colonial past. In the autumn and winter of 2013, outsiders frequently voiced their frustration with the organisations' behaviour.[12] The work at the Humboldt Forum took place behind closed doors, despite a provisional three-storey exhibition space known as the Humboldt Box located at the Forum's construction site. The Humboldt Lab Dahlem (henceforth: HLD) organised exhibitions and 'experiments' to accompany the Forum preparations. With a budget of more than 4 million euros, the Humboldt Lab was perceived as the Humboldt Forum's showcase, yet it too had not taken a public position on German colonialism in the autumn of 2013.

Yet on my first day at the Museum, the seemingly clear-cut opposition between outside activist and museum insider collapsed. A Museum staff member referred to the Humboldt Forum as 'an ultra-conservative project led by old white men'.[13] That view was no exception among staff members. Throughout the duration of my research, museum staff routinely criticised the Forum. Part of their problem, they often said, was the absence of a stated programme and a clear idea of who would define it. 'No one wants to work for a project that is at the centre of criticism', I wrote in my fieldnotes. 'Museum staff lack identification with the Forum.'[14] Some were unaware of the brochure 'The Humboldt Forum: "To Be in Touch with as Much of the World as Possible"', highlighting the disconnect between experts working closely with the collections and those representing the Forum. I realised then that the SPK's leadership had not only *not* responded to the activists; they had not communicated effectively with their own staff. Neither did they seem to then have heeded the recommendations of the Forum's international advisory board for the Ethnological Museum's and Museum of Asian Art, made in 2011, that the organisation address colonialism and its latter-day repercussions (Heizmann and Parzinger 2012). The Museum's Africa department curators, however, *had* defined colonialism as a central topic of their research and exhibition plans as early as 2008.[15]

Behind the scenes at the Ethnological Museum, then, were numerous opinions and positions, not a single unified view. My work at the Museum complicated the idea of a straightforward binary opposition—one between those denying Germany's colonial past and those facing up to it, between those against and those for the Humboldt Forum, between the postcolonial and the neo-colonial.

Being affected: making *Object Biographies*

In December 2013, HLD approached me and Verena Rodatus, the museum apprentice (*Volontärin*) working in the Africa department, to ask us whether we would like to curate an exhibition on 'looted art' (*Beutekunst*). The HLD was under pressure to present critical voices and reflect the current state of the academic literature on German colonialism and provenance. Verena Rodatus and I would occupy a kind of insider–outsider position. We would both be temporarily employed, we were new to the field, and we were not on staff at the Ethnological Museum. As one of the HLD's leaders explained to us, it was 'obvious to everyone' that the provenance of cultural artefacts needed to be addressed, but no official 'proactive position' was likely in the near future. Neither the Ethnological Museum nor the SPK had the personnel and funds to deal with those questions because their curators were in the final stages of determining their object lists for the Humboldt Forum. The HLD, by contrast, had enough resources at its disposal to fund such work.[16]

Initially, we were unsure whether to accept the offer. We worried that the Museum or the SPK would distance itself from our criticisms because we were temporary employees, limit the project's critical scope or take over the project without changing their general stance. Working within the organisation, and being associated with the Humboldt Forum would restrict our room to maneuverer. Going from anthropologist and museum apprentice to public curators felt like a risk, one that could possibly drive a wedge between us and our immediate peers. We later noted our concern that we would be 'discredited by critics because of our institutional affiliation' (April 2014).

Our concern was not unjustified. The HLD's first efforts had received bad press (*Probebühnen*, March, June, September 2013),[17] and it underwent an external review. The evaluators found that HLD had ignored or inadequately addressed the general expectations of ethnological museums and the Forum's critics in particular, and the news had started to leak (Mörsch et al. 2014). The HLD's projects had been met with hostility even by museum staff, some of whom criticised the HLD as 'appropriating the objects for a second time'.[18] Some associated with the HLD found their experience emotionally challenging. 'I'd better do a good job so as not to lose my friends', one curator said in a meeting. Another recounted how she had been publicly faced with 'overt hostility, simply because I was working for the Humboldt Forum.' One person reported crying when a friend refused to say hello to her on the street. 'It's not nice when everyone turns away, like that', someone else said.[19]

Nevertheless, we decided to accept the offer in the hope of helping change the system from within. We developed the exhibition, titled *Object Biographies*, in conversation with the Africa department's curators. A crucial issue for the exhibition was provenance research, which we had already conducted for the Humboldt Forum as part of our individual work. Our objective was to address the Museum's ties to German colonialism head-on by taking the collection's history and the trajectories of specific objects as the exhibition's starting point. We were interested in which stories had *not* been told, who and what was absent or rarely visible in the Museum's own story. With the help of contemporary voices and research, both from Europe and Africa (von Oswald and Rodatus 2017), we wanted to arrive at a more expansive understanding of the Museum's collections. It would be the first show at the Ethnological Museum to put the violent history of German colonial rule on centre stage.

From participant observation to observant participation

When I decided to co-curate the exhibition, my position changed from being a scholar and stipend recipient to a curator, from being a 'participant observer' to being an 'observant participant'. Becoming a 'participant' changed my conception of 'distance' and 'scientific objectivity' in the field.

Jeanne Favret-Saada's notion of affect in her work on witchcraft in rural France has helped me think through the particularities of my situation (Favret-Saada 1977). The field of museum anthropology is obviously very different from that of witchcraft in France—not to mention, less deadly. Still, Favret-Saada's idea that researchers are affected by their work challenges the relationship between 'observation' and 'participation' in a way that was also useful for my field. Favret-Saada argues that earlier accounts of witchcraft are usually written from the perspective of anthropologists who were interested in observation, rather than participation. She recalls that academics had long reduced witchcraft to an 'accusation' and depicted it as 'a medicine for the illiterate and ignorant people' (Favret-Saada 2012). By contrast, she describes that the people she encountered wanted her to become a 'partner'. They would only communicate with her once she too had been, as she put it, 'taken'. She describes the feeling of participating in the field as 'being affected', without knowing whether or not she was actually bewitched herself.

Being affected and affecting the field

Alhough metaphors like being 'taken' were not unknown in my field—the former museum director Clémentine Deliss once asked me if I had been 'turned' by 'museum anthropology', as in 'turned like a zombie'[20]—the field of ethnological museums is also shaped by binary oppositions like those that Favret Saada describes in her field.

Favret-Saada argues that participation can be an instrument of knowledge. To understand the 'intensities' that come when working within a field, one must experience them (Favret-Saada 2004: 4–5). Researchers participate in and contribute to developments in the field: they are both affected by the objects of study and affect them. Being affected also means that one loses control over how one is positioned in the field. In conventional 'participant observation', the researcher can remain 'just' an anthropologist. Not so in the polarised atmosphere of Berlin, where the mere fact of collaborating with this state organisation meant being assigned a position. Unlike empathy, Favret-Saada argues, being affected tells the researcher about her own feelings and not necessarily the feelings of those who are the subject of research (Favret-Saada 2012; 1977). Being affected means becoming the person about whom the anthropologist is ultimately writing. In this way, the anthropologist's own doubts, instabilities and anxieties become tools for analysis. Here, what Sharon Macdonald describes as the 'anthropological approach'— the 'commitment to trying to see and experience life-worlds from the point of view of those who live them and within the context of which they are part' (Macdonald 2013: 9)—becomes the personal, physical experience that is the researcher's own 'life-world'.

My approach to the field changed as I sought ways to exhibit the Museum's objects publicly while balancing a complicated mixture of political and marketing interests, decision-making processes, legal regulations and professional convictions. As an insider, I began to look at the work of museum curators differently. Instead of focusing solely on identifying 'mistakes'—like many external critics of exhibitions in ethnological museums—I became more in tune to their complexities and contradictions.

Curating contested collections

At the Ethnological Museum the curators of colonial collections were aware of the expectations to respond to activist critique and recent academic research, and the relationship between German colonialism and anthropology, in particular. For decades, researchers, archivists and curators had worked on the history of colonial violence and theft. The difficulty lay in collaboratively addressing that history in a politically explosive climate.

Did our project challenge or perpetuate the museum's role as a 'colonial instrument' (Boast 2011)? *Object Biographies* addressed not only *what* was being told but *who* was telling the story. Who was allowed to speak, and from which position and how? This also concerned the composition of our team and what has been called the 'delegation of interpretative sovereignty' (*Deutungshoheit abgeben*) and the politics of representation more generally.

I often felt defensive and apologetic when working on and writing about the exhibition. I was worried about being *perceived* as perpetuating colonial injustice and of *actually* perpetuating colonial injustice from within a contested organisation.[21] Ambivalent feelings continued to accompany me as I tackled the collection's colonial legacy and the question of how best to discuss and exhibit that legacy from my privileged position within the Museum.

As questions of colonial provenance and restitution garnered more and more public attention, those publicly representing the HLD and the Ethnological Museum found the SPK's silence on those issues increasingly difficult. In January 2015, in response to a parliamentary inquiry by the Green Party, the Federal Government Commissioner for Culture and the Media, Monika Grütters, announced that 'the government, including the SPK, defends the position that no unlawfully acquired objects should be kept within the collections of the State Museums Berlin, regardless of the time period from which they stem'. It was, in other words, an official guarantee that every object displayed in the Humboldt Forum would undergo provenance research and that this research would be 'made transparent' (Deutscher Bundestag 2015: 2–3). The government position marked a shift in public and political debate that set the *legality* of collections against the *legitimacy* of owning them. The shift, in turn, was closely related to activist activities, including a long correspondence between activist organisations and the SPK (Prosinger, Mboro, and Kisalya 2013; Kathmann 2014; Prosinger and Mboro 2014; Parzinger 2014), and the sudden cancellation of a public event at the Haus der Kulturen der Welt, which No Humboldt 21! interpreted as a refusal of Humboldt Forum representatives 'to dialogue' with them in public (No Humboldt 21! 2014a). In December 2014, *No Humboldt 21!* published a press release containing a list of the human remains and 'war loot' (*Kriegsbeute*) (No Humboldt 21! 2014b) in the museum collection.

Critique and complicity

In *Object Biographies*, we addressed Germany's colonial history by narrating different stories of the objects' provenance. We decided to focus on the violent history of two figures from the historic kingdom of Kom, located in present-day Cameroon. We understood that when provenance research identifies illegitimate modes of acquisition, the political consequences can be significant. What does it mean to display colonial loot within an organisation that has yet to take an official position on colonialism? The question points to a paradox that often confronted me in my work: the constant risk of legitimising or strengthening a contested organisation when working within it, even when that work is critical. The fear of involuntary complicity accompanied me as I prepared *Object Biographies* and thought about the possible public response.

In March 2015, HLD managing director Agnes Wegner wrote an email to the SPK's legal department (*Justiziariat*) saying that she was 'troubled'. She described her unease at a public event.[22] Seated below several *No Humboldt 21!* posters asking 'Ever seen looted art?', she found it hard to justify the presence of war trophies in the museum collections, though she felt institutionally bound to do just that. 'I often reach my limits, and words fail me.' She asked for advice and legal consultation and attached the exhibition texts of Objects Biographies, to inquire about the communications strategy for the exhibition.[23]

With regards to ownership and restitution, the common ground at the SPK consisted in arguing that the collection had been legally acquired within the framework of international colonial-era law,[24] and that any claims on artefacts would be beyond the statute of limitations. Accordingly, restitution could occur only 'from an ethical, political or moral point of view.' The duty of the museum was to uphold the principles of 'keeping, conserving, making accessible'. 'If we give the objects to non-museum contexts, we are breaking the law. For better or worse, the museum perspective is: What has once entered the museum stays in the museum'.[25]

This position expressed the legal limbo that objects acquired in the colonial era often find themselves. 'Law, by its nature, crystallizes the general consensus at a particular time', Lyndel Prott writes. 'There was no consensus on the (il)legality of colonization before 1960', when the United Nations Resolution on Decolonization was adopted (Prott 2009: 103; see also Schönberger 2016). And it was clear that legality at the time of acquisition was the decisive legal standard applied by the SPK. For instance, in 2012, Hermann

Parzinger stated that 'what was right then cannot be wrong today' ('Was damals Recht war, kann heute nicht Unrecht sein') (Parzinger 2012). The problem for the SPK and the Humboldt Forum, however, was that the legitimacy of the legal argument had now come under public scrutiny.

3.4 Ever seen looted art? *Poster by No Humboldt 21!*[26]*, Creative Commons Licence.*
3.5 Prussian cultural heritage? *Poster by No Humboldt 21!*[27]*, Creative Commons Licence.*

The difficulty of drawing a clear line between legality and legitimacy became evident when we received the wall texts from the SPK's communication department, ten days before the exhibition was scheduled to open. As we learned, the *Justiziariat* and the Humboldt Forum's communication department had the right to control and eventually amend every text that had a possible 'link with restitution' (*Restitutionsbezug*).[28] Words and entire sentences were missing; others were added new. For example, in the phrase 'unknown and sometimes problematic histories', the SPK deleted 'and sometimes problematic'. It also expunged the question 'Which histories are told, and which ones are silenced?' In the introductory text, we claimed to shed 'critical light on the museum's networks and practices'. The new version read that "we are taking a new look at the Ethnological Museum, which has long confronted itself with its own collection history and will not only be showing objects in the Humboldt Forum, but also presenting the history of those objects.'

Needless to say, I was not happy with the result. I talked with Agnes Wegner, who thought it best if she and the two Africa curators jump into the fray. In their communications with the SPK, they argued that our texts were scientifically correct, and that the exhibition project had been approved by the Museum's and HLD's directors with the explicit aim of making the Museum's collection histories 'transparent'. They also noted that SPK was out of step with academic scholarship, which in the 1990s had begun to identify looted art in the collection. A denial or concealment of that information risked exposing the Humboldt Lab Dahlem to ridicule.[29]

After several exchanges, Wegner and the two Africa curators were able to reverse almost all the changes. But the process had shed a spotlight on the hierarchical nature of the SPK and its difficulty to take a public stand on the histories of its colonial collections and the issues of ownership and restitution. The emotional rollercoaster of the ordeal—I went from feeling outraged to feeling deprived of authorship—had left me exhausted.

Being affected helped me to understand the curators' difficult position: how emotionally draining it was to engage critically with an organisation while having to defend it, especially one so complex and hierarchical, and the resulting lack of control over the final results, authorship and public communication.

Collaboration and control

While planning the exhibition, we repeatedly reminded ourselves of our privileged role in the museum. As part of an evaluation workshop, we invited the scholars Friedrich von Bose and Nora Sternfeld to comment on our team. They recommended that we rethink the team's composition in order to break with conventional modes of representation. In particular, they pointed out that we failed to include a person of colour who would be 'critical of reproduction (*reproduktionskritisch*) and able to address appropriation (*Aneignung*) from a Black, anti-racist and activist position.'[30]

After discussing their recommendations, we decided not to change our curatorial team. Instead, we invited two art historians with academic experience in the field, Mathias Alubafi and Romuald Tchibozo, to provide a written statement (Alubafi) and contribute to a larger research project on *bocios* in Benin and Berlin (Tchibozo). Romuald Tchibozo raised difficult questions about our position in the 'decolonisation of research'. We examined different power asymmetries present in the project. These included the ability to acquire a visa and travel, the restricted access to the collections and the inability to move the objects beyond the walls of the museum. The control of the exhibition authorship and its products was defined by the organisation, while the budget lay in our hands (Tchibozo 2015; Oswald and Rodatus 2017: 218–19).

Our curatorial duo also contributed to maintaining the power asymmetry. We were only partly committed to giving up our privileged position within the project and to opening up the process (Oswald and Rodatus 2017: 218). In Bernadette Lynch's words, despite 'a commitment to the contact zone', in terms of both encounter and 'coercion, radical inequality, and intractable conflict' (Mary Louise Pratt quoted in Clifford 1997:192), 'we somehow continue to face the Other with fear, and work hard to exercise control' (Lynch 2014: 6). Neither Alubafi nor Tchibozo was part of the curatorial team; they had joined the project after we had defined its general concept. And though we aimed for a particular understanding of collaborative museology for the project, in which the collaborator is defined 'as expert in a knowledge not present in the museum,' we afforded insufficient space to this 'right to co-determination' (Landkammer 2017: 278). Hence, despite our efforts, we risked repeating, reproducing or reinscribing colonial mechanisms and power structures. Addressing past injustices does not mean that one is sure to avoid reproducing similar injustices in the present.

Reflexivity and performance

Verena Rodatus and I published an article on *Object Biographies* that pondered the challenges of decolonising research and exhibition-making. Consider the following representative passage:

> We agree with Nora Landkammer, who argues that 'decolonisation should concentrate on organisational development and on understanding community engagement as an all-encompassing practice for institutions (Landkammer 2017: 278).' This would include prioritising and institutionalizing access to the collections and to the exhibition space for those who have been denied access, contribution and co-production in the making of the museum (Oswald and Rodatus 2017: 219).

This is all well and good, but we failed to consider that this kind of self-reflective writing about the exhibition served *us* as a curatorial team by facilitating our own positioning especially with regards to the exhibition's aftermath and academic reception. By contrast, those who had contributed from Benin, in particular those who were unable to travel—such as David Gnonhouévi, Romuald Tchibozo's student who had organised the research trip to Benin—stood to gain little.

Looking back, I feel ambivalent about our observations. Writing can be a highly performative act of self-reflectivity meant to divert responsibility. Friction and conflict remain because the consequences of such reflections are rarely taken seriously. What would 'prioritising and institutionalising access' mean for those who have been denied access?

The ambivalence lies in the fact that appropriation goes hand in hand with defensiveness, apology, reflexivity—and holding on to power. Could gestures of 'inviting' and 'collaborating', as long as they come from *within* the confines of a museum's structures and practices, be anything other than patronising? Is it possible to avoid paradoxical appropriation? Would the alternative be to *not* engage in these debates, to leave one's place to others, or to listen? Is there a possibility of sitting with and enduring these moments of fragility?

Conclusion

Being affected enables reflection on how the colonial is imbricated in the present. Through it, I noticed how elements of our exhibition maintained and reproduced asymmetries between the Global North and the Global South despite our efforts to address them explicitly. The exhibition confronted us with the presence, reappearance, effects and continuities of the colonial past in our everyday practice and decision-making.

Being affected and using it as a research tool complicate the research of curatorial practice. In the case of *Object Biographies*, being affected shifted the analysis beyond binaries, and pointed to the paradoxes, tensions and ambivalence of working with colonial collections from within a contested organisation. By being implicated and being part, I could grasp how and why people grew weary and became defiant. I was confronted with the effects of organisational hierarchies, the anticipation of critique, the uncertainty of how my work would be publicly received and my contributions to reproducing the structures and mechanisms I was critical of. At root were questions of curatorial agency and change. When does one become complicit? When is it possible to contribute to political and organisational change?

Shortly after the exhibition's opening, the SPK published its long-awaited statements on the 'treatment of human remains' and 'non-European collections' (Stiftung Preußischer Kulturbesitz 2015a; 2015b). It confirmed the SPK's focus on provenance research and the deployment of shared heritage. Critics understood 'provenance' as a way to delay questions of restitution[31] and interpreted 'shared heritage' as a tactic of avoiding returns (No Humboldt 21! 2015). Then, in May 2015, Hermann Parzinger shifted course and published an article about the Humboldt Forum titled 'Berlin's Rebuilt Prussian Palace to Address Long-ignored Colonial Atrocities' (Scaturro 2015). Announced as a 'collaborative project' a month later, the Museum's curators would put into practice the abstract and undefined notions of 'shared heritage' and 'provenance'.[32]

Between 2013 and 2015, a process of negotiation emerged in which politicians, organisations and activists sought to identify and forge a moral consensus on German colonialism. Through this process, the behaviour of the SPK was, like the resulting consensus itself, more reactive than proactive, and often at odds with the Ethnological Museum staff. Meanwhile, the debates around the collections' fate increased awareness of Germany's colonial history (Koalitionsvertrag 2018).

I close these reflections by asking about the role that I can take as a white, privileged academic from within the Ethnological Museum, an organisation shaped by colonial ideology? To what extent can I bring about change from this position? As I have argued, curatorial struggles tend to centre around tensions: critique and complicity; collaboration and control; reflexivity and performance. Within complex organisational structures and mechanisms, which side becomes predominant will forever be uncertain and ambiguous. Balancing and withstanding the inherent contradictions is a central (emotional) challenge in curating contested collections. As Nanette Snoep, then director of the Ethnographic Collections of the State of Saxony, stated in 2016: 'It is not enough to talk a little bit about colonial history, put it in a small showcase, and that's it. The malaise stays.'[33]

Acknowledgements

This chapter was written as part of the *Making Differences: Transforming Museums and Heritage in the Twenty-First Century* project, at the Centre for Anthropological Research on Museums and Heritage (CARMAH), funded by Sharon Macdonald's Alexander von Humboldt Professorship. I would like to thank Verena Rodatus and Agnes Wegner for their reflections and remarks on different versions of this text. I am grateful to the museum staff at the Ethnological Museum who agreed to be part of this research. My gratitude also goes to Sharon Macdonald for her many comments and thoughts and for the helpful edits of this chapter. This text is a result of innumerable conversations about curating with Christine Gerbich, who has my gratitude for her helpful and critical point of view. Finally, I would like to thank Patrick Wielowiejski, Aida Baghernejad and Francis Seeck for discussing white guilt, tears and fragility with me.

Notes

1 This chapter is based on the chapter entitled 'Being affected. A methodological approach to working through colonial collections', in the book 'Working Through Colonial Collections. An Ethnography of the Ethnological Museum in Berlin', Leuven University Press, 2022.

2 The following quotes are transcriptions from the video recording of the event *Preußischer Kulturbesitz? Postkoloniale und entwicklungspolitische Perspektiven auf das Humboldt-Forum – Zum Umgang mit Kulturgütern und Human Remains aus der Kolonialzeit* (*Prussian Cultural Heritage? Postcolonial Perspectives and Perspectives from Development Policies on the Humboldt-Forum – Dealing with Cultural Assets and Human Remains from the Colonial Era*) at the Werkstatt der Kulturen, 22 October 2013, organised by members of *No Humboldt 21!* https://www.youtube.com/watch?v=QEojPEqZDSY (accessed 20 February 2020).

3 The point of view expressed in this chapter is solely mine, even if I sometimes use 'we' to describe Verena Rodatus' and my curatorial ambitions and approach with regard to *Object Biographies*.

4 The German title is 'Das Humboldt-Forum. "Soviel Welt mit sich verbinden als möglich." Aufgabe und Bedeutung des wichtigsten Kulturprojekts in Deutschland zu Beginn des 21. Jahrhunderts'. The brochure was available in German and English, https://www.preussischer-kulturbesitz.de/en/newsroom/media-library/documents/document-detail/article/2013/11/27/media-the-humboldt-forum-to-be-in-touch-with-as-much-of-the-world-as-possible.html (accessed 23 May 2019).

5 Examples of key literature on the relationship between museums and colonialism include Clifford 1988; Thomas 1991; Karp and Lavine 1991; Coombes 1997; Clifford 1997; and Gosden and Knowles 2001.

6 The works of the historians Andrew Zimmermann and Glenn Penny analyse the relation between colonialism, anthropology, and museums in the Berlin collections (Zimmerman 2001; Penny 2002).

7 'Kleine Anfrage der Abgeordneten Clara Herrmann (Bündnis 90/Die Grünen) vom 28. Juni 2013 (Eingang beim Abgeordnetenhaus am 01. Juli 2013) und Antwort (Postkoloniale) Auseinandersetzung mit dem Humboldt Forum', Drucksache 17 / 12 360, http://www.clara-herrmann.net/sites/default/files/AnfrageKolonialisierung.pdf, published 28 June 2013, (accessed 20 April 2018).

8 'Kleine Anfrage der Abgeordneten Niema Movassat, Christine Buchholz, Sevim Dagdelen, Annette Groth, Heike Hänsel, Inge Höger und der Franktion Die Linke.

Weiterer Umgang mit menschlichen Gebeinen aus ehemaligen deutschen Kolonien und anderen Überseegebieten', http://dip21.bundestag.de/dip21/btd/18/000/18000 10.pdf, published 23 October 2013, (accessed 20 April 2018).

9 a The exhibition 'Anti-Humboldt-Box' was organised by *Artefakte//anti-humboldt* (Brigitta Kuster, Regina Sarreiter, Dierk Schmidt) and *AFROTAK TV cyberNomads* (Michael Küppers-Adebisi) in cooperation with Andreas Siekmann and Ute Klissenbauer, and was exhibited in different locations.

10 For more information on the organised events, see the association's website, http://www.no-humboldt21.de/programme2/ (accessed 25 April 2019).

11 A special issue of the internet journal *darkmatter*, edited by *Artefakte//anti-humbolt*, was released in October 2013. 'Afterlives' brought together discussions and scholarly analysis regarding the politics of representation, restitution and historiography regarding the Humboldt Forum.

12 Several participants at a conference in Dahlem voiced this frustration (fieldnotes from 10 December 2013).

13 Extract from my field diary, 14 October 2013.

14 Extracts from my fieldnotes, from 8 November 2013, 11 November 2013 and 2 December 2013.

15 Plans for the Africa department exhibition going back to 2008 note the presence of colonial war loot in the collection (König 2012: 24). An early concept of the permanent exhibition—introduced by Paola Ivanov in 2012—states that colonial history will occupy a central role in the exhibition. This position was repeated in the exhibition plans published by Peter Junge and Paola Ivanov in 2015 (Ivanov 2012; Ivanov and Junge 2015).

16 Fieldnote from 11 December 2013.

17 Examples include Pataczek 2013; and Fuhr 2013. However, while the exhibitions received relatively little attention, some reviews were positive and encouraging (Wulff 2013; and J. König 2013).

18 Fieldnotes from 23 February 2013.

19 Personal communications and conversations with the author. Fieldnotes from 23 February 2013, 17 March 2014 and a conversation in 2016.

20 Discussion of the author's presentation of her PhD project at the Musée du Quai Branly-Jacques Chirac as part of the seminar 'Ecologie des collections', on 7 May 2017.

21 Mary Elizabeth Moore describes her feelings about white privilege in similar terms, fearing that her acting 'would be perceived as a racist act and could well *be* a racist act' (Moore 2019, 254 highlighted in original; see also DiAngelo 2018).

22 10 March 2015, 'Blind Spots: Berlin' (Blinde Flecken: Berlin), https://www.hebbel-am-ufer.de/programm/pdetail/gespraech-blinde-flecken-berlin/, consulted 02.05.2019.

23 10 March 2015, 'Blind Spots: Berlin' (Blinde Flecken: Berlin), https://www.hebbel-am-ufer.de/programm/pdetail/gespraech-blinde-flecken-berlin/ (accessed 2 May 2019).

24 For an extensive review of the legal frameworks for requesting returns, see Splettstößer 2019: 57–71.

25 Fieldnotes from 08 October 2014. The representative explained the legal situation to Verena Rodatus and me during a meeting about communication strategies for *Object Biographies*.

26 www.africavenir.org/de/projekte/projekte-deutschland/dekoloniale-einwaende-gegen-das-humboldt-forum.html

27 www.africavenir.org/de/projekte/projekte-deutschland/dekoloniale-einwaende-gegen-das-humboldt-forum.html

28 Email from legal department, 12 March 2015.

29 Resumé of email exchanges from 12–17 March 2015.

30 Notes from a workshop, 19 June 2014, Ethnological Museum of Berlin.

31 See for example Häntzschel 2018; and Zimmerer 2019.

32 In the following years, the Museum's Africa curators continued to initiate further research and curatorial projects with organisations and individuals in Tanzania, Namibia, Angola, and Cameroon.

33 This is a retranscription of an interview with Nanette Snoep at Leipzig's Grassi Museum für Völkerkunde, 19 April 2016.

References

Boast, R. 2011. 'Neocolonial Collaboration: Museum as Contact Zone Revisited', *Museum Anthropology*, 34(1): 56–70.

Bose, F. von. 2016. *Das Humboldt-Forum. Eine Ethnografie seiner Planung*. Berlin: Kulturverlag Kadmos.

Clifford, J. 1988. *The Predicament of Culture: Twentieth-Century Ethnography, Literature, and Art*. Cambridge, MA: Harvard University Press.

Clifford, J. 1997. *Routes: Travel and Translation in the Late Twentieth Century*. Cambridge, MA: Harvard University Press.

Coombes, A. E. 1997. *Reinventing Africa: Museums, Material Culture and Popular Imagination in Late Victorian and Edwardian England*. New Ed edition. New Haven: Yale University Press.

Deutscher Bundestag. 2015. 'Schriftliche Fragen mit den in der Woche vom 5. Januar 2015 eingegangenen Antworten der Bundesregierung. Drucksache 18/3711'.

DiAngelo, R. 2018. *White Fragility: Why It's So Hard for White People to Talk About Racism*. Boston: Beacon Press.

Eckert, A. 2007. 'Der Kolonialismus im europäischen Gedächtnis', *Aus Politik und Zeitgeschichte*, no. 1–2/2008.

Eckert, A., and A. Wirz. 2013. 'Wir nicht, die Anderen auch: Deutschland und der Kolonialismus', in R. Römhild, S. Randeria, and S. Conrad (eds), *Jenseits des Eurozentrismus. Postkoloniale Perspektiven in den Geschichts- und Kulturwissenschaften*, 2nd ed., 506–25. Frankfurt am Main: Campus Verlag.

Favret-Saada, J. 1977. *Les Mots, La Mort, Les Sorts. La Sorcellerie dans le Bocage*. Paris: Gallimard.

Favret-Saada, J. 2012. 'Being Affected. Translated by Mylene Hengen and Matthew Carey'. *HAU : Journal of Ethnographic Theory*, 2(1), 435–45.

Favret-Saada, J., A. Esquerre, E. Gallienne, F. Jobard, A. Lalande, and S. Zilberfarb. 2004. 'Glissements de terrains. Entretien avec Jeanne Favret-Saada'. *Vacarme*, no. 28, 4–12.

Fuhr, E. 2013. 'Fernseh-Doku : Berlins Stadtschloss hat ein Beutekunstproblem', 16 December 2013. https ://www.welt.de/kultur/kunst-und-architektur/article122994919/Berlins-Stadtschloss-hat-ein-Beutekunstproblem.html (accessed 2 March 2022).

Gosden, C., and C. Knowles. 2001. *Collecting Colonialism. Material Culture and Colonial Change*. Oxford: Bloomsbury.

Häntzschel, J. 2018. 'Vertröstungen', *sueddeutsche.de*, 12 April 2018, https://www.sueddeutsche.de/kultur/debatte-vertroestungen-1.4238454 (accessed 2 March 2022).

Haubrich, R. 2013. 'Berliner Schloss: Ein kleiner Staatsakt zur Grundsteinlegung', 12 June 2013. https://www.welt.de/kultur/kunst-und-architektur/article117070873/Ein-kleiner-Staatsakt-zur-Grundsteinlegung.html (accessed 2 March 2022).

Heizmann, K., and H. Parzinger. 2012. 'Workshop des Internationalen Advisory Board zur Neupräsentation der Sammlungen des Ethnologischen Museums und des Museum für Asiatische Kunst im Humboldt-Forum', in H. Parzinger (ed.), *Jahrbuch Preussischer Kulturbesitz 2011*, XLVII:293–317. Berlin: Gebr. Mann Verlag.

Ivanov, P. 2012. 'Fragenkatalog für Ausstellungsdesigner: Sammlung Afrika / Modul: Ostafrika in der Synästhetischen Handelslandschaft des Indischen Ozeans (Arbeitstitel).'

Ivanov, P., and P. Junge. 2015. 'Afrika Im Humboldt-Forum – Planungsstand 2014', *Baessler-Archiv Beiträge Zur Völkerkunde* 62: 7–20.

Karp, I., and S. Lavine (eds). 1991. *Exhibiting Cultures: The Poetics and Politics of Museum Display*. Washington: Smithsonian Institution Press.

Kathmann, D. 2014. 'Antwortemail der SMB – SPK vom 16.01.2014'. http://www.no-humboldt21.de/politik/ (accessed 2 March 2022).

Koalitionsvertrag. 2018. 'Ein neuer Aufbruch für Europa. Eine neue Dynamik für Deutschland. Ein neuer Zusammenhalt für unser Land. Koalitionsvertrag zwischen CDU, CSU und SPD'.

König, J. 2013. 'Wenn der alte Indianer wieder lächelt'. Deutschlandfunk Kultur. 16 October 2013. https://www.deutschlandfunkkultur.de/wenn-der-alte-indianer-wieder-laechelt.1013.de.html?dram:article_id=265436 (accessed 2 March 2022).

König, V. 2012. 'Die Konzeptdebatte'. *Baessler-Archiv Beiträge zur Völkerkunde*, 59: 13–60.

Landkammer, N. 2017. 'Visitors or Community? Collaborative Museology and the Role of Education and Outreach in Ethnographic Museums', in C. Mörsch, A. Sachs, and T. Sieber (eds), *Contemporary Curating and Museum Education*, 269–80. Bielefeld: transcript. http://lib.myilibrary.com?id=978508 (accessed 2 March 2022).

Lutz, H., and K. Gawarecki (eds). 2005. *Kolonialismus und Erinnerungskultur: Die Kolonialvergangenheit im kollektiven Gedächtnis der deutschen und niederländischen Einwanderungsgesellschaft*. Niederlande-Studien. Münster: Waxmann.

Lynch, B. 2014. '"Whose Cake Is It Anyway?": Museums, Civil Society and the Changing Reality of Public Engagement', in L. Gouriévidis (ed.), *Museums and Migration: History, Memory and Politics*. London; New York: Routledge. https://ucl.academia.edu/BernadetteLynch (accessed 2 March 2022).

Macdonald, S. 2013. *Memorylands: Heritage and Identity in Europe Today*. London: Routledge.

Moore, M. E. 2019. 'Disrupting White Privilege: Diving beneath Shame and Guilt', *Religious Education,* 114(3): 252–61. https://doi.org/10.1080/00344087.2019.1615206 (accessed 2 March 2022).

Mörsch, C., N. Landkammer, A. Chrusciel, and C. Seefranz. 2014. 'Interne Anfangserhebung für eine Begleitforschung zum Humboldt Lab Dahlem. Fokus: Probebühne 1 (März – Mai 2013), Erhebungszeitraum: April – September 2013'.

No Humboldt 21! 2013. 'Stop the Planned Construction of the Humboldt Forum in the Berlin Palace!' 7 March 2013. http://www.no-humboldt21.de/resolution/english/ (accessed 2 March 2022).

No Humboldt 21 !. 2014a. 'Pressemitteilung des Kampagnenbündnisses „No Humboldt 21!" Stiftung Preußischer Kulturbesitz verweigert Dialog zum Humboldt-Forum und zur Rückgabe von menschlichen Gebeinen aus Afrika'. http://www.no-humboldt21.de/deutschland-muss-menschliche-gebeine-und-kriegsbeute-aus-kamerun-togo-tansania-und-ruanda-zurueckgeben/ (accessed 2 March 2022).

No Humboldt 21 !. 2014b. 'Pressemitteilung des Kampagnenbündnisses „No Humboldt 21!". Deutschland muss menschliche Gebeine und Kriegsbeute aus Kamerun, Togo, Tansania und Ruanda zurückgeben'. http://www.no-humboldt21.de/deutschland-muss-menschliche-gebeine-und-kriegsbeute-aus-kamerun-togo-tansania-und-ruanda-zurueckgeben/ (accessed 2 March 2022).

No Humboldt 21 !. 2015. 'Bündnis „No Humboldt 21!" kritisiert die aktuellen „Grundpositionen" der Stiftung Preußischer Kulturbesitz zum Umgang mit ihren außereuropäischen Sammlungen'. https://www.africavenir.org/de/newsdetails/article/pm-buendnis-no-humboldt-21-kritisiert-die-aktuellen-grundpositionen-der-stiftung-preu/print.html (accessed 2 March 2022).

Oswald, M. von, and V. Rodatus. 2017. 'Decolonizing Research, Cosmo-Optimistic Collaboration? Making Object Biographies', *Museum Worlds,* 5(1): 211–23.

Parzinger, H. 2011. 'Das Humboldt-Forum. Soviel Welt mit sich verbinden als möglich. Aufgabe und Bedeutung des wichtigsten Kulturprojekts in Deutschland zu Beginn des 21. Jahrhunderts'. Edited by Stiftung Berliner Schloss – Humboldtforum.

Parzinger, H. 2014. 'Sammlungsbestände aus Tanzania. Ihre Anfrage vom 12.02.2014 / Antwort Der SPK Vom 16.04.2014'. http://www.no-humboldt21.de/politik/ (accessed 2 March 2022).

Pataczek, A. 2013. 'Der Schemel des Schamanen Das dritte Humboldt-Lab in den Museen Dahlem'. 24 October 2013. https://www.tagesspiegel.de/kultur/der-schemel-des-schamanen-das-dritte-humboldt-lab-in-den-museen-dahlem/8976098.html (accessed 2 March 2022).

Penny, H. G. 2002. *Objects of Culture. Ethnology and Ethnographic Museums in Imperial Germany*. Chapel Hill, NC: University of North Carolina Press.

Prosinger, J., and M. S. Mboro. 2014. 'Offener Brief an SPK'. http://www.no-humboldt21.de/politik/(accessed 2 March 2022).

Prosinger, J., M. S. Mboro, and D. F. Kisalya. 2013. 'Anfrage zum Sammlungsbestand der Stiftung Preußischer Kulturbesitz und speziell des Ethnologischen Museums Berlin und des Museums für Vor- und Frühgeschichte'. http://www.no-humboldt21.de/politik/ (accessed 2 March 2022).

Prott, L. 2009. 'The Ethics and Law of Returns', *Museum International,* 61(1–2): 101–6.

Scaturro, M. 2015. 'Berlin's Rebuilt Prussian Palace to Address Long-Ignored Colonial Atrocities', *The Guardian*, 18 May 2015, sec. World news. http://www.theguardian.com/world/2015/may/18/berlins-rebuilt-prussian-palace-to-address-long-ignored-colonial-atrocities (accessed 2 March 2022).

Schaper, R. 2013. 'Grundsteinlegung für einen Hybrid', *Der Tagesspiegel Online*, 6 November 2013. https://www.tagesspiegel.de/meinung/das-neue-schloss-fuer-berlin-grundsteinlegung-fuer-einen-hybrid/8334582.html (accessed 2 March 2022).

Schönberger, S. 2016. 'Restitution of Ethnological Objects: Legal Obligation or Moral Dilemma?', in Deutscher Museumsbund (ed.), Positioning Ethnological Museums in the 21st Century., *Museumskunde*, 81:45–48. Berlin: Deutscher Museumsbund.

Stiftung Preußischer Kulturbesitz. 2015a. 'Statement Regarding the Approach of the Stiftung Preußischer Kulturbesitz (Prussian Cultural Heritage Foundation) to Handling Human Remains in the Staatliche Museen Zu Berlin (National Museums in Berlin) Collections'. https://www.preussischer-kulturbesitz.de/schwerpunkte/provenienzforschung-und-eigentumsfragen/umgang-mit-menschlichen-ueberresten.html (accessed 2 March 2022).

Stiftung Preußischer Kulturbesitz. 2015b. 'Die Außereuropäischen Sammlungen der Staatlichen Museen zu Berlin -Grundpositionen der Stiftung Preußischer Kulturbesitz zum Umgang und zur Erforschung der Provenienzen'. https://www.preussischer-kulturbesitz.de/fileadmin/user_upload/documents/mediathek/schwerpunkte/provenienz_eigentum/rp/grundhaltung_spk_aussereuropaeische-slg_dt_final.pdf (accessed 2 March 2022).

Tchibozo, R. 2015. 'Absent Objects and Academic Collaboration: The Case of the Bocio.' Online documentation of Humboldt Lab Dahlem. http://www.humboldt-forum.de/en/humboldt-labdahlem/project-archive/probebuehne-6/object-biographies/positions (accessed 2 March 2022).

Thomas, N. 1991. *Entangled Objects: Exchange, Material Culture, and Colonialism in the Pacific*. Cambridge, MA: Harvard University Press.

Wulff, M. 2013. 'Was die Dahlemer Museen für das Berliner Stadtschloss planen'. *Morgenpost*, 17 October 2013. https://www.morgenpost.de/kultur/berlin-kultur/article120978296/Was-die-Dahlemer-Museen-fuer-das-Berliner-Stadtschloss-planen.html (accessed 2 March 2022).

Zimmerer, J. 2013. 'Kolonialismus und kollektive Identität: Erinnerungsorte der deutschen Kolonialgeschichte', in J. Zimmerer (ed.), *Kein Platz an der Sonne: Erinnerungsorte der deutschen Kolonialgeschichte*, 9–40. Frankfurt a.M.: Campus Verlag.

Zimmerer, J. 2019. 'Die größte Identitätsdebatte unserer Zeit', *sueddeutsche.de*, 20 February 2019, sec. kultur. https://www.sueddeutsche.de/kultur/kolonialismus-postkolonialismus-humboldt-forum-raubkunst-1.4334846 (accessed 2 March 2022).

Zimmerman, A. 2001. *Anthropology and Antihumanism in Imperial Germany*. Chicago: University of Chicago Press.

Beyond Compare
Juxtaposition, Enunciation and African Art in Berlin Museums

Nnenna Onuoha

> And then they die in their turn. Classified, labelled, conserved in the ice of showcases and collections, they enter into the history of art, paradise of the forms where the most mysterious relationships are established. We recognize Greece in an old African head of 2000 years; Japan in a mask from Logoué; and still India; Sumerian idols; our Roman Christ; or our modern art. But at the same time it receives this title of glory, Black art becomes a dead language and that which is born over its death is the jargon of decadence.
> (Marker, Resnais and Cloquet, *Les Statues Meurent Aussi*, 1953)

What is and is not considered art is entirely subjective and often fiercely contested. Historically, art museums in Europe have excluded works from other—and othered—cultures, relegating them to the realm of the ethnographic. However, the subsequent accession of non-Western artworks into these institutions is not necessarily corrective, and has itself been sharply criticised, notably in *Statues Also Die (Les Statues Meurent Aussi)*, the source of the above quote. Perhaps the best-known documentary about African sculpture, the 1953 filmic essay is directed by Chris Marker, Alain Resnais and Ghislain Cloquet. The filmmakers criticise the confinement of 'Black art' to Le Musée de L'Homme, an ethnological museum, as against the contemporaneous displays of European pieces in the Louvre, an art museum (Wilson 2006: 22). They nevertheless caution against the newfound designation of African sculpture as art. Receiving this 'title of glory', they warn, can be just as violent as prior exclusion from art institutions: so much so, in fact, that they liken the attendant processes of being 'classified, labelled, conserved' to death.

Half a century later, similar concerns about stark institutional divisions between objects associated with Africa and Europe, art and the ethnographic, inform another trio, curators at the Berlin State Museums *(Staatliche Museen zu Berlin)*: Julien Chapuis, Jonathan Fine and Paola Ivanov. They co-curated *Beyond Compare: Art from Africa in the Bode Museum (Unvergleichlich: Kunst aus Afrika im Bode-Museum)*, an exhibition placing

African art from Berlin's Ethnological Museum *(Ethnologisches Museum)* beside European pieces in the Bode Museum, an art museum.

This chapter interrogates the use of juxtaposition as a method of enunciation (Bhabha 2004: 31) in *Beyond Compare*, suggesting that, in its treatment of the past, present and future of African collections at the Berlin State Museums, the exhibition re-inscribes some of the same modes of Eurocentricity that it otherwise claims to transcend. As *Statues Also Die* warns, the exhibition of sculptures from Africa in the Bode Museum, 'classified, labelled, conserved' and juxtaposed with other examples of European art, perpetuates the violence of exoticisation: continuing stereotypical, ethnocentric and colonial perceptions that reduce living sculptures to museum objects.

I begin at the exhibition's opening display.

'...But this Is comparison, isn't it?'

'I'm really interested to know,' I overhear, 'what do you think about this?' Five steps away, on the other side of the vitrine at which I stand taking photographs, two visitors take in the display titled 'Becoming Art?' ('Wie wird Kunst zur Kunst?'). In a glass case of about one-metre in height, two cast-metal figurines of roughly the same size have been arranged side-by-side. Both are humanoid, unclothed and with their arms bent upwards. Despite these similarities of posture, their visual forms are markedly different. Whereas one is reminiscent of sculptures from early West African kingdoms such as Oyo and Benin, the other resembles Roman statues. Labels hint at their dissimilar origins, identifying them as 'Statue of the goddess Irhevbu or of Princess Edeleyo' and 'Dancing putto with a tambourine', respectively. Together, they comprise the first of many such experimental juxtapositions throughout Berlin's Bode Museum as part of *Beyond Compare*. Staring at the figurines, I wonder what it means, curatorially, to juxtapose pieces in a way that seemingly invites comparison, yet to title the exhibition—and perhaps—provocatively so—'Beyond Compare' or, as the German version has it, 'Incomparable' ('Unvergleichlich')? From across the glass, snatches of conversation from my fellow visitors drift over once more. 'They are saying "Beyond Compare"', the one tells the other, his tone mirroring my own bewilderment, 'but this is comparison, isn't it?' I take this visitor question as a point of departure to examine the use of object pairings in the exhibition. Close-reading the opening display 'Becoming Art?', I ask: How is juxtaposition used in *Beyond Compare* and to what extent does the exhibition's depiction of the trajectory of these African artworks fulfil its promise to transcend a mere compare-and-contrast model?

This chapter consists of four sections. The first introduces *Beyond Compare*, analysing its use of juxtaposition and comparison and arguing that they are performances of cultural diversity rather than enunciations of cultural difference (Bhabha 2004: 34–35). Instead of problematising institutional divisions between the sculptures from both continents, the exhibition, I contend, reinforces these binaries in three main ways: its historicisation of African art in the Ethnological Museum's past, its contextualisation (or lack thereof) of African art within the Bode Museum's present and its conceptualisation of African art in the Humboldt Forum's future. In the second section, I use historiographical methods to challenge the exhibition's construction of a past in which African objects were purely ethnographica, incomparable with European art. Citing early 20th century museum catalogues, I suggest that this historicisation, while providing convenient justification for the exhibition, is inaccurate. Moreover, it contributes to the exoticisation of the exhibited African art. In the third section, I examine the placement of the object pairings in the physical space of the galleries. I show that *Beyond Compare,* by failing to interrogate the Bode Museum setting, replicates the Eurocentric gaze in the present. Whereas the African statuettes have been brought into the museum for the exhibition, most of their European counterparts remain in their original display positions. Given that the Bode Museum's galleries are arranged according to regional and chronological themes, this results in a situation in which the included African objects are visually and contextually othered, reinforcing hierarchies of cultural supremacy in art museums. Lastly, the fourth section considers *Beyond Compare* within the wider context of the newly opened Humboldt Forum. Specifically, *Beyond Compare* was conceived as a test for a universal exhibition concept titled *On the Way to the Humboldt Forum.* Zooming in on the concept of the encyclopaedic museum, I outline how ideas of universality flatten the various colonial 'emplacements' (Foucault 1998: 178) in which these objects as well as the museums that contain them are enmeshed, subsuming a range of perspectives under a dominant Western framework.

Art from Africa in the Bode Museum

Beyond Compare

Running from October 2017 until November 2019, 'Beyond Compare: Art from Africa in the Bode Museum' was a special temporary exhibition curated by Julien Chapuis, Jonathan Fine and Paola Ivanov. Its aim was to 'introduce superlative works of art from Africa from the Ethnologisches Museum into the peerless sculpture collection of the Bode Museum.'[1]

Founded in 1873 as an amalgamation of various royal cabinets of art, Berlin's Ethnological Museum—originally the Royal Ethnological Museum *(Königliches Museum für Völkerkunde)*—is one of the largest collections of non-European artistic, cultural and historical items in the world. It contains objects, sound recordings, photographs, films and written texts from Africa, Asia, the Americas, Australia and the Pacific, many of which were acquired during the colonial era. In 2017, pending the relocation of the collection to the Humboldt Forum—a multi-museum complex situated in the reconstructed Berlin Palace *(Berliner Schloss)* on the city's Museum Island—the museum suspended exhibitions at its former base in Dahlem (Staatliche Museen zu Berlin 2019). In the meantime, selected pieces from its African collection were selected for display in the Bode Museum as part of *Beyond Compare* (Chapuis, Fine and Ivanov 2017: 6). The Bode Museum, which is also located on Museum Island, began as the Kaiser Friedrich Museum, an institution devoted to the high art of the Renaissance. At its opening in 1904, the museum stunned visitors by displaying both painting and sculpture side-by-side, 'a presentation strategy that differed radically from that of traditional museums'.[2]

Echoes of the Bode Museum's foundational practice of experimental juxtaposition ripple through the design of *Beyond Compare* more than a century later. Within the exhibit, artwork from the Ethnological Museum's Africa collection is set beside European sculptures in twenty-two object pairings spread throughout the two floors of the Bode Museum's permanent collection, as well as through hundreds of other objects grouped under six broader themes in the basement-level special exhibitions room. These pairings are intended to catalyse conversations between the artworks from either continent, as well as among visitors who come to see them. As the museum website explains:

> These experimental juxtapositions reveal possible correlations and differences between the objects, and raise multiple questions. What causes us to view objects as similar or different? What insights can we gain from the joint display of works of art with different histories? Why were some objects classified in the past as 'ethnological' and others as 'art'?[3]

This intention to provoke contemplation and debate (Staatliche Museen zu Berlin, *Beyond Compare*: 10) is evident in the various subheadings under which the pieces are paired—including 'Opposite or Complementary?' 'Dissimilar Similarity,' 'Must a Portrait be True to Life?' and 'The Gaze'.

4.1 The temporary exhibitions room in the basement contains objects grouped by six main themes. Photograph by Nnenna Onuoha, 2019. Reproduced courtesy of the Ethnological Museum, State Museums of Berlin.

Aside from inviting viewers to consider various juxtapositions, *Beyond Compare* also points to specific similarities and differences between the objects. In the section of the print catalogue devoted to the opening object pairing, each paragraph begins with a direct comparison: 'Both works show...Neither object was conceived...Both objects were acquired...The two objects were understood...The differences between the two objects was emphasized'. (Staatliche Museen zu Berlin: 132–35) The text articulates specific convergences and divergences in style and perception that the curators want to underscore.

This brief description of the exhibition outlines how its object pairings frame African sculpture against their European counterparts. Though I refer to both juxtaposition and comparison in my analysis, these two complementary processes are not quite the same. I understand juxtaposition as the method employed by museum exhibits, catalogues, audio guides, etc. whereby disparate objects are placed near each other, side-by-side or in other assemblages to facilitate conversation (Thomas 2010: 7). The response mode afforded by juxtaposition is comparison, i.e. considering objects or ideas simultaneously and in relation to each other, in order to rank or outline similarities and differences (Malraux 1978: 14). This exhibition employs both processes.

In separate conversations with curators Jonathan Fine and Julien Chapuis, both said that they had intended for the juxtapositions to provoke comparisons that would subsequently unsettle the ways in which sculpture from Europe and Africa are associated with categories like art and ethnographica. 'We wanted the public to consider not merely that these African sculptures are art, but also that these European statues are ethnographic.' Reflecting on some of the feedback to the exhibition, however, Fine concedes that this second aim—othering European art—may not have been as successful.

Difference and diversity

In his book *The Location of Culture*, Homi K. Bhabha distinguishes between diversity and difference as approaches for engaging a culture. Whereas cultural diversity is described as an "epistemological object...a category of comparative ethics, aesthetics or ethnology," which relies on the idea of historically disparate societies, and reinforces binaries about past and present, tradition and modernity, cultural difference is a more discursive process. When cultural difference is enunciated, meanings and symbols can, rather than remaining fixed, be 'appropriated, translated, rehistoricized, and read anew.' (Bhabha 2004: 37) The enunciation of difference creates a third space where it becomes possible to transcend the exoticism of cultural diversity that has been created by the hegemonic, Western gaze, and instead develop more liberated, critical and hybridised conceptions of culture. *Beyond Compare* positions itself as wanting to do exactly this: moving past stereotypical modes of depiction in which African art has historically been placed, and provoking visitors to rethink preconceptions of what art is or the status European sculpture in the hierarchy of art.

Appointed curator for the Ethnological Museum in 2015, Fine had been struck by the institutional traditions in the Berlin State Museums—and German museums more generally—which, since the 19th century, had separated non-Western and Western artefacts into separate collections. He conceived of the idea of an exhibition that would trouble these outdated categorisations of Western as art and non-Western as ethnographic. With the Bode Museum on board, he set out to create a format that would exhibit African and European sculpture together. The format would create space within which to shatter the binary divisions between art and ethnographica and to make way for new ways of relating to the objects. *Beyond Compare* aimed to use juxtaposition as a means for the enunciation of difference.

4.2 Beyond Compare's official exhibition imagery features a logo with a painted pink X. Photograph by Nnenna Onuoha, 2019. Reproduced courtesy of the Ethnological Museum, State Museums of Berlin.

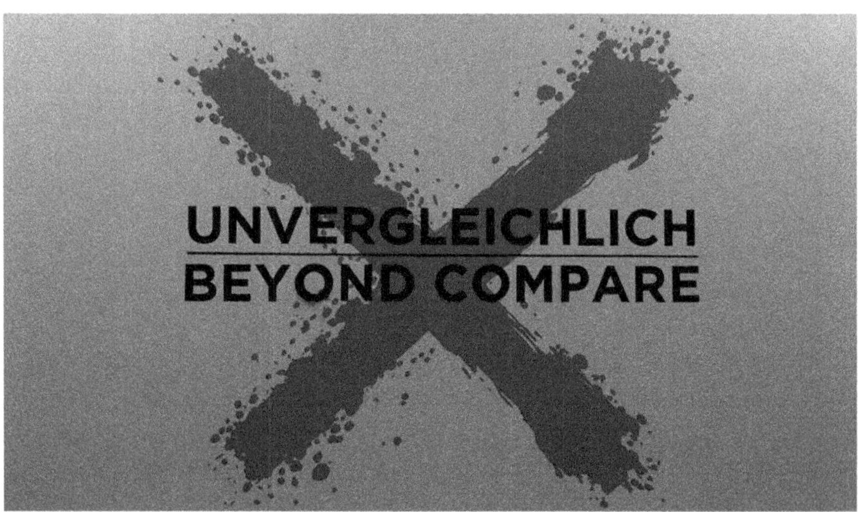

This intention is evident in the design of the exhibition logo, which features a pink cross over 'Beyond Compare' and 'Unvergleichlich.' Visually, the "X" symbolises disavowal. As the title suggests, *Beyond Compare* wants to transcend earlier, racist and Eurocentric instances of evolutionary theory and scientific racism by ethnologists and earlier dismissals of African sculpture as primitive by art historians. On a related note, the 'in' of '<u>in</u>comparable' ('<u>Un</u>vergleichlich') makes clear that comparison itself relies on subjective hierarchies of value that merit scrutiny (Staatliche Museen zu Berlin, *Beyond Compare*: 10–11).

Whereas the exhibition's message that African sculptures from the Ethnological Museum should be considered 'art' is more accessible, the other side of this assertion, which sought to displace the assumption that the objects from the Bode Museum were the standard of art, and instead inspire their consideration as ethnographic objects, is largely lost in translation. Consequently, the exhibition seems to uphold European art as a standard with which the African sculptures now have the honour of being compared. Though the exhibition wants to unsettle fixed, dominant narratives, it ends up reinforcing them, making the museum, as Coombes describes, 'a repository for contradictory desires.' (Coombes 1997: 2) It is precisely these contradictory outcomes of underlining rather than overturning essentialised cultural categories, performing diversity instead or enunciating difference, that I unpack in the sections that follow.

To do this, let us return to my position beside the vitrine.

4.3 In addition to the exhibition catalogue, Beyond Compare is also accompanied by a smartphone app. Photograph by Nnenna Onuoha, 2019. Reproduced courtesy of the Ethnological Museum, State Museums of Berlin.

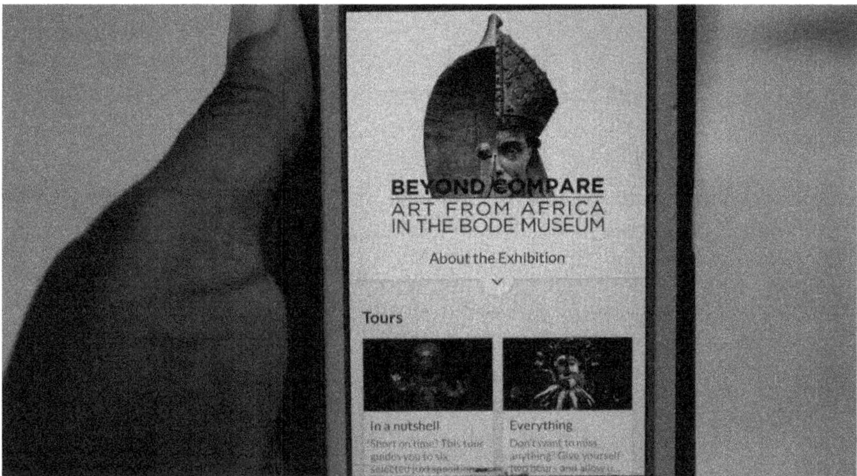

African art in the history of the Ethnological Museum

Unthinkable?

I consult the exhibition's dedicated smartphone application, also called Beyond Compare. The app provides supplementary information to accompany the museum labels. The extras generally comprise high-definition photographs of the artefacts, audio interviews of the curators describing the pairings, background text on, say, the provenance of objects, and, occasionally, video footage of the conservationists who prepared the artwork for display. Having opted for 'Everything' i.e. all twenty-eight stations of the virtual guide, I 'Begin Tour', and play the first audio file. Over headphones, Jonathan Fine explains:

> The figure from Nigeria was acquired as an example of metal-casting in the kingdom of Benin. It was not acquired for its artistry. Today we understand both sculptures as very important works of art, but at the time they were acquired only one of them was considered art. Art from Benin is often concerned with decoration, with form, and one sees that splendidly with this sculpture: it's three-dimensionality, it's stability, the woman's beautiful skin. The details of the sculpture's ornamentation are depicted: the scarifications on her body; the very shiny, flat surfaces on her skin are really shown down to the smallest detail. While for the sculpture from Donatello, it's important to show the moment when the putto pulls back his hand before he strikes his tambourine, when he shifts his weight from one foot to another, and how he pivots in this moment of dancing and playing. All that is to say that despite the formal similarity of both sculptures, each has a completely different goal, a completely different artistic intention. The idea of comparison per se wouldn't have occurred to the people

> who acquired the sculptures for Berlin's museums. It was unthinkable that they would even put them in the same category.
> (Bode Museum, *Beyond Compare [Exhibition App]*)

Two points stand out in Fine's description. First, and most immediately apparent, is the comparison of style, i.e. the aesthetic dissimilarity between the two figurines. Fine observes that the Benin sculpture emphasises corporeal details whereas the Italian one focuses more on bodily movement. A second takeaway, which serves to justify the importance of this exhibit's existence today, is the claim that the ways in which these artworks are considered within the museum space has changed significantly since they were originally acquired. Descriptions of a moment in which 'only one of them was considered art' and 'the idea of comparison...wouldn't have occurred' signal that their juxtaposition is a drastic departure from past norms.

This sense that the exhibition is radical in its use of juxtaposition, and that putting African and European objects together is something heretofore 'unthinkable', is echoed in the print catalogue, where Fine writes that 'the two objects were understood quite differently... difference...was emphasized by the institutions in which each was held and displayed.' (Staatliche Museen zu Berlin, *Beyond Compare*: 134) But who were 'the[se] people who acquired the sculptures for Berlin's museums'? And did the idea of comparison really never occur to them?

The Benin Bronzes

'Statue of the goddess Irhevbu or of Princess Edeleyo' was one of thousands of artworks looted from the Kingdom of Benin by the British during the punitive expedition of 1897. Erroneously christened the Benin Bronzes,[4] these pieces 'immediately caused a stir in the professional circles' ('erregten-sie gleich in Fachkreisen lebhaftes Aufsehen') of the European art world (Heger 1921: 4). That August, at the annual gathering of the German Anthropological Society (Deutsche Anthropologische Gesellschaft) in Lübeck, Justus Brinckman, the director of Hamburg's Decorative Art Museum (Museum für Kunst und Gewerbe), delivered a lecture on the Bronzes that left German museums scrambling to acquire as many pieces as possible.

Franz Heger, the director of Vienna's Ethnological Museum recalled that this lecture brought to light the great importance of collecting these Benin antiquities, especially in Germany (Kunst & Kontext 2018: 70–71). The following year, more than half of them ended up in German museums and private collections, sourced from Lagos and London, acquired on auction from the British government and through mass art dealers (Staatliche Museen zu Berlin, *Beyond Compare*: 134; Coombes 1997: 60; 'Königreich Benin—was fehlt?': 68–72; Bode Museum, *Beyond Compare [Exhibition App]*). The scramble for the Bronzes was especially competitive between the Hamburg Decorative Arts Museum under Brinckmann, and Berlin's Ethnological Museum, led at the time by Felix von Luschan. When Fine says that 'the idea of comparison per se wouldn't have occurred to the people who acquired the sculptures for Berlin's museums" he was no doubt thinking about von Luschan (Bode Museum, *Beyond Compare [Exhibition App]*). But wouldn't it?

Felix von Luschan

Felix von Luschan served as assistant to the Director of the Ethnological Museum from 1886 and Director of the Africa and Oceania Department from 1905. He was also the Humboldt University's[5] first chair in anthropology. In competition with Brinckman, von Luschan oversaw the acquisition of hundreds of the Benin Bronzes for Berlin's Ethnological Museum. He also wrote several reports and museum catalogues on the subject. Two publications illustrate von Luschan's views on the Benin Bronzes: *The Karl Knorr Collection of Benin Antiquities in the Museum for Countries and Ethnology in Stuttgart (Die Karl Knorrsche Sammlung von Benin-Altertümern in Museum für Länder und Völkerkunde in Stuttgart)*, published in 1901, and *The Antiquities from Benin* (*Die Altertümer von Benin*), a ten-volume catalogue of the Ethnological Museum's complete collection of Benin Bronzes, published in 1919.

In the 1919 catalogue, von Luschan specifically mentions the 'Statue of the goddess Irhevbu or of Princess Edeleyo', which at the time was known as 'Big Round Figure of a Woman with Raised Hands' ('Große Rundfigur einer Frau mit erhobenen Händen'). One paragraph about the Bronzes, which he originally wrote in 1901 and then republished verbatim two decades later in the catalogue, is of particular interest:

> Turning to the technique of these works of art, we arrive at one of the most important sections of our investigation. These Benin works are at the highest level of European casting technology. Benvenuto Cellini could not have done better and no one before him or after him to this day could have done so either. Technically, the bronzes are at the highest level of achievement.
>
> (Wenden wir uns nun zur Betrachtung der Technik dieser Kunstwerke, so gelangen wir zu einem der wichtigsten Abschnitte unserer Untersuchung. Diese Benin-Arbeiten stehen nämlich auf der höchsten Höhe der europäischen Gusstechnik. Benvenuto Cellini hätte sie nicht besser giesen können und niemand weder vor ihm noch nach ihm, bis auf den heutigen Tag. Diese Bronzen stehen technisch auf der höchsten Höhe des überhaupt Erreichbaren).
> (von Luschan 1901: 11; and von Luschan 1919: 15)

Not only does von Luschan refer to the Bronzes as 'works of art' ('Kunstwerke'), he declares them to be "at the highest level of European casting technology...at the highest level of achievement.' Elsewhere in the catalogue, he likewise praises how they have been fashioned with 'utmost care and virtuosity' ('größter Sorgfallt und Virtuosität').

Von Luschan was not alone in his regard for the Bronzes. Heger, too, described them as being 'at a level of perfection hardly reached in Europe at the time' ('auf einer Höhe der Vollendung, wie sie in dieser Zeit kaum in Europa erreicht worden ist').(Heger 1921: 9). Such pronouncements are at odds with *Beyond Compare*'s assertions that, upon acquisition, the aesthetic value of the African pieces was not appreciated. Equally questionable is the statement that it would have been 'unthinkable' to compare these works with European sculpture at the time. On the contrary, not only does von Luschan compare the Bronzes with works of the famed Italian sculptor Cellini; elsewhere in the text he likens them to German carvings from Nuremburg and to art from France, Portugal, Holland, etc. Although *Beyond Compare* repeatedly justifies its importance by alluding to a past in which thinking about African sculpture in relation to European ones was inconceivable, the historical record suggests that comparison did in fact occur.

Exoticising the past

Rather than being purely historical, these age-old dichotomies between art and the ethnographic, Africa and Europe that *Beyond Compare* sets out to remedy seem, in part, to be 'invented traditions' (Hobsbawn and Ranger 2014). This is not to say that they are completely false. In line with racist, colonial assumptions of the time, Africa was indeed generally regarded as inferior. In Britain, for instance, esteem for the Bronzes was so low that the government refused to allocate funds for their acquisition, paving the way for Germany's large-scale stockpiling of them. And across Europe, debates raged as many scholars who could hardly conceive of Black Africans creating anything so masterful rushed to attribute the craftmanship of the Bronzes to various foreign influences. Dismissive attitudes towards African peoples and cultures were rampant in the late 19th century. They still are.

However, *Beyond Compare*'s suggestion that calling these objects 'art' and comparing them with European works is something new, begs questioning. While it may have been possible that African sculptures were never juxtaposed with their European counterparts in the physical space or catalogued within the same museum collections, von Luschan's writing demonstrates that these comparisons certainly abounded on paper in that era. Instead of acknowledging these nuances, *Beyond Compare* simplifies the history of African objects in the Ethnological Museum, erasing the impact that they had on the art world upon their arrival in Berlin. In essence, then, this particular interpretation of history falls short of any real enunciation; instead it confines the past of African art in Berlin to the category of ethnographic.

Having examined how the exhibition minimises African objects within the history of the Ethnological Museum, I now turn to how its juxtapositions function in the present. How are African objects situated within the physical space of the Bode Museum?

African Art in the galleries of the Bode Museum

Aesthetic context

A section in the exhibit's printed catalogue titled 'Becoming Art?' provides an account of the conditions under which 'Dancing putto with a tambourine' and 'Statue of the goddess Irhevbu or of Princess Edeleyo' were first displayed in the Bode Museum and Ethnological Museum, respectively. Whereas the putto's placement alluded to its original cultural setting, no such care was paid to the Benin sculpture, which we are told was exhibited in a 'crowded display case':

> The difference between the two objects was emphasized by the institutions in which each was held and displayed. As a masterpiece of Renaissance art, the putto was given

> pride of place in the Kaiser-Friedrich-Museum...to evoke a sense of the culture in which the [works was] created...In one stroke, Bode emphasized Donatello's position in the artistic pantheon, the importance of the sculptures that seemed to have absorbed his influence, and the pre-eminence of the museum itself for possessing these key works. The Benin sculpture, by contrast, was considered an ethnological specimen and relegated to a crowded display case alongside dozens of other objects from Benin without attempting to evoke its original aesthetic context.
> (Staatliche Museen zu Berlin, *Beyond Compare*: 134.)

The use of 'relegated' here emphasises the curator's conviction that this lack of attention to crafting a more careful contextual background for the statuette diminished its appreciation in the eyes of others. Having read this critique of how the pieces were first shown, and understanding this exhibit to be, at least in part, a response to those circumstances, I find it impossible not to apply the same aesthetic and contextual analysis to the exhibit before me. In what ways does the juxtaposition of the figurines overcome these stated inequalities?

In the Basilica

'Becoming Art?' stands at the front entrance of the Bode Museum's Basilica, a two-floor high exhibition space at the centre of the museum. In this glass case next to the putto, the Benin statuette is no longer 'crowded' in. Visitors can walk around the display and enjoy a clear, undisturbed 360° view of the statue, and even notice the inventory numbers on the backside from its early days in the Ethnological Museum. But what of the second half of the critique? Having criticised earlier displays for failing to provide one, does *Beyond Compare* situate the Benin sculpture in an appropriate cultural context?

The set-up is clean, and minimal: the sculpture stands in a glass case accompanied only by the other half of the pairing, the putto. At first glance, the putto seems equally bereft of context. At least, this is the idea given by the exhibition's catalogue and smartphone app, which provide only close-ups of the objects. Yet the picture they paint is incomplete. In reality, the pairings are not in a vacuum, but in the material space of the Bode Museum, an institution largely created around European Renaissance art. In person, *Beyond Compare* offers an unequal contextualisation of the two sculptures being juxtaposed. Take a close look at the glass case, and you see two objects paired in seemingly the same manner. Step back and suddenly one sculpture fits in while the other is out of place. The larger context for the glass box is the Bode Museum's Basilica. With six reconstructed altars, each replete with religious paintings and sculptures, the space replicates a Florentine chapel from the Renaissance era. In terms of architecture and the objects it contains, the Basilica provides the perfect context for the putto.

Continue to look around and even more signs of what belongs in this room, and what does not, emerge. To the bottom left, less than a metre away from the glass case is a box of museum pamphlets about the putto and how it was discovered in a Florentine church-setting not unlike the Basilica. Separate from *Beyond Compare*'s labels, this double-sided, A3 text provides further detail and photos about the putto and its history in the Bode Museum. Even without scrutinising the context of this text visually, the mere presence of this information contributes to the putto's aesthetic positioning within this exhibition space. While it may seem unusual to expect any museum to pay so much explicit attention to the walls within its objects are displayed, it is important to note that such in-depth contextualisation is entirely in character with the Bode Museum. In front of each of the miniature altars, exhibition images display the architectural plan of the room, and a brief text provides information on 'The "Basilica" as a Museum Space'. It is therefore striking that in a setting so self-aware, such a level of spatial consideration has not been extended to the art from Africa.

Othering the present

4.4 The two statues, 'Statue of the goddess Irhevbu or of Princess Edeleyo'(right) and 'Dancing putto with a tambourine' (left), minimally arranged, in a glass case. Photograph by Nnenna Onuoha, 2019. Reproduced courtesy of the Ethnological Museum, State Museums of Berlin.

4.5 The glass case stands at the entrance to the Bode's Basillica; to its bottom left is the supplementary material about the putto. Photograph by Nnenna Onuoha, 2019. Reproduced courtesy of the Ethnological Museum, State Museums of Berlin.

4.6 & 4.7 The supplementary materials, as well as the general aesthetic of the Basillica, provide context to the putto while leaving the Benin statue out of place. Photograph by Nnenna Onuoha, 2019. Reproduced courtesy of the Ethnological Museum, State Museums of Berlin.

4.8 Plans and exhibition texts indicate that the Bode is no stranger to considering how its own walls and architectural style influence the experience of exhibitions. Photograph by Nnenna Onuoha, 2019. Reproduced courtesy of the Ethnological Museum, State Museums of Berlin.

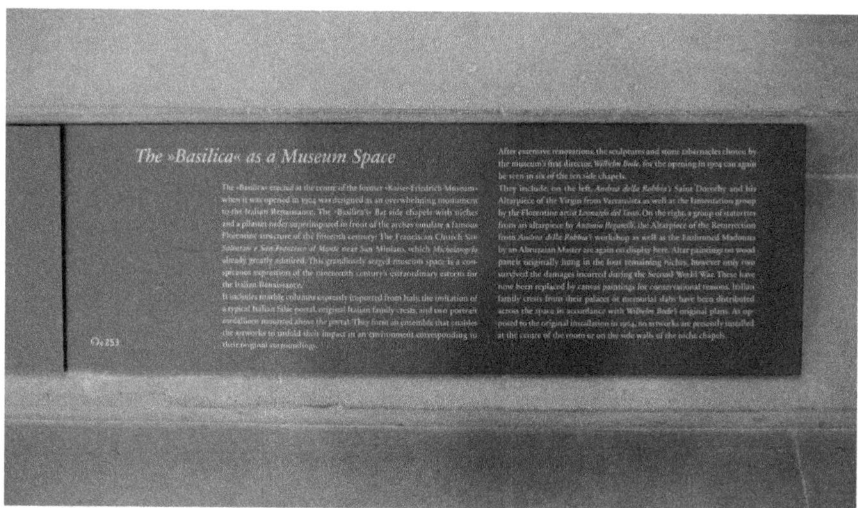

4.9 The two sculptures are juxtaposed not only with each other, but more broadly with the physical space of the Bode Museum as a whole. Rather than rejecting the distinction between African sculpture as ethnographic and European sculpture as art, the placement in the Bode Museum seems to highlight and even reinforce it. Photograph by Nnenna Onuoha, 2019. Reproduced courtesy of the Ethnological Museum, State Museums of Berlin.

The putto was originally part of the baptismal font of the Sienna Cathedral. Its placement in a large two-story room of other Renaissance artworks 'evoke[s] a sense of the culture' and 'emphasize[s] Donatello's position in the artistic pantheon'. By comparison, the Benin statue is displayed 'without attempting to evoke its original aesthetic context'. And such is the case throughout the other pairings of the exhibit. Whereas the African art has been brought into the Bode Museum to provide visual rhymes, the European objects are almost all displayed in their original, temporal, stylistic and geographically-appropriate contexts.

Although the exhibition seems to want to challenge the distinctions between art and anthropology, Africa and Europe, the way in which the art from Africa is incorporated into space of the Bode Museum more broadly reinforces hierarchies of what is art and, by extension, of what belongs in a museum and what does not. Though within the pairings the objects seem on equal footing, within the broader museum experience the African sculptures are out of place while the European sculptures fit right in. The exhibition appears to neglect the other levels of juxtaposition—and alienation—between the objects, their physical space and the aesthetic context of the Bode Museum.

Following the examination of how African art is othered within the Bode Museum at present, I turn to plans for the future. How will African art be conceptualised at the Humboldt Forum?

African Art in the Humboldt Forum

On the Way to the Humboldt Forum

Beyond Compare is one of a series of temporary, cross-cultural exhibitions launched in 2017 by the Berlin State Museums under the name *On the Way to the Humboldt Forum (Auf dem Weg zum Humboldtforum)*.[6] Late that year, the Ethnological Museum and the Asian Art Museum (Museum für Asiatische Kunst) closed their doors in Dahlem as they prepared to relocate their collections to the Humboldt Forum in the newly rebuilt Berlin Palace (Berliner Schloss). The series allowed visitors to see parts of the Asian and African collections until the Humboldt Forum opened to the public. Most of the temporary exhibitions took place at European art museums such as the Bode Museum and the Museum for Decorative Arts (Kunstgewerbemuseum).

Bringing these Asian and African collections in dialogue with European ones through juxtaposition demonstrates the State Museums' objective of becoming a 'universal' institution. Like the new Humboldt Forum, the temporary exhibitions promise to place Asian and African pieces together with European ones so that visitors can consider them collectively. In an interview titled 'Comprehending the World in its Entirety', the director of the State Museums, Michael Eissenhauer, indicated that such comparative methods are to become a part of the State Museums' identity. 'Transcend[ing] the boundaries between collections', he explained, 'are already a matter of course for an encyclopaedic or 'universal' museum like the Staatliche Museen zu Berlin.'[7]

The encyclopaedic museum

This plan for an encyclopaedic or 'universal' museum grew out of the 2002 Declaration on the Importance and Value of the Universal Museum. Signed by 18 major museums in the West—including the Berlin State Museums—the declaration was a response to calls for the repatriation of inappropriately acquired objects to their communities of origin. The declaration argued, controversially, that the objects had become part of their host countries' own heritage and that their new locations provided more insightful context than the artefacts might otherwise have in the communities from which they were taken (Cleveland Museum of Art 2003).[8]

Elsewhere in the interview, Eissenhauer associates the exhibition series, and by extension the Humboldt Forum, with a much older, genealogy of universal museum: late-16th-century cabinets of curiosities (*Kunstkammer*).

> This is the idea that we want to revive in the Humboldt Forum, where world cultures will be brought together with the historical cultures of Europe. The exhibition 'Art from Africa in the Bode Museum' provides a foretaste of this, as do other exhibitions like 'New Neighbours' or 'Vis à Vis: Asia Meets Europe', which showcase the collections of the Ethnologisches Museum and the Museum für Asiatische Kunst on the Museumsinsel and at the Kulturforum.[9]

The juxtapositions are meant to reflect the broader visitor experiences anticipated to accompany the opening of the Humboldt Forum, when, according to *Beyond Compare*'s curators, 'visitors will be able to see objects from all over the world in close proximity to the archaeological and European art historical collections on Museum Island.' (Staatliche Museen zu Berlin, *Beyond Compare*: 6) *On the Way to the Humboldt Forum* was, in other words, a curatorial experiment with a 'brand new exhibition concept'[10] that could be adopted once the Humboldt Forum was completed and the objects were returned to permanent exhibition.

For some Berliners, however, the most important outcome of the *Beyond Compare* was the inappropriateness of exhibiting colonial collections in buildings such as the Bode Museum and the Berlin Palace.

The Berlin Palace

I return to *Beyond Compare*'s opening vitrine, this time on a thirty-person tour of the exhibition led by activists Mnyaka Sururu Mboro and Christian Kopp, as part of a conference on restitution. Voicing their myriad oppositions to the exhibition concept, Mboro and Kopp repeatedly stress the inappropriateness of the building itself:

> Though it may be good to have African and European art in the same room, to break down institutional divisions, this building [the Bode Museum] as a 'Temple of European Art' which pays homage to the German founding fathers is as ill-fitting as the Humboldt Forum.
>
> With their royal, imperial structures, both of them are the wrong place to present objects from colonial contexts.

Built with profits from the slave trade and filled with statues of German colonial monarchs and officials, the Bode Museum, Mboro and Kopp emphasise, is a violent home for African art. For them, the temporary display of colonial-era African art in the Bode Museum was just as inappropriate and condemnable as their permanent relocation at the Humboldt Forum.

Since the launching of the Humboldt Forum as a space to 'Be in Touch with as Much of the World as Possible', activist groups such as *No Humboldt 21* and *Berlin Postkolonial* have opposed it on the basis that its non-Western collections were acquired through colonial violence. They have also condemned the plans to display these objects in the refurbished palace of Hohenzollern monarchs—who were responsible for and profited off of 'the enslavement of thousands of people from Africa as well as genocides and concentration camps in Germany's former colonies'[11]—as disrespectful, asserting that they glorify the colonial past. Moreover, they point out that gathering all non-Western art into one museum, while Western art continues to be exhibited in a variety of museums, reinforces hierarchies that position European art as superior and art from Asia, Africa, etc. as other.

Universalising the future

Understandings of non-Western cultural artefacts that seek to grasp 'the world in its entirety'[12] are framed by dominant narratives. In the case of *Beyond Compare* and the Humboldt Forum, the narratives arise from the architecture of the space and the Western gaze of the museums' directors and curators. As one visitor to *Beyond Compare* remarked to me: 'The exhibition doesn't seek to understand non-European culture in its own terms.' Of course, the mere fact of a European perspective on non-Western cultures is not in and of itself the subject of critique here; rather, it is the fact that the European perspective is presented as somehow broader and more generalised. Its 'universal' claim effectively otherises all others, and often precludes them from consideration. (Abungu 2004) In this way, *Beyond Compare*, like the idea of an encyclopaedic museum in general, ends up reinforcing the stereotypical divisions it purports to undo.

'So what is the basis of their universal value?' the former director of the National Museums of Kenya, George Abungu, asks with regard to the Declaration on the Importance and Value of the Universal Museum. 'Are Universal Museums based solely in Europe and North America?' (Abungu 2004) Abungu's challenge exposes the forms of othering inherent in the idea of the encyclopaedic museum, not least those concerning who makes the decisions and which perspectives get to be designated as 'universal'. Despite being presented as neutral, universality often erases the various 'emplacements' (Foucault 1998: 178), such as colonialism, within which these objects and the museums that contain them are enmeshed (Curtis 2012: 79). In the case I have considered here, the emplacements that universality seeks to erase are nowhere more obvious than in the architecture of the Bode Museum and Humboldt Forum themselves.

Conclusion

As the first, most popular, most intricate and longest running of all the exhibitions that comprised the *On the Way to the Humboldt Forum* series, *Beyond Compare* can perhaps give us some hints about what kinds of critical cultural spaces and modes of engagement we can expect from the recently opened Humboldt Forum.

In this chapter, I have focused on the use of juxtaposition in *Beyond Compare*, paying particular attention to how the exhibition frames the past, present and future of African art in Berlin museums.

My first example focused on how the exhibition material situates African artworks within the Ethnological Museum's past. The exhibition told the story of an earlier era in which the African objects were considered purely ethnographic, European sculptures were considered art and the two were utterly incomparable. Despite the undeniable racism of the late 19th and early 20th centuries, this account is inaccurate. Many of these objects in Berlin *were* admired for their aesthetic value—so much so, in fact, that theories accounting for their origins abound, the presumption being that such masterpieces could not have been created by Africans. In erasing this nuance, *Beyond Compare* oversimplifies history, and creates an exaggerated past in which African sculpture is utterly alienated from the European art world.

As a second point of analysis, I examined how the object pairings are set within the Bode Museum. The exhibition brings African objects into the museum and places them next to European pieces. But the museum's geographic and chronological presentation means that the European objects are contextualised by the gallery and the other objects, whereas the African objects seem incongruous with their surroundings. By failing to consider the physical space, *Beyond Compare* further amplifies the African objects' out-of-placeness in the Bode Museum.

Lastly, I have focused on how African collections fit into the Humboldt Forum's future. *Beyond Compare* is part of the series *On the Way to the Humboldt Forum*, which tests out comparative methods for giving visitors a glimpse of 'the whole world in its entirety'. However, 'universal' approaches often disguise the very real colonial entanglements built into the structures of these museums such as the acquisition of colonial collections. By framing dominant narratives from the West as shared, the idea of a 'universal museum' silences other perspectives and reifies existing hierarchies.

Ultimately, then, though *Beyond Compare* seeks to undo stereotypical, Eurocentric perceptions and disrupt institutionalised cultural distinctions, it re-inscribes hegemonic ways of engaging with African art. Rather than enunciating difference, the exhibition performs diversity, subjecting the sculptures to the very fate that *Statues Also Die* cautioned against so long ago.

Acknowledgments

This research was completed with funding from Sharon Macdonald's Alexander von Humboldt Professorship as part of the project *Making Differences: Transforming Museums and Heritage.*

Notes

1 *Beyond Compare: Art from Africa in the Bode-Museum*, Press Release, https://www.artsy.net/show/bode-museum-beyond-compare-art-from-africa-in-the-bode-museum (accessed 8 November 2018).

2 Staatliche Museen zu Berlin, 'Staatliche Museen Zu Berlin: Museums & Institutions – Bode-Museum – About Us – Profile', Staatliche Museen zu Berlin, https://www.smb.museum/en/museums-institutions/bode-museum/about-us/profile.html (accessed 25 March 2019).

3 Bode Museum, *Beyond* Compare: *Art from Africa in the Bode Museum*, version 1.16.2, iOS, English (Berlin: Staatliche Museen zu Berlin – Preußischer Kulturbesitz, 2017).

4 The Bronzes are actually made of brass.

5 Originally *Friedrich-Wilhelms-Universität.*

6 The other exhibits include *Vis-à-vis: Asia Meets Europe (Asien Trifft Europa)*, co-organised by the Museum for the Decorative Arts (Kunstgewerbemuseum) and the Asian Art Museum (Museum für Asiatische Kunst); *China and Egypt: Cradles of the World (China und Ägypten. Wiegen der Welt)*, by the Neues Museum and the Shanghai Museum; *Exchanging Gazes Between China and Europe (Wechselblicke Zwischen China und Europa) 1669–1907*, by the Berlin Art Library (Kunstbibliothek); and *Faces of China Portrait Painting of the Ming and Qing Dynasties (Gesichter Chinas Porträtmalerei der Ming- und Qing-Dynastie) 1368–1912*, by the Kulturforum.

7 Staatliche Museen zu Berlin, 'Interview with Michael Eissenhauer: 'Comprehending the World in Its Entirety'', 22 November 2017, http://www.smb.museum/en/whats-new/detail/michael-eissenhauer-im-interview-die-welt-als-ganzes-begreifen.html (accessed 22 November 2017).

8 Cleveland Museum of Art, Staatliche Museen zu Berlin, and The British Museum, Declaration on the Importance and Value of Universal Museums (Cleveland Museum of Art, 2003), http://archive.org/details/cmapr4492 (accessed 22 November 2017).

9 Staatliche Museen zu Berlin, 'Interview with Michael Eissenhauer: 'Comprehending the World in Its Entirety'', 22 November 2017, http://www.smb.museum/en/whats-new/detail/michael-eissenhauer-im-interview-die-welt-als-ganzes-begreifen.html (accessed 22 November 2017).

10 Berlin, 'Staatliche Museen Zu Berlin'.

11 No Humboldt 21, *Resolution*, http://www.no-humboldt21.de/resolution/english/ (accessed 15 December 2019).

12 Staatliche Museen zu Berlin, 'Interview with Michael Eissenhauer: 'Comprehending the World in Its Entirety'', 22 November 2017, http://www.smb.museum/en/whats-new/detail/michael-eissenhauer-im-interview-die-welt-als-ganzes-begreifen.html (accessed 22 November 2017).

References

Abungu, G. 2004. *The Declaration: A Contested Issue*. Paris : ICOM.

Bhabha, H. K. 1994. *The Location of Culture*. London: Routledge.

Chapuis, J., J. Fine, and P. Ivanov (eds). 2017. *Beyond Compare: Art from Africa in the Bode Museum*. Berlin: Braus.

Coombes, A. E. 1997. *Reinventing Africa: Museums, Material Culture and Popular Imagination in Late Victorian and Edwardian England*. New Haven: Yale University Press.

Curtis, Neil G.W. 2012. 'Universal Museums, Museum Objects and Repatriation: The Tangled Stories of Things', in Bettina Messias Carbonell (ed.), *Museum Studies: An Anthology of Contexts*, 2nd ed., 73–81. Chichester: John Wiley & Sons.

Foucault, Michel. 1998[1984]. 'Different Spaces', in James D. Faubion (ed.), *Aesthetics, Method, and Epistemology*, 175–85. New York: The New Press.

Heger, F. 1921. 'Merkwürdige Altertümer aus Benin in West-Afrika': Anläßlich der Herausgabe des Werkes Dr. F. v. Luschan 'Die Altertümer von Benin'. Wien.

Hobsbawn, E., and T. Ranger (eds). 2012. *The Invention of Tradition*. Cambridge: Canto Classics.

Luschan, F. v. 1919. *Die Altertümer von Benin*. Band I. I. Vol. I. X vols. BV040795509 Museum für Völkerkunde, Berlin. Veröffentlichungen aus dem Museum für Völkerkunde 8. Berlin: Georg Reimer.

Luschan, F. v., and Linden-museum Stuttgart. 1901. 'Die Karl Knorrsche Sammlung von Benin-Altertümern in Museum Für Länder Und Völkerkunde in Stuttgart". *Sonderabdruck Aus Dem XVII u. XVIII. Jahresbericht Des Württ.Vereins Für Handelsgeographie*. Stuttgart: W. Kohlhammer.

Malraux, A. 1978. 'Museum without Walls', in A. Malraux, *The Voices of Silence*, 13–131. Princeton, N.J.: Princeton University Press.

Marker, C., A. Resnais, and G. Cloquet. 1953. *Les Statues Meurent Aussi*. B&W, 16mm, Documentary.

Schlothauer, A. 2018. 'Königreich Benin—was fehlt?', in *Kunst & Kontext: Außereuropäische Kunst und Kultur im Dialog*,15: 60–79.

Thomas, N. 2010. 'The Museum as Method', *Museum Anthropology*, 33(1): 6–10.

Wilson, E. 2006. *Alain Resnais (French Film Directors)*. Manchester: Manchester University Press.

Polarised Public Perceptions of German Colonialism
Visitor Comments at the DHM *German Colonialism* Exhibition

Harriet Merrow

In 2016–2017 the German Historical Museum (Deutsches Historisches Museum; DHM) held its exhibition *German Colonialism: Fragments Past and Present*. One of the museum's most-attended exhibitions to date (with 135,845 visitors),[1] it opened at a time in Germany when the country's colonial past and postcolonial continuities were gaining wider public recognition. *German Colonialism* looked at the long-neglected history of colonial occupation, exploitation and violence in the former German colonies, and drew both high praise and stark criticism from visitors and the press. This varying reception is evident in the 1,842 comments made in the exhibition's visitor books. These express often polarised views about this history and how it is exhibited.[2] Indeed, *German Colonialism* divided the visitors' opinions to an extent that members of the museum's staff had rarely witnessed.[3]

German Colonialism was the first major exhibition at the DHM on the topic. Of the Museum's more than 200 temporary exhibitions over the previous two decades, only two had addressed colonialism: *Namibia—Germany: A Shared History* (2004–2005) and *Tsingtao—A Chapter of German Colonial History in China 1897–1914* (1998). The Museum's permanent exhibition, established in 2006 and since refurbished, contained only a small section on German colonialism. This had been criticised by activists and scholars for its Eurocentrism as well as for 'marginalising and simultaneously de-contextualising the significance of the colonial agenda in Germany's history' (Wegener 2018: 192; author's translation). In marginalising colonialism within German history, the museum was not alone. Until recently, giving attention to German colonialism was largely the preserve of specialised historians and persevering activists (see Förster 2019: 80; and Gross/Konitzer 2020: 341–46). German school curricula generally give only cursory or no attention to the topic (Kerber 2005: 92), although this is now beginning to change (Hille 2020). This has left a large gap in many Germans' knowledge of their country's history, as visitors themselves often acknowledged in the *German Colonialism*'s visitor books.

In this chapter, I examine the reception of *German Colonialism*, especially as evident in the visitor books. Thus far, little research on the public perception of German colonialism has been published. While those who choose to attend an exhibition on this topic—and the share who leave written comments—cannot necessarily be seen as representative of a broader German public, the entries nevertheless provide an insight into a range of often markedly different understandings of, and opinions about, the colonial past and Germany's treatment of this history.[4]

The *German Colonialism* exhibition

In late 2014, as debates over German colonial heritage were intensifying, staff members at the DHM saw a prime opportunity to respond with the largest-scale exhibition on German colonialism to date (Schröder 2016). The result was an exhibition that divided the critics. Some hailed it as highly educational and reflecting the Zeitgeist (Ewert 2017), observing that it 'benefitted from the general political situation in Germany' which made the exhibition more 'politically charged' (Hitz 2016). Others accused it of being 'overtly moralistic' (Kilb 2016 and Speicher 2016) and of 'keeping visitors on a short leash' in terms of their individual assessment of the historical reprehensibility on display (Fanizadeh 2016).

German Colonialism was located on the basement level of the museum's modern I.M. Pei building, and covered a wide range of topics within just 1,000 m^2 of floorspace. A 'Prologue' introduced the German colonial past and was expanded in seven subsequent sections, and an eighth section focused on the 'Post-colonial Present'. The 'Prologue' consisted of a length of wall panels with small-print text summarising the history of 18th-century Prussian exploitation in parts of today's Ghana, and later colonial expansion in East and West Africa and in Oceanic and Chinese territories under Emperor Wilhelm II and the unified German Reich's first chancellor, Otto von Bismarck. The final sentence of the text panels pointed out that, despite the fact that numerous objects were collected in colonised regions, the perspectives of the colonised are largely absent (Hartmann 2016: 251).

Accordingly, *German Colonialism* primarily exhibited mostly German artefacts from colonial contexts. The majority of the approximately 500 objects on display was from the DHM's own collection, with most others coming from other German institutions. Objects included advertising materials for imported goods from the colonies, missionaries' educational materials, letters home, and clothing, as well as scientific research equipment. The few objects that were not from Germany included the famous Nama-leader, Hendrik Witbooi's bible (which has since been repatriated). Two so-called *colon* carvings, from 'Nigeria or Cameroon' (DHM 2016: 30–31) and West Africa, respectively—the former portrayed a pale, thin Christian missionary cloaked in black from head to toe; the latter, a condescending-looking colonial officer with long, exaggerated features—were also on display. These showed colonised peoples as active subjects and contributed towards illustrating several complex 'micro-stories' of the colonial past (Hartmann 2016: 262).[5]

The exhibition was loosely chronological but also delved into particular themes in order to explore these in more depth and sometimes in order to indicate continuities across time. Themes included the prevalent racism among Christian missionary groups, the many brutal 'punitive expeditions' against colonised peoples and 'the first genocide of the 20th century' against the Herero and Nama in today's Namibia (Zimmerer 2016: 138). The exhibition also addressed the varying strategies that German governments employed in dealing with their colonial past in both East and West Germany.[6] The final section, 'Post-colonial Present', gave an overview of colonial-racist continuities in German society, such as street names with colonial backgrounds, and racist words and phrases still in use today. 'Post-colonial Present' was located such that visitors had to walk through it as they moved between other sections. This, the curators planned, would also help visitors to perceive continuities between the past and the present.[7] Unfortunately, as will be discussed further below, this layout contributed to many visitors perceiving the exhibition as 'disorganised'[8] and 'chaotic'.[9] Before turning to these and further results of an analysis of the comments in the visitor books, however, I first describe how the analysis was conducted.

Analysing visitor books

Visitor books can be seen as collections of the visiting public's views about an exhibition, offering diverse insights on its content and the responses it evoked. Visitors may choose to write in the books for a myriad of reasons: Some may see visitor books as vehicles for communicating with a museum's staff, for instance to address curators, guides and sometimes the service staff with general impressions, praise or complaints. Others might perceive their entry simply as a record of their visit, a documentation of their presence in the exhibition space. In *German Colonialism*'s books, for instance, numerous comments were written by school classes visiting the exhibition and leaving page-filling 'I was here'-entries with few—if any—references to the exhibition.[10]

Depending on the sentiment expressed, as well as on the information the commenters choose to share, writing in the visitor book can also be highly significant to those leaving their 'mark': 'As an African-American and member of the diaspora, it was gratifying & appalling to see the display. [...] In Hotep (peace) and solidarity with Africans the world over. [...] Houston, TX'[11] By including specific information about oneself like one's age, gender, ethnicity, place of residence, even one's academic degree, a visitor might attain a sense of visibility—and in doing so, a sense of empowerment—within the hegemonic space of the museum. This visibility is of particular significance when one looks at the great number of visitors who can't or choose not to write in the visitor book.

Bearing in mind the multiple factors that could conceivably keep a visitor from writing in a visitor book, the analysis of the comments by those who *do* leave a response is still a compelling method of gauging exhibition reception.[12] Visitor books can be analysed in a 'relatively informal and open' (Macdonald 2005: 124) manner. In these cases, entries in visitor books might serve the function of supplementing observant participation or interviews to create an overall impression of an exhibition's reception.

Others have used the visitor book as a source for quantitative analysis. This type of analysis has in some cases been developed specifically for, and with, museum staff aiming to utilise visitor feedback to improve museum management (Miglietta et al. 2012). In other cases, such as museum audience analyst Andrew Pekarik's approach of coding, categorising and counting, a quantitative analysis of visitor comments was used to explore visitors' reactions to specific issues addressed in an exhibition (Pekarik 1997: 59). In the case of *German Colonialism*'s visitor books, I employed a quantitative method similar to Pekarik's, whereby the coding, categorising and counting of entries in the visitor books was supplemented with qualitative data gathered through observant participation, interviews and media analysis.

My approach to the *German Colonialism* visitor books with additionally gathered data allowed me to contextualise visitor comments in a larger framework. Nevertheless, my insights gained through visitor book analysis must be viewed circumspectly, as it cannot be known to what extent these comments reflect a wider public. Since only 1,842 of the total 135,845 visitors (a mere 1.3%) left a comment in the books, the collection of views and opinions certainly can't be seen as equivalent to a general index of exhibition reception. Crucially, the visitor book may have been used especially by those visitors who felt particularly strongly about the exhibition or the topic of colonialism. Therefore, the sample of opinions and views may suggest a more polarised perception than is reflective of the general public.

German Colonialism's visitor books: methodology

In most cases, comments within the visitor books entailed carefully articulated and thought-out formulations of sentiments, though some entries indicate a more superficial engagement with the subject matter of the exhibition. Based on how directly the *German Colonialism* visitor book entries referenced the exhibition's contents and themes or did not do so, I categorised comments broadly as either 'engaged' or 'not very engaged'. The comments placed firmly in the category 'engaged' were those with references to the exhibition's content, or those which made general statements addressing colonial heritage (i.e. 'Reparations Now!!').[13] While I saw the aforementioned entries by school classes that stated little more than names and dates (and sometimes a bit of profanity) as clearly belonging to the 'not very engaged' category, I ended up excluding from this category many other one-liners that could have easily been deemed 'less engaged'. One-liners were simple Thank You's and unelaborated praise such as 'Great exhibition'[14] or 'Sehr interessante Ausstellung […]!'[15]

In addition to this, I placed each comment in the categories 'praising' and 'critical' in order to gauge the overall reception of the exhibition as recorded in the visitor books. Doing this made those comments from which I inferred a critical reaction to, or acclaim for the exhibition visible and quantifiable. This was not always an easy task, as comments could not be consistently identified as belonging in just one—at times, in any—of these major categories. The praising comments in the visitor book were comparatively easy to identify and count, though the categorisation of comments as either 'praising' or 'critical' required some careful deliberation in certain cases: a quote about 'half-truths being the worst lies'[16] attributed to Churchill could have been directed at the curators and their choice of content—or may well have been left in contemplation of the erstwhile propaganda tactics of colonial officials in the early 20th century. Though this type of comment is one reason that several visitor book entries are in none of the major categories, the selection of the broad terms 'engagement' and 'praise/criticism' enabled me to code and count nearly all of the visitors' entries within this system.

The result of this subjective analytical approach was a quantitative representation of the divided public reception of the DHM's exhibition. The close reading of the comments in the course of categorising and counting them individually allowed me to attach further codes to the entries and thus identify several themes within the books. In the following, I discuss three of these themes that are echoed in (or are relevant to) discussions on German colonial heritage beyond a visitor book's pages: the reflection of Germany's colonial remembrance practices; the curators' alleged bias; and the occurrences of passionate visitor interaction.

German Colonialism's visitor books: results

Of the 1,842 entries, a total of 1,082 showed characteristics of an 'engaged' visitor, such as references to specific exhibition content, a formulation of an opinion about the exhibition (or colonialism *per se*), or an emotional response. 687 of all comments were 'praising', while 376 were 'critical'. 242 comments were critical of certain aspects while praising others, in which the critique primarily took place in the form of complaints about specific design details like lighting or font sizes. A total of 491 entries (most of which fell into the 'not very engaged' category) fit neither in the 'praising' nor the 'critical' classifications. 47 entries were written in alphabets that I could not read (Japanese, Korean, Cyrillic, etc.) and therefore were not factored into any of the four major categories.

Of the 687 appreciative comments, 224 were written by non-German speakers, who spanned forty-four different countries and five continents.[17] Only thirteen 'critical' remarks were written by non-German visitors, constituting only about one-thirtieth of all 'critical' entries. This contrast may indicate how the museum-as-host is afforded respect and/or gratitude by non-German commenters—most of whom described themselves as tourists—who might already feel distinctly like 'guests' in the country.[18] The contrast between the proportions of positive versus negative comments by non-German visitors may also reflect a greater distance to the subject matter of the exhibition—a 'guilt-free' objectivity not available when the atrocities on display are of one's own difficult heritage.

Twenty-two entries—by visitors from the UK, Belgium, France, the USA, Australia and Russia—noted the need for similar exhibitions on their own countries' colonial pasts:

> 'As a French [person, H.M.], thank you for this lesson. We must take an example.'[19]

> 'Excellent! V. thought-provoking + unflinchingly self-critical. Wish the Brits could do something similar! [Name] (A Brit in Berlin)'[20]

> '[...] The honesty in the interpretation of the past is refreshing. I wish we could be so forthcoming/open/honest in Australia about our colonial past + its impact on our indigenous people. [...]'[21]

Many of the 'praising' comments from non-German visitors referred to the exhibition's 'honesty' and 'courage', as well as their perception of Germany, as a whole, being admirably capable of examining its own contentious heritage. Among the 'critical' comments from non-German visitors, just two expressed disapproval of the 'negative' portrayal of German colonialism, with one anonymous visitor calling for Germans to revere the country's past and its 'help' in former colonies' 'development';[22] and one Belgian commenter complaining about the 'condescending' tone of the texts, specifically their 'ad nauseam [...] repetition'[23] of anti-racist content.

Themes such as the 'appropriateness' of the exhibition at a particular time in Germany or mentions of particular exhibits became apparent through a more detailed reading and subsequent coding of the previously broadly categorised visitor books entries. Codes I used included 'school curricula', 'politically correct', 'sarcastic' and 'racist'. The following three themes that I identified in the visitors' comments do not necessarily represent the most-addressed topics but nevertheless depict visitors' sentiments that were written often and in various formulations throughout the books' 567 pages. For instance, the 'appropriateness' of an exhibition on German colonialism was the focus in a wide range of 'critical' and 'praising' comments, indicating, among other things, a divided public perception of the need for colonial remembrance in present-day Germany.

The visitor book on the topic of colonial remembrance in Germany

The need for and appropriateness of a more in-depth reflection of the German colonial past and its postcolonial continuities was addressed in various forms of wording.[24] This included comments about the exhibition as a timely and 'overdue' contribution to colonial remembrance:

> 'The contents of this exhibition are long overdue! Effects of colonialism are becoming more visible day by day. [...]'[25]

> '[...] For a long time, colonialism did not seem to be a topic of critical historical reappraisal. Fortunately, this has changed in recent years. This exhibition makes a very important contribution to this. [...]'[26]

Several visitors drew a connection between the need for a wider recognition of Germany's colonial heritage and the current German political climate, referring to the popularity of far-right political views, the growing prevalence of racist attacks and nationalist ideology:

> '[...] In times of increasing racism in our society, this critical and honest confrontation of history is more important than ever! [peace symbol]'[27]

> '[...] Many thanks for the courage to show an exhibition like this, especially in times of increasing racism and the AFD! This should shatter their world view! [...]'[28]

> 'It's so important to remember the past in times of growing populism and nationalism. [...]'[29]

On the other hand, the visitor books also offered some insight into the thought processes of visitors who were seemingly sympathetic to populist and nationalist views similar to those peddled by the far-right party AfD (Alternative for Germany). The social anthropologist Jonathan Bach has described the difficulty of some Germans to accept the remembrance of colonial-era evils alongside National-Socialist and GDR-era evils with explicit reference to the right-wing AfD's opposition to the process (Bach 2019). The visitor book mirrored certain talking points of this far-right party, even including multiple uses of the term 'Schuldkultur' ('culture of guilt'), which they use in reference to the extensive memory work that has gone into remembrance of the Holocaust, and to complain about current German generations having to still bear senses of guilt for the past. Several visitors staunchly opposed the exhibition's negative appraisal of the German colonial past, complaining that Germany has had to deal with a great 'burden' of historical evils as it is:

> 'Unfortunately, the exhibition is partly one-sided. The British and others would certainly frame their history on this topic differently, more positively from their point of view. Why do we always have to present our history in a negative light? [...].'[30]

> '[...] One-sided, the typical German self-flagellation! Germany was not one of the 'great' colonial powers. [...] It's called the past because it is in the past. [...] Since my birth in 1945 I have been made to feel guilty as a member of a 'perpetrator nation'. [...]'[31]

Beyond this, numerous comments by visitors who expressed discomfort with the growing recognition of colonialism accused the curatorial team of a 'biased' approach to the history. While several used terms such as 'one-sided' or 'leftist', twenty-one visitors referred to the exhibition as being 'pro-GDR':

> '[...] The exhibition is biased: FRG [Federal Republic of Germany] = unreflective. GDR [German Democratic Republic] = grasped this part of history. [...]'[32]

Another attribute of many visitors' comments about the exhibition's 'one-sidedness' was the claim that it was also 'politically correct'. In the following, I will give a more detailed look at these instances and the implications of such accusations.

The visitor book on 'political correctness' and a 'biased' exhibition

Visitors' opinions of *German Colonialism* were often coloured by their impressions of the museum's or the curatorial team's perceived 'bias', which they shared in often vehemently expressed entries. Accusations of bias were attached to a variety of issues, first and foremost the exhibition's perceived positioning regarding anti-colonialism. Criticism was levelled against the exhibition makers for being both too anti-colonial, as well as for not distancing themselves *enough* from the colonial 'ethos'.[33] Some, for instance, stated in rather broad terms that the portrayal of the exploitative and inhumane facets of colonialism weren't highlighted enough.[34] A handful of visitors perceived a specific, identity-based bias within the curatorial team: a 'white', 'voyeuristic' gaze. This was criticised, for instance, as an indication of Germans' 'unwillingness to confront' their colonial legacy:

> 'A very white perspective. Very uncritical. [...] All in all, this is a voyeuristic reproduction of colonial-racist conditions & resembles part of a German unwillingness to confront our structures & our own positionality.'[35]

By contrast, a common point of criticism was the curators' 'one-sided' ('einseitig') approach to the topic, leading to a far too 'negative' portrayal of colonialism, as well as a 'vilification' of Germans:

> 'Extremely one-sided and biased presentation in the interest of an ideological anti-colonialism. This sort of one-sidedness does not belong in a public institution!'[36]

> 'In my opinion, this exhibition contains and conveys too much 'German-hatred'. What a shame! Objectivity looks different.'[37]

Numerous visitors deemed the curators' work to be pandering to a 'left-leaning mainstream' which aimed to 'propagandistically' over-emphasise the evils of the German colonial past as well as its problematic postcolonial continuities.[38] This criticism was often marked by either sarcasm or reference to 'politically correct' language throughout the exhibition:

> 'Much is correct [...] BUT overall a leftist view of history dominates, which makes the exhibition a politically correct exhibition [...]!'[39]

In general, the term 'political correctness' describes the avoidance of discriminatory speech and the use of agreed-upon self-designations of groups, in order to not further marginalise those historically disenfranchised. Over the last years, *accusations* of 'political correctness' have begun to allude to an 'oversensitivity' or 'squeamishness' of individuals who promote non-discriminatory and inclusive language (Hayn 2010: 338–39). In some instances, even the slightest suggestion to stop using discriminatory language is decried as 'threatening one's freedom of speech' (ibid.).[40] Researchers have asserted that those who tend to accuse something of being 'PC' are most often not directly affected by derogatory phrases or terms (ibid.: 340), and therefore can't easily empathise with those affected by hegemonic speech. In an ironic turn, these 'hegemonic speakers' will often claim authority in the evaluation of various words' hurtfulness or prejudice, enabled precisely by their supposed un-affectedness and 'rationality' (ibid.: 340–41).

Interestingly, the visitor book showed some ambiguity around the term 'political correctness', which was not used solely in a negative manner (as accusation), but also as a praiseworthy attribute of the exhibition.[41] However, an aversion to the 'politically correct' as a suspected threat to freedom of speech, as well as the tendency to link 'PC-ness' with the curators' 'emotionality' and 'consternation' was evident in numerous visitor book entries:

> 'The exhibition is unfortunately all-out 'politically correct'. Despite the justified criticism of colonialism, it would have been good to treat this historical phenomenon in a more nuanced way and with less of the fake consternation. [...] Dr. [initials]'[42]

In several instances, visitors criticised the curators' careful treatment of problematic language in exhibition texts *without* attaching the label of 'political correctness'. For example, various comments expressed frustration with the curators' treatment of racist German heritage and their use of anti-discriminatory formulations (such as the 'Gender-Sternchen', i.e. 'Besucher*in', to include women and non-binary persons in historic narratives).[43] The two entries below show a similar backlash to what could be called an alleged 'reverse racism'[44] encountered in the exhibition, by which the commenters felt offended:

> '[...] If we're called 'palefaces' or 'long-nosed', we aren't offended either. [Signature] [...]'[45]

> 'I'm taking my evil white husband home with me now.'[46]

In addition to these types of responses to the portrayal of German colonial history's close entanglement with white supremacy, dozens of visitors wrote offensive comments in the visitor books, employing racist stereotypes as well as slurs in their entries. It was noticeable, however, that such comments were always 'answered' by other visitors with anti-racist views. As the following, final, theme demonstrates, visitor interaction in the books mirrors the overall polarisation of opinions expressed throughout the books' pages as well as in person: in a sense, the recurrent interactivity in the comments is a microcosm of the divided perception of German colonialism in general.

The visitor book as a space of visitor interaction

My methodological approach employed participant observation and interviews in addition to visitor book analysis. This enabled me to hear and observe several in-person visitor interactions concerning specific topics addressed in the exhibition. Over the course of my fieldwork these interactions occurred numerous times at the ends of guided tours, where (sometimes long) disputes about issues like the changing of colonial-racist street names took place among members of the tour group. Particular exhibits that dealt with extreme colonial violence or the enduring effects of German colonialism, such as everyday racism, also sparked debate among some visitors.

The visitor books also showed similar visitor interaction. Indeed, one DHM staff member said that the amount was 'unprecedented', with an unusual level of detailed reference to previous comments.[47] Two visitors even remarked that the book was the 'best part of the exhibition',[48] and one comment likened the exhibition and its visitor book to a 'öffentlicher Verhandlungsort' ('public space of negotiation').[49] This echoes descriptions in previous research of visitor books 'as a kind of virtual public sphere, something like an Internet message board' (Reid 2005: 8; quoted in Macdonald 2005: 123). In the case of *German Colonialism*'s visitor books this is especially apt, with the placement of responses on pages looking like social media interfaces, with some replies to previous entries written in the margins of already-full pages, while others were squeezed in between two entries. But some were visually unlike such interfaces, written at oblique angles squeezed around the original comment. This was often the case with statements that elicited multiple responses on one page:

5.1 A full page of the visitor book showing lively interaction by commenters.

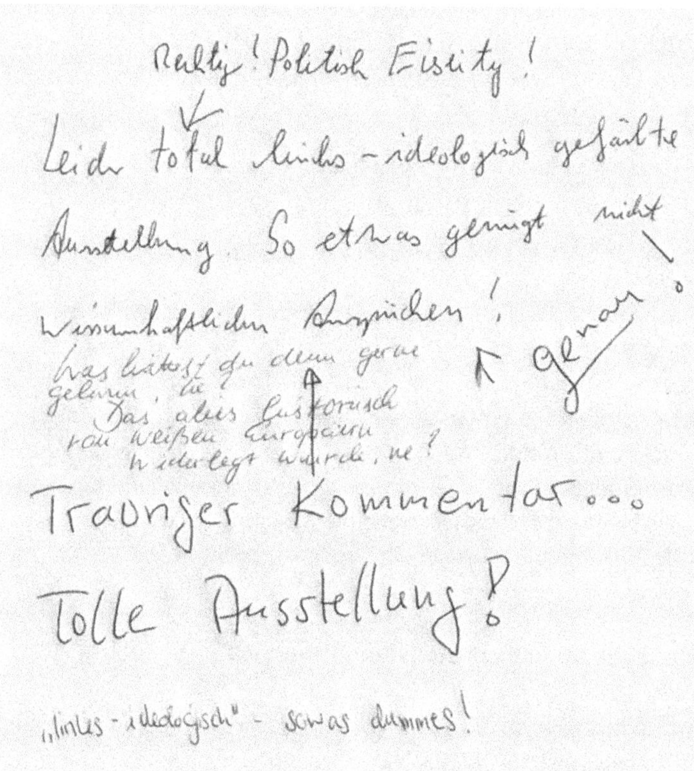

'Unfortunately, this is a totally left-ideologically coloured exhibition. Something like this does not meet scientific standards!'[50]

'Correct! Politically one-sided!'[51]

'exactly!'[52]

'What would you like to have seen, huh? That everything was historically disproved by white Europeans, right?'[53]

'Sad comment... Great exhibition!'[54]

'"left-ideological"—such nonsense!'[55]

Particularly controversial comments, for instance those containing the reproduction of racist stereotypes and the use of racist epithets, were often crossed out and rendered barely legible. One such message that included an offensive, white supremacist viewpoint and the use of the German N-word, was 'censored' in this way. Additionally, three separate visitors condemned the racist visitor on the same page, calling the original commenter a 'Nazi' and a 'Nazi pig', and remarking on the sad circumstance that the exhibition apparently 'hadn't deepened every visitor's understanding' of Germany's racist past and present.[56]

Attempted communication in the visitor book was not limited to interaction between visitors, but also took place in the form of addressing the museum or the curatorial team. As *German Colonialism* refrained from naming any of the exhibition's curators within the exhibition hall—a widespread convention of exhibition-making (Muttenthaler and Wonisch 2006: 39)—the authors of the displayed content were unknown to most visitors. Nevertheless, numerous entries directly addressed the museum and the (unknown) curators of *German Colonialism* in messages that also sum up the polarised visitor reception. This took the form of praise and thanks for their diligent work, corrections of, or additions to, specific exhibition texts as well as criticism in an array of intensity and crudeness:

> '[...] A very special thanks to [the guides, H.M.] and the curators for [their presentation of, H.M.] this long-repressed topic!'[57]

> '[...] Thank you to the exhibition makers. Keep going! [Signature]'[58]

> '[...] Important opportunities were missed to show colonial continuities, which could have been seamlessly connected to the existing exhibits, for example, in the context of advertising for products such as coffee. [...]'[59]

> '[...] The curators obviously had no interest in a differentiated look at colonialism. What a pity! Opportunity wasted. [Name]'[60]

> '[...] The 'easy' language option is degrading, propagandistic and in many parts simply wrong!!! The German Historical Museum should be ashamed, the organisers of this exhibition should be ashamed!'[61]

In the context of *German Colonialism*, addressing the museum actually made a difference in specific cases: while some museums let 'visitor books pile up and gather dust' (Macdonald 2005: 131) in storage rooms without making use of the collected material, staff at the DHM did make use of the comments at least once. After a noticeable proportion of complaints were made about the inscrutable structure of the exhibition, a change was made to exhibition signage. However, I am unaware of the DHM undertaking any systematic examination of the *German Colonialism* visitor books after the exhibition closed. This is an unfortunate circumstance, since the books offer such a prime opportunity for exploring visitor reception, which a handful of commenters astutely noted and communicated to the envisioned recipients of the books' comments:

> '[...] The entries in this visitor book are also very fascinating! Maybe towards the end of the exhibition you could say/write something about the disputes and criticisms? [...]'[62]

> 'Rarely was a visitor book so meaningful & interesting! Please evaluate! [...]'[63]

Needless to say, I agree.

Conclusion

The visitor books from the DHM's special exhibition *German Colonialism: Fragments Past and Present* offer a lens into diverse understandings and assessments of the exhibition and of German colonialism itself. The analysis of the collected 1,842 entries was fascinating—at times tedious, at times baffling, even infuriating—work. The fervour evident in many comments, as well as the passionate interactivity within the pages demonstrate just how strongly a large proportion of the commenters felt about the exhibition and the developments around colonial remembrance in Germany.

The exhibition, which opened in late 2016, came at a time when Germany's contentious colonial legacy was gaining wider public recognition. In preceding years, it had become increasingly apparent that the country had suffered from 'amnesia, neglect, and misguided thinking' (Bach 2019: 63), which had led to a lack of public remembering of colonialism. One contributing factor in this is certainly the near absence of German colonialism in school curricula, leading to a gap in knowledge that a single large-scale exhibition like *German Colonialism* cannot easily amend. Nevertheless, following decades of the Museum's own scant attention to German colonial history in the DHM's permanent and temporary exhibitions, *German Colonialism* perhaps marked a turning-point not only for the museum but in public culture more broadly. In the years since the exhibition closed, it has remained in the Zeitgeist, finding mention in news articles about postcolonial matters such as current reporting on street renaming initiatives (Thewalt 2020), or in renewed calls for reparations to the descendants of the Herero and Nama (Maihofer 2018).

As numerous comments in the visitor books noted, Germany is not the sole former colonial power that has inadequately (or ineffectively) faced its past and its postcolonial present. As Matthew Stanard has written with regard to the European context, '[...] European countries are only now coming to terms with the fact that they have not come to terms with decolonization' (Stanard 2019: 23). This absence of understanding of the past is now being challenged by more and more Europeans who are eager to see meaningful and lasting changes to neo-colonial and Eurocentric presentations of colonialist histories. However, this chapter also shows clearly that there is a divided perception about the necessity for a reappraisal of the German colonial past, in addition to a divided opinion about which methods should be employed in doing so. For example, the analysed comments show that one hinderance to reappraisal could be an opposition to the use of exclusively non-discriminating language, which was often criticised in the books with the use of the dog whistle term 'political correctness'. Comments such as those admonishing the exhibition's 'bias' or 'PC-ness', along with all the other critical entries in the books—especially those addressing the museum or the curators directly—can be seen as an attempt at participating in the public discourse on German colonialism. For that matter, every entry indicating a level of engagement with the exhibition's content can be read as a form of active participation in these debates, in addition to representing a visitor's partaking in one 'ritual' of the museum visit (Macdonald 2005: 125). Of course, it is necessary to reflect on the possibility of missing voices in the pages of exhibitions' visitor books. In general, the contents of a visitor book represent a limited sample of visitors' responses and certainly can't be straightforwardly interpreted as equivalent to a general public's exhibition reception. Since the choice to write in the book may have resulted from particularly strong feelings about the exhibition (or the topic of colonialism), the sample of opinions and views may suggest a more polarised perception than is reflective of the total number of visitors. Nevertheless, what is recorded in visitor books does provide an indication of the views of some members of the general public, indicating certain tendencies, concerns, interests and modes of expression.

Beyond what this research says about contemporary debates around Germany's reappraisal of its colonial heritage, this chapter's insights may be relevant for future conceptualisations of exhibitions on colonialism. One insight could be the necessity to bring an understanding—mentioned in the exhibition prologue's crucial final sentence—about the absent perspectives of those formerly colonised to the forefront of future exhibitions with a decolonising agenda. This is merely one aspect of any decolonial curatorial practice that reflects on the hosting institution's entanglements with colonial collecting agendas. Furthermore, the high level of interactivity between the pages of the visitor books, as well as the many comments which demonstrate some visitors' substantial knowledge of the exhibition's topic, highlight a readiness of museumgoers to share their expertise, or to enter into 'dialogue' with other visitors' statements. A method of anticipating and engaging with lively interactivity could be to use participatory interactive modules in the exhibition space (i.e. opinion polls, or publicly shared and rearrangeable comment cards) that are continually augmented with each visitor's mark left in the space.

Future exhibitions on this topic may elicit a different overall reception due to the fact that even within these few past years the debate on colonial heritage has gained further momentum, and understanding of this difficult heritage is more widespread. When that time comes, I hope that there will be books or other media for visitors to record their views and, moreover, that these will be analysed, and their insights drawn upon. Through more extensive visitor research, including visitor book analysis, the German museum landscape's exhibition projects of the near future that look at Germany's colonial heritage could help build a deeper knowledge of the public's perception of this past and its enduring consequences.

Acknowledgments

This research was conducted in the context of the Master's degree programme in European Ethnology at the Humboldt University Berlin, and was completed as part of the project *Making Differences: Transforming Museums and Heritage*. Vital guidance and support were generously given by Sharon Macdonald, Duane Jethro and Larissa Förster.

Notes

1 See Stiftung DHM (2019): 23.

2 I received written permission to publish my analysis of *German Colonialism*'s visitor books from a DHM staff member. I gained access to these fascinating visitor books with the help and support of Larissa Förster while she was a research fellow and I was a student assistant at the Centre for Anthropological Research on Museums and Heritage.

3 A museum staff member noted this in an interview from 20 August 2019.

4 As an example of these diverse views, social anthropologist Jonathan Bach's 2019 essay *Colonial Pasts in Germany's Present* shows the differing opinions on the past and future treatment of German colonial heritage within German parliament.

5 One such story unfolded from the black and white photograph of King Njoya of Bamum (today in Cameroon), shown in a Prussian-style uniform which he fashioned in order to benefit diplomatically from assimilating his appearance to the German colonial officials. King Njoya's efforts, however, were not rewarded by the German colonisers, who consistently reciprocated gifts and offerings with inferior return gifts (Hartmann 2016: 253).

6 As the curators' display showed, the West German state had not extensively addressed—and certainly not problematised—German colonial heritage, whereas this past played a prominent role in East German history education and was seen as a clear precursor of Fascism and National Socialism. For more, see Gross/Konitzer (2020: 335).

7 I learned this from a museum staff member in an interview from 20 August 2019.

8 Visitor book entry 327 (p. 109): 'Wichtig, leider sehr ungeordnet.' Signed by a male visitor from Copenhagen.

9 Visitor book entry 440 (p. 146): '[...] Interessant, wenn auch wirr. [...]' Unsigned and undated.

10 Remarkably often, groups of pupils also left their Instagram and Snapchat account names, asking for 'followers' and 'likes' on their social media pages.

11 Visitor book entry 174 (p.54): Dated 28 October 2016, signed by a female visitor from Houston, Texas. Original emphasis.

12 Writing in visitor books can pose difficulties as it requires literacy and the ability to put pen to page. Further, a visitor may not be interested in the 'ritual' of closing an exhibition visit by leaving a response, or perhaps a visitor may feel overwhelmed by a given subject, and deem their opinion comparatively ineffectual. Beyond this, the decision not to leave a comment might not be a 'decision' at all: some visitors might want to write a response, but simply cannot locate the book, or haven't the time to stand in queue behind others already occupying it.

13 Visitor book entry 48 (p. 15). Undated and unsigned.

14 Visitor book entry 420 (p. 138). Undated and signed by group.

15 Visitor book entry 660 (p. 223). Undated and signed by a German visitor.

16 Visitor book entry 367 (p. 123): 'Es gibt keine schlimmere Lüge als die Halbwahrheit; W. Churchill' Undated and unsigned. I deemed the content 'critical' due to the con-

text of the surrounding entries with similar criticism of the museum and the curators.

17 Many commenters noted their (non-German) nationalities, which were all over the map: Great Britain, Mexico, USA, New Zealand-Aotearoa, Brazil, Italy, Finland, France, Namibia, Greece and many more. Most of these entries were in English or in a mixture of English and another language.

18 On the culturally different understandings of the visitor book and its purpose, see Ina Ross' 2017 analysis of the visitor book in the Madhya Pradesh Tribal Museum in Bhopal (Ross 2017: 104).

19 Visitor book entry 1078 (p. 345): 'En tant que francais, je vous remercie pour cette lecon. Nous devons en prendre exemple.' Undated and unsigned.

20 Visitor book entry 1086 (p. 349). Undated and signed by a female visitor from Great Britain.

21 Visitor book entry 1705 (p. 510). Undated and signed by a male visitor from Australia.

22 Visitor book entry 318 (p. 107). Dated 11 November 2016 and unsigned.

23 Visitor book entry 289 (p. 98). Dated 8 November 2016 and signed by male Belgian visitor.

24 Though the specific term 'continuities' (or a German direct translation) was used by only one visitor (entry 201, p.61), the repeated use of 'immer noch' (meaning 'still' or 'ongoing') demonstrates how important the notion of the enduring consequences of colonialism were to individual visitors.

25 Visitor book entry 1661 (p. 494): 'Die Inhalte dieser Ausstellung sind längst überfällig! Auswirkungen des Kolonialismus werden heute Tag für Tag deutlicher sichtbar. [...]' Dated 17 April 2017 and signed by a female German visitor.

26 Visitor book entry 1793 (p. 542): '[...] Kolonialismus schien für lange Zeit kein Thema der kritischen historischen Aufarbeitung zu sein. Das hat sich in den letzten Jahren glücklicherweise verändert. Diese Ausstellung leistet dazu einen ganz wichtigen Beitrag. [...].' Undated and signed by a prominent German politician.

27 Visitor book entry 177 (p. 55): '[...] In Zeiten, in denen Rassismus sich wieder vermehrt durch unsere Gesellschaft zieht ist ein kritischer Blick und eine ehrliche Auseinandersetzung mit der Geschichte wichtiger denn je! [Peace-Symbol]' Dated 29 October 2016 and unsigned.

28 Visitor book entry 168 (p. 52): '[...] Ich danke für den Mut eine solche Ausstellung gerade in Zeiten des immer stärker werdenen Rassismus und der AFD zu machen! Es müsste deren Weltbild zerlegen! [...]' Dated 27 October 2016 and signed by a female museologist.

29 Visitor book entry 1717 (p. 518): 'So wichtig in Zeiten aufstrebenden Populismus und Nationalismus an die Vergangenheit zu erinnern. [...].' Dated 22 April 2017 and unsigned.

30 Visitor book entry 714 (p. 236): 'Die Ausstellung ist leider zum Teil einseitig. Die Briten u. a. würden ihre Geschichte zu diesem Thema gewiß anders, aus deren Sicht positiver, gestalten. Warum müssen wir unsere Geschichte immer nur negativ darstellen? [...].' Dated 31 December 2016 and initialled.

31 Visitor book entry 1451 (p. 426): '[...] Einseitig, die typische deutsche Selbstgeißelung! D war keine der 'großen' Kolonialmächte. [...] Die Vergangenheit heißt so weil sie

nun mal vergangen ist. [...] Seit meiner Geburt 1945 muß ich mich als Angehöriger eines 'Tätervolkes' schuldig fühlen. [...]' Dated 27 March 2017 and signed by a male German visitor from Berlin.

32 Visitor book entry 146 (p. 44): '[...] Die Ausstellung ist tendetiös [sic]: BRD= unreflektiert. DDR= haben diesen Teil der Geschichte begriffen. [...].' Dated 23 October 2016 and signed.

33 cf. Visitor book entry 337 (p. 113): 'Sehr ärgerlich: Unstrukturiert, verwirrend, ohne klare Aussage, einige Texterläuterungen sind erschreckend wenig distanziert vom DEUTSCHEN KOLONIALISMUS-ETHOS der damaligen Zeit! Wer hat das konzipiert?' Undated and signed.

34 cf. Visitor book entry 695 (p. 230): '[...] Und auch die von den Deutschen verübten Gräueltaten hätten deutlicher herausgestellt werden müssen [...].' Dated 30 December 2016 and signed by female German visitor.

35 Visitor book entry 1813 (p. 551): 'Eine sehr weiße Perspektive. Sehr unkritisch. [...] Alles in allem eine voyeuristische Reproduktion von kolonial-rassistischen Verhältnisse [sic] & reiht sich in den deutschen Unwillen ein, die eigenen Strukturen & Positionierung zu hinterfragen.' Undated and unsigned.

36 Visitor book entry 29 (p. 10): 'Äußerst einseitige, tendenziöse und propagandistische Präsentation im Sinne eines ideologischen Anti-Kolonialismus. Solche Einseitigkeiten gehören nicht in ein öffentliches Museum!' Undated and unsigned. Original emphasis.

37 Visitor book entry 1261 (p. 368): 'Aus meiner Sicht leider eine Ausstellung, die zu viel 'Deutschenhass' enthält und vermitteln soll. Schade! Objektivität geht anders.' Dated 08 March 2017 and signed on behalf of a family.

38 Visitor book entry 1416 (p. 416): 'Desinformative Ausstellung, völlig einseitig beleuchtet. Keinerlei Differenzierung und Einordnung in den historischen Kontext. Man kommt sich vor wie in einer linksradikalen Propagandaausstellung. Abstoßend. Leider.' Undated and unsigned.

39 Visitor book entry 671 (p. 224): 'Vieles ist richtig [...] ABER insgesamt dominiert eine Linke Geschichtsauffassung, was die Ausstellung zu einer politisch korrekten Ausstellung macht [...]!' Dated 29 December 2016 and signed.

40 Criticism of this kind was not levelled against *German Colonialism* in the press, though recent exhibitions on the topic of colonial entanglements have faced this 'PC'-critique in the media coverage: ethnologist and curator Julia Binter, for instance, was criticised for her employment of 'politically correct' speech in the 2017 exhibition 'Der Blind Fleck'. Her 'refusal to spell out contentious work titles as recorded in the museum's archive, including, for example, the N-word,' was 'just the beginning of a more sweeping postcolonial 'censorship', claimed [...] Germany's leading liberal newspaper *Die Zeit*' (Binter 2019: 591). The author of the review asserted that this supposed censorship 'starts with a few innocent '*****', but it leads to an anti-hegemonic obligation of peace' (Rauterberg 2017).

41 See the visitor book entry 1398 (p. 410): 'Hervorragende Ausstellung, insbesondere der inklusive Ansatz und die weitgehende politische Korrektheit sind beispielgebend. [Signature]' Dated 23 March 2017 and signed.

42 Visitor book entry 81 (p. 25): 'Die Ausstellung ist leider [...] uneingeschränkt 'politisch korrekt' ausgerichtet. Bei aller Berechtigter Kritik am Kolonialismus wäre es gut gewesen, dieses historische Phänomen differenzierter und ohne ständige Betroffenheits-Attitüde zu behandeln.' Undated, initialled by a Swiss visitor with a doctorate.

43 The curators included a disclaimer about their approach to racist language near the beginning of the exhibition, for instance the capitalisation of 'Black', or their use of unaltered historical source texts that contained racial epithets.

44 See Roussell et al. (2017): 'Given the systemic nature of racism, reverse racism cannot occur [...]' (2–3). Though the concept of 'reverse racism' has long been dismantled, complaints about 'racism' against white people are often made in the course of debates regarding white supremacist heritage.

45 Visitor book entry 222 (p. 66): '[...] Wenn man uns 'Bleichgesichter' oder 'Langnasen' nennt, sind wir doch auch nicht beleidigt. [Signature] [...].' Dated 03 November 2016 and signed by a male German visitor from Berlin.

46 Visitor book entry 672 (p. 224): 'Nehme jetzt meinen bösen weissen [sic] Mann mit nach Hause.' Undated and unsigned.

47 This is from an interview with a DHM staff member from 20 August 2019.

48 See visitor book entries 1313 (p. 384): 'Dieses Buch ist das Beste an der Ausstellung!' and 1320 (p. 385): 'Dieses Buch ist das beste an der ganzen Ausstellung! [heart symbols]'. Both undated and unsigned. Of course, there is '[...] no independent access to, or guarantee of, sincerity' (Macdonald 2005: 122), and it is possible that the comments were sarcastic criticisms of the exhibition.

49 Visitor book entry 707 (p. 234): '[...] Ich habe das Gefühl in einem öffentlichen Verhandlungsort zu sein, nicht nur weil sie sehr besucht wird, sondern weil sie so viele Gefühle und Gedanken wachruft—siehe Besucherbuch. Manche rassistische Kommentare hier zeigen, dass diese Ausstellung nötig ist [...].' Undated and signed.

50 Visitor book entry 381 (p. 126): 'Leider total links-ideologisch gefärbte Ausstellung. So etwas genügt nicht wissenschaftlichen Ansprüchen!' Undated and unsigned.

51 Visitor book entry 382 (p. 126): '← richtig! Politisch einseitig!' Undated and unsigned.

52 Visitor book entry 383 (p. 126): '← genau!' Undated and unsigned.

53 Visitor book entry 384 (p. 126): 'Was hättest du denn gerne gesehen, he? Dass alles historisch von weißen Europäern widerlegt wurde, ne?' Undated and unsigned.

54 Visitor book entry 385 (p. 126): 'Trauriger Kommentar... Tolle Ausstellung!' Undated and unsigned.

55 Visitor book entry 386 (p. 126): '"links-ideologisch"—sowas dummes!' Undated and unsigned.

56 See the visitor book entry 286 (p. 96): 'Danke für die Ausstellung, auch wenn diese nicht allen zum besseren Blick auf die Geschichte verhilft. [Signature]' Dated 07 November 2016 and signed by visitor with a doctorate.

57 Visitor books entry 1102 (p. 354): '[...] Ein ganz besonderer Dank an Sie und die Kuratoren zu diesem lange verdrängten Thema!' Dated 19 February 2017 and unsigned.

58 Visitor book entry 430 (p. 142): '[...] Danke an die Ausstellungsmacher. Machen Sie weiter! [Signatur]' Dated November 22, 2016.

59 Visitor book entry 968 (p. 315): '[...] [Es] wurden wichtige Chancen verpasst, koloniale Kontinuitäten aufzuzeigen, was bspw. im Kontext von Werbung für Produkte wie Kaffee nahtlos an die vorhandenen Exponate hätte anschließen können. [...]' Undated and signed by visitor from Berlin.

60 Visitor book entry 891 (p. 285): '[...] Die Kuratoren haben offenbar kein Interesse an einen differenzierten Bild des Kolonialismus gehabt. Schade! Chance vertan.[...]' Dated 1 January 2017 and signed by a male German visitor.

61 Visitor book 1447 (p. 425): '[...] Die 'einfache Sprache' ist entmündigend, propagandistisch und in vielen Teilen schlicht falsch!! Das Deutsche Historische Museum sollte sich schämen, die Konzeptoren dieser Ausstellung sollten sich schämen!' Undated and unsigned.

62 Visitor book entry 1523 (p. 452): '[...] Auch sehr faszinierend sind Einträge in diesem Gästebuch! Vielleicht könnte man gegen Ende der Ausstellung etwas zu den Auseinandersetzungen und Kritiken sagen/schreiben? [...]' Undated and signed by a German female visitor.

63 Visitor book entry 514 (p. 175): 'Selten war ein Besucherbuch so vielsagend u. interessant! Bitte auswerten! [...]' Undated and signed.

References

Bach, J. 2019. 'Colonial Pasts in Germany's Present', *German Politics and Society*, Issue 133, 37(4): 58–73.

Binter, J. T. S. 2019. 'Beyond Exhibiting the Experience of Empire? Challenging Chronotopes in the Museum', *Third Text*, 33(4&5): 575–593.

Deutsches Historisches Museum (ed.). 2016. *Deutscher Kolonialismus—Fragmente seiner Geschichte und Gegenwart*. DHM: Berlin.

Ewert, B. 2017. 'Keine Bildungsbürger auf Reisen: Wie das DHM Kolonialismus entzaubert', *Neue Osnabrücker Zeitung*, 29 April 2017. www.noz.de/deutschland-welt/kultur/artikel/887878/keine-bildungsbuerger-auf-reisen-wie-das-dhm-kolonialismus-entzaubert#gallery&0&0&887878 (accessed 22 June 2020).

Fanizadeh, A. 2016. 'An der pädagogisch kurzen Leine', *taz*, 16 October 2016. www.taz.de/Kolonialismus-Ausstellung-in-Berlin/!5347101/ (accessed 22 June 2020).

Förster, L. 2019. 'Der Umgang mit der Kolonialzeit: Provenienz und Rückgabe', in Edenheiser, I., and L. Förster (eds), *Museumsethnologie. Eine Einführung. Theorien—Debatten—Praktiken*. Berlin: Dietrich Reimer Verlag GmbH: 78–103.

Gross, R., and Konitzer, W. 2020. 'Koloniale Objekte und deutsche Vergangenheitspolitik', in Schanetzky, T., T. Freimüller, K. Meyer, S. Steinbacher, D. Süß, and A. Weinke (eds), *Demokratisierung der Deutschen—Errungenschaften und Anfechtungen eines Projekts*, 333–348. Göttingen: Wallstein Verlag.

Hayn, E. 2010. '"Political Correctness". Machtvolle Sprachaushandlungen und sprachliche Mythen in Diskussionen um "Politische Korrektheit"', in A. Nduka-Agwu and A. Hornscheidt (eds), *Rassismus auf gut Deutsch. Ein kritisches Nachschlagwerk zu rassistischen Sprachhandlungen*, 337–343. Frankfurt a.M.: Brandes & Apsel.

Hille, P. 2020. 'How German schools miss out country's colonial history', *Deutsche Welle*. https://www.dw.com/en/how-german-schools-miss-out-countrys-colonial-history/a-55230081 (10 October 2020).

Hitz, J. 2016. 'Sonderausstellung zur deutschen Kolonialgeschichte: Der lange Schatten des deutschen Kolonialismus', *Deutsche Welle*, 14 October 2016. www.dw.com/de/sonderausstellung-zur-deutschen-kolonialgeschichte-der-lange-schatten-des-deutschen-kolonialismus/a-36039693 (accessed 20 July 2021).

Kerber, A. 2005. 'Kolonialgeschichte in deutschen Schulbüchern—kritisch oder kritikwürdig?', in H. Lutz, K. Gawarecki (eds), *Kolonialismus und Erinnerungskultur. Die Kolonialvergangenheit im kollektiven Gedächtnis der deutschen und niederländischen Einwanderungsgesellschaft*, 81–93. Münster: Waxmann.

Kilb, A. 2016. 'Grimmige Arier am Kilimandscharo', *Frankfurter Allgemeine Zeitung*, 21 October 2016. www.faz.net/aktuell/feuilleton/kunst/deutscher-kolonialismus-im-deutschen-historischen-museum-in-berlin-14481515.html (accessed 20 February 2020).

Macdonald, S. 2005. 'Accessing Audiences: visiting visitor books', *Museum and Society*, 3(3): 119–136.

Maihofer, G. 2018. 'Wie sollte Europa mit seinen Kolonialverbrechen umgehen?', *Der Tagesspiegel*, 29 January 2018. www.tagesspiegel.de/kultur/tagung-an-der-akademie-der-kuenste-wie-sollte-europa-mit-seinen-kolonialverbrechen-umgehen/20901176.html (accessed 1 July 2020).

Miglietta, A. M., Boero, F., Belmonte, G. 2012. 'Museum management and visitors book: there might be a link?', *Museologia Scientifica*, 6(1-2): 91–98.

Muttenthaler, R., Wonisch, R. 2006. *Gesten des Zeigens. Zur Repräsentation von Gender und Race in Ausstellungen*. Bielefeld: transcript.

Pekarik, A. J. 1997. 'Understanding visitor comments: The case of *Flight Time Barbie*', *Curator—The Museum Journal*, 40(1): 56–68.

Rauterberg, H. 2017. 'Mit ***** fängt es an', *Die Zeit*, 31 August 2017. Issue 36:40.

Reid, S. E. 2005. 'In the name of the people: The Manège affair revisited', *Kritika: Explorations in Russian and Eurasian History*, 6(4): 1–43.

Ross, I. 2017. 'Uncharted Territory: Visitor books of Indian museums. The Madhya Pradesh Tribal Museum in Bhopal—a case study', *Museum and Society*, 15(1): 100–113.

Roussell, A., K. Henne, K. S. Glover, and D. Willits. 2017. 'Impossibility of a "Reverse Racism" Effect', *Criminology & Public Policy*, 18(1): 1–12.

Schröder, C. 2016. 'Kontinente in Ketten', *Der Tagesspiegel*, 16 October 2016. www.tagesspiegel.de/kultur/ausstellung-dhm-deutscher-kolonialismus-kontinente-in-ketten/14692744.html (accessed 19 February 2020).

Speicher, S. 2016. 'Mit der Nilpferdpeitsche', *Süddeutsche Zeitung*, 17 October 2016, Bavarian Edition: 11.

Stanard, M. G. 2019. *The Leopard, the Lion and the Cock. Colonial Memories and Monuments in Belgium*. Leuven: Leuven University Press.

Stiftung Deutsches Historisches Museum. 2019. *Tätigkeitsbericht 2017/18*. Berlin: Stiftung Deutsches Historisches Museum.

Thewalt, A. 2020. 'Die Umbenennung von Straßen kann nur ein Anfang sein', *Der Tagesspiegel*, 03 February 2020. www.tagesspiegel.de/berlin/deutsche-kolonialgesc

hichte-die-umbenennung-von-strassen-kann-nur-ein-anfang-sein/25499054.html (accessed 20 June 2020).

Wegener, F. 2018. 'Kolonialismus im Kasten? Ein alternativer Museumsguide', in C. Dätsch (ed.), *Kulturelle Übersetzer—Kunst und Kulturmanagement im transkulturellen Kontext*, 191–206. Bielefeld: transcript.

Zimmerer, J. 2016. 'The First Genocide of the 20th Century—On the Problems of Confronting Germany's Colonial Legacy', in S. Gottschalk, H. Hartmann, S. Müller, A. Scriba (eds), *German Colonialism—Fragments Past and Present*, 138–145. Berlin: Stiftung Deutsches Historisches Museum.

Changing Street Names
Decolonisation and Toponymic Reinscription for Doing Diversity in Berlin

Duane Jethro

The autumn chill had begun to creep into our bones by the end of the three-hour postcolonial tour through Berlin.[1] As the last afternoon sun dissolved into the Spree river, we stood around and listened to the activist and public intellectual Joshua Kwesi Aikins describe the significance of this final Kreuzberg tour stop at May-Ayim-Ufer. He had by then taken us along streets with names that he explained were either outright racist, such as M-Straße in the district of Mitte, or marked with colonial traces such as those in what is called the African Quarter in the district of Wedding. These street names had long gone unchallenged and black activists had struggled for years to change them.[2] The renaming of May-Ayim-Ufer was a milestone, he said. It had originally been named Gröbenufer after Major Otto Friedrich von der Gröben, an 18th-century German explorer. In 2007 activist groups such as the Initiative for Black People in Germany (ISD) agitated in the district council (Bezirksverordnetenversammlung, BVV) that the street name be changed. Gröben, they argued, had participated in advancing the early German colonial enterprise by, among other things, establishing the fort Großfriedrichsburg in Ghana on behalf of the Great Elector Friedrich Wilhelm as a way station for the trade in African slaves. After two years of persistence, activists succeeded in persuading BVV members and local residents that Gröbenufer should instead be named after the poet, activist, feminist and educator May Ayim (see MacCarroll 2005; Konuk and Janovich 1997; Florvil 2020).

The renaming was not just a decommemoration of a problematic street name (Gensburger and Wustenberg fc). It was simultaneously about the commemoration of a leading feminist in the black German movement. A plaque installed on site further affirmed this double function: the headline states that it is May-Ayim-Ufer formerly known as Gröbenufer, and it recounts in German and English the history of the former street name, state's why it was problematic, provides a short biography of May Ayim and explains how the renaming came about. This is not a substitution of one name for another, or the erasure of a name for another. Instead, it set a precedent for what Aikins repeatedly referred to as shifting perspectives on commemorations (Aikins 2012). By that he meant critically intervening in existing public commemorative signage so that one historical narrative is more emphasised than the other.[3] This is a negation of substitution or erasure, and an embrace of the idea that decommemoration and commemoration go hand in hand. This was an important first step, Aikins said, for 'decolonising public space' and creating a decolonial urban future. [4] Standing alongside the plaque at the conclusion of the public tour, he expressed pride in having helped facilitate what was then the first activist-initiated street renaming in Berlin (see Author Unknown 2016).

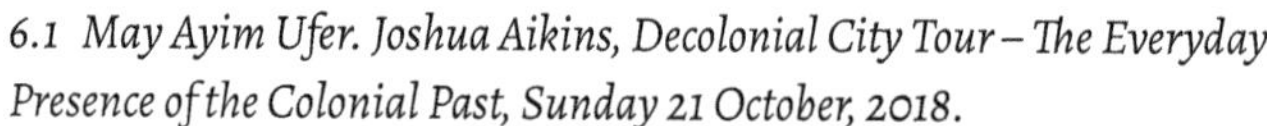

6.1 May Ayim Ufer. Joshua Aikins, Decolonial City Tour – The Everyday Presence of the Colonial Past, Sunday 21 October, 2018.

Walking off into the noisy, hustle and bustle around Schlesisches Tor U-Bahn station at the conclusion of the tour, I wondered what precisely the decolonisation of public space meant? What could a decolonial urban future look like? It led me back to thinking about the kinds of commemorative interventions I had witnessed and researched in South Africa, my home and another region of my research focus. There, a similar but more wide-ranging state-sponsored project to change urban streetscapes, geographic designations and apartheid commemorative culture has been underway since the mid-1990s. It was enacted as a cultural policy of reconciliation and nation building, which explicitly eschewed punitive removal, substitution and renaming. New statues and museums were built to diversify the commemorative landscape. Street and place renaming was also implemented as symbolic reparation and historical justice, the assumption being that some signs and place names celebrating figures from the apartheid past needed to be changed to create a more inclusive post-apartheid society.[5] The Department of Arts and Culture described it as 'decolonising the heritage landscape by replacing colonial names with the names that reflect a post-colonial, post-apartheid, democratic South Africa'.[6] Here, it was implied but never asserted that decolonisation was an exercise in the removal of old, problematic names and substituting them with new, more representative ones.[7]

At the time, my understanding of decolonisation was shaped by more recent experiences in South Africa where, in 2015, the Rhodes Must Fall movement revived and amplified the term 'decolonisation' as part of their call for the transformation of the University of Cape Town. The movement targeted the symbolic culture, signs, symbols, institutional structures and curricula. While the term certainly has other genealogies and histories (see Tuck and Yang 2012; Mignolo and Walsh 2018), it was the concept of decolonisation formulated in South African higher education contexts that informed my interpretation of the commemorative interventions in Berlin. And it is precisely these assumed shared universal ideas of the relationship between race, identity and commemoration that through the course of my research would also be productively troubled.

In this chapter I follow Joshua Kwesi Aikins's tour as I explore the arguments made by activists about why references to the German colonial past are problematic, why renaming is necessary and how they see renaming as a restorative, commemorative act. Building on previous research by other scholars of colonial legacies and street names (Jacobs and Sprute 2019), I also bring in arguments and alternative commemorative strategies proposed by residents, civic organisations and political groups opposed to renaming, showing how they frame the debate as a purely civic matter of rights to belonging, as facts explicitly not about race. Unpacking the conflict through a South African perspective, I show how attempts to rename street and place names are commemorative acts of doing diversity. This activism concerns an attempt to diversify Berlin's urban geography and the history it commemorates, a struggle over race as a term in which German belonging can be staked. Claims to and about names are also claims to the possibility of diverse German identification. The renaming debate is the urban setting in which the renegotiation of German identity takes place.

Street renaming as commemorative intervention

In Berlin, on our tour of the city, Joshua Kwesi Aikins asserted the symbolic force of renaming, emphasising its importance and relevance for a more diverse and inclusive city. The existing names, and those we would encounter on this tour specifically, were, Aikins suggested, exclusionary. These ideas were asserted again and again on other tours of the city, such as those offered by Berlin Postkolonial e.V, run by the activists Christian Kopp and Mnyaka Sururu Mboro. Walking the city while following the traces of colonialism and interpreting the colonial past was itself activist work.

If, as the urban geographer Maoz Azaryahu argues, 'street names communicate official representations of the ruling socio-political order' (2009: 53), for Aikins and colleagues, certain streets and places in Berlin discriminate against black Germans, and exclude them from full membership as city residents and German citizens. Not only were some street and place names offensive, but the city had failed to name streets in honour of figures and histories that black Germans and the city's African diaspora could identify with. Read as a city-text, as a grand narrative of history and power in an urban space (Azaryahu 1990; 1996), the numerous walking tours that keep tourists busy illustrate how densely historicised the city streets are. This is, however, as black activists emphasised, a story of a white German past. Street names, in that sense, are 'convenient and popular political symbols, a fact not generally recognized' (Azaryahu 1986: 581). Activists work to point out and persuade the public and local politicians to recognise that existing 'street names reflect and manifest a certain political identity' that is one-sided and exclusionary towards them (ibid.).

The history of apartheid naming and renaming in South Africa sharply illustrates the ties between political authority, naming and the racialisation of space that Aikins and others draw attention to. Until 1994, city maps represented the apartheid state's political vision of the primacy of the colonial past and a racially divided social order. Street and place names reflected this reality and the apartheid state's authority over history in urban space (Murray et al. 2007). Moreover, apartheid-era street names referenced or concealed real material histories of violent forced removal, segregation and the erasure of urban memory, as in the case of District Six in Cape Town and other suburbs across South Africa (Field 2001; Kentridge 2013; Rassool and Prosalendis 2001). Apartheid-era naming policy was explicitly engineered as urban spatial violence aimed at concretising associations between race, place and power.

In a city like Cape Town, policies of apartheid urban segregation provided a convenient map for neoliberal market policy during the post-apartheid period, further reinforcing racialised residency across the city. Affluent, scenic, touristic suburbs under Table Mountain remain overwhelmingly white as market logic has kept working class black residents at the distant periphery on the Cape Flats. As a black South African, I have personal experience traversing the city from the township to the town centre, effectively navigating the urban history of spatial woundedness. Yet the pathways created by my inherited assumptions about race, street and place names in Cape Town led me astray in Berlin. Navigating this city was different. It bore its own map of race, and indeed, histories of political transition, that include names of figures linked to WWI and WWII, National Socialist resistance, the Holocaust, the Cold War division and reunification (see Azaryahu 1997). These are different histories of purposeful and calculated segregation. They are also not merely layered upon each other as separate and distinct ages, following Andreas Huyssen's (2003) claim about Berlin as an urban palimpsest. Rather, they cross over, intersect, converge and diverge, and even clash in surprising ways. Berlin, we will see, is a multi-directional urban memoryscape (Rothberg 2009) that is not easy to navigate.

Certainly, Berlin was no apartheid city, and activists had never claimed that it was. Neither was it racially segregated. And despite having an area called the 'African district', which I discuss in detail later, it does not have a distinct area for the working-class African diaspora that is common in other big European cities. Berlin activists' complaints were not they had been formally segregated through racialised urban housing policies. To be sure, gentrification was contributing to transformation in the city that could lead to such segregation. Instead, theirs was an argument about symbolic exclusion in that the symbolic culture of street and place names was exclusionary, discriminatory and offensive to black Germans and residents from the African diaspora. One major point of difference was that while the idea of symbolic exclusion and racial offense was taken for granted and widely understood in South Africa in Berlin activists had to repeatedly make this very case. They had to point out why certain street and place names were problematic, and they often needed to argue vociferously for years for them to be changed. It was tiresome work that reinforced a sense that black struggles in the city had yet to receive true recognition.

The streets they identified led off of popular, tourist maps of the city, and wound their way into a history of blackness that increasingly and awkwardly was surfacing in mainstream public conversation about race and the German colonial past. The historians Fatima El-Tayeb (1999; 2001) and Grada Kilomba (2008) have argued that the notion of race as referring to blood ties, and the visible markers thereof, still codes dominant, contemporary notions of national identity in Germany (see also Florvil and Plumly 2018; and Florvil 2013; Ha 2014). Indeed, as the literary studies scholar Michele M. Wright points out, for many white Germans, the relationship between blackness and German identity is largely unintelligible: 'many white Germans are either resistant or incapable of imagining someone who is both Black and German ... Afro-German identity is not the antithesis in the dialectic of (white) German subjectivity: it is simply non-existent' (2003: 298). 'German-born individuals of African descent' are considered to be temporary residents who have a real home elsewhere and are seen as just passing through (Campt 1993: 110). There was a direct link between this disavowal of identity and street names. As the anthropologist Jenny Engler (2013) has pointed out, street renaming was about black Germans making a case for belonging: 'The claims to rename racist or colonial streets in Berlin are often rejected with reference to a German identity that is thought of as exclusively white and based on a shared [white] past' (2013: 50). Percolating in the struggle for street names was the issue of the terms in which German identity could be formulated. The German colonial enterprise in Africa, and the place names and institutions that covertly commemorate it, are particularly visible to black Germans. It is visible, moreover, as a period of trauma with which they can identify, and which, they argue, links to present day racism that continues to go largely unaddressed. Street signs commemorating the names of German colonial officers, for example, are prime examples of continuing offense.

Those who identify as Afro-German share a common experience of having ties to the African continent, being racialised and self-identifying as black in a majority white European society (Lennox 2017). They also share the German language and culture. This is, however, no homogenous group. Organisations that represent different constituencies in the broader black community active in Berlin, such as Each One Teach One (EOTO),

Berlin Post-Koloniale, the ISD and others have their own varying interests, geographic and political orientations, and participate in local debates about the terms of black Germanness. While key identifiers such as people of colour and BIPOC (black, indigenous and people of colour) are commonly used, the term Afro-Deutsch (Afro-German) has gained currency, but not exclusivity, as a distinctive identifier and subject position that many black Germans can step into. I use 'Afro-German' below as the most common (if still debated) term for Germans who identify as having a black, African background.

The term emerged out of an awakening in social consciousness that occurred among black Germans in the late 1980s during the American poet Audre Lorde's literary collaboration with a group of black German women. The publication *Showing Our True Colours*, which grew out of that workshop, coined 'Afro-Deutsch' as an inclusive label for framing a common black German experience. May Ayim and others built on this new sense of identification to co-found the (ISD) in Germany as an organisation that campaigned for black German cultural issues and to advocate against racism and discrimination. Following the fall of the Berlin Wall, Ayim and others contested the terms of German reunification, citing rising, violent East German racism and ongoing exclusion through public renaming practises, such as the 1991 renaming of the Mohrenstraße Ubahn station in Berlin, which I elaborate on below. This became more strident starting in the 2000s, when Afro-Germans and diasporic groups led the renaming initiative as a sustained point of civic protest.

The anthropologist Damani Partridge points out (2012: 17) that Afro-Germans are simultaneously citizens and non-citizens, incorporated and excluded on the basis of race. Illustrating this distinction between white German belonging and black exclusion, another activist interlocuter remarked that, 'when you're controlled [passport is checked] in the US or elsewhere [as a black person] people don't ask you if you belong there. Whereas in Germany they do'. It was a telling analogy with strong resonances after the 2020 Black Lives Matter protests following George Floyd's murder. In context, the remark was meant to convey the idea that black Germans were prevented from fully occupying the dominant national subject position and enjoying all its civic benefits. This would include the authority to contest inappropriate signage in their city. Contesting colonial legacies was in many ways, then, an attempt to secure this right to civic recognition based on a claim to historic presence and agency.

Identifying as black and African, but not German, I also stepped into and moved through a category of non-whiteness and blackness that allowed me to appreciate the dynamics of race, identity and commemorations being contested in the city. The sometimes confusing subject positions available to me both opened up and closed off access to logics circulating in this field of identity politics and commemoration. I could identify with the experience of being excluded from being seen as European, which Afro-Germans often highlighted. My race was readily apparent to conservative individuals suspicious of race and identity politics, but also to black Germans. Despite my enjoying the freedom of being able to move through such positions of race, by any calculus Afro-Germans were often far more materially privileged than me. Our shared blackness was to some extent also illusory, perhaps even merely situational. In research settings I have often shared with my colleagues and interlocuters a sense of *Bruderschaft*, to reference a colloquial German expression for kinship of a kind, that also concealed complicated hierarchies of privilege that marked us out as different even while it instantiated a claim to affinity. Yet these differences were far from my mind as our bus made its way through the city in preparation for our tour of the places important for black Germans in Berlin.

The Afrikanisches Viertel

Our bus wound its way through the suburb of Wedding on its way to what is known as the *Afrikanisches Viertel*, or the African Quarter. The district name refers to the many African street and place names concentrated in the area. It also maps an urban history of Germany colonial exploits in Africa. The street names also referenced the names of colonised African nations as well as German colonial officials involved in that project. As our bus pulled off, Aikins rose, introduced himself and attended to issues of housekeeping. Among other practical matters, he warned us about a possibility that we could be approached by those whom he referred to as 'revisionists'. Evoking a potent historical designation (see Lewerenz 2011; Dedering 1993), he said that the revisionists could be local residents who disagreed with the arguments he and other activists make about the German colonial past and their attempts to change street names.[8] If it did so happen that we were approached by individuals speaking 'rapid German', he warned, we were just to refer them to him. It appeared that revisionists were everywhere. Sometimes 'revisionists even come on these tours', he ominously remarked.[9]

We alighted and walked into the African Quarter. This suburb in the north of Berlin was established in the late 19th century. It was Carl Hagenbeck, an animal trader who proposed the idea of building a zoo in the district, in the Rehberge Park, modelled on a type he'd built in Hamburg. He imagined that it would show not only animals but also peoples from Germany's African colonies. Fortunately this did not come to pass, but an African colonial profile was etched into the landscape starting with the Togostraße and the Kameruner Straße. These colonial commemorative aspects would be accentuated post-WWI as the district became a piece of post-war urban propaganda. The streets and squares retrospectively mapped 'Germany's African land grab' as 'more than 20 [street signs were erected] between 1899 and 1939, long after Germany had lost its colonial territories during the First World War' (Stevenson 2017: 38; van der Heyden 2002: 261–263). We stood gathered around on the corner of Swakopmunder Straße, a street named after the former German colonial port city in Namibia. Aikins explained in his introduction that the tour was to point out 'traces of the colonial past that exist in the present in the Berlin cityscape' and to explain how they continued in the present. Moreover, it was about 'tracing continuities from slavery and colonial times through National Socialism to the present'. He highlighted that Berlin, and the African quarter in particular, was 'a place of contestations', a place of 'quarrels and activism' where different layers of history 'wrestle' with each other. It was not about seeing huge construction sites, big monuments, memorials or museums. Rather, the tour was about surfacing 'subtle traces', and the African Quarter, he emphasised, was full of them.

6.2 Afrikanisches Viertel. Joshua Aikins, Decolonial City Tour – The Everyday Presence of the Colonial Past, Sunday 21 October, 2018.

Aikins also took a moment to reflect on his own position as an expert. One could not relate historical information, especially information about such a sensitive subject, without explaining one's own position, he stressed. 'We cannot be objective if we do not share the perspective from where we come from'. He was a Ghanaian German, a father of two and a scholar working in political science in Germany. The point was not to be objective: taking a perspective is at odds with the idea of a universal rational standard. Rather, it was an effort to be transparent and open, to reveal one's position rather than assume oneself to be making a universal claim. Asserting transparency and evidentiary truth are discursive tactics employed by activists and revisionists alike when positioning themselves vis-à-vis the body of factual historical knowledge.

Further along on our walk we paused on Petersallee. This street, Aikins explained, had originally been named after the notorious colonial official Carl Peters, who had advocated for the establishment of the colony of German East Africa in what is now Tanzania. Labelled 'Hanging Peter' by the late-19th-century German press for the murder of his mistress and her secret lover, Peters was also chastised by politicians in Berlin for his brutal treatment of Africans. The district municipality rededicated Petersallee in 1986 to the anti-Nazi resistance fighter Hans Peters.[10] Aikins pointed out that, following protests, the city planned to rename part of the street Maji-Maji-Allee to commemorate the Maji-Maji war of resistance (Gwassa 1973; Giblin and Monson 2010). Aikins then noted that we were standing on the corner of Nachtigalplatz, a public square named after Gustav Nachtigal, an official known for establishing colonies in Togo and Ghana. In light of these jarring colonial histories, activists were campaigning to have this square renamed too.

Continuing to trace the concentration of colonial markers in the quarter, we were led into to the *Dauerkleingarten* 'Togo', a recreational green space of fenced-off garden allotments. Another German iteration of the notion of a 'colony', the *kolonialer Garten* refers to an area of enclosed allotments where residents in urban spaces can plant gardens.[11] Standing at the entrance to the Togo Allotment Association, Aikins explained that 'Togo' was established as a piece of colonial propaganda in 1939 by the Nazi state. He drew our attention to the different flags flown inside the garden. One in particular, he noted, referenced the garden's historical origins in the 1930s. At this point, a middle-aged couple passed our group and entered the garden, muttering 'this is not OK. This is not OK' in German. What exactly was not OK was not made clear despite earnest enquiries from tour participants.

A short walk past the garden led us to Lüderitzstraße, which was named after the aristocratic and colonial pioneer Adolf Lüderitz and the namesake of Lüderitz in Namibia. The city bore this name, Aikins said, because an agent working on behalf of Lüderitz had swindled large tracts of land from the local Nama people. It was for that reason that activists wanted to rename the street after Cornelius Fredericks, a leader in the resistance against German colonialism. By advocating for the renaming of two streets and Nachtigalplatz, rather than all the streets in the quarter, activists aimed to transform its public profile from one bearing the legacy of colonial figures into a place of learning about Africa, the horror of the German colonial enterprise and the significance of African historic resistance.

As we exited the Quarter, Aikins directed us to an information board on Otawistraße, near the Rehberge U-Bahn station. An emblem of the prevailing clash of perspectives about the African Quarter, it illustrated the complicated local politics in which the renaming debate was situated. Unveiled on 8 June 2012, the information board was the product of a political compromise reached between the Social Democratic Party and the Christian Democrats, who in the 2011 local elections had campaigned for and against street renaming, respectively. To come to an agreement in the local parliamentary coalition, the parties decided to suspend the debate and instead install an information board recounting the colonial history of the district. Yet the well-meaning overture was not without controversy. Activists argued that the narrative proposed by the district council softened the history of the quarter. Unable to achieve a shared text, activist NGOs and the municipality agreed to include one version of the district's history by the ruling coalition and another by activists.[12] When it was unveiled, however, the text relating the local government's version was prominently positioned to greet oncoming pedestrian traffic, while the activists' text faced a wall. Naturally, another struggle over the reorientation of the plaque ensued.

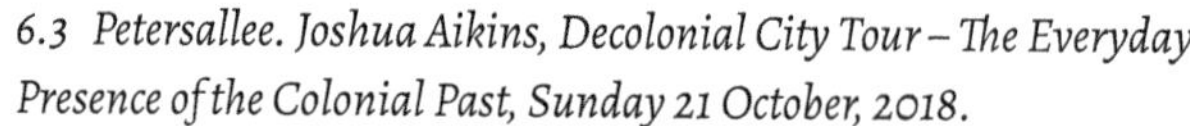
6.3 Petersallee. Joshua Aikins, Decolonial City Tour – The Everyday Presence of the Colonial Past, Sunday 21 October, 2018.

A number of local residents also opposed the renamings (see Förster et al. 2016). This was not necessarily because they held positive views of colonialism, however. For example, the Pro-Afrikanisches Viertel, a local residents' organisation, mobilised sophisticated arguments aimed at rededicating rather than renaming streets, to signify new, more acceptable historical figures and places.[13] They stood against renaming but also the honouring of German colonial history and memory, the spokesperson for the organisation argued. They felt that their proposals for the rededication of existing names was a reasonable compromise and argued that they were trying to make a positive difference in the area. They objected to the way the renaming process was being 'pushed through' the district parliament to the detriment of district residents who they felt were not being taken seriously. They saw rededication, rather than renaming, as the way forward.

Rededication was the retention of the original names for streets and places but reinscribing the original dedication behind it. The rededication of the Petersallee to Hans Peters, they argued, was a good model, which had been more cost-effective and less disruptive. Yet the kinds of rededications that they proposed did not entirely free existing names of their colonial baggage. For example, in the case of the Lüderitzstraße, they proposed to keep the name and rededicate the street after the city rather than the person, Lüderitz. They claimed that the city had decided to keep its own name and so the rededication would honour the city rather than the person. This work around did not negate the fact that the sign continued to honour Lüderitz the person if only by one degree of separation.

Moreover, Pro-Afrikanisches Viertel argued that it would mobilise around the renaming issue to establish a partnership with the city of Lüderitz for educational exchange and learning, so as to strengthen ties between Africa and the Afrikanisches Viertel. In so doing, they seemed to be styling themselves as activists and advocates for African partnership through rededication rather than renaming. At every turn of the official renaming process, Pro-Afrikanisches Viertel posted information on flyers and their website about the district and the heavy-handed approach of local politicians and activists. The organisation stressed their marginalisation and the 'ideological way' in which the renaming process was being handled. For Pro-Afrikanisches Viertel, the struggle to keep the existing street names in the African Quarter was about claiming recognition for the civic rights of local residents through what they saw as dispassionate appeals to reason, strident legal action, public relations and concrete plans for African partnership.

M-Straße

We left the district and travelled across the city from Wedding to a spot in Mitte near the location on Wilhelmstraße where the Berlin Africa Conference of 1884 was held. European powers arrogated the authority to themselves to establish distributed domains of influence, marked by the drawing of artificial borders at that meeting. Aikins noted that this history had painfully shaped the experience of space and belonging for Africans, and continues to do so today. To counter this history of unacknowledged spatial violence, Berlin activists had gathered funds for a plaque marking the site where the conference had taken place. The plaque contrasts with the official information boards dotting the inner city, which mostly focus on National Socialist and GDR history. Activists hold a demonstration every year on 26 February—the final day of the conference—to memorialise the violence that it represents.

Aikins then guided us across the street and stood on a square at the M-Straße U-Bahn station.[14] Located in former East Berlin, the station received the name in 1991 during a time when names commemorating the GDR past were being changed to fit the reunification agenda. Activists soon called out the renaming of the station after M-Straße, arguing that reunification politics was serving to exclude black German residents. The station has since been a rally point for anti-racist activism and has repeatedly been vandalised, and has even led the transport authority to take an official stance (see Jethro and Merrill fc).[15] The painful history of the street—now home to the Department of Justice, the Institute for European Ethnology of the Humboldt University, several luxury hotels and a shopping mall—is hidden in plain sight. The word *Mohr* is an offensive, if archaic, racial slur, and the German dictionary, Duden, indicates that the term is discriminatory. Despite its clear racist undertones, however, the history of the street's name is complex enough to have complicated straight-forward renaming efforts. The street name was first registered in 1706, with the name making reference to a group of black African residents who were seen to make use of it. Historians disagree whether this group was invited as a special delegation by the Prussian Royal family, or whether they were a group of slaves brought to the city as part of the sale of the Groß-Friedrichsburg fort in Ghana to Great Elector Friedrich Wilhelm of Prussia.

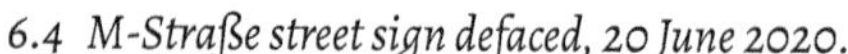

6.4 M-Straße street sign defaced, 20 June 2020.

Aikins stressed that activists were campaigning to have the street renamed because the etymology of *Mohr* emphasises the backwardness of people of colour and because the word is directly linked to early German colonial activities and slavery. Finally, the name is problematic today because it continues to carry negative associations for black people who do not use it as a self-descriptor. It was for these reasons, he argued, that an alternative name had been put forward: that of the German philosopher Anton Wilhelm Amo, a recognised, distinguished black intellectual who was born in Ghana but educated at the University of Halle (see Lochner 1958, Abraham 1964; Sephocle 1992). Renaming the street after him would publicly commemorate a black intellectual in Germany who had worked to subvert the colonial past and the legacies against which activists struggled. It would publicly recognise black intellectual history in Germany and make the case that Africans are part of Germany's history (see Diallo and Zeller 2013).

6.5 'Decolonize the City'. M-Straße Ubahn Station defaced, 23 July 2020.

Activists were not the only ones to advocate for this street name to be changed. As Jenny Engler explains, local councilman Christoph Ziermann proposed in 2004 a motion to rename the street on the grounds that it was offensive. He argued that in very few other places in Germany – in museums, in the public sphere, in the education system – was there such an explicit reference to the country's colonial history. He also believed that the German black community should be included in the process of finding a new name. 'The search for a new name,' his motion declared, 'should take place in cooperation with the black community in Berlin to make sure that the new name signals a postcolonial, anticolonial and equality-based representation of Africa' (Engler 2013: 48). Unfortunately, his efforts ran up against a lack of sustained political will. The case is a reminder that renaming is a local political issue and often leads to heated debates, with district elections being contested explicitly on the back of parties taking positions on either side of the argument. As the case of the African Quarter also showed, commemorative debates and identity politics are very much entwined with local city politics.

The M-Straße debate has its own history of debate and resistance. The historian Ulrich van der Heyden, a leading scholar of German colonialism who has written extensively on the history of M-Straße, argues that the street took its name from a visiting African delegation who stayed in nearby barracks (van der Heyden 2008). The issue, he believed, came down to an acknowledgment of the facts, which in his estimation showed a history of African and German partnership. As to the word *Mohr*, he argued that it arose from a historically specific idea of Otherness that was not discriminatory toward black Africans today. His arguments were used by Pro-Mohrenstraße, an organisation that was led by a retired lawyer, Bodo Berwald, and that opposed activists' renaming efforts. The spokesperson for Pro-Möhrenstraße said that the street name was not offensive because the German etymology of the word *Mohr* was different to the English *Moor* and did not carry the same racist connotations. Moreover, the street already has a heritage going all the way to the 18th century, when it was first designated; renaming the street would rob it of that heritage. As in the case of Pro-Afrikanisches Viertel, members of Pro-Mohrenstraße were motivated by a sense of civic duty and justice. Their case was about the right to be heard as local residents. They argued that activists were conflating historical facts in order to push through an ideologically-loaded agenda. Again, they mobilised 'the facts of history', 'cold reason' and 'objectivity' in arguing that activists were making emotive and ideologically skewed claims. It was decidedly not about race, they maintained. And even if it was, it concerned notions of race that lay in the past and not in the present, the argument went.

As the M-Straße debate raged on, activists in 2014 began to stage an annual protest that playfully engaged issues of discrimination and renaming in Berlin. The Street Renaming Festival forcefully inverts existing politics of commemoration and reclaiming blackness in the city. Organised by the ISD in partnership with other activist groups in Berlin and across Germany, the festival takes place annually in late August to coincide with the International Day of the Remembrance of the Slave Trade and Its Abolition. It features musical and cultural performances and tributes of solidarity showing how street renaming is tied to the repatriation of objects and human remains from Berlin's museums. It often includes contributions by migrants and other minorities and links into their struggles. The event concludes with a collective performance in which participants are invited to show their support for the name Anton-Wilhelm-Amo-Straße by holding up mock street signs bearing the philosopher's name. This is always a joyous moment, and provides a celebratory photo opportunity. This festival is part of the work of doing diversity in Berlin, and shows how entwined issues of race are with the urban struggle for recognition.

Conclusion

In August 2020, following weeks of Black Lives Matter protests after the police murder of George Floyd in the U.S., the Senate for the BVV of the district of Mitte voted to rename M-Straße to Anton-Wilhelm-Amo-Straße. It was a momentous, timely announcement arriving on the eve of the 2020 street renaming festival. After a years-long campaign, public and political perspectives appeared to be shifting towards recognising the causes of the Afro-German community. While, at the time of writing in early 2022 the street name has not yet been changed, it is indeed true that the Berlin city map was changing in the ways that activists had hoped.

The renaming projects I have described here revolve around issues of civic authority, race, identity and national belonging. In that sense, the struggle to change street names is, I submit, part of doing diversity. Not only were activists trying to diversify markers in the urban geography so that they are more inclusive and representative. They were also making a case for recognising contemporary black residents and the histories of black life in Berlin and Germany. Race has been a crucial aspect in the debate over street names. In the case of M-Straße, activists mobilised race for claiming recognition: the name needed to be changed, they argued, because that name was offensive. But that sense of offense was not shared by local residents and some historians, who claimed that the histories on which this claim was being made were false or entirely misconstrued. Clearly, what was playing out here was a dispute about what constituted race and racism, both then and now. For activists, the dispute was an important point of identification, recognition and denial. To be able to effectively make claims to and about public space was to close the gap between being black and being German. They adroitly navigated questions of race and rarely confronted it with allegations of outright racism, which could trigger legal action. Both sides approached the issues through arguments, facts and evidence, believing that the best rational argument, rather than the strongest moral appeal, would ultimately win out.

This stands in marked contrast with how arguments about engaging with problematic commemorations in South Africa were framed and engaged. Race was taken for granted as a primary historically informing criterion of the past in South Africa. In the context of colonisation and apartheid, renaming and transforming the urban landscape was presented as a matter of historic justice. In South Africa, decolonisation functioned as a rhetorical strategy for uniting ideas of commemoration, race, identity and the past. It was against that backdrop, and especially the student movements of 2015 and 2016 that I encountered Aikins's use of the term decolonisation to describe the work of urban activist projects in Berlin. As I thought it through in context and comparison, I came to see how important and beguiling decolonisation was. It enabled activists to frame renaming efforts as a challenge to uncritical commemorations of Germany's colonial past and a promotion of Afro-Germans' national belonging in the present. The idea of decolonisation could facilitate solidarity among people of colour in the struggle over urban signage because it was an appealing message that invited a wide range of actors to identify with the cause.

But while these struggles were similar to those in South Africa, this use of the term decolonisation glossed over important current and historical differences—as it probably also did in South Africa. Seeing street renaming as a form of doing diversity means recognising the politics of occlusion that goes hand in hand with mobilisations of identity. Certainly, activists and activist groups were not unaware of those cleavages. What it does allow is new questions about how and where the Afro-German struggle creates entry points with and for other non-white minorities with claims to commemorative real estate in Berlin. One wonders, say, about the future claims to heritage made by Turkish Germans and how they fit into a black struggle for diversification and for the diversification of commemoration in the city generally.

The efforts I have described in this chapter are better observed up close. My anthropological approach of renaming was meant to deepen the usual analysis of street renaming debates, which frequently takes place at a remove. Thinking with Berlin activists, and occupying a space of solidarity, challenged my own historically informed perceptions of race, urban space, and of what it means to be black, Other and yet to belong. This research was an active occasion of doing diversity. The solidarities and differences that the struggles I participated in and tried to understand troubled my embodied assumptions about belonging and my scholarly training, which told me to keep my distance. As the activists I met sought to change perspectives on commemorations, my perspective changed on how identity could be brought to bear in such debates. This had consequences for perceiving dynamics in South Africa and Berlin, for recognising how in these struggles categories of blackness could emerge and yet also collapse in on each other. It also had consequences for thinking about what an engaged anthropology of museums and heritage can be today. I realised that taking a position and reading the debate from the activists' perspective made sense as a contribution not only to social transformation but also to a vibrant, public anthropology where my scholarly knowledge could be put to work. I understood that it was in the streets that socially significant heritage debates were being waged in earnest and where important shifts in perspectives were occurring with significant repercussions both in and beyond the academy.

Acknowledgements

This research was completed with funding from Sharon Macdonald's Alexander von Humboldt Professorship as part of the project *Making Differences: Transforming Museums and Heritage in the Twenty-First Century*. I would like to especially also thank my interlocuters at various NGO's and activist organisations and colleagues for their time, knowledge, generosity and warmth of spirit during a lively, heated time of commemorative change in Berlin.

Notes

1 Decolonial City Tour - The Everyday Presence of the Colonial Past, 21 October 2018.
2 I use the abbreviation 'M-Straße' out of solidarity with activists and black city residents who find the official street name racist and discriminatory. The chapter builds largely on the public tour narrative of following the city's colonial traces. This is but one version of the narrative; there are other ways of exploring the colonial past in Berlin.
3 The anthropologist Jenny Engler, while discussing the case of M-Straße in Berlin, believes that the process inverts perspectives on commemorations, therefore referencing the activist assertion about the shifting of perspectives.
4 Decolonial City Tour - The Everyday Presence of the Colonial Past, 21 October 2018.
5 Ibid.
6 Ibid.
7 Other references are scant. For example, the word appears in the 2017/2018 and 2016/2017 annual reports, where it explicitly refers to geographical names and to the transformation of the education sector, but no clear definitions are provided. Nevertheless, it is worth remarking on the mobilisation of a word that calls to mind the struggles for independence and, more recently, the transformation of institutions of higher learning and inherited systems of thought and practise associated with apartheid.
8 The term 'revisionist' has a potent cultural and political genealogy in Germany going back to the early 20th century. It refers to historians who tried to revise the facts about the colonial past to suggest that allies had lied about the German colonial project, especially their brutal treatment of African subjects. Revisionists portrayed

Africans as willing, even enthusiastic, accomplices, and emphasised the 'positive', beneficial outcomes of the colonial project.

9 Increasingly—as the organisers of a leading post-colonial activist tour group dishearteningly mentioned—incidents of confrontational opposition from members of the public were making walking tours with smaller groups more difficult to host in the area. Revisionism, activists wanted to assert, was not merely a code for an outdated form of historical misrepresentation; it was also an active, present-day form of denial that could lead to real public hostility.

10 While noble, activist groups subsequently discovered that the rededication was unlawfully enacted and was no longer binding, which opened the way for its outright renaming.

11 On the history of these gardens in Germany, see Gert Gröning, 'The Politics of Community Gardening in Germany', accessed at http://www.cityfarmer.org/german99.html#develpgerman, 1 June 2019.

12 The full text of the information board is available here: https://pro-afrikanisches-viertel.de/downloads/pdf/BVV-Beschluss_Texttafeln.pdf (accessed 1 June 2019).

13 See 'Argumente': https://www.pro-afrikanisches-viertel.de/index.php/argumente (accessed 1 June 2019).

14 See note 1 on the politics of the designation of the abbreviated, M_Straße, and my use of it in text.

15 On 3 July 2020, the Berlin Transport Company, a private company, announced that due to global protests against racism and white supremacy triggered by the death of George Floyd, they would be renaming the Ubahn station Glinka Straße, after the Russian composer. This was subsequently rescinded when Glinka's antisemitic links and references in his work were made public. The motion has been stalled until M-Straße is renamed.

References

Abraham, W. 1964. 'The life and times of Anton Wilhelm Amo', *Transactions of the Historical Society of Ghana*, 7: 60–81.

Aikins, J. K. 2012. 'Berlin Remix – Straßenumbenennungen als Chance zur postkolonialen Perspektivumkehr, in K. N. Ha (ed.), *Asiatische Deutsche – Vietnamesische Diaspora and beyond*, 288–304. Berlin, Hamburg: Assoziation A.

Author Unknown. 2016. *Dossier: Stadt neu lesen Koloniale und rassistische Straßennamen in Berlin*. Berlin: Berliner Entwicklungspolitischer Ratschlag e.V.

Azaryahu, M. 1986. 'Street Names and Political Identity', *Journal of Contemporary History*, 21(4): 581–604.

Azaryahu, M. 1990. 'Renaming the Past: Changes in 'City Text' in Germany and Austria, 1945–1947', *History and Memory*, 2(2): 32–53.

Azaryahu, M. 1996. 'The power of commemorative street names', *Environment and Planning D: Society and Space*, 14(3): 311–330.

Azaryahu, M. 1997. 'German reunification and the politics of street names: the case of East Berlin', *Political geography*, 16(6): 479–493.

Azaryahu, M. 2009. 'Naming the Past: The Significance of Commemorative Street Names', in L. D. Berg, and J. Vuolteenaho (eds), *Critical Toponymies: the Contested Politics of Place Naming*, 53–70. London: Ashgate.

Campt, T. 1993. 'Afro-German Cultural Identity and the Politics of Positionality: Contests and Contexts in the Formation of a German Ethnic Identity', *New German Critique*, 58, winter: 109–126.

Diallo, O., and J. Zeller (eds). 2013. *Black Berlin: Die deutsche Metropole und ihre afrikanische Diaspora in Geschichte und Gegenwart*. Berlin: Metropol Verlag.

Dedering, T. 1993. 'The German-Herero war of 1904: revisionism of genocide or imaginary historiography?', *Journal of Southern African Studies*, 19(1): 80–88.

El-Tayeb, F. 1999. '"Blood Is a Very Special Juice": Racialized Bodies and Citizenship in Twentieth-Century Germany', *International Review of Social History*, 44(7): 149–169.

El-Tayeb, F. 2001. *Schwarze Deutsche: der Diskurs um 'Rasse' und nationale Identität 1890–1933*. Berlin: Campus Verlag.

Engler, J. 2013. 'Renaming Streets, Inverting Perspectives: Acts of Postcolonial Memory Citizenship in Berlin', *Focus on German Studies*, 20: 41–62.

Field, S (ed.). 2001. *Lost Communities, Living Memories: Remembering Forced Removals in Cape Town*. Cape Town: New Africa Books.

Florvil, T., and V. D. Plumly (eds). 2018. *Rethinking Black German Studies: Approaches, Interventions and Histories*. Berlin: Peter Lang.

Florvil, T. 2013. *Writing Across Differences: Afro-Germans, Gender, and Diaspora, 1970s–1990s*. PhD Thesis. Department of History. University of South Carolina.

Florvil, T. 2020. *Mobilising Black Germany: Afro-German Women and the Making of a Transnational Movement*. Champaign: University of Illinois Press.

Förster, S., S. Frank, G. Krajewsky, and J. Schwerer. 2016. 'Negotiating German colonial heritage in Berlin's Afrikanisches Viertel', *International Journal of Heritage Studies*, 22(7): 515–529.

Gensburger, S. and J. Wustenburg (eds). Forthcoming. *(De)commemorations: Making Sense of Contemporary Calls for the Removal of Statues and the Renaming of Places*. London: Berghahn Books.

Giblin, J., and J. Monson. 2010. *Maji Maji: Lifting the Fog of War*. Leiden: Brill.

Gwassa, G. C. K. 1973. *The Outbreak and Development of the Maji Maji War; 1905–1907*. Doctoral dissertation, University of Dar es Salaam.

Ha, N. 2014. 'Perspektiven urbaner Dekolonisierung: Die europäische Stadt als "Contact Zone"', *sub\urban. Zeitschrift für Kritische Stadtforschung*, 2(1): 27–48.

Huyssen, A. 2003. *Present Pasts: Urban Palimpsests and the Politics of Memory*. Stanford: Stanford University Press.

Jacobs, C., and P. Sprute. 2019. 'Placing German Colonialism in the City: Berlin Postkolonial's Tour in the African Quarter', *Global Histories: A Student Journal*, 5(2): 110–117.

Jethro, D., and S. Merrill. Forthcoming. 'Next Stop M_Straße: the BVG and toponymic reinscription in Berlin', in S. Gensburger, and J. Wustenburg (eds), *(De)commemorations: making sense of contemporary calls for the removal of statues and the renaming of places*. London: Berghahn Books.

Kentridge, I. 2013. '"And so they moved one by one": Forced Removals in a Free State Town (1956–1977)', *Journal of Southern African Studies*, 39(1): 135–150.

Kilomba, G. 2008. *Plantation Memories: Episodes of Everyday Racism*. Münster: Unrast.

Konuk, K, and N. Jancovich. 1997. 'With love, in memory and in honour of May Ayim', *Journal of Gender Studies*, 6(1): 71–72.

Lennox, S. 2017. *Remapping Black Germany: New Perspectives on Afro-German History, Politics, and Culture*. Massachusetts: University of Massachusetts Press.

Lewerenz, S. 2011 'Colonial Revisionism'. *Postcolonial Europe and Its Empires, Postcolonial Literatures*: 224–25. Edinburgh: Edinburgh University Press.

Lochner, N. 1958. 'Anton Wilhelm Amo: A Ghana Scholar in Eighteenth Century Germany', *Transactions of the Historical Society of Ghana*, 3(3): 169–179.

MacCarroll, M. 2005. *May Ayim: A Woman in the Margin of German Society*. PhD thesis. Florida State University.

Mignolo, W., and C. E. Walsh. 2018. *On Decoloniality*. Durham: Duke University Press.

Murray, N., N. Shepherd, and M. Hall. 2007. *Desire Lines: Space, Memory and Identity in the Post-Apartheid City*. London: Routledge.

Partridge, D. J. 2012. *Hypersexuality and Headscarves: Race, Sex, and Citizenship in the New Germany*. Bloomington: Indiana University Press.

Rassool, C., and S. Prosalendis (eds). 2001. *Recalling Community in Cape Town: Creating and Curating the District Six Museum*. Cape Town: District Six Museum.

Rothberg, M. 2009. *Multidirectional Memory: Remembering the Holocaust in the Age of Decolonization*. Stanford: Stanford University Press.

Sephocle, M. 1992. 'Anton Wilhelm Amo', *Journal of Black Studies*, 23(2): 182–187.

Stevenson, P. 2017. *Language and Migration in a Multilingual Metropolis: Berlin Lives*. London: Springer.

Tuck, E., and K. Yang. 2012. 'Decolonization is not a metaphor', *Decolonization: Indigeneity, Education & Society*, 1: 1–40.

van der Heyden, U. 2002. 'Das Afrikanisches Viertel', in U. van der Heyden, and J. Zeller (eds). *Kolonialmetropole Berlin: Eine Spurensuche*, 261–263. Berlin: Berlin-Ed.

van der Heyden, U. 2008. *Auf Afrikas Spuren in Berlin: Die Mohrenstraße und andere koloniale Erblasten*. Berlin: Tenea.

Wright, M. M. 2003. 'Others-from-within from without: Afro-German Subject Formation and the Challenge of a Counter-Discourse', *Callaloo* 26(2): 296–305.

Dis-Othering Diversity
Troubling Differences in a Berlin-Brussels Afropolitan Curatorial Collaboration

Jonas Tinius

Curatorial practices that address Europe's colonial legacies through contemporary art frequently engage with constructions of alterity, difference, and otherness. Many target the ways in which institutions of artistic and cultural production reproduce ethnic and geographic forms of othering. The practices on which I focus in this chapter build on a range of critiques articulated in anti-racist, feminist, and intersectional approaches to curating and artistic production (Bayer, Kazeem-Kaminski and Sternfeld 2017, Oswald and Tinius 2020). At the heart of those practices is a 'double presence of difference', that is to say, difference as both a subject of positive identity-formation and an object of critique, an obstacle to social justice and a political strategy for its attainment (Ndikung and Römhild 2013).[1] Markers of identity such as race, gender, class, and regional and cultural belonging can indicate symptoms of structural discrimination and exclusion, yet they also allow for the formulation of subject positions that can challenge hegemonic, normative, and canonical structures.

In recent decades, and across a variety of transnational contexts, the notion of diversity has captured many of the tensions implicit in earlier debates on class, nation, race, identity politics, and difference. Damani Partridge and Matthew Chin suggest that we may indeed 'use the current discourse on diversity as a lens to think about question of economic disparity and social justice' (2019: 202; see also Appadurai 2013). By asking, 'Who benefits from diversity, and who might be forgotten?', they argue that we can 'productively engage with the different kinds of work [that] are being done under "diversity"' (2019: 202; 206). Drawing on Sara Ahmed's analyses of the ways in which diversity works in 'institutional life' (2012), my research has sought to understand the practices of curators working in Berlin, and the complex means by which they strategically operationalise an anti-racist diversity agenda in identifying larger issues of exclusion in public cultural institutions. I describe these practices as a form of 'curatorial troubling' in which curators seek to 'stir up potent responses' (Haraway 2016: 1) to structural forms of exclusion.

For this contribution, I draw on fieldwork conducted between mid-2016 and late-2019 with the Berlin art space SAVVY Contemporary, the BOZAR Centre for Fine Arts in Brussels (Belgium), and Kulturen in Bewegung, a smaller cultural institution in Vienna (Austria) engaged in anti-racist cultural production.[2] The collaboration was initially meant to focus on Afropolitanism, and much of the programming across the three countries focused on African diasporic life in Europe.[3] Due to a number of conflicts arising over the representation of Africa in predominantly white cultural institutions, especially between SAVVY Contemporary and its director Bonaventure Soh Bejeng Ndikung and BOZAR's director Paul Dujardin, the project inadvertently became itself an example of the work and effects of diversity agendas in European cultural institutions.

This chapter describes how Ndikung and his colleagues reframed a large EU-funded project, initially focusing on Afropolitanism and Afropean identity by turning it around, suggesting it look instead at the ideas of Africanness in institutions that conduct projects on Africa.[4] The project eventually was renamed to indicate the shift: *Dis-Othering: Beyond Afropolitan & Other Labels*.

Dis-othering is a term coined by Ndikung for institutions to analyse their own practices of othering. I was invited as an ethnographer to join the advisory committee of Mapping Diversity, a quantitative data-gathering effort within the Dis-Othering project managed by the BOZAR 'Africa desk'. The aim of Mapping Diversity was to investigate conceptions and policies of diversity in public culture and art organisations in Austria, Germany and Belgium. Specifically, its task was to examine the extent to which curatorial projects focusing on diversity (i.e. the presence of persons of African descent in shows about Africa curated by European cultural institutions) are themselves lacking the diversity they purport to exhibit. As such, the survey was entangled in the problem it sought to address, namely, the reification of markers of difference such as race, nationality, ethnicity and gender. How can a survey designed to challenge geographically-bound categories of otherness operate without reproducing them?

This chapter traces the paradoxes of curatorial practices that hope to trouble the reification of diversity. It shows how efforts to expose a lack of diversity at cultural institutions can reinforce the markers it seeks to undo. Focusing on this double presence of difference as both the subject and the outcome of the diversity survey, I argue that the querying of diversity is always implicated in the unresolved and ongoing reproduction of difference. The curatorial probing of diversity for tackling social injustice can also shed light on the complexity of similar problematisations of difference in the fields of contemporary art, exhibition-making and museum practice.

Curatorial troubling

By late 2017, I had conducted fieldwork for nearly a year on three galleries and project spaces in Berlin focused on German colonial legacies, migration, and constructions of difference (Tinius 2018, 2020, 2021). I was planning to conclude the official research phase when I received a text message from Bonaventure Soh Bejeng Ndikung and Antonia Alampi, the founder and one of the then co-directors, respectively, of one of my principal fieldwork partners, SAVVY Contemporary. They wanted to talk. We arranged a meeting at SAVVY Contemporary, located in the Wedding district of Berlin. At the meeting, which took place among the many books and magazines of SAVVY

Contemporary's archive, Ndikung and Alampi told me about their collaboration with BOZAR and expressed regret about the way the project had developed: the inclusion of people of colour in major European cultural institutions was lagging behind the demographic realities of the cities in which these institutions were located, Brussels and Berlin in particular.[5] Their concerns echoed what Damani Partridge and Matthew Chin describe as the way in which 'diversity has come to mean a sprinkling of color or the contingent presence of the "disadvantaged" in otherwise majoritarian "White" or upper-class/high-caste institutions' (2019: 198). In Ndikung's view, BOZAR's project on the African diaspora was merely symbolic and risked reducing Africa to a mere theme or project, which Ndikung found particularly inappropriate for a major cultural institution in a former colonial metropolis with ongoing ties to the African continent. As Antonia Alampi noted, 'for them "Africa" is just a show', while 'for us', an engagement with practices of othering 'is why we exist'. The problem for the two curators was not their partnership with a large institution on an EU-funded project about Africa, but what the consequences of such an engagement would be. The two curators were worried that the project on Europeans of African descent would end up being another project in which an institution 'cloaks itself with a thin veil of recognising the diversity of its cities' without drawing any consequences in terms of its programming or hiring policies. The two curators criticised the institutional appropriation of difference—in this case, the label 'African' and 'Afropolitan'—for the purposes of appearing inclusive.

Ndikung and Alampi wanted to know how an institution like BOZAR could conduct a small albeit significant project on Africa and Afropolitanism without instrumentalising people of colour as temporary tokens to make the project appear inclusive. They also wondered how SAVVY, an organisation doing critical, mostly independent and, by extension, financially precarious work with artists from Africa and the African diaspora, could collaborate with BOZAR without falling prey to the same logic of appropriation. When, they wondered, does collaboration signal approval and complicity? Alampi and Ndikung thought a mapping survey of the actual employment statistics of large state-funded institutions could provide some 'hard facts'.

Alampi and Ndikung did not describe the mapping survey as a form of strategic essentialism whose purpose was to identify people of colour working in art and cultural institutions. Rather, its purpose was, in keeping with their Dis-Othering concept, to provoke reflection on whiteness and diversity in an organisation like BOZAR that aimed to carry out a large project on its institutional ties to Africa. The survey was part of a complex attempt to address a practice that Alampi and Ndikung believed was especially strong in the areas of art and culture: the promotion of diversity in certain types of temporary projects while keeping the institutional landscape largely unchanged. They were grappling with how they could trouble the tokenism of 'diversity' while still partnering with major institutions.

After our conversation, I agreed to join the mapping survey project. I was curious how the curators would negotiate the shift from identifying the 'African' ties of public cultural organisations in Belgium, Germany, and Austria to analysing these institutions 'policies on and reckoning with diversity'. For the curators, conducting a quantitative survey with markers of difference was a political and moral challenge that ran counter to the ways in which they sought to *problematise* statistical science. They were already worried about the double presence of difference and were reluctant to develop a survey that would promote diversity while reaffirming markers of difference (race, ethnicity, gender) that they sought to undo in most of their curatorial work. They thus suggested that my role could be to document their efforts to deal with the basic conundrum. They believed that the inclusion of an ethnographer like me who was outside the project yet implicated in its work could be productive. Moreover, the additional perspective could provoke or illuminate the negotiations of the categories used by the organisations in question. The outside observation, they hoped, might add a layer of observation on the production of conventional notions of diversity in cultural organisations and in the survey project itself. In Alampi's words, the survey's point was to pose the question, 'Who is talking about whom when it comes to diversity and difference?'

The origins of Dis-Othering

During the months after our meeting, I became acquainted with the Dis-Othering project and its partner staff from Kulturen in Bewegung in Vienna and from the Africa desk at BOZAR, including its director, Kathleen Louw. It seemed curious to me that a project could so abruptly shift gears. What started as a study focused on Afropolitanism in Europe swerved to an interrogation of its own premises and of diversity in Europe's cultural institutions. How did this come about?

Ndikung's official curatorial statement of the Dis-Othering project begins with an observation that hints at the need to use and reformulate received notions of difference.

> Just in the nick of time when we, by repetition and reiteration, start believing our own concepts that we have postulated and disseminated...we seem to be experiencing a quake that pushes us ...to reconsider who and how one bears historical Othering, reconsider the mechanisms of rendering Other, as well as reconsidering who represents whom or who tries to shape whose future in contemporary societies and discourses (2019: 3).[6]

SAVVY's curatorial troubling is marked by self-aware political positioning.[7] The 'quake' that made them reconsider forms of othering was triggered in part by 'geographical specification-ing' (2019: 3): the museum practice of highlighting specific regions of the world for a temporary period of time. As Ndikung puts it:

> What does it mean to put together an 'Africa exhibition' or an 'Arab exhibition' today, as we see in the New Museum, MMK Frankfurt, BOZAR Brussels, Fondation LV and many other museums in the West? (...) [H]ow would one represent the 54 African countries, thousands of African languages, and communities within such an exhibition? These issues necessitate re-questioning and reconsidering (2019: 4).

Ndikung identifies seven ways that Dis-Othering responds to a 'geographical specification-ing' often promoted under the heading of soft-power diplomacy and inclusion. Most importantly from my perspective, Ndikung writes that 'Dis-Othering starts with the recognition of the acts and processes of othering' (2019: 5). In this sense, the concept of Dis-Othering is already a Dis-Othering practice insofar as it positions the curator in a conscious and critical relation to host institutions. As Ndikung elaborates, Dis-Othering considers how

> social identity building is not made by projecting on the so-called 'Other,' but rather a projection towards the self. A self-reflection. A boomerang. ... It is about acknowledging and embodying the plethora of variables that make us be (2019: 5).

Ndikung describes a position in which institutional introspection and subjective self-analysis can be mobilised for the purposes of anti-discrimination. It is a position that reshuffles the genealogies of Othering—in line with the efforts of Seloua Luste Boulbina (2007), Arjun Appadurai (1986), and Michel-Rolph Trouillot (2003)—using new postcolonial language that is at once poetic and political. The project statement is a gesture of 'theoretical accounting' (Smith 2015: 15) that situates and affirms Ndikung's epistemological jurisdiction vis-à-vis other institutions while shifting the discussion of othering to one of institutional self-critique. As Ndikung wrote in an earlier version of the text, the curatorial statement is 'a reaction to the invitation to exercise Afropolitanness'.[8]

The SAVVY's curatorial concept bears the imprint of this critique in its subtitle: Beyond Afropolitan & Other Labels. The subtitle pokes fun at the tokenistic usage of the prefix 'Afro-' in cultural institutions. But the criticism voiced by Ndikung and the Berlin team went further. As later became evident during the project's final conference in May 2019, their criticism was not a response merely to BOZAR's engagement with minorities, particularly of African descent.[9] It also targeted the way that institutions, which work on 'Africans', or those of 'African descent' (or 'afro-descendant'), do not include those people among its permanent staff; instead they invite them to contribute to programming temporarily on an unpaid or low-paid basis. BOZAR is a 'differentiating institution' in the sense that it produces geographically-bounded, tokenistic, and even racialised images of Africa. As Ndikung writes, SAVVY was concerned that their project might serve a similar function for BOZAR, leading to a 'parasitical incorporation' of critical work in an otherwise 'white' institution that, in their eyes, did little to further more substantial engagement with African scholars, artists, personnel, publics, and programming (2017). Ndikung and Alampi's Dis-Othering project was meant as a critique of institutional 'othering' practices and well-intended 'conceptual labels' such as Afropolitan, which ignore the broader context and fail to look at 'what they actually do and what processes of identity construction they encourage'.[10]

The critical reorientation, which I observed unfold during fieldwork in Brussels at BOZAR and at SAVVY Contemporary in Berlin, brought a level of critical reflection to the ways in which institutions and projects can produce difference. Dis-Othering

> is not about the 'Other'—which is just the 'product'. The project is a deliberation on the amoebic and morphed methodologies employed by institutions and societies at large in constructing and cultivating 'Otherness' in our contemporaneity. It is about the commodification and the cooption of the 'Other', strategies of paternalization used in the cultural field.[11]

Ndikung, Alampi, and their expanded team are part of Berlin's ecology of cultural institutions. Their organisation is diverse in terms of its inclusion of women and people of colour, and other directors of cultural institutions in Berlin and beyond regard them as the vanguard of a progressive post-colonial agenda. In a conversation with me, Ndikung and Alampi said that their position was a double-edged sword. On the one hand, they were pleased with the recognition they received for issues regarding contemporary art from African perspectives; on the other, they worked with larger institutions whose desire for 'representation' relied on a merely temporary inclusion of African perspectives. Ndikung and Alampi's curatorial troubling led them, therefore, to a sub-project: interrogating policies on diversity.

The mapping diversity survey

The SAVVY mapping survey was designed to assess diversity at major cultural institutions in Germany, Belgium, and Austria. Initially, it focused on the distribution of class, race, and gender among curatorial and executive personnel. In view of the difficulty of attaining such sensitive data and several SAVVY team members' 'discomfort with the simple positing of such markers of identity as "facts"', Ndikung and Alampi decided that the survey should also examine the ways in which cultural organisations understand diversity. The survey concentrated on directorial staff because the SAVVY curators and other members of the mapping survey team felt that it was on this level that decisions about personnel, programming, and public outreach—the three p's—would be made.

In the first few months, the partners discussed the scope of the survey via email and in online meetings. Due to the limited funding for research (the Berlin team relied on external funding from small grants and private research scholarships), they restricted the survey to institutions mainly involved in arts or culture production and kept the number to five institutions per country from its three largest cities. Moreover, they decided to use institutions in which at least 70 percent of the funding comes from public sources. Publicly funded institutions, they argued, could reasonably be expected to take into account the demographics of the city and country that finance them.

Selection, data and privacy

Choosing which institutions to survey proved contentious. Team members were uncertain whether it would be a good idea to identify institutions based on 'best practice', 'worst practice', or name recognition. Some wondered whether the project should focus on different types of institutions (universities, museums, performance venues) or on different organisations within a broad institutional category (cultural sector, public sphere, programming)? The framing would affect the ultimate selection. For instance, programming staff at a museum are different from programming staff at a small-scale art space. In a similar vein, SAVVY Contemporary would feature as a 'best-practice' type of organisation given the high percentage of women and persons of colour working there, while BOZAR would be seen a 'bad practice' institution, with its white middle-class director and its predominantly white executive staff. Long debates ensued about whether the aim would be to expose the assumed lack of diversity in one institution or to provide statistical facts about the diversity in another. For example, the SAVVY team identified the Humboldt Forum as a case to be 'exposed', but the idea was abandoned due to the institution's complicated organisational structure (Häntzschel 2017; Macdonald, Gerbich, and Oswald 2018).

The Mapping Diversity advisory committee found that while the data gathered might not be on the scale of larger regional or national surveys, the project stood to provide meaningful data on the diversity of staff in decision-making positions along with their particular understanding of diversity. But the committee suggested that it would be helpful not only to approach institutions via formal email inquiries but also to interview 'gatekeepers', i.e. directors or head curators most likely to decide whether or not to send the surveys to their core staff. Hence, the team invited gatekeepers from the institutions selected for the survey to meetings in the hope of convincing them to participate.

After consultations with the BOZAR legal department and the legal team of the Creative Europe programme, the Mapping Diversity teams formulated short ethical and legal statements.[12] But the country teams remained unclear about how to transmit the survey data to the participating institutions. Although they broadly agreed on the use of anonymous data, some wondered whether this would miss the point of the project, which was to determine how major public cultural institutions deal with diversity. Would producing general statistics for each country be meaningful? Might it be necessary to specify and differentiate the data? How would the data help identify particular kinds of diversity. Would not the project's ethical and political commitment to anonymity make it impossible to make meaningful statements about diversity? The conundrum here was the tension between 'private' and 'political' data. Some participants might refuse to share 'private' data to conceal sensitive information. Yet the 'private' data seemed likely to provide the most relevant insight into the politics of diversity.

Gatekeeper interviews

The issues regarding data use continued in the gatekeeper interviews. For instance, a representative from a well-known German cultural institution expressed discomfort about the project's results and how the data would be put to use. The team members believed that the collaborative nature of the project— all of the partners involved were cultural institutions, after all—would help establish trust and encourage participation. But some gatekeepers were not convinced. 'We don't want our data to be used in some form of artistic project where the outcome and form is unclear to us', one respondent said. Other interviewees expressed scepticism on other, altogether opposite grounds. The links of the project to universities—including my presence in the interviews as a white male anthropologist—raised concerns that the data would be used in academia and therefore detached from a shared artistic context.

On a whole, the gatekeepers made clear to the team that, while they were sympathetic to the general aims of the project and were happy to participate in the interviews, we could not distribute the results of our survey. For it was not 'sufficiently clear' what would happen with the survey, whether public authorities could access the data or whether the project would reframe the data in ways beyond the institutions' control. Participating institutions from Austria were worried that the information might be used against them by the government, which at the time was composed of a right-wing coalition between the ÖVP (Austrian People's Party) and FPÖ (Freedom Party of Austria). Tonica Hunter, the then research lead for Kulturen in Bewegung, commented on the situation during a talk at the final BOZAR symposium:

> Several institutions that participated in our 'let's talk about Dis-Othering' symposiums who then agreed to be included in the mapping, later declined for various reasons...We found the pattern pertinent given the tense political situation in Austria in view of its black-blue government and the threatened (and real) cuts to the cultural sector. The diversity of cultural institutions is not an easy topic for institutions, who seem to believe that the exercise will lead to critique rather than to the kind of insight that could help bring about improvements and address shortcomings.

The issue, therefore, was not only about managing data but also about the mapping itself. As the project team noted during the final conference in Brussels, the term mapping is associated with colonial practices such as systemic governmental control, geographic information systems, and other forms of knowledge acquisition, which have often targeted marginalised peoples (Rose 2007).

7.1 Olani Owunnet, Naomi Ntakiyica, athe nd Jonas Tinius during panel on the Mapping Survey at Dis-Othering Symposium, BOZAR, May 2019. Photograph by Lyse Ishimwe.

As the process unfolded and interviews were coordinated, the project's advisory committee (of which I was a member in my capacity as research coordinator and ethnographer) decided that it would be helpful to document the survey deliberations. It had become evident to most participants that almost every step of the survey—from design and implementation to analysis—involved a fundamental questioning of the survey categories and the purpose they were meant to achieve. The team members recorded the deliberations in several kinds of documents, regularly contributed new documents, and reviewed the contents. The process was also discussed with team members during the final *Dis-Othering* Symposium at BOZAR in Brussels in 2019.

Survey design

The mapping coordination team at SAVVY Contemporary discussed at length the precise organisation of the survey. Each of the research teams had access to the survey software SurveyMonkey, which provides a fairly straightforward interface for designing surveys (similar to website design software like Weebly or WordPress) and for sharing surveys and exploring data sets in visualised form.

The teams decided on a 40-question survey, beginning with drop-down optional questions on economic issues and general questions covering age, nationality, location, gender, sexual orientation, religious orientation or belief, immigration history, and education. These included an 'other' category and several open boxes. Next was a set of broader questions about the diversity of staff, diversity policies, job criteria, and general assessments such as 'How important is diversity to your institution?' and 'Do you think you contribute to the diversity of a) the public/audience, b) the programmes/curatorship or c) the personnel?' For many of the questions, the survey requested elucidation, including prompts such as 'If yes, why and how?' or 'If yes, please elaborate'. These allowed for critique and disagreement to avoid implicit bias.

The research team members held intense discussions about which markers of identity were considered 'sensitive', including ones liable to discrimination such as gender, country of birth, nationality, ethnic background, and sexuality. They collected several of the categories from existing surveys in Germany such as online discrimination questionnaires conducted by the Humboldt-Universität zu Berlin. The teams included 'current nationality' and 'nationality at birth' to account for migration and changes of nationality over time. A particular contentious category was 'ethnic background'. Some team members disputed the relevance or existence of 'ethnicity'; and everyone rejected the category of race, which, despite its frequent use in the Anglophone world, was not considered appropriate in Continental Europe. Instead, the team decided to specify the difficult notion of 'ethnos' by asking respondents whether they belong 'to an ethnic minority which is not linked to recent migration'. All questions related to ethnicity came with the option 'Prefer not to say'. Team members agreed that the survey categories could not be assumed to be 'exhaustive'. Furthermore, though questions about nationality had a long list of drop-down options, they included the box 'Add your current nationality / nationality at birth, if it is not on the list'. Participants were also given the choice to choose multiple nationalities, with options ranging from pre-defined countries to open boxes.

7.2 Screenshot of a survey question in the SurveyMonkey app during the test phase.

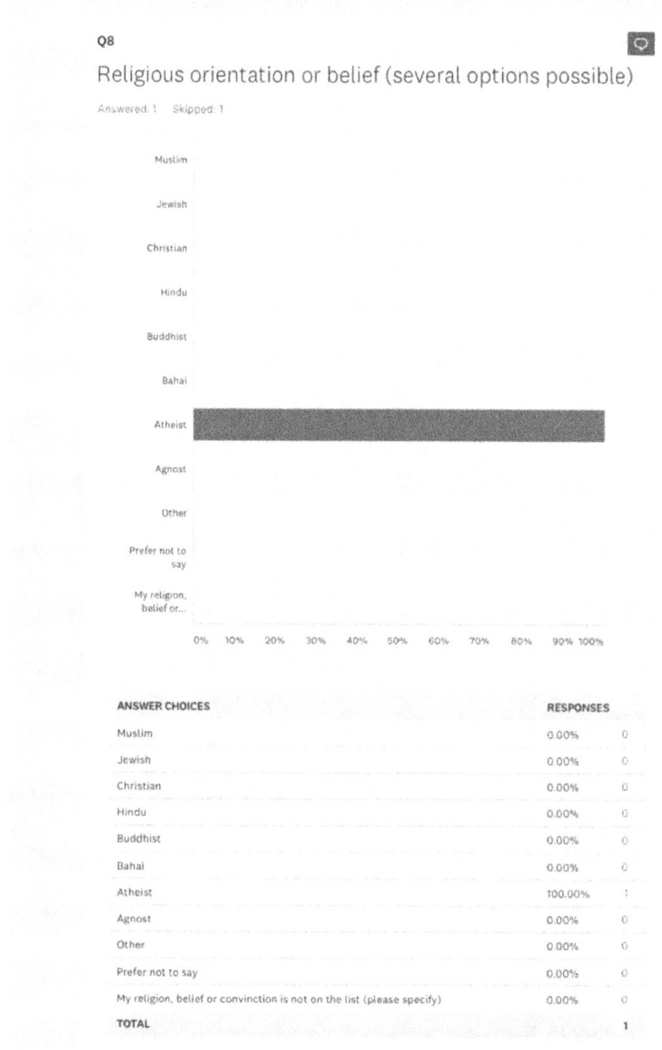

ANSWER CHOICES	RESPONSES	
Muslim	0.00%	0
Jewish	0.00%	0
Christian	0.00%	0
Hindu	0.00%	0
Buddhist	0.00%	0
Bahai	0.00%	0
Atheist	100.00%	1
Agnost	0.00%	0
Other	0.00%	0
Prefer not to say	0.00%	0
My religion, belief or convinction is not on the list (please specify)	0.00%	0
TOTAL		1

The team members discussions revealed a broader problem when it came to diversity: the multiplication of differences extended the problem of difference by 'maximising' differentiation. Yet, it also became evident that the categories that were most contentious were also the ones that mattered most to team members. This suggested that the core of the 'diversity' problem in the survey involved categories of identity that themselves created discomfort. These included the concepts of race, sexuality, sexual orientation, and their translatability (or *un*translatability, as with *race* and the German *Rasse*, which immediately recalls Nazi racial ideology). In our online video conferences several members self-identified as persons of colour or of African descent. It was noticeable that the positionality of the team members across categories of whiteness, sexual orientation, and institutional affiliation played a role in the discussion, and many were reluctant to fix a category that they experienced as discriminatory. Their response revealed the non-neutrality of the categories, and how the meaning of the categories change depending on who is using them (e.g. me as a white German male versus a person of colour). The challenge here lay not in maximising the number of diversity markers, but in crafting a survey that overcomes discrimination without reifying difference.

Conclusion

Curatorial practices seeking to create infrastructures for 'greater diversity' within cultural institutions often essentialise difference for strategic purposes. The process is as paradoxical as it is unavoidable. Yet some institutions adopt elements of strategic essentialism without reflecting on the difficulties of diversity. BOZAR and the Dis-Othering project are a case in point: a well-intended project ended up causing such a stir within its own team that the project turned on itself and became a study of failure and critical self-reflexivity. This is not an isolated problem. The language of wokeness and strategic criticality pervades capitalist and cultural institutions alike (Ahmed 2021, Boltanski and Chiapello 2007 [1999], Bose 2017, Leary 2018). The risk here is that 'diversity' becomes a technocratic issue, packaged in 'proposals' and handled by short-term 'diversity managers' who serve to conceal underlying structural inequalities instead of addressing them.

In this chapter, I focused on two dimensions of difference-making for two different ends. First, I considered the criticisms of BOZAR and the reformulation of the SAVVY Contemporary project on Dis-Othering in response. The revised SAVVY project shaped the terms used in the mapping diversity project, which speaks not of 'difference', but of 'Othering' and 'Dis-Othering'. These depart from a particular genealogy of postcolonial theory and thought. These include Afropeanism, in which the practices of SAVVY Contemporary are situated, and more recent institutional discussions on diversity management, which echo through the Humboldt Forum exhibition addressed by Sharon Macdonald.

Dis-Othering is a curatorial neologism that has an ethnographic function insofar as it describes a particular problem and situation. It is a form of curatorial troubling coined by Ndikung and Alampi to facilitate critical thinking about the way in which public cultural institutions produce geographically-bounded ideas of cultural otherness. The questions that led to the mapping diversity survey in the Dis-Othering project centred on representation and infrastructure: who can represent whom? In whose interest is diversity work done? How can projects critically reflect on the *undoing* of Othering practices, and turn their gaze onto themselves?

A second dimension of difference-making that I addressed is how 'diversity' became the central problem of the Mapping Diversity survey. The attempt to interrogate what diversity and diversity-work means for cultural institutions led to an ambivalent and often contradictory discussion of how to define diversity without recreating the categories that the project as a whole sought to question. The group discussions—and the references to similar surveys (Marguin and Losekandt 2017)—illustrates the primacy of 'diversity' in the project.

The core analytical contribution of this chapter is to draw out the tensions of difference: on the one hand, difference can be a problem (producing geographical, cultural, and even racialised distinctions between 'Europeans' and 'Africans') and an obstacle (preventing non- or post-racial forms of artistic expression). At the same time, difference and diversity are part of the performative consequences of the survey, which risked reproducing the very essentialism of diversity work that the project as a whole wanted to overcome.

Perhaps, as a participant mentioned at the final BOZAR conference, the significance of the project lies in sparking a conversation about diversity agendas within and among cultural institutions. Due to the reasons I outlined above, the mapping survey did not produce the scale and scope of quantitative results that the curators initially hoped for, and the reasons for this failure are themselves testament to the broader problem the survey sought to address. Too little money, time, and human resources were allocated to the mapping project, which, as the BOZAR manager of the project commented, could have been the subject of an entire EU-project itself—as could failure itself (Appadurai and Alexander 2019). Yet, within the boundaries and limitations of the project, the survey helped sensitise the participating institutions to the complexity and multiple forms of difference at play. And it began a conversation about the need to reflect on, refine, and dis-other strategic mobilisations of diversity in the cultural field and beyond.

Acknowledgements

The fieldwork for this chapter was conducted during a research fellowship for *Making Differences: Transforming Museums and Heritage in the Twenty-First Century*, at the Centre for Anthropological Research on Museums and Heritage (CARMAH). The fellowship was funded by Sharon Macdonald's Alexander von Humboldt Professorship. I am grateful to Sharon Macdonald along with Arjun Appadurai, Bonaventure Soh Bejeng Ndikung, Antonia Alampi, Lynhan Balatbat-Helbock, Olani Ewuett, Tonica Hunter, Kathleen Louw, Naomi Ntakiyica, Elena Ndidi Akilo, and Nikolai Ssorin-Chaikov for their helpful comments.

Notes

1 At the time of writing, one of the discussions involving members of SAVVY Contemporary coalesced around the debate on the overwhelming presence of white men. See the open letter by the organisers (https://conversations.e-flux.com/t/open-letter-regarding-lack-of-diversity-in-nrw-forum-exhibition/8345) and a video recording of an event at the Red Salon of the Berlin Volksbühne (http://www.youtube.com/watch?v=G2zejVIrAdI), which included several of the interlocutors mentioned in this chapter. All links were last accessed on 8 February 2022.

2 Further project partners include the Royal Museum for Central Africa (Tervuren), Afropean London, and Obieg Magazine (Poland). The Dis-Othering project website at BOZAR can be found here: https://www.bozar.be/en/calendar/dis-

othering#event-page__description (last accessed, 8 February 2022). The Dis-Othering project was funded by the EU's Creative Europe programme, which possesses a budget of 1.46 billion euros.

3 The concept of Afropolitanism has its roots in pan-African theoretical texts, but now includes a broader set of reflections on the relationship of urban space to African cultural production and to diasporic citizenship practice (Weheliye 2005). The concept has thus moved from Africa's post-independence era to the postcolonial theorisation of transnational forms of belonging.

4 *Afropean: Notes from Black Europe* (2019), by Johny Pitts, an affiliated member of the project discussed in this chapter, engages with the notion in order to overcome the 'hyphenated identities of Afro-and' (personal communication).

5 Ahead of the 2019 European elections, a *Guardian* newspaper op-ed with the heading 'Why is Brussels so White? The EU's Race Problem That No One Talks About' (2019) states that 'Migrants, minorities and people of colour are almost absent from tomorrows' list of prospective MEPs.' As the author, Sarah Chander, writes, the representation of people of colour in the European parliament is 'less than 3%, and Italy's Cécile Kyenge is the sole black woman.'

6 The concept was written in response to BOZAR's interest in collaborating with SAVVY Contemporary. It was subsequently revised and updated by the curator to reflect the ongoing processes and experiences in this collaboration. The project statement can be found on the SAVVY Contemporary website: www.savvy-contemporary.com/site/assets/files/4038/geographiesofimagination_concept.pdf (last accessed 8 February 2022).

7 In a chapter co-authored with Sharon Macdonald, I reflect on the recursivity of such concepts in curatorial discourse (Tinius and Macdonald 2019). Marcus Morgan and Patrick Baert's book *Conflict in the Academy* (2015), on positioning theory and the role of discursive statements in the creation of intellectual spheres, is a relevant point of comparison.

8 In June 2019, when I finished a first draft of this piece, the shortened earlier statement could still be found on the BOZAR website here https://www.bozar.be/en/calendar/dis-othering#event-page__description. It had since been removed.

9 The conference Race, Power and Culture: A Critical Look at Belgian Cultural Institutions (22–24 May 2019) stirred up a heated discussion and even a boycott of BOZAR. Various attendees, among them members of the original advisory committee, felt that they had been lured to participate on false promises, only to appear as tokens of a thinly veiled diversity agenda.

10 The quote appears in the shorter version of Ndikung's curatorial concept on the BOZAR website.

11 Ibid.

12 Excerpts of the invitation email include these passages: 'The survey is anonymous. It has been reviewed by the legal department of the Centre of Fine Arts (Brussels) (project leader), and assessed compliant with the new EU General Data Protection Regulation (GDPR). The collected survey data: is collected for scientific research only; will be accessible only to a scientific committee comprising a total of 6 researchers from the three partner countries, who will perform a qualitative

analysis of interview material and quantitative results, and direct the graphic and digital visualisation of survey results; will not be shared with any other research or projects (3rd parties); will be destroyed after 2 years'.

References

Ahmed, S. 2012. *On Being Included: Racism and Diversity in Institutional Life.* Durham, NC: Duke University Press.

Ahmed, S. 2021. *Complaint!* Durham, NC: Duke University Press.

Appadurai, A. 1986. *The Social Life of Things: Commodities in Cultural Perspective.* Cambridge: Cambridge University Press.

Appadurai, A. 2013. 'Diversity and disciplinarity as cultural artifacts', in C. McCarthy, W. Crichlow, G. Dimitriadis, and N. Dolby (eds), *Race, Identity, and Representation in Education*, 2nd ed., 427–437. London, New York: Taylor and Francis.

Appadurai, A., N. Alexander. 2019. *Failure.* Cambridge, UK: Polity Press.

Baert, P., and M. Morgan. 2015. *Conflict in the Academy. A Study in the Sociology of Intellectuals.* Basingstoke: Palgrave.

Bayer, N., B. Kazeem-Kaminiski, and N. Sternfeld (eds). 2017. *Kuratieren als antirassistische Praxis. Kritiken, Praxen, Aneignungen.* Berlin: de Gruyter.

Boltanski, L., and È. Chiapello. 2007 [1999]. *The New Spirit of Capitalism.* Trans. Gregory Elliott. London, New York: Verso.

Bose, F. von 2017. 'Strategische Reflexivität. Das Berliner Humboldt Forum und die postkoloniale Kritik', *Historische Anthropologie,* 3: 409–417.

Boulbina, S. L. 2007. 'Being Inside and Outside Simultaneously. Exile, Literature, and the Postcolony: On Assia Djebar', *Eurozine.* 02 November 2007. www.eurozine.com/being-inside-and-outside-simultaneously/ (accessed 8 February 2022).

Chander, S. 2019. 'Why is Brussels so white? The EU's race problem that no one talks about', *The Guardian,* 19 May 2019. www.theguardian.com/commentisfree/2019/may/19/eu-race-problem-european-elections-meps-migrants-minorities (accessed 8 February 2022).

Häntzschel, J. 2017. 'Verstrickung als Prinzip', *Süddeutsche Zeitung,* 20 November 2017. www.sueddeutsche.de/kultur/kulturpolitik-verstrickung-als-prinzip-1.3757309 (accessed 8 February 2022).

Haraway, D. J. 2016. *Staying with the Trouble. Making Kin in the Chthulucene.* Durham, London: Duke University Press.

Law, J., and R. Williams. 1982. 'Putting Facts Together: A Study of Scientific Persuasion', *Social Studies of Science,* 12(4): 535–558.

Leary, J. P. 2018. *Keywords. The New Language of Capitalism.* Chicago: Haymarket Books.

Macdonald, S., C. Gerbich, and M. von Oswald. 2018. 'No Museum is an Island: Ethnography beyond Methodological Containerism', *Museum & Society,* 16(2): 138–156.

Marguin, S., and T. Losekandt. 2017. *Studie zum Berliner Arbeitsmarkt der Kultur- und Kreativsektoren.* Berlin: Bildungswerk Berlin der Heinrich-Böll-Stiftung.

Ndikung, B. S. B. 2017. 'The Globalized Museum? Decanonisation as Method: A Reflection in Three Acts', Mousee Magazine. www.moussemagazine.it/the-globalized-museum-bonaventure-soh-bejeng-ndikung-documenta-14-2017/ (accessed 8 February 2022).

Ndikung, B. S. B. 2019. 'Dis-Othering as Method. LEH ZO, A ME KE NDE ZA', Curatorial Concept, published online. Berlin: SAVVY Contemporary. www.savvy-contemporary.com/site/assets/files/4038/geographiesofimagination_concept.pdf (accessed 8 February 2022).

Ndikung, B. S. B., and R. Römhild. 2013. 'The Post-Other as Avant-Garde', in D. Baker, and M. Hlavajova (eds), *We Roma: A Critical Reader in Contemporary Art*, 206–225. Amsterdam: Valiz.

Oswald, M. von, and J. Tinius. 2020. 'Introduction: Across Anthropology', in M. von Oswald, and J. Tinius (eds), *Across Anthropology. Troubling Colonial Legacies, Museums, and the Curatorial*, 17–44. Leuven: Leuven University Press.

Partridge, D. J., and M. Chin. 2019. 'Interrogating the Histories and Futures of "Diversity": Transnational Perspectives', *Public Culture*, 31(2): 197–214.

Pitts, J. 2019. *Afropean: Notes from Black Europe*. London: Penguin.

Rose, N. 2006. *The Politics of Life Itself. Biomedicine, Power, and Subjectivity in the Twenty-First Century*. Princeton: Princeton University Press.

Smith, T. 2015. *Talking Contemporary Curating*. New York: ICI.

Tinius, J. 2018. 'Awkward Art and Difficult Heritage: Nazi Art Collectors and Postcolonial Archives', in T. Fillitz, and P. van der Grijp (eds), *An Anthropology of Contemporary Art*, 130–145. London: Bloomsbury.

Tinius, J. 2020. 'Porous Membranes: Hospitality, Alterity, and Anthropology in a Berlin District Gallery', in M. von Oswald, and J. Tinius (eds), *Across Anthropology. Troubling Colonial Legacies, Museums, and the Curatorial*, 254–277. Leuven: Leuven University Press.

Tinius, J. 2021. 'The Anthropologist as Sparring Partner: Instigative Public Fieldwork, Curatorial Collaboration, and German Colonial Heritage', *Berliner Blätter*. 83: 65–85.

Tinius, J., and S. Macdonald. 2019. 'The Recursivity of the Curatorial', in R. Sansi (ed.), *The Anthropologist as Curator*, 35–58. London: Bloomsbury.

Trouillot, M.-R. 2003. 'Anthropology and the Savage Slot: The Poetics and Politics of Otherness', in *Global Transformations. Anthropology and the Modern World*, 7–28. New York: Palgrave.

Weheliye, A. G. 2005. 'Sounding Diasporic Citizenship', in *Phonographies: Grooves in Sonic Afro-Modernity*, 145–197. Durham, NC: Duke University Press.

Diversity Max*
Multiple Differences in Exhibition-Making in *Berlin Global* in the Humboldt Forum

Sharon Macdonald

Diversity has come to be considered an obvious good thing in most areas of public culture, including in the museum and heritage sector. Numerous programmes and initiatives have been designed to 'increase diversity' and to 'diversify'. These generally entail the implicit assumption that the aim should be to achieve as much diversity as possible. In other words, their goal is what I here call (using an orthography that I will explain later) 'diversity max*'.

In this chapter, my aim is not to question whether diversity is or is not a good thing. With caveats, I mostly agree that it is.[1] Rather, taking the assumed goodness of diversity, and the quest for more of it, as my starting point, I examine how exhibition-making is undertaken in a context of diversity-proliferation. In particular, I am interested in the question of 'maxing out' on diversity, either in the sense of achieving—or aiming to achieve—some kind of maximum coverage or of otherwise reaching limits on the range or forms of diversity included. Whether such coverage is deemed possible, or to what extent, depends on certain usually implicit, or only semi-explicit and taken-for-granted ideas about what 'diversity' means and how it is understood to operate, as well as about the practice through which diversification is attempted and realised. This is not to say, however, that such implicit or semi-implicit understandings of diversity are necessarily either fully shared or coherent. On the contrary, there may be multiple and even discrepant understandings at work without this necessarily being fully evident to participants collectively engaged in practice. This can have consequences for what a maximisation of diversity might mean and entail, including for whether it is imagined as even possible or desirable.

The questions that I raise here were prompted by conducting ethnographic fieldwork—as part of the multi-researcher museum and heritage project, *Making Differences*—with a team of progressive curators as they created a new exhibition in Berlin.[2] In multiple ways, they sought to make an exhibition that would be 'inclusive' and 'diverse' as well as for 'everybody' (words that they themselves used). Some of the questions are, however, also debated within political theory, if not always in quite the same way.

Putting some of these debates into conversation with ethnography, as I seek to do in this chapter, makes it possible to examine the specific language, context and practices that give shape to positions that might otherwise be only abstract or that might play out in other ways. It also highlights 'sticking points' or complications in the realisation. In this way, ethnography contributes to the task of understanding the workings of specific institutions that some political theorists see as vital for avoiding the analytical pitfalls of institution-blind extrapolations from 'formal political systems' (Tully 2004: 87). In the ethnographic case that I discuss, institutional, or even more locally specific, conditions—for example, the remit to address a 'public' whose 'diversity' is itself at issue—shape what is done and how. The fact that some of the dilemmas that arise are ones that are seen as rather intractable within political theory makes it unsurprising that they pose difficulties for curators. At the same time, however, I suggest that there are possibilities within the specific institution of the exhibition that allow, to some extent at least, for these to be accommodated or even brought productively together.

The ethnographic case is that of the curatorial team making the 4000m2 non-temporary exhibition called *Berlin Global*, which opened in 2021 in the Humboldt Forum. A large, costly and contested cultural development in Berlin, the Humboldt Forum houses exhibitions from various museums in a reconstructed city palace and is widely proclaimed as being a significant—if far from unproblematic—public statement about Germany and its worldview today. Especially in light of Germany's histories of Holocaust and colonialism, as well as experiences of migration and racism, how this new high-profile memory institution performs 'diversity' is of great political importance, as well as of considerable academic and public interest (see the Introduction to this volume). *Berlin Global* positions itself as addressing 'the diversity of Berlin—a city whose most striking feature is its heterogeneity,' as the first sentence in the exhibition's catalogue puts it (Leimbach and van Dülmen 2021: 5). Moreover, it has been flagged up by others involved in Berlin cultural institutions as 'a model project in terms of diversity'.[3] How it does diversity is, therefore, of considerable significance for the high-profile Humboldt Forum, as well as for cultural production more widely in the capital and beyond.

Below, I first explain the orthography of my title, which also highlights the broader ambiguity of diversity discourse as a signalling of diversity in relation to specific currently neglected differences versus invoking unlimited potential differences. I then look at the dominant model of 'diversity'—as the 'non-European' or 'other'—within the Humboldt Forum in relation to which *Berlin Global* was at least partly formulated. This is followed by other understandings of diversity—including that of migrants, of the non-mainstream, of subcultures, of lifestyles, or of everybody—that were mobilised or that otherwise arose, and how these were variously negotiated and accommodated. In the concluding discussion, I consider how these could be brought productively together, while also looking further at the limits of diversity max* and its wider implications.

Asterisked diversities

At a table strewn with papers, cups, biscuits and fruit, a group of women and men are discussing what in German is called 'gender-sensitive language' (*gendersensible Sprache*) or 'gender-correct language' (*gendergerechte Sprache*). At issue is whether they will use this in the planning document that will present the exhibition, at that time provisionally called *Berlin und die Welt* (Berlin and the World) to the public. What this language entails is using orthographic forms for certain nouns (usually for jobs or roles—such as curator or director) that do not use masculine forms as generic but indicate feminine—and all in-between—ones too, through specific linguistic suffixes. Most of those present at the meeting are nodding in ascent at using this, though there is at least one furrowed brow and a question of whether this language will also be used in the finished exhibition. If so, the questioner suggests, he thinks this might be confusing for visitors. Somebody else says that she too has been wondering about this. A freelance member of the team who has a lot of expertise in gender issues says that it is very important to bring greater awareness to these issues and that the finished exhibition definitely should do so. Several people nod, others look thoughtful. For now, however, it is agreed that the decision concerns the text for the document.

How the gender-sensitive language works is that compound nouns for roles, such as professions, are created that indicate feminine as well as masculine versions. So, for example, beginning from the fact that there are the words *Kurator* and *Kuratorin* (the 'in' indicating the feminine form) for male and female curators respectively, a compound form is created using either an underscore or 'Gendergap' (as it is sometimes also called in German), as in *Kurator_in*, or an asterisk, as in *Kurator*in*. These forms are taken to indicate not only 'either/or' but also further possible genders and sexualities.[4] In the meeting, it was argued that * especially opens up the latter and the decision was reached, for the document at least, to use the asterisk, referred to as *Sternchen*, literally 'little star'.

In using * in the orthography in my title, then, I am, like the curatorial team, harnessing its capacity to point to multiple possible—potentially even as yet unrecognised—diversities. Although the orthography was designed to address gender diversity—and although this was the focus of the use of the asterisk in the team discussion—I use it to indicate other diversities too. This is congruent with the team's attempt to consider many kinds of diversity, as I discuss further below. In using it in my title, I also position it as one might a number to indicate 'to the power of', thus drawing on its indeterminacy to signal potentially limitless multiplication, which is the topic of my diversity-max discussion.

For the curatorial team, using the asterisk in the text and presentation to be presented to the press and public in July 2016, felt bold and even a bit risky. It was, though, just one concern amidst the much bigger question of how the overall exhibition plans would be received within the wider context of the Humboldt Forum. The fact that the Humboldt Forum had been so much under the gaze of critical commentary—including for questions relating to difference and diversity—made this especially acute.

Diversity in the Humboldt Forum

A discourse of diversity had already been widely deployed to promote and legitimate the Humboldt Forum (see von Bose 2016) and this has continued. Berlin's main tourism-promotion organisation, Visit Berlin, for example, introduced an entry on the City Palace/ Humboldt Forum in 2020 as follows: 'a palace is being rebuilt in the heart of the city, not as a seat for kings and Kaisers—but as a museum for the whole world and all the diversity of its cultures'.[5] Although this appears to be an all-encompassing use of 'diversity', in practice it is used most often to index what are called 'the non-European collections' (*die außereuropäische Sammlungen*), namely those of the Ethnological Museum and the Museum of Asian Art, which occupy the largest areas of the reconstructed palace. For Visit Berlin and other organisations supporting this development, the non-European objects are regarded as bringing a welcome cultural diversity to Berlin and, at the same time, giving positive recognition to that non-European diversity through its incorporation into the important cultural venue of the Humboldt Forum (Macdonald 2016; von Bose 2016). A very different view, however, is held by groups such as Berlin Postcolonial, which regard the Humboldt Forum as a Eurocentric and colonial project (see Introduction and von Oswald, this volume), and argue that not only does this entail an implicit 'self' being juxtaposed with 'the other', but also 'Europe [being] constructed as the superior norm'.[6] Far from enriching culture, in this view, the Humboldt Forum's dominant model of diversity merely replicates limited binary formulations of difference, sustaining a hierarchical relationship between Europe and the rest of the world.

As planning for the Humboldt Forum had already been underway for many years by the time that it was decided, in 2015, to include a permanent space dedicated to Berlin, what was to become *Berlin Global* began in a context in which many parameters were fixed, politics were prickly and debate was heated. Under the leadership of Paul Spies, who in 2016 moved from Amsterdam to take up the directorship of the Berlin City Museum (Stadtmuseum Berlin) and the Chief Curatorship of what was usually referred to as 'the Berlin Exhibition' (*die Berlin Ausstellung*) in the Humboldt Forum, a team of curators—variously freelancers or from the City Museum or *KulturProjekte Berlin* (a Federal State non-profit cultural organisation which was jointly responsible, together with the City Museum, for the exhibition)—devised an approach that positioned the Berlin Exhibition as a kind of hinge, connecting with other parts of the Humboldt Forum, especially the displays upstairs of the Ethnological Museum and Museum of Asian Art, which Paul Spies, sometimes tongue-in-cheek referred to as 'the world above'. This connecting is evident in the working title, *Berlin and the World,* as well as in the Exhibition's stated aim to show Berlin's 'entanglement with the world' ('*Berlins Verflochtenheit mit der Welt*'; *Berlin und die Welt* 2016: 5). The wording of this aim is an outcome of much discussion of the potential dilemma inherent in the working title, namely that in the very act of trying to indicate the city's links with, and being part of, wider global relationships, it risks setting up a division between Berlin and the rest of the world and even of replicating an idea of diversity as being brought to Berlin by the world beyond, a double-bind that occurred, as described below, in other instances too.

In emphasising Berlin as entangled with other parts of the world, the curatorial team stressed that Berlin's impact elsewhere was not necessarily positive but could be damaging and destructive. In so doing, they addressed criticisms that the exhibition might be city marketing. In addition, however, they were responding to concerns voiced by activists, such as Berlin Postcolonial, and others, that the Humboldt Forum would give inadequate attention to colonial entanglements, especially with respect to the ethnological collections. Frequently discussed in team meetings, the curators sought to bring missing critical attention to colonialism, and related issues of racism, into the Humboldt Forum.

Many members of the team had knowledge of critical and postcolonial perspectives, and they augmented this during the exhibition-making process, by, for example, consulting experts in this area—such as one who highlighted ways in which images might be incipiently racist—and themselves undertaking anti-racist training. As part of this critical awareness, they not only attempted to avoid perspectives such as exoticism and stereotyping but also planned to point out how certain exhibitionary practices involving the display of other cultures have been part of the means of disseminating such negative representations. In so doing, the curatorial team aimed to bring critical attention to the model of diversity as the difference of the (non-European or exotic) other that they feared might be promulgated in other parts of the palace.

Double-binds and dilemmas in displaying diversity

In trying to devise ways of referring in the exhibition's display to problematic modes of representing diversity, however, the curators faced a double-bind—namely, that they might be seen to be reproducing the representations that they were seeking to criticise (see also Tinius, this volume). The clearest instance of this concerned curators' attempts to include discussion of *Völkerschauen*—'human shows', sometimes also called 'human zoos'. Especially popular in the late nineteenth and early twentieth centuries, these displayed living people, usually from countries outside Europe, in supposedly natural—but usually stereotypical and old-fashioned—scenes from their home countries. One such in Berlin in 1896, for example, was part of an exhibition that attracted an audience of over seven million people (Geppert 201: 56). The plan for *Berlin Global* was to discuss such shows in an exhibition area called 'Entertainment' (*Vergnügen*), the idea being that this would show that popular entertainment connected with other parts of the world could have negative dimensions. The difficulty came to a head when the designers (from the company Krafthaus/Facts & Fiction) proposed showing images of the shows in display-cases that would resemble large snow domes, in which one side would show original posters or photographs of the shows and the other would have information such as quotes about the poor living conditions to which performers were subjected. The designers argued persuasively that the display-cases would evoke the idea of ethnological display and of touristic practice, critically reminding visitors of their own role as tourists. After reflection, however, the curators decided that the double-bind risk that visitors would view the human zoos voyeuristically, replicating rather than challenging the problematic gaze, was too great, and the snow domes were, so to speak, dropped and the human show content later cut entirely. This is just one instance of a sticking point that is familiar from theory, in this case especially from discussion within anthropology about the discipline itself, which in its attempts to highlight and discuss difference may risk overemphasising it and even exoticising (e.g. Kapferer 2013). In exhibition-making, however, the problem is all the greater due to the visual and three-dimensional content and the fact that publics may well not read accompanying texts.

If the Berlin team tried to avoid reproducing the reductive model of diversity as the difference of the other—and even to confront it—what did they turn to instead? What was entailed by the max* approach to diversity that they took? Here I turn first to why what became *Berlin Global* was sometimes regarded as a model diversity project.

Model diversity and participation

In referring positively to the not yet opened Berlin Exhibition for its anticipated approach to diversity, Sandrine Micossé Aikins, the director of the new organisation Diversity Arts Culture, did so, she said, on account not only of its approach to personnel but also the diversity (*Vielfalt*) of perspectives that would be brought into the exhibition. At the time when the interview was conducted the then ten-person core curatorial team consisted of three men and seven women, of whom three of the latter identified as 'people of colour'—to use the terminology that, after much discussion, came to be used within the team, and the rest as white. Two of the people of colour, both identifying as Turkish-German Berliners, had been recruited as part of a concerted effort to do what was specifically referred to as diversifying the team. It had been expected that this diversification would have resulted in also recruiting somebody from the black community, and it was still hoped that this would be possible. While gender and colour were most often remarked upon in explicit considerations of the diversity of the team, other kinds of difference were also sometimes commented upon as significant in the media and by the team themselves as important. These included the mix of West and East Germans, with one team member having been brought up in East Berlin; and the mix of countries, with not only Paul Spies but two other members of the original curatorial team being from the Netherlands. Within the team, the fact that not all team members identified as heterosexual was also occasionally mentioned; and it was sometimes reflected upon whether the team should also be diversified further to include a greater range of physical diversity, in relation to ableism, as well as of social background.

The diversity of team members was considered important to helping the team themselves not just represent but also perceive and potentially include a 'diversity of perspectives,' as Aikins had put it. As their attempts to appoint new members had not resulted in the team becoming more diverse—and as the team size inevitably limited the amount of diversity it was possible to include—they sought to expand the range of inputs through their consultations with others (including some who they called 'critical friends' who were consulted over a longer time-period), and through various areas within the exhibition that would be left open for changing content suggested by different groups themselves. All of this was in order to 'bring in' more—and more diverse—perspectives.[7]

In trying to achieve this, however, the curators did not want to replicate what they saw as a problematic position of themselves just representing the perspectives of others. Rather, they sought modes in which diverse individuals and groups might be enabled to represent themselves. The key word here was 'participation'. This was the subject of extensive discussion among the curators, including by a sub-group that wrote up a guiding document about it, drawing on literature including Nina Simon's categorisation of different types of participation (2010). The considerable thought—and hours and hours of discussion—given to it was itself an indication of just how seriously they took the task they had set themselves, as was the fact that they also established a post specifically to initiate and manage participative work. Many participative projects were undertaken during the exhibition's making, bringing collaboration with a wide range of individuals and groups, including artists, schools and local initiatives of various sorts. The number of collaborations, although substantial, was, however, necessarily limited by the time available. Indeed, as participative work is typically intensive and time-consuming, attempting to diversify could lead to a paradoxical limiting of coverage. This is just one of the constraints that diversity max* may bump up against in practice. So how, in the face of that, was diversifying, with its necessary selection, done?

Especially significant in the case of *Berlin Global* was the idea of diversifying beyond the status quo and the 'usual suspects.' In addition, selection was often in relation to particular topics already selected. Important too, however, were operational dimensions of selection, a matter to which ethnography is well-placed to attend. The curators' own networks—sometimes connected to their previous exhibition or community work—were often a starting point in the selection of participants, sometimes one contact leading to another. They asked friends for further contacts; and in curatorial meetings they shared information about people that they had heard about, perhaps also from the news or other exhibitions. Through the many participative projects established, the selection of certain exhibition content was to varying degrees delegated. Thus, for example, a refugee Syrian journalist was invited to interview refugees from various countries, herself playing a role in choosing at least some of the further participants. Or, to take another example, fashion school students worked together to select examples of 'Berlin style' and create some of the content for the part of the exhibition dealing with fashion.

It is beyond the scope of this chapter to look in more detail at how the participative approaches in *Berlin Global* worked, how participants experienced the collaboration and how visitors viewed the results. Research into this is underway within the *Making Differences* project.[8] As *Berlin Global* embraced participative approaches to an unusual extent, such research can make an important contribution to the wider understanding of how participation operates within museum practice. Not least, it can help show the extent to which it succeeds in diversifying, and in what ways. In the following section, I look further at the various understandings of diversity—which also shaped how selections were made—that were present during the making of *Berlin Global*. These different understandings, as well as certain dynamics and tensions between them, are also present, as will be shown, within political theory.

Expanding and constraining diversities

In July 2016, after intense months of discussion of the use of asterisks and far more, the Berlin exhibition-team presented the principles—referred to as the concept—that would guide their exhibition, together with some proposed content, to the press and public. This included the following statement about diversity:

> The exhibition is intended to reflect the diversity of society, which is shaped by migration, diverse lifestyles and lived realities. It should give space for diverse, quite

> contradictory, unexpected perspectives on Berlin, including beyond the mainstream (Spies et al. 2016: 4).

Although short and perhaps not especially striking at first glance, the statement is a condensed result of a struggle over certain difficulties. While not explicitly articulated as such, a core dilemma concerned whether diversity is understood in terms of multiple differences that result in everybody being regarded as different in some way, or whether difference is more specifically difference from what in the quote is expressed as 'the mainstream'.

This is a tension that has also fuelled debates in political theory. Giving recognition to difference rather than operating a liberal 'politics of universalism', as philosopher Charles Taylor (1994) has famously written, has been a major development in many societies since the later twentieth century. As he explains: 'Where the politics of universal dignity fought for forms of nondiscrimination that were quite "blind" to the ways in which citizens differ, the politics of difference often redefines nondiscrimination as requiring that we make these distinctions the basis of differential treatment' (1994: 39). What this opens up, however, is the question of what counts as a difference that deserves such differential treatment—and who gets to decide and how. Here it is worth noting (as also pointed out in the Introduction to this volume), that museums and heritage—especially those with high social and cultural status—can be regarded as especially significant cultural agencies on account of their historically-based legitimating role and capacity to make difference visible for the public.

As various commentators have pointed out (e.g. Smits-Leutoff 2018, Vertovec 2019), both in public life and in academic theorising, there has been a tendency towards identification of more and more differences—towards, we might say, diversity max*. Political sociologists Raphael Baehr and Daniel Gordon refer to this as diversity's 'fractal dynamic' (2018: 979). Intersectionality—how differences may intersect to create more specific differences, e.g. black women—contributes further to this by creating even more specific differential conditions that need to be recognised. Not only does this create an issue of coverage, it also comes together with a tendency to identify more and more specific differences beyond those of relatively clearly discriminated against 'minorities' (to use the language in which these early claims were made) that were the focus of the earlier politics of difference.

The proliferative dynamic was evident in the making of *Berlin Global*. At a public presentation of the exhibition plans in 2019, audience members posed questions, some asking about content they hoped to see there. One question was whether the exhibition would include anything about eating, and specifically about *Curry Wurst* (the famous Berlin hot dog with curry-flavoured ketchup). 'Yes', replied Chief Curator Paul Spies, 'Curry Wurst will be included, in [the exhibition area on] Entertainment'. Further, however, diverging from the content that was in fact planned at that point but showing, perhaps, the way that a diversity max* impulse had taken hold, discursively at least, he continued: 'What many people don't know is that there are many kinds of curry in the world, not just that of the powder sprinkled on the *Wurst*.' Then, after reiterating the hope to have a flexible structure in order to include other topics and groups that could not be part of the permanent opening exhibition, he remarked: 'Maximal is maximal.'

Yet, where does 'maximal' end? The problem with allowing an endlessly proliferating form of diversity is that it dilutes the significance of any particular diversity. This is especially the case when difference is individualised, leading to the conclusion that 'everybody' is different in some way. Feminist critics (e.g. Fraser 2000) have been at the forefront of arguing that such expansion of the recognition of difference in effect undermines the very political efficacy for which it was devised—namely to address marginalised positions in relation to a privileged mainstream.

In the statement about diversity within the concept document of the Berlin exhibition—and even more so in the thoughtful and sometimes lengthy discussions of the team that led to it—there is awareness of this problem, signalled directly by the reference to 'beyond the mainstream.' However, the statement does not call *only* for inclusion of non-mainstream difference. Rather, it attempts to ensure that the non-mainstream is present but without defining diversity exclusively in these terms. The phrase 'the diversity of society' leaves open what is referred to—Berlin, Germany, the world? Moreover, the reference to 'lifestyles and lived realities'—rather fuzzy and open-ended designations—opens up an unlimited expansive understanding of diversity. While these two positions—diversity as beyond the mainstream and diversity as all kinds of lifestyles and lives—tend to be seen as opposed at an abstract level within political theory, within the context of exhibition-making, they can be practically accommodated. In effect, the exhibition attempts to speak to as many people as possible while at the same time giving as much recognition as feasible to the usually marginalised. Both of these are, however, necessarily limited by the fact that there is an inevitable 'max'—the inherent limitlessness of diversity. As such, the question of which specific differences and diversities to address does not go away entirely.

Migration

Although the statement on diversity in the 2016 concept document above does not specifically mention possible differences such as those of gender, sexuality or age (though some are mentioned elsewhere in the document), it does refer to migration, and indeed does so before anything else. This reflects the fact that migration is seen as a core concern for the exhibition. It was one of the first topics to be listed for inclusion in the exhibition's planning when the team did their initial brainstorming sessions, and some of the first freelancer team members had expertise in exhibiting migration. Within the framework of Berlin and the World—which gave priority to highlighting global interconnectedness—it was clearly vital that migration should be foregrounded in this way and that it should thread throughout the exhibition. On the one hand, giving priority to migration could push against the limitless expansion of diversity. On the other, unless 'migration' is reduced to a homogenous difference of 'the migrant', migration itself opens up to the expansion of difference in that there are potentially numerous different realisations of migration (i.e. from different places, at different times, with different genders, sexualities, religions, lifestyles etc). As such, even foregrounding migration only partially limits diversity proliferation. At the same time, however, migration sets up a further dilemma over which the curators struggled and that led them to emphasise certain already-present tendencies in addressing diversity.

Migration was considered crucial as a vector between Berlin and the rest of the world, and integral to highlighting the diversity of Berlin. In initial plans, it was listed as one of eight 'aspects' of the exhibition. These aspects were thematic areas, the others being: Images of Berlin, Revolution, Free Space, Entertainment, War, Boundaries and Fashion. Migration was, thus, the only one that could be said to be 'a diversity', though other aspects could certainly also accommodate it, as was intended. Although the initial idea was that these aspects would not map directly onto space—one reason why they were called 'aspects'—once thinking about the exhibition layout began, they came, almost by default, to do so, and by the time of the concept document in July 2016 they were presented as such. Putting migration into one space, however, contained it and meant that the diversity that it signalled was less prominent than it would otherwise have been, and it ran the risk that migration would be seen as separate from all of the other aspects. Later, however, initially for practical reasons, migration was moved to the last room in the exhibition. The conceptual advantage of this quickly became clear. Placed at the end of exhibition, migration could act as a kind of 'apotheosis'—this was the word Paul Spies enthusiastically and semi-jokingly used— giving migration greater significance once again.

Simmering in the background during all of this, however, was the dilemma that the topic of migration raises—namely, that it seems to single out people with what in Germany is called *Migrationshintergrund*—a migratory background. Such a singling out could easily inadvertently create an implicit category of non-migrant Berliners who might thus be seen as somehow the 'real' Berliners. Moreover, given the incipient binarism of the exhibition's then title, *Berlin and the World,* it could map onto this, equating migrants with the world beyond Berlin. All of this came to a head in a meeting of the curators with 'critical friends' (selected external advisors—of which I was one), at which several of us, including me, raised these points.[9] Following discussion, it was decided instead to emphasise the multiple positionings of individuals in relation to other places—i.e. not just that of migrating into Berlin. This meant an emphasis on more diverse forms of interconnections. Various possible terms were discussed as alternatives to 'migration' and that of '*Verflechtungen*'—a word that had already figured in some previous discussion and text—was deemed to best capture the idea. Often translated as 'entanglements', the German suggests something less untidy, more like braiding or plaiting together. Following weeks of further discussion and some misgivings—and even a public plea made for alternative suggestions—'interconnection' was selected as the English wording to be used. While in general the move to interconnections was regarded as good, in order to avoid the dilemmas posed by using migration, there was also concern that it might relativise issues faced by migrants, such as discrimination and border regimes. But precisely by raising this concern, the exhibition-makers attempted to address this.

Interconnections

In terms of doing diversity, what happened in relation to migration, then, was a shift from a model of relatively discrete differences—often talked about in terms of 'communities'—to a much broader idea of interconnection. A move in the max* direction, it more readily allowed consideration of various and complicated migration stories, and supported the exhibition's attempt to highlight multiple possible connections across difference. In many ways, this was an articulation of something that was already being put into practice, and that drew on critique made by some of the team members (Miera and Bluche 2014). To gather stories and objects for this area of the exhibition, then, rather than contacting a specific 'community', curators sought out organisations in which participants came together from a wide range of diverse, and often multiple, countries and experiences. Furthermore, rather than asking them about their migration routes—a trope in which migration reaches its apotheosis in the new country—they were asked to talk about their connections with various other places, within Germany, as well as beyond, which were not necessary tied to their migration experiences.

Within the exhibition, this is realised in the *Interconnection* area by exhibits such as 'audio portraits', in which speakers tell of their 'interconnected lives' (as the text panel describing this puts it) and sometimes narrate their experiences of discrimination and exclusion. These are accompanied by art work created by the Tape That collective and consisting of different designs and selected objects that feature in the narratives (Images 81. and 8.2). At computer terminals, visitors can input six cities that are meaningful to them in various ways—places where relatives live or for which they feel longing, as well as where they have lived. The responses then turn into lines on a spinning globe—even if all of the responses are within close geographical proximity (Image 8.3). This exhibit resembles the large globe near the beginning of the exhibition (Image 8.4), which likewise suggests the world as criss-crossed by many and various routes. This motif is also present in the exhibition's background design, also created by Tape That, which consists of lines in a 'network of perspectives'.

Visitors' own interconnections, the idea of individual connections—and thus individualised diversity—is threaded through the exhibition via each visitor being invited to don an armband with a chip that records their responses to particular questions. At the end of the exhibition, in an area called the Lounge, they can input this and be shown what percentage of other visitors replied in what way to each question. On a card, they then receive a question—such as 'What does security mean to you?' or 'What does tradition mean to you?'—with the suggestion to discuss this with other visitors who are present. To encourage this, the area is filled with large green cushions in the form of gigantic tree-creepers (Image 8.5), given the witty name of '*Berlianen*'—blending together the word 'Berlin' with that for tree-creeper, *liana*. The idea is, then, to make connections with others, finding possible commonalities, though also differences. Individuals are not here classified into categories, then, but neither does the exhibition end simply with a celebration of diversity for its own sake. Instead, the possibility for multiple connection and difference is opened up but it is not left without implications. Rather, it leads to questions whose answers may have consequences that visitors are encouraged to consider—and that might even result in visitors changing their minds.

8.1 *Tape That sound portraits and artworks. Photograph by Thomas Beaney. Reproduced courtesy of Stadtmuseum Berlin and Kulturprojekte Berlin.*

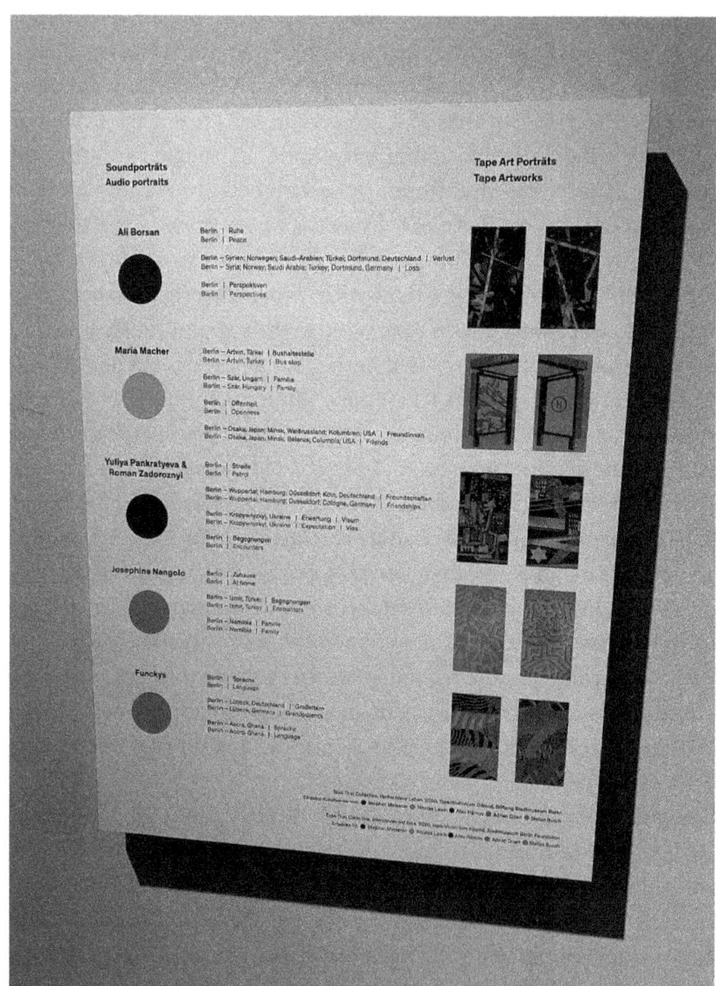

8.2 Interconnections area in Berlin Global. Photograph by Thomas Beaney. Reproduced courtesy of Stadtmuseum Berlin and Kulturprojekte Berlin.

8.3 Computer terminal showing visitors' connections. Photograph by Thomas Beaney. Reproduced courtesy of Stadtmuseum Berlin and Kulturprojekte Berlin.

8.4 Globe showing multiple connections near the beginning of Berlin Global. Photograph by Thomas Beaney. Reproduced courtesy of Stadtmuseum Berlin and Kulturprojekte Berlin.

8.5 Berlianen in Berlin Global. Photograph by Thomas Beaney. Reproduced courtesy of Stadtmuseum Berlin and Kulturprojekte Berlin.

Concluding discussion

In the making of *Berlin Global*, then, diversity was understood both expansively and also in terms of difference from the mainstream, with the inequalities and discrimination that could come with the latter. Yet rather than these being incommensurable, as they may seem in the abstract, they come together within the exhibition to fulfil different functions—sometimes to bring in more of the difference that has been left out and often, indeed, to highlight this very fact (e.g. in consideration of migrants), and at others to attempt to recognise the potential multiplicity of the diversity of members of the public and their possible interconnections. But this is not just about putting theoretical alternatives alongside each other in practice. Rather, the challenge to the status quo involved in 'beyond the mainstream' is coupled with a provocation to visitors to move beyond their usual connections and to recognise and make others.

In neither of these formulations of diversity, however, is its maximisation endless. Limits are set by constraints of space and time, as well as by prior interests and personal connections. They are at least in part also set by the very imagination of what might constitute a difference—though opening up the possibility for visitors to provide input and for others to get in touch and exhibit within the space mitigates this to some extent. Yet, the fact of limits does not in any case invalidate the attempt to include as much diversity as possible—to be as diversity max* as can be. Certainly, there needs to be careful examination of the kinds of assumptions that might creep in, shaping selections in unexamined ways. But compared with approaches that try to fill a predetermined hit-list of diversities, or to map them (see Tinius, this volume), the max* approach keeps options open. Moreover, it does not rule out being accompanied by the aim to select particular diversities on account of their having been underrepresented, or due to a story considered important to be told. And it does not rule out *not* covering certain differences. In the catalogue of *Berlin Global*, this is aptly put by Paul Spies and Brinda Sommer when they write that 'a diversity of voices does not mean whateverism' (Spies and Sommer 2021: 16). '[O]n the contrary', they continue, 'it requires a stance. However, we do not want to instruct anyone with our stance; rather, we understand it as an invitation for discussion' (ibid.).

The question of the limits of diversity max*—of where it maxes out—are, of course, not only numerical but also political. Who is included and who is excluded is another way of putting the questions raised above. A diversity max* impulse, however, raises the issue of how much of the political spectrum should be given space or voice in the exhibition. During the making of *Berlin Global* this was directly addressed by Paul Spies in a lecture (subsequently published, 2018) titled 'Populists, No Thanks! Or: Populists Welcome!' ('Populisten, nein danke! Oder: Populisten Willkommen!'). The lecture illustrated a thoroughly diversity max* approach, noting that people define themselves as different from their neighbours through numerous differences of style or preference (p.186). If museums were not to just attempt to speak to 'communities, often described as 'minorities' (p.186)—but to truly address 'culture for all'—then what about groups such as populists? Was that a step too far or should the museum only speak with politically-correct thinking people? Describing an attempt to work with populists (right-wing football fans) in Amsterdam Museum, during his time there as director, Spies' argued that museums should have the courage to try to engage with the broadest spectrum of society—including those with what the curators themselves might regard as repugnant views.

So far, *Berlin Global* has not done this, though Paul Spies has suggested that it might be considered in the future for one of the free spaces of the exhibition. Also, however, he accepts arguments from some of the other curators that in deciding which diversities to include, a line should be drawn to exclude those who would themselves seek to exclude diversity.

The difficulties over diversity—including diversity max*—are certainly not restricted to the *Berlin Global* exhibition. What kind of model of diversity to deploy, how to put it into operation and who to involve in the process and how are questions for all exhibitions. So too are those of where to draw the lines. As evident in this case, and brought to light especially through ethnographic research into the details of the specific case, some of these difficulties are inherent in the very idea of diversity—its proliferative or fractal tendencies, the risk of categorical models, and the double-bind of attempting to highlight problematic forms. Others, however, come into play in the making—the search for appropriate metaphors and terms, scenographic design and even the diacritics of language.

Regarding the latter: the asterisk made it through to the finished exhibition. Berliners are addressed as Berliner*innen and visitors as Besucher*innen, and so forth, thus invoking, within these categories and orthographically at least, a potentially limitless diversity.

Acknowledgments

I am grateful to the Alexander von Humboldt Foundation for supporting this research through its award of an Alexander von Humboldt Professorship. The *Making Differences*: Transforming Museums and Heritage project received further funding from the Museum für Naturkunde Berlin and the Prussian Cultural Heritage Foundation. I heartily thank the curatorial team of what became *Berlin Global* for allowing an anthropologist on board; special thanks for comments on drafts of this chapter go to Frauke Miera, Daniel Morat, Brinda Sommer and Paul Spies. I also thank members of the *Making Differences* team and other researchers within CARMAH (the Centre for Anthropological Research on Museums and Heritage) for their helpful comments, in particular: Christoph Bareither, Nazli Cabadag, Larissa Förster, Christine Gerbich, Hannes Hacke, Duane Jethro, Margareta von Oswald, Katarzyna Puzon and Jonas Tinius. Mike Beaney commented on more than one version and helped me to see it through. Any remaining errors or misjudgements are my responsibility.

Notes

1 For caveats, see the Introduction to this volume and, among others, Ahmed 2007.

2 *Making Differences: Transforming Museums and Heritage in the Twenty-First Century* was funded by my Alexander von Humboldt Professorship (2015–2022), together

with further funding from the Humboldt-Universität zu Berlin, the Museum für Naturkunde Berlin and the Prussian Cultural Heritage Foundation. For further details, see the Introduction to this volume and https://www.carmah.berlin/making-differences-in-berlin/ (accessed 30 March 2022).

3 All translations from German throughout are by me unless otherwise specified. This quote is from Sandrine Micossé-Aikins in a discussion with Claudia van Laak in 'Diversität im Berliner Kulturbetrieb—"Wir können der Anfang von etwas Neuem sein"', 25 August 2019, https://www.deutschlandfunk.de/diversitaet-im-berliner-kulturbetrieb-wir-koennen-der.911.de.html?dram:article_id=457039 (accessed 30 November 2020).

4 It is indicative of many other comments that I have witnessed during my fieldwork concerning the curatorial team of what became *Berlin Global*. Though some see the underscore as doing this too. For discussion, see, for example: https://link.springer.com/chapter/10.1007/978-3-531-91972-0_90; https://www.tagesspiegel.de/politik/geschlechtergerechte-sprache-kommt-das-gendersternchen-jetzt-in-den-duden/22573778.html (accessed 30 November 2020).

5 https://www.visitberlin.de/en/humboldt-forum-berlin-city-palace (accessed 30 November 2020). In the German version of this, the word *Vielfalt* is used for 'diversity'. The terms *Diversität* and *Vielfalt* are often used more-or-less interchangeably for 'diversity', though the latter is of more longstanding and wider use, and includes the variety or kinds of media that might be used, while *Diversität* is more likely to be used for contemporary diversification initiatives.

6 http://www.no-humboldt21.de/resolution/ (last accessed 30 November 2020). The issues were intensified further by questions over the provenance and possible restitution of objects from the ethnological museum—see Förster, this volume.

7 I have already discussed notions of 'perspective' and 'multiperspectivity' in the Humboldt Forum, as well as in anthropology. See Macdonald 2023.

8 This research is being conducted by Irene Hilden and Andrei Zavadski. Participation has also been a focus in work for *Making Differences* at various other museums in Berlin. See the chapters by Gerbich and by Garbellotto and Nadim, this volume; and Puzon 2019; Macdonald, Gerbich, Gram, Puzon and Shatanawi 2021.

9 The professors of social anthropology, Ayşe Çağlar and Regina Römhild, both of whom have been critical of certain models of migration (e.g. Çağlar 2001; 2016; Römhild 2014; 2017), were especially vocal, and Regina proposed the term *Verflechtungen*. In a recent study (Macdonald 2023), I provide some further discussion of the use of this term within the exhibition.

References

Ahmed, S. 2007. 'The language of diversity', *Ethnic and Racial Studies*, 30(2): 235–56.

Baehr, P., and D. Gordon. 2018. 'Paradoxes of diversity', in W. Outhwaite, and S. Turner (eds), *Sage Handbook of Political Sociology*, 977–988. London: Sage Publications.

Bose, F. von. 2016. *Das Humboldt Forum. Eine Ethnografie seiner Planung*. Berlin: Kadmos.

Çağlar, A. 2001. 'Constraining metaphors and the transnationalisation of spaces in Berlin', *Journal of Ethnic and Migration Studies*, 27(4): 601–13.

Çağlar, A. 2016. 'Still "migrants" after all those years: foundational mobilities, temporal frames and emplacement of migrants', *Journal of Ethnic and Migration Studies*, 42(6): 952–969.

Fraser, N. 2000. 'Rethinking recognition', *New Left Review*, 3: 107–120.

Geppert, A. 2010. *Fleeting Cities. Imperial Expositions in Fin-de-Siècle Europe.* Heidelberg: Springer.

Kapferer, B. 2013. 'How anthropologists think: configurations of the exotic', *Journal of the Royal Anthropological Institute*, 19: 813–836.

Leimbach, S., and M. van Dülmen. 2021. 'Exhibition, experience, city walk', in M. van Dülmen, S. Leimbach, P. Spies, and B. Sommer (eds), *Berlin Global*, 4–7. Berlin: Distanz Verlag.

Macdonald, S. 2016. 'New constellations of difference in Europe's 21st Century Museumscape', *Museum Anthropology*, 39(1): 4–19.

Macdonald, S. 2023. 'Multiperspectivity and anthropological engagements in heritage-making. Challenges from the Humboldt Forum, Berlin', in E. Gilberthorpe, and F. de Jong (eds), *Anthropological Perspectives on Global Challenges.* London: Routledge.

Macdonald, S., C. Gerbich, R. Gram, K. Puzon, and M. Shatanawi. 2021. 'Reframing Islam? Potentials and challenges of participatory initiatives in museums and heritage', in K. Puzon, S. Macdonald, and M. Shatanawi (eds), *Heritage and Islam in Europe*, 212–230. Abingdon: Routledge.

Miera, F., and L. Bluche. 2014. 'Inclusive collecting strategies of city museums in a diverse society: Thoughts on the implementation of multi-perspectivity beyond group categories', in P. Innocenti (ed.), *Migrating Heritage. Experiences of Cultural Dialogue in Europe*, 177–188. Farnham: Ashgate.

Puzon, K. 2019. 'Participatory matters: Access, migration and heritage in Berlin Museums', in H. Oevermann, and E. Gantner (eds), *Securing Urban Heritage: Agents, Access, and Securitization*, 31–46. Abingdon and New York: Routledge.

Reus-Smit, C. 2018. *On Cultural Diversity: International Theory in a World of Difference.* Cambridge: Cambridge University Press.

Römhild, R. 2014. 'Diversität?! Postethnische Perspektiven für eine reflexive Migrationsforschung', *Kultur, Gesellschaft, Migration*, 255–70. Wiesbaden: Springer.

Römhild, R. 2017. 'Beyond the bounds of the ethnic: for postmigrant social and cultural research', *Journal of Aesthetics and Culture*, 9(2): 69–75.

Simon, N. 2010. *The Participatory Museum.* Santa Cruz: Museum 2.0.

Spies, P. 2018. 'Populisten nein danke! Oder Populisten, willkommen! Fünf Ansätze aus dem Amsterdam Museum für ein offene Museum', *Szenographie in Ausstellungen und Museen VIII.*: 186–93.

Spies, P. et al. 2016. *Berlin und die Welt: Konzept der Ausstellung des Landes Berlins im Humboldt Forum.* Berlin.

Spies, P., and B. Sommer. 2021. 'Totally interconnected', in M. Dülmen, S. Leimbach, P. Spies, and B. Sommer (eds), *Berlin Global*, 14–17. Berlin: Distanz Verlag.

Taylor, C. 1994. 'The Politics of Recognition', in A. Gutman (ed.), *Multiculturalism: Examining the Politics of Recognition*, 25–73. Cambridge, MA: Princeton University Press.

Tully, J. 2004. 'Recognition and dialogue: the formation of a new field', *Critical Review of International Social and Political Philosophy*, 7(3): 84–96.

Vertovec, S. 2019. 'Talking around super-diversity', *Ethnic and Racial Studies*, 42(1): 125–139.

Diversifying the Collections at the Museum of European Cultures

Magdalena Buchczyk

In June 2019, the Museum of European Cultures (Museum Europäischer Kulturen, Staatliche Museen zu Berlin, or "MEK") hosted a conference titled What's Missing? Collecting and Exhibiting Europe. The conference discussions explored how historical collections could tell more diverse stories (Edenheiser 2020: 15), and participants called for the inclusion of a greater variety of objects, people and narratives. Amid heated public debates about diversity, the What's Missing? proceedings laid out a path for museums like the MEK to rebuild their collections and change their public perception.

This chapter examines the ways in which the MEK has diversified its collections. It is based on archival and ethnographic research I conducted at the MEK between 2019 and 2020, which includes grey literature, archival material, semi-structured interviews with the curatorial and education team, as well as notes taken during the regular curatorial meetings. Rather than focusing on participatory or project-based collecting (Tietmeyer & Meijer-van Mensch 2013), I consider the everyday acquisition activities of the curatorial team, and identify how the diversity of the collections have been shaped over time. Against the historical morphology of the collection, I discuss how diversity is understood by members of the MEK's curatorial team. I go on to explore the MEK's new collection policy and recent object acquisitions as attempts to diversify. I argue that collection diversification initiatives are rooted in the past, in curatorial practices and in anticipated potential futures.

Describing diversity

> The MEK differs from other ethnological museums and museums of everyday life due to its European perspective and its thematic focus on diverse cultural identities and cultural contacts (Collection Concept 2019, 7).
>
> The goal of the MEK collection is to preserve contemporary and historic manifestations of cultural identities in Europe, to allow comparisons to be formed between them and to highlight differences and similarities. The objects in the collection

> reflect the diversity of cultural identities in Europe, reveal cultural contacts and represent the formation of groups, hybridities and boundaries (Collection Concept 2019, 8).

Diversity plays a central role in the MEK's understanding of its collections. Yet in my conversations with museum curators, I observed a range of ideas and practices. As one curator remarked, the team tends to 'think diversity *(Vielfalt)* in different directions'. One basic difference centred on its definition. Many of the curators with whom I spoke distinguished between *Vielfalt* and *Diversität* (see Macdonald in this volume). According to one senior staff member, *Diversität* describes the social aspects of diversity such as ethnicity, migration history, gender, sexuality or dis/ability. *Vielfalt* is a broader and vaguer term indicating plurality or heterogeneity in general. For her, the collection's temporal, spatial and social plurality are examples of *Vielfalt*. The temporal plurality is the period of time covered by the collections, that is, from the 18th to 21st centuries. The social plurality of the collections refers to the classes from which the objects are drawn. Most of the collections stem from lower- and middle-class material culture, because historically, upper-class material culture was the exclusive domain of art and design museums, and the Museum of European Cultures features objects from everyday life. Spatial plurality refers to the geographical scope of the collections. Though the museum is devoted to 'European cultures', the majority of its objects are from German-speaking regions.

In my conversations with museum staff, diversity in the sense of *Vielfalt* was both an attribute and a benchmark. Some stressed the collection's variety. As one curator remarked:

> I think that it is really hard to find a similar collection of such great diversity. We really have everything from a spoon to a bridal gown, and everything in between.

But despite the MEK's vast and heterogeneous collections of objects and images, others pointed out signs of bias. One curator discussed how difficult it was to find non-Christian objects in the historical collections while preparing an exhibition on life rituals. She complained that the collections were uneven, 'in some areas already diverse (vielfältig), in others not at all'. Depending on the topic, the collections could yield a diversity of examples or it could be spotty and uninspiring.

One curator, who had worked for decades at the museum, pointed to the recent shifts in curatorial practices:

> I would say that diversity (*Diversität*) is much more important to us today than it was in the past, when we might have chosen a particular population group [or] social class as our research topic. We don't really work that way anymore.

The curator suggested that there was a significant shift away from specialist topic areas to *Diversität*. Rather than documenting the material culture of a group, such as working-class women, museum acquisitions now focus on capturing topics from different perspectives.

During a discussion on *Diversität* with a senior curator, she initially questioned the usefulness of the idea for the museum:

> With an object, I do not ask myself, 'Is that diverse?' That's not a question I'm posing. Instead, I ask myself: 'Does this represent an interesting perspective, which so far has not been present in the collection?'

But then, paradoxically, she described strategies for making the museum more diverse:

> I strongly believe that from the gender perspective, I'm more interested in feminist objects per se. And of course a perspective that is beyond 'majority German'. I think that's very important. No matter what that is. Is that POC (people of colour) or is this Turkish community, or are they the children of Vietnamese contract workers from East Germany? And otherwise, I'm looking at many things—that's where the question of class comes into the equation.

The curator restated the importance of diversity as a matter of representation and a commitment to bringing in new perspectives. Here, the emphasis was on the targeted inclusion of missing protagonists within the collections (Aksoy 2020). Another member of the museum indicated that the work of *Diversität* required ongoing attention to the ways in which different perspectives are tied with power relations:

> Diversity is always about keeping an eye on what is the 'majority society' and what are 'minorities'. What is considered 'normal' and what is not seen as normal. And what are the positions of social power, what are the positions from which one makes oneself very difficult to hear, or that usually do not appear.

In her view, the task of shaping the collection was to determine the missing perspectives and critically examine the normative frameworks that reproduce majority positions and unequal structures.

During the conversations, the members of the curatorial team pointed to some of the challenges related to collection diversification. They noted that diversity could be mobilised to different ends and might risk becoming an institutional exercise in ticking boxes. Moreover, instrumental attempts at collection diversification might reproduce privilege rather than challenge it. Another curator raised concerns that *Diversität* was an empty slogan that concealed wider challenges in curatorial practice:

> Diversity is a worn-out term that is often used in such a political field. I have the feeling that it is also often used as a fig leaf. My colleague...talks about a feel-good museology. That's where this term would actually fall in for me, when you talk about diversity in the museum. Nevertheless, I don't want to completely rule out the possibility that I might use it in some public circumstances, because I can't handle it any other way.

For her, diversity is both a hollow phrase and a cover for other issues. Practice centred on diversity, she argued, ends up being about the museum rather than the underlying issues that led to the problem of diversity. A member of the educational team shared with me another challenge to diversity-oriented practice in the museum. She found that diversity was perplexing and obstructive for educational work. Tackling many different and complex topics within one exhibition space might risk making museum displays illegible and confusing for visitors.

While the idea of diversity is a key part of the museum's mission, it seems to escape definition. The MEK curatorial team not only conceptualised diversity 'in different directions' but also emphasised divergent practices of collection diversification. Given the fuzzy boundary between *Vielfalt* and *Diversität*, it is impossible to determine a single institutional model for collection diversity. What the narratives seemed to agree on was that diversification was an evolving idea that reflected changing institutional practices. Indeed, the different priorities of collection diversity, the commitments of the curatorial team, the ways of doing diversity and their effects have been shaped over time. The next section looks at the historical origins of the collections and focuses on the processes that led to the current the composition of the collections and how they affect curatorial work today.

Reshaping diversity

The MEK collection is the outcome of historically contingent ideas of diversity and difference. The main portion of the collection originated in the Museum of German Costume and Household Products, which was initiated by fears that industrial culture would erase the regional diversity of the countryside (Virchow 1890, Hartung 2010, Tietmeyer 2013). Vernacular objects such as clothing or crafts were classified as indicators of distinct regional, cultural landscapes (*Kulturlandschaften*). The aim was to collect the 'tangible folklore' of German peoples ranging 'from Tyrol to Schleswig-Holstein, from the Lithuanian border to the Flemings, from the Transylvanian Saxons to the Vasken Forest' (Jahn 1889: 336). This acquisition practice was embedded in the tradition of language island research (Sprachinselforschung), which explores how 'Germanic Sprachinseln (islands of German speakers), have clung tenaciously to the soil of their forebears even as the tides of German borders have ebbed and flowed around them' (O'Donnell et al. 2010: 1). Within this cultural island imaginary, the collection worked to showcase 'the various regions of Germany in the characteristic features of the population, in their clothing and in household products' (Jahn 1889: 337). Ideas of territorialised difference and regional diversity informed collection practices in the early stages museum and, as I show below, its successor institutions.

A key development took place in the 1930s, when the institution was relocated to the Bellevue Palace in central Berlin. Additional room in the palatial museum allowed the reorganisation of the collections and the introduction of modern conservation and storage practices. To improve collection documentation and care, the new thematic groups indicated the make and function of objects (Tietmeyer and Vanja 2013). Rather than cultural landscapes, the artefacts became grouped into subsections such as 'household and living', 'work and profession' and 'religion and cult'. Additionally, labels indicated the materials of the objects. New categories such as "Textiles and Jewellery" became divided into functional subsections such as domestic textiles, patterns and children's clothes. It was also during this period that the institution renamed itself the Museum of German Folklore and began to focus on nationalist themes. In 1935, the exhibition of German Peasant Art linked the collections to 'race and space, folk art and people's morals' and displayed archaeological records demonstrating two thousand years of ongoing German settlement in Europe (Ausstellung Deutsche Bauernkunst 1935: 9). In line with the notions of folklore in Nazi Germany, particular interest was paid to expatriate Germans (*Auslandsdeutsche*) and ethnic German material culture (Tietmeyer and Vanja 2013: 389). Within the nationalist paradigm, the collection showcased the Germanness of the objects, highlighting their rural origins and their membership in the ethnic nationhood.

The museum's work was interrupted by the outbreak of Second World War. Despite various attempts to protect the objects, the museum lost up to 80% of its collection (Pretzell 1962: 108). After the war, the what remained ended up in separate museums in East and West Berlin. Both tried to make up for the war losses by soliciting public and private donations and finding objects equivalent to the lost artefacts, even if it meant shopping at flea markets. (Not surprisingly, many of the objects lacked proper documentation.) Post-war acquisitions reinforced the material-functional classification of objects, and focused on German-speaking territories and German language islands.

9.1 The Scottish section of the museum store retains some of the classifications used in the Ethnological Museum's European Department. Reproduced courtesy of the Museum of European Cultures, Staatliche Museen zu Berlin.
9.2 The museum library catalogue bears the material traces of the divided and ever-changing history of the institution. The catalogue still distinguishes between 'Island', 'Dahlem' and 'Europe' collections and retains the distinct numbering systems of the predecessor institutions. Reproduced courtesy of the Museum of European Cultures, Staatliche Museen zu Berlin.

The emphasis on retrieving lost collections became less pronounced in the 1980s. On both sides of the Iron Curtain, the museums refocused on collections representing life in the city and acquired several industrially-produced objects (Neuland-Kitzerow 2005: 156). (In East Berlin, this acquisition focus was part of the GDR's aim to create a record of working-class material culture (Hauptaufgaben 1978).) One example of the new focus was the shift in textile acquisitions. Prewar curators were interested in 'Sunday best' clothing rather than worn-out, everyday garments. By contrast, the post-war curators in the folklore museums in East and West Berlin were the first to collect day-to-day urban attire. The new object groups included pieces made with recycled fabrics and working-class fashions.

The acquisitions were accompanied by new levels of documentation that included descriptions of textile techniques and object biographies. For the first time, records also documented reasons for damage or repurposing. On both sides of the Berlin Wall, museums opened their collections to everyday visual culture with new acquisitions of non-professional photography, vernacular design, advertising and personal archives. This led to the creation of a more diverse record of urban material culture and new kinds of object data. At the same time, the reshaping of priorities brought about new distinctions within the collection. For instance, curators in the GDR lacked interest in 'bourgeois' material culture, resulting in a bias towards working-class artefacts in their urban collections.

In 1992, just a few years after the fall of the Berlin Wall, the East and West Berlin museums reunited. In 1999, their collections became merged with of the European section of the Ethnological Museum (EM), which was located in Dahlem in what used to be West Berlin. The EM regarded Europe as composed of distinct ethnic, national and regional entities. The objects indicated the cultures of the 'Scots', the 'Italians' or the 'Sami'. The commercial collectors and traders of so-called ethnographica who had acquired many objects for the museum had recorded little information regarding provenance. What is more, because EM curators acquired objects based on their own geographical area of specialisation, large parts of the collection documented incremental changes in material culture within narrow areas of expertise (such as a series of Slovakian shirts showing local textile techniques).

Along with undocumented records of territory, community and culture (De Cesari 2017), the reunification brought to the new museum some of the missing, pre-war objects. As the boxes arrived from across the former Iron Curtain, many objects came without records. Some of those artefacts have been yet to be identified and continue to occupy the mysterious 'X' shelf in MEK storage. To find a coherent narrative for the partially unidentified and overlapping collection objects, museum curators opted for a thematic and comparative approach that reimagined the historical collection through a new, Europeanised lens (Früh 2014).

Ten years after the fall of the Wall, the institution was renamed the Museum of European Cultures, becoming part of the reunited State Museums of Berlin (Staatliche Museen zu Berlin) and the Prussian Cultural Heritage Foundation (Stiftung Preussischer Kulturbesitz). The MEK set out on a course that diverged from its preceding institutions:

> The name of the new museum may suggest that it will exhibit all of Europe's national cultures or even show all of Europe in its facets. Besides that claim being presumptuous, it is downright impossible to address all European cultural forms in their temporal, spatial and social dimensions. Rather, it will comparatively explore the commonalities and the differences in the diversity [*Vielfalt*] of European cultures (Karasek and Tietmeyer 1999: 19).[1]

As the statement suggests, museum made diversity (*Vielfalt*) and difference (*Unterschied*) as key concepts in the construction of a new institution. In its quest to understand European cultures, the museum did not want to represent all of Europe (De Cesari 2017) but to showcase a cross-section of topics:

> Tracing the diversity [*Vielfalt*] of these cultural phenomena across national borders, researching them in a comparative manner and documenting them through additional collections is one of the fundamental tasks of the Museum of European Cultures and will be the basis for future events and exhibitions. Particular emphasis

> is placed on the study of cultural contacts and the presentation of their effects and consequences, since it is the voluntary or forced encounters between people of different [*verschiedene*] cultures that have made Europe what it is today: Europe's shape is the result of different cultural contacts (Karasek and Tietmeyer 1999: 19).[2]

For the MEK, Europe was a sum of intertwined local and national cultures (Kaiser, Krankenhagen and Poelhs 2014: 30) linked by 'cultural contacts' through migration, trade, travel or media. The contacts were envisioned as building blocks of shared cultural affinities within Europe as a wider 'cultural whole'. Implicit in this new narrative of a Europe made from 'different cultural contacts' is its separation from 'non-European cultures' (außereuropäische Kulturen) (1999: 31):

> Despite its cultural diversity, [Europe] is characterised by an equal unity, which is decisively based on the Judeo-Christian religion. Through religious, social, economic and political relations, cultural contacts have been established in which the media—a means of transferring information—occupy a special position. Because of these interconnections, Europeans of different nations share common cultural traits (Karasek and Tietmeyer 1999: 13).[3]

In this formulation of difference, Europe is a 'community united by a common fate' (*Schicksalgemeinschaft*) in the Judeo-Christian tradition. Here, religious-cultural boundaries delineated what was held in common and what appeared as different. As de Cesari observes:

> This kind of strategic Europeanization did not fully purge the collection of its built-in biases—in particular, the enduring legacy of nineteenth-century academic and museum practices. Such a legacy is exemplified by the emphasis on Christianity, reflected in the large number of nativities that fill two exhibition rooms, as well as by the distinct cultural-geographic understanding of "Europe" embedded in the collection itself (de Cesari 2017: 28).

Much of these implicit categories were, as de Cesari notes, built into the historical collection.

The 2011 collection exhibition highlighted this new model of diversity and difference. The display used themes of travel, trade, media, fashion and food to illustrate points of cultural contact across Europe. One room used textiles to highlight identities and their geographical boundaries. A display case presented mannequins in various clothing styles— professional attire, uniforms, festive costumes—from a myriad of regions across Europe. At the back of the room, an art installation titled *The Europeans* presented an outfit stitched from fragments of maps, regional craft patterns and pop culture themes. Although the installation was meant to show that European identity was a construct, the majority of the objects perpetuated the idea of spatialised diversity and regionalism. Indeed, the exhibition's comparative cross-section of localised sartorial identity echoed the territorial taxonomies typical of the 19th-century *cultural landscape* (de Cesari 2017: 29). In 2019, the curators decided that the exhibition was no longer in line with current museum practice. They wanted to reimagine the museum's collections and address some of the inherent problems of comparing historical objects.

My interlocutors often stressed that the collections left them ambivalent, as the following statement from the What's Missing? conference shows:

> The historical collections are both a blessing and a curse: they form the basis of a museum's very existence, but they were originally collected under the paradigm of 'salvage anthropology', often according to national, regional and/or ethnic categories. Their historical narratives do not sufficiently represent current social developments or even complex, diverse pasts (Edenheiser 2020: 15).

For example, one MEK team member felt that diversity is a matter of perspective and that the collections still have an untapped potential for novel inquisitive approaches:

> We bring in diversity through our questions. And the collections themselves, as they were created at that time, are of course also diverse in themselves. But it also depends above all on the questions we ask. If I make an exhibition on the subject of sustainability...then I look at the objects that we have collected from people who made objects out of necessity, as in the postwar period, when goods were scarce. This famous steel helmet, which was then converted into a sieve, we have multiple objects like this. Or how clothes were mended because one had nothing else. So the variety depends on our questions and there are actually no limits. Because everyday life, culture, is already very diverse [*vielfältig*] in itself.

By contrast, historical collections can pose a curatorial stumbling block that forecloses on diversity. The curators frequently noted the challenge of providing insights into Europe's complex past from biased collections such as traditional folk costumes or Christian wax votive offerings. For example, the museum's pre-war collections mostly cover rural, German-speaking regions. What is more, provenance in the original 19th-century collection is patchy and the objects acquired from 'flea markets' after the war are undocumented. As one curator noted, 'What we are missing are the stories. We find them important now. A hundred years ago no one would have thought so'. Although the curator was aware of the historical reasons for the lack of documentary information, she still found it paralysing. Moreover, the separation of the museum into two institutions during the Cold War resulted in duplicates and gaps; many objects from East and West Berlin have gone unused. Quite a few objects were relegated to storage as obscure remnants of earlier curatorial preoccupations.

The MEK collections are, in other words, a veritable curate's egg. Their historical legacy brought specific epistemic categories framing the ways in which the objects have been understood and displayed (Bowker and Star 1999). These categories developed over time, ranging from cultural landscapes to ethnic, material and functional ideas of diversity and difference. Some of the collection's *Vielfalt* might feel outdated for contemporary curators. Some curators wanted to include queer diversity and other marginalised perspectives such as refugee and decolonial vantage points in the museum's social mission. But the legacy of the collections continues to shape museum practice as curators contend with unknown provenance, a sense that the objects have become irrelevant and worries that they will unintentionally reinforce old categories. As the 2011 show demonstrated, although work with the historical collection can go beyond established categories, it can also perpetuate the very framework that it wants to challenge (von Oswald 2019). The next section explores the ways in which the curatorial team works to implement diversity at the institutional level and to address the problems of past collections. What can curators do to overcome outmoded categories and biases? Instead of provisional initiatives such as research projects and temporary exhibitions, which are often regarded as tokenistic (Aksoy 2020: 20), I focus on the museum's new Collection Concept.

Enabling diversity

Starting in 1999, the MEK began to introduce new approaches to acquisitions based on modern, participative principles (e.g. Karasek and Tietmeyer 1999, Tietmeyer, E., & Meijer-van Mensch 2013). Recently, those new approaches were enshrined in the MEK's Collection Concept, part of an institution-wide reckoning with the collections' gaps, biases and future possibilities. The Concept describes the MEK collections as a 'memory in which the diversity [*Vielfalt*] of European cultures and ways of life in the past and the present can be preserved for posterity' (Collection Concept 2019: 6). The museum is a depository of material and immaterial culture that makes visible past and present diversity. But as the Concept stipulates, the MEK collections must also be a driver of social change through participation, inclusion and stakeholder dialogue. They must initiate debates and provide insights into questions of European identity, now and in the future. As one curator emphatically put it:

> No longer do we want to collect and show how people used to live. That was a mistake in the past, it remains a mistake today and it will continue to be a mistake tomorrow. We are no longer positivistic. Those times are over. We are not encyclopaedic.

To meet the museum's new objectives, curators must perform regular reviews of the collections and determine what is missing in key areas. For example, the museum intends to supplement the craft objects in the historical collection with more artefacts documenting intangible cultural heritage. It also wants to fill gaps in the collections by introducing participatory acquisition and exhibition projects (Puzon 2019). Participation is at the heart of the museum's efforts to incorporate outside perspectives from external experts, community members and other stakeholders.

The Concept also calls for a 'significant leap' in efforts to document social developments and material culture over time amid a profusion of mass-produced artefacts (Macdonald and Morgan 2018). The museum wants to stop collecting entire series of objects and minimise incremental acquisitions. For example, the museum will no longer collect every type of mug for its collection of drinking vessels. Instead, it has decided to acquire the first recyclable coffee cup, which indicates a new practice. Other core elements of the Concept include deaccession, digitisation, more precise categorisation and a greater emphasis on intangible material culture.

The Concept lays out a list of specific criteria for proposed acquisitions. The first set of criteria concerns the acquisition's fit with the overall vision of the museum. The second defines benchmarks for the condition of new objects and the resulting conservation and institutional costs. The third set of criteria requires sufficient provenance data and supplementary biographical information for any object it acquires. Finally, and most importantly, the criteria stipulate that communities and other stakeholders be actively engaged in the collecting process. The aim here is to foster a participatory model of acquisitions and prevent the creation of 'pet collections', that is, collections that are likely to be of more interest to the curator than anybody else.

In line with the historical collections, the MEK's current acquisition practice takes into account areas such as work and trade, religion, belief and ritual and visual culture. At the same time, the team has identified new themes that reflect pressing social issues. The new priorities include identity formation, Europe in a global context, sustainability and the relationship between culture and nature. In other words, new objects need either to correspond with existing key categories or advance new selected areas of interest. In this way, the Concept aims to shape the history of the collections and set a new plot line going forward.

Hastrup, while discussing the ways in which past experience affects the future, has argued that plots provide frameworks for action: 'It is a profound matter of responding-, response being made within a moral horizon and within a social context that we interpret and project forward as we go along' (2005: 11). Decision-making, in other words, responds to both the past and to an anticipated future. In this regard, the Concept provides a plot for the development of the MEK collection. But it also captures the fundamental ambiguity of distancing the museum from existing narratives. On the one hand, the collection is supposed to be enriched by new perspectives from a variety of stakeholders. Objects need to be forward-facing, moving through collection groups and responding to changing social contexts, so as to build accountability and social relevance into the museum's curatorial practice. On the other hand, the Concept is embedded in the infrastructure, ordering practices, routines and internal logics of existing holdings. At the same time, the Concept significantly limits the types of artefacts that qualify for a place in the collections. Although meant to include a diversity of positions, the Concept's 'plot space' privileges certain objects while precluding those that do not confirm to existing categories. Below I consider the MEK's decision-making in a few specific instances and the ways that the new procedures both go beyond and conserve certain institutional practices.

Injecting diversity

> Now every object is presented and discussed in our advisory circle. Only then do we say, yes, okay, we can acquire this. It is important that it doesn't proceed any other way.... Even trivial criteria play a role. We need to consider whether we have space for the object.

In an April 2019 meeting, the museum's curatorial team proposed a number of objects for the collection. The discussion began with two donations—sketches made by a famous illustrator and a commemorative coffee set. These were accepted because the sketches complemented the existing graphic and advertising collection, and the coffee set was considered a developmental leap—it represented the material culture of everyday commemorative elements for the First World War. The team then discussed a T-shirt and other Brexit-related merchandise. The objects were accepted because they captured both the mundane and the commercial aspects of the Brexit public debate. They were a good fit with a collection linked to contested ideas of Europe and supplemented the Brexit collection, which included a DIY protest sign.

The next object up for discussion was Kraftwerk's Trans-Europe Express album. The curator who proposed it argued that it bore witness to the ways in which European nations were connected through transport infrastructure, capturing an emerging idea of Europe as a space in which, through trains or cheap flights, visitors can travel the Continent as a package experience. In contrast to the Brexit object or the commemorative coffee set, the album sparked controversy. One curator suggested that it is easier to find objects reflecting wider European issues at a local level. Another maintained that it is more challenging to acquire a truly Pan-European object. As the curatorial team considered other options, the discussion grew heated. One participant argued that European objects could not simply be defined as anything made in the EU because the MEK is not a museum of the European Union.

As the discussion continued, some offered proposals for alternative objects. One curator mentioned a fur coat that was already part of the collection. It was made with transnational techniques in a diverse community in Transylvania, taken abroad by migrants and reconceptualised in a diaspora community in Germany. Another noted that objects of war such as a gas mask from the First World War could be considered quintessentially European. Unlike the Kraftwerk album, the gas mask was part of everyday wartime life across the Continent. As the discussion proceeded, more and more questions emerged—how is the construction of Europe reflected by its material culture? Should the museum be collecting Interrail tickets instead of music albums? The conversation demonstrated that the category of Europeanness, as crucial as it is for MEK's acquisition practice, remained open to interpretation.

The album did not pass the MEK admission test because the majority of the team members believed that it was neither an everyday object nor sufficiently European. It was not clear how the object would accord with the collections and how would it be used in future exhibitions. As the group debated different examples, the discussion turned to another potential acquisition: an ivory silk wedding gown in the Wedding Dreams exhibition, which ran from September 2018 to July 2019. With a large bow on the chest, a ruffled border and long train, the dress was a centrepiece of the show. The wedding gown had initially been displayed at the Kunstgewerbemuseum as part of a collaboration between a high-street fashion retailer (H&M) and an Amsterdam fashion house (Viktor & Rolf). The piece bridged the domains of mass-produced fashion and crafted designer pieces and was considered an pop-culture masterpiece.

The MEK wanted to acquire the dress not as a designer outfit but as an example of Europeanness and the diversity of the European experience, immigration and global connectedness. The piece was bought by a French woman living in London for a wedding that took place in Las Vegas. Manufactured in Bangladesh for a Dutch designer and Swedish clothing brand, the object was a product of the global supply chain network on which Europe's fast fashion relies. The curator suggested that the dress stood out not only because of its unique story, but also because it documented how wedding rituals intersect with popular culture. As ideas of the dream wedding have evolved over time, the wedding dress has shown the ever-changing patterns of markets and material culture, status aspirations and gender normativity. In this light, the dress represents a "leap" in the wider wedding attire category. Moreover, it speaks to the themes of global Europe, non-sustainability in the mass production of textiles and identity formation. Finally, the object met the main criteria of the Concept regarding provenance, biography and condition. As a result, the curatorial team agreed to go ahead with the acquisition.

According to the Concept, MEK collections must have the ability to address current and future questions of European identities (Concept 2019: 8). Objects such as the wedding dress and the Kraftwerk album allow us to explore how such a multiplicity of possible futures is imagined by the curators. In the case of the album, the group felt that its Europeanness was unclear. By contrast, the dress tells more than one story. It can contribute to multiple future exhibitions while creating different points of contact within the historical collections. The dress, in other words, occupies a clear place within the plot space of the Concept.

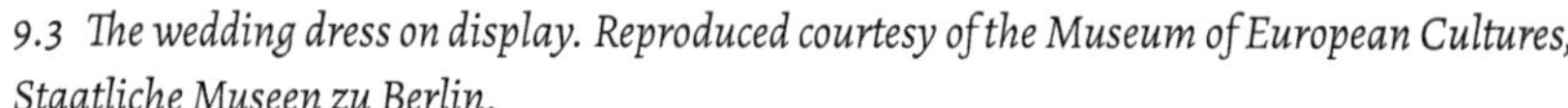

9.3 The wedding dress on display. Reproduced courtesy of the Museum of European Cultures, Staatliche Museen zu Berlin.

The deliberative practices on display in the above cases are meant to build consensus on new acquisitions and limit the influence of particular curatorial passions. Paradoxically, however, the MEK's consensus-driven approach might ultimately perpetuate a flattened idea of Europeanness (De Cesari 2017: 30). For objects that tick all the right boxes could end up being approximations of many things rather than strong statements about a particular issue or phenomenon. They could be the curatorial equivalent of eager-to-please diplomats that are unwilling to trouble, complain, disagree, disturb or make a stink. A practice that privileges a multiplicity of meanings and future uses could produce what Sharon Macdonald calls "diversity lite" (2018)— watered-down collections that stay clear of more eccentric and controversial examples of material culture. (For more, see Macdonald in this volume.)

When it comes to diversifying the collections, then, the Concept might hurt as much as it helps. Requirements to fill gaps and make leaps might result in the rejection of material culture that lie outside the museum's existing holdings and categories of difference. At any rate, the criteria for new objects affords little space for radically different artefacts and experiences, potentially undercutting the museum's ambition to showcase marginalised 'lenses'. The ultimate outcome, however, will depend on the extent to which the team treats the Concept criteria as requirements or suggestions. Judging by the specific instances I discussed above, the Concept is likely to open up new avenues of diversity while foreclosing and sanitising others.

Anticipating diversity?

> By collecting objects from the present, we make the cultural history of the future. What do you call that? Anticipatory collecting.... Of course, we address present questions in the exhibitions...but the collections are for the future.

Given the uneven diversity of the collections and the long history of institutional changes and renamings, MEK curators have been careful in their decisions about what should be acquired and what should be preserved for the future. If past is prologue, then the museum for which they are collecting today might be an entirely different institution tomorrow. The subject of the museum's future triggered a host of hopes and fears among museum staff. One curator wanted to remove "European" from the museum's name and refocus on global contexts. She felt that the distinction between European and non-European cultures was artificial. Another curator told me that the MEK might be reinvented as a women's museum given the predominant role played by women in historical material culture and in the make-up of the curatorial team and museum visitors. A third curator presented me with what she believed was the worst-case scenario, namely the possibility that the MEK would become

> a museum for German folklore that is politically instrumentalised, because there are nationalist aspirations all over Europe and the basic idea of the museum is a very nationalist one. It would really be a nightmare if the political tides turned in such a way that someone would again regard the costumes and objects as a mark of German identity.

But she added that she didn't think she was ready to talk about the future. "I think that we are still at the beginning...like a butterfly that has just emerged from a cocoon." Although the metaphor seems to sound a hopeful note, the curator's worries about a nationalist future are bound up with Germany's past.

As Hastrup has argued, 'actions take place within a moral horizon and within a social context that we interpret and project forward as we go along' (Hastrup 2005: 11). However the collections develop, curatorial decisions will take place within their own moral horizon as they summon a new possible future. Just as worries about a vanishing future drove early museum curators to acquire objects of traditional regional culture amid a rapidly industrialising countryside, the MEK's staff has worked to diversify its collections in an effort to stave off certain future scenarios while encouraging others. Injecting diversity into the collections may prevent the return of nationalism, and it is likely to correct past mistakes as it builds out neglected areas and centres those once marginalised. By diversifying its collections and pulling into them into the present, as it were, the MEK could even expand beyond its current scope and focus instead on sustainability or the entanglements of a global Europe. At any rate, all diversification activities are quintessentially future-oriented—be they preventative, corrective or aspirational.

Conclusion

For museums that have come to embrace social responsibility, diversification poses a major challenge. MEK curators understand how much is at stake in *what* is missing from the collections, and *who*. But diversification does not happen all at once. I have argued in this chapter that past ways of doing and undoing diversity can encumber diversification in the present. The MEK curatorial team, guided by the new Collection Concept, has worked to jettison outmoded forms of diversity (e.g. drawing differences along *ethnic* or *regional* lines) and introduce others, though my discussion of recent acquisitions indicate that efforts to diversify may remain ultimately reinforce some pre-existing categories of difference. Indeed, while the Collection Concept may improve transparency and reduce incrementalism, it could also result in a sanitised 'diversity lite' that perpetuates longstanding practices.

This raises wider questions about how everyday museum work is shaped by the future. Some recent studies have turned their attention to worry about the future loss of diversity and its effect on heritage practice. DeSilvey and Harrison (2020) argue that collections articulate forms of managing endangerment. This can be seen in the past accumulation of heritage material (e.g. salvage collecting) as well as in current attempts to tackle the challenge of material profusion (Morgan and Macdonald 2020). However, the case of the MEK demonstrates that collection diversification is also about responding to a museum's past and enacting different approaches for its future.

What can we learn from the MEK as we begin to address the bigger issue of doing diversity in museums? My ethnographic study shows that curators continuously lay the groundwork for a future that permeates their everyday decision-making and affects their ways of doing diversity. The decisions and non-decisions about which objects to acquire plant the seeds of different museum futures. As many museums seek to diversify, understanding their work requires insight into particular museum practices and initiatives and the broader temporal frameworks of specific collections. The success of diversification hangs in the balance of confrontations with the past and aspirations for the future.

Acknowledgements

The research for my work was undertaken as part of a Humboldt Postdoctoral Fellowship during the years 2019–2021. I am grateful to Elisabeth Tietmeyer, Iris Edenheiser, Judith Schühle, Jana Wittenzellner, Jane Redlin, Beate Wild, Irene Ziehe, Fatma Gul, Tina Peschel, Sofia Botvinnik, Andrea Aßinger, Kirstin Csutor, Christian Krug, Salwa Joram and Christine Binroth, and all staff members of the Museum of European Cultures for generously sharing their practice and insights, and for their comments on earlier drafts of the paper. Many thanks to Sharon Macdonald for her patient editorial guidance, to CARMAH community members for their feedback and to Jennie Morgan and the other panellists at Future Museum: Collections and Collecting for their thoughtful comments on the paper I delivered at the 5th biennial conference of the Association of Critical Heritage Studies in London.

Notes

1 "Der Name des neuen Museums mag suggerieren, alle Nationalkulturen Europas auszustellen oder gar ganz Europa in seinem Facetten zu zeigen. Abgesehen von der Vermessenheit eines solchen Anspruches ist es geradezu unmöglich, alle europäischen Kulturformen in ihrer zeitlichen, räumlichen und sozialen Dimension zu thematisieren. Vielmehr sollten durch komparistische Verfahren die Gemeinsamkeiten, aber auch Unterscheide in der Vielfalt europäischer Kulturen verdeutlicht werden. Die Erklärung von kulturellen Zusammenhängen und Prozessen in Europa sowie den Folgen des Kulturkontaktes mit Außereuropa soll zu den weiteren Aufgaben des MEK gehören."

2 "Der Vielfalt dieser Kulturphänomene über staatliche Grenzen hinweg nachzuspüren, vergleichend zu erforschen und durch ergänzende Sammlungen zu belegen, gehört zu den grundlegenden Aufgaben des Museum Europäischer Kulturen, muss die Grundlage für künftige Veranstaltungen und Ausstellungen sein. Dabei wird auf die Erforschung von Kulturkontakten und der Darstellung ihrer Auswirkungen und Folgen besonders Gewicht gelegt, haben doch freiwillige oder erzwungene Begegnungen zwischen Menschen verschiedene Kulturen Europa erst zu dem gemacht, wie es sich heute darstellt: Europas Gestalt ist das Ergebnis von unterschiedlichen Kulturkontakten."

3 "Trotz ihrer kulturellen Vielfalt wird sie durch eine ebensolche Einheit charakterisiert, die maßgeblich auf der jüdisch-christlichen Religion basiert. Durch religiöse, soziale, wirtschaftliche und politische Beziehungen kommen bis heute Kulturkontakte zustande, bei denen die Medien – Mittel des Transfers von Informationen – eine besondere Stellung einnehmen. Aufgrund dieser Verflechtungen weisen die Europäer unterschiedlichen Nationen gemeinsame Kulturzüge auf."

References

Antoš, Z. 2014. '"Collecting" the present in ethnographic museums', *Etnološka istraživanja*, (18/19): 115–128.

De Cesari, C. 2017. 'Museums of Europe: Tangles of memory, borders, and race', *Museum Anthropology*, 40(1): 18–35.

Aksoy, S. 2020. 'What's Missing? – Sticking to the Margins', in I. Edenheiser, E. Tietmeyer, and S. Boersma (eds), *What's Missing? Collecting and Exhibiting Europe*, 9–23. Berlin: Reimer.

Ausstellung Deutsche Bauernkunst 1935. *Katalog der Ausstellung der Staatlichen Museen für Deutsche Volkskunde, Berlin – Schloss Bellevue*. Berlin: Druck Wilhelm Limpert.

Bowker, G. C., and S. L. Star. 1999. *Sorting things out: Classification and its consequences*. Cambridge, MA: MIT Press.

Collection Concept for the Museum Europäischer Kulturen—Staatliche Museen zu Berlin. 2020. https://www.smb.museum/fileadmin/website/Museen_und_Sammlungen/Museum_Europaeischer_Kulturen/02_Sammeln_und_Forschen/MEK_Sammlungskonzept_EN.pdf (accessed 23 June 2021).

DeSilvey, C., and R. Harrison. 2020. 'Anticipating loss: rethinking endangerment in heritage futures', *International Journal of Heritage Studies*, 26(1): 1–7.

Edenheiser, I. 2020. 'Introduction: Towards new Filters and Relations', in I. Edenheiser, E. Tietmeyer, and S. Boersma (eds), *What's Missing? Collecting and Exhibiting Europe*. Berlin: Reimer.

Früh, A. 2014. 'Politics of Memory and Institutional Change: Remembering the German Democratic Republic at the Museum Europäischer Kulturen', *Studia Universitatis Cibiniensis. Series Historica*, (XI sp): 215–239.

Hartung, O. 2010. *Kleine deutsche Museumsgeschichte: von der Aufklärung bis zum frühen 20. Jahrhundert*. Köln, Weimar: Böhlau Verlag.

Hastrup, K. 2005. 'Performing the world: Agency, anticipation and creativity', *The Cambridge Journal of Anthropology*, 25(2): 5–19.

Hauptaufgaben (Die) der Museen der DDR bis 1980, in NMk 21, 1978, 4–8.

Jahn, U. 1889. 'Nachricht: Das neubegründete Museum für deutsche Volkstrachten und Erzeugnisse des Hausgewerbes zu Berlin', *Zeitschrift für Völkerpsychologie und Sprachwissenschaft*, 19: 334–343.

Kaiser, W., S. Krankenhagen, and K. Poehls. 2014. *Exhibiting Europe in museums: Transnational networks, collections, narratives, and representations (Vol. 6)*. New York: Berghahn Books.

Karasek, E, and E. Tietmeyer. 1999. 'Das Museum Europäischer Kulturen: Entstehung—Realität—Zukunft', in E. Karasek (eds), *Faszination Bild. Kulturkontakte in Europa*, 7–19. Potsdam: UNZE-Verlag.

Macdonald, S. 2018. *Diverse museum diversities*. https://www.zflprojekte.de/zfl-blog/2018/10/20/sharon-macdonald-diverse-museum-diversities/ (accessed 17 March 2022).

Macdonald, S., and J. Morgan. 2018. 'What not to collect?: Post-connoisseurial dystopia and the profusion of things', in P. Schorch and C.McCarthy (eds), *Curatopia*. Manchester: Manchester University Press.

Morgan, J., and S. Macdonald. 2020. 'De-growing museum collections for new heritage futures', *International Journal of Heritage Studies*, 26(1): 56–70.

Neuland-Kitzerow, D. 2005. Sammlungen–als kulturhistorisches Gedächtnis und Inspiration, in G. Mentges, N. Schack, H. Jenss, and H. Nixdorff, *Kulturanthropologie des Textilen*, 151–168. Berlin: Edition Ebersbach.

O'Donnell, K. M., R. Bridenthal, and N. Reagin (eds). 2010. *The Heimat abroad: the boundaries of Germanness*. University of Michigan Press.

Oswald, M. von. 2019. 'Troubling Colonial Epistemologies in Berlin's Ethnologisches Museum: provenance research and the Humboldt Forum', in M. von Oswald, and J. Tinius (eds), *Across Anthropology: Troubling Colonial Legacies, Museums, and the Curatorial*. Leuven: Leuven University Press.

Pretzell, L. 1962. 'Zur Situation des Museums für Deutsche Volkskunde in Berlin', *Zeitschrift für Volkskunde*, 57/58.1961/62: 104–111.

Puzon, K. 2019. 'Participatory matters: Access, migration and heritage in Berlin Museums', in H. Oevermann, and E. Gantner (eds), *Securing urban heritage: Agents, access, and securitization*, 31–46. Abingdon and New York: Routledge.

Tietmeyer, E., and K. Vanja. 2013. 'Das Museum Europäischer Kulturen und der Nationalsozialismus. Eine Geschichte der Anpassung in zwei Teilen', in J. Grabowski, and P. Winter (eds), *Zwischen Politik und Kunst. Die Staatlichen Museen zu Berlin in der Zeit des Nationalsozialismus*, 387–408. Köln: Böhlau.

Tietmeyer, E. 2013. 'The Challenge of "Displaying Europe". Experiences of the Museum Europäischer Kulturen—Staatliche Museen zu Berlin', in C. Whitehead, S. Eckersley, R. Mason (eds), *Placing Europe in the Museum*, 61–73. Milano: MELA Books.

Tietmeyer, E., and L. Meijer-van Mensch (eds). 2013. *Participative Strategies in Collecting the Present*. Berlin: Panama Verlag.

Virchow, R. 1890. *Vorwort. Kurzer Führer durch die Sammlung des Museums für Deutsche Volkstrachten und Erzeugnisse des Hausgewerbes in Berlin.*

Collecting Diversity
Data and Citizen Science at the Museum für Naturkunde Berlin

Chiara Garbellotto, Tahani Nadim

Natural history museums are purveyors of diversity. Indeed, by way of taxonomy—the description, identification and naming of species—natural history museums actively produce the diversity they disseminate. Natural history museums generally embrace the position that diversity, or, more precisely, biodiversity, is vital for the health of the planet. With the alarming decline of biodiversity worldwide, natural history collections are experiencing renewed attention. A recent report for the International Council of Museums (ICOM) emphasises their central role in the 'conservation of global biodiversity': 'Understanding what species live where is a foundation of understanding biodiversity and nature conservation. Specimen labels provide basic information on what species occur where, or at least where they once occurred' (McGhie 2019: 15).

The passage from the ICOM report outlines two interdependent issues that sit at the heart of this chapter. First, biodiversity draws its meaning and practice from both biological and sociological categories. Sometimes biodiversity is used to denote the diversity of life in all its biological, cultural and social forms, which accords with the definition of biodiversity by the Convention on Biological Diversity (CBD). At other times, it refers exclusively to the diversity of non-human species. The ambiguity of the term, which indicates both diversity and biodiversity, captures the interpenetration of the biological and the social, nature and society. The criss-crossing of these concepts is particularly central for understanding the duality of bio/diversity. As Subramaniam observes, 'western societies (at least since Darwin) have struggled with the biological questions of variation alongside political questions of diversity and difference' (Subramaniam 2014: 10).

The second issue relates to the labels and other data points typically attached to museum objects providing proper names, taxonomic designation and provenance. For biodiversity sciences, such data are crucial for creating and managing biodiversity, especially amid increasing digitisation and the use of data-based tools. The history of science has shown how the nature and value of diversity have been co-produced by the material-semiotic devices used to record it—taxonomic tables, indices, double-entry book-keeping, museum collection designs, drawers and the like.[1] How we document diversity is thus co-constitutive of how we cognitively, politically and experientially apprehend it.[2] Consequently, the data practices that have emerged in the past 10 years are critical for understanding the relationships between the biological and the social that implicate 'diversity'.

What difference do digital data make when it comes to the nature of bio/diversity? In posing that question, we seek to go beyond the standard issues of access, speed and preservation and attend instead to the specific relations—between people, objects, politics, environments and institutions—that are compelled, maintained or, at times, severed in data practices. To do so, we examine a particular case of citizen science that exemplifies the evolution of museum digitisation efforts. *Forschungsfall Nachtigall*, a project devoted to the study of nightingales, was initiated by the Museum für Naturkunde Berlin to encourage public participation in science. The project is an example of lay people and scientists working together in the production of data and scientific knowledge. It also shows how biodiversity—in this case, that of nightingales—can be a vehicle for social diversity through the inclusion of non-scientists ('citizens') in the research process. In this chapter we speak of 'data creatures' to denote both nightingales and citizens made in and through the data practices designed to capture biodiversity and social diversity. We borrow the term from Jennifer Gabrys's work on citizen sensing. According to Gabrys, 'citizen-sensing' projects are processes of '*creaturing data*, where actual environmental entities that come together are creations that materialize through distinct ways of perceiving and participating in environments' (2017: 13). In our chapter, the term 'data creature' serves a two-fold purpose: it foregrounds the making of data in the constitution of bio/diversity and focuses on the coeval becoming of entities and distinct ways of assembling (in) data.

While histories of science have shown how lay knowledges have always been a core part of scientific knowledge-making, the term citizen science has gained spectacular traction in recent years (Kimura and Kinchy 2016; Strasser et al. 2019). Knowledge and memory institutions as well as various sciences have responded to calls for more participation and transparency by enrolling lay people through specifically designed research projects, from mapping galaxies to deciphering historical shipping log books. But these developments have also sparked critical responses, triggered not least by the reduction of participation to data gathering and the lack of critical reflection of citizen science projects on the exclusions, politics and economics involved. Questions about the particular form of 'citizen' or 'science' in use, the struggles over what constitutes legitimate knowledge and expertise and the underlying institutional interests are usually not part of the project design. Our chapter addresses some of these problems by following data practices of the *Forschungsfall Nachtigall* project, from nightingales in Berlin public parks to digital spectrograms in data workshops and the Museum's Animal Sound Archive. We use the notion of 'data creatures' to propose a particular constellation of citizen and natural history object.

The natural history museum and bio/diversity

Forschungsfall Nachtigall began in 2018 as a two-year research project funded by the Federal Ministry of Education and Research (BMBF) as part of a programme to increase co-operation between science and 'citizens'. The nightingale project aimed to study nightingales' 'dialects' and habitat requirements in Berlin (2018) and Germany (2019) by generating a map of nightingale locations and collecting recordings for bioacoustic analyses. Both the map and the recordings were to be created through the collective efforts of volunteers who would venture into Berlin late at night and in the early morning to capture nightingale songs on their smartphones.

The drive to include mainstream citizens in scientific research has been a central concern of European research policy for the past several years. Horizon 2020, a framework programme governing Europe's research priorities, set aside explicit funding for efforts to involve civil society in research and innovation. In their guidelines for the programme, the German government states that science and innovation need to be 'closer to the people' to ensure 'public transparency and acceptance of scientific processes' (Federal Government Position Paper 2017: 14). It further stresses that 'digital transformation...offers new possibilities for exchange and communication', which can ultimately contribute to 'reawakening people's interest in Europe' (Devictor and Bensaude-Vincent 2016: 8). Citizen science is a tool to address three distinct contemporary issues: the apparent 'disconnect' between Brussels and the 500 million people that live in the European Union; the increasing scepticism towards scientific methods and results; and the yet-to-be realised potenial of digital technologies.

The government guidelines require that citizen science 'be distinguished from civic participation, which refers to the possibility of (political) participation in political decisions and processes, for example to further develop our model of society' (Federal Government Position Paper 2017: 14 fn. 6). The disclaimer is curious because the very name 'citizen science' makes an explicit appeal to the political. Moreover, it indirectly references the untenable division between science and society. It is this tension that we want to address when situating bio/diversity in museum data, not least because museums have become a key site for doing and promoting citizen science. The Museum für Naturkunde Berlin was one of the founding members of the *Bürger schaffen Wissen—Wissen schafft Bürger (GEWISS)* platform, a portal and advocacy programme for German-based citizen science projects. It also hosts ECSA, the European Citizen Science Association, and runs its own citizen science projects such as the nightingale project.

This chapter is based on ethnographic fieldwork carried out by Chiara Garbellotto, who accompanied parts of the nightingale project as a participant observer, and on research carried out by Tahani Nadim on 'data creatures' (Nadim 2022). In what follows, we present this citizen science project before focusing on nightingales and citizens as forms of data creatures produced by data practices. Following the work of feminist science & technology studies at the intersection of sociology and cultural anthropology, the chapter contributes to debates concerned with tracking the interpolations of nature and culture (Franklin, Lury, and Stacey 2000; Haraway 2018) and with the infrastructural powers of datafied classification systems (Bowker and Star 2000).

The nightingale project

The biologists, PhD students and other museum team members with whom the first author spoke described the nightingale project as a 'modular network' comprising different activities, research practices and foci. The project had three main components. The first was an education programme designed for seventh- and eighth-graders in Berlin schools to foster awareness of conservation, encourage direct contact with nature and assess students' knowledge of nightingales. This assessment consisted of questionnaires before, immediately after and eight weeks after scientist-led excursions into Berlin's urban nature. In addition, a second set of questionnaires targeted the correlation between individual learning and motivation and the provision of information about the project's research and context.

The second component consisted of an artistic exploration of the nightingale's symbolism in different cultures. It was accompanied by the collection of biographical anecdotes and memories related to the birds from a second cohort of project participants, which the project team variously referred to as 'refugees', 'new citizens' and 'new Berliners'. (On the use of essentializing categories, see Gram and Tinius in this volume). In the first year, the collection was expanded to include other participant contributions such as written stories and recorded audios transcribed by the project team. The work revolved around activities such as crafting and sewing bird puppets, live music, cross-stich and poetry performances. A map of Berlin designed and sewn by the members of the *Nachtigall Projekt* group on a black textile localised the stories gathered. With the unfolding of the project, this became the place where stories and images were narrated and stitched together.

The third and final component of the project focused on the collection of nightingales' songs by citizen scientists and their visualization through a digital, interactive map on the project's website. Data collection was enabled by the popular and free-of-charge app Naturblick developed by the museum in 2015. Funded by the Federal Ministry for the Environment, Nature Conservation, and Nuclear Safety, the app is meant to enable 'conscious access to nature in the city' for valuing and supporting this nature'. This app allows people to 'discover city-nature' by recording and identifying animals and plants through image and sound. It integrates different taxonomic keys that let users answer a series of questions about the anatomy or morphology of the yet-to-be identified species, and optical pattern recognition that pulls up similar-looking flowers or trees. Participants in the nightingale project used the app during guided tours, though any app user could feed data to the project. Aside from the collection of song data, this component included two free workshops on bioacoustics analysis, which was used to study the songs that had been recorded and collected via the app.

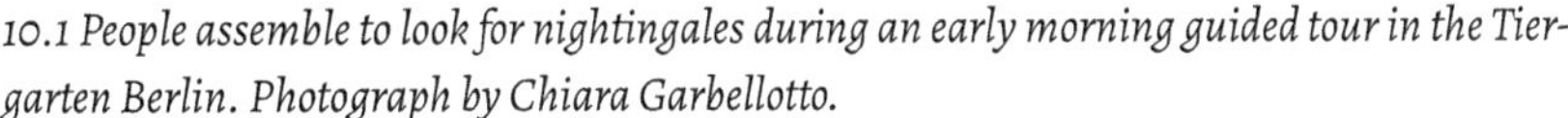
10.1 People assemble to look for nightingales during an early morning guided tour in the Tiergarten Berlin. Photograph by Chiara Garbellotto.

This brief outline of the project shows that it brought together realms conventionally thought of as scientific (bioacoustics, natural history) with realms conventionally thought of as social or cultural (museum pedagogy and informal learning, story-telling, cross-stich). Jenny Reardon, in her work on diversity in modern genetics, has observed how these realms 'are inextricably interconnected and come into being together' (Reardon 2001: 381). And indeed, non-scientists have been constitutive of modern natural history that began with colonial expansions in the 15th century. The history of natural history has been made by amateurs, from colonial officers collecting specimens to hobby breeders recording the character traits of peas and finches and sharing them with Charles Darwin and other scientists. In what might be the first museum-led citizen science project, Hugo Gonwetz, the director of the natural history museum in Gdansk (then a part of the German Empire), sent out questionnaires in the early 1880s to local groups asking for data on fauna and flora (Nyhart 2009: 244). In this capacity, the museum assumed an informational and, we would argue, governmental function as a producer and arbiter of bio/diversity. The museum not only enrolled lay people in its official activities, it catalogued the species diversity of a territory, a territory *contested* across the political upheavals that marked German-Polish relations from the partitions in the 18th century to the end of Second World War.

The biological perspective

In her history of the 'biological perspective' in Germany, Lynn Nyhart examines the changes in structural and social relations that occurred in Museum für Naturkunde Berlin in the late 19th century. According to Nyhart, the 'biological perspective' replaced classical natural history and its focus on system classification with a concern for evolution, ecology and biogeography. The 'biological perspective' introduced what was to become the dominant view of nature as an interdependent and functionalist entanglement of organisms and their environments. The rise of modern biology compelled the new naturalists to venture outside and study living organisms in situ (see also Kohler 2006). Moreover, it prompted museum curators and researchers to use specimens as evidence for complex ecological dynamics outside the museum. In moving from stable form to function, and from collection to environment, the value of diversity and the meaning and measurement of difference changed, too. Diversity became a scalar phenomenon that still encompassed morphological differences at the individual level but could now also include many other levels as well, from microbial communities to ecoregions. Importantly, diversity was rendered into a tractable object for experimental systems, something that could be manipulated and scientifically verified (Kohler 2002). This shift is indicative of much broader changes that looked to science for delivering and shoring-up social facts by appealing to 'nature' or innate 'biology'. Not coincidentally, the late 19th century also saw the invention of a scientific theory of society in the work of Émile Durkheim, who published sociology's foundational text, *The Rules of Sociological Method*, in 1895. Social and cultural differences could now be reified as natural differences and their function related to the progress and well-being of society as a social whole. Difference, in the form of variation, thus attained a new valence. Patterns of variation were studied and evaluated by an increasing repertoire of differentiating techniques with regard to phenotype, behaviour, ecology and genetics (Subramaniam 2014). Natural history museums were central actors in the circulation and popularisation of these ideas. According to Nyhart, the spread and institutionalisation of the 'biological perspective' manifested itself in the invention of new display formats such as dioramas and coincided with two further transformations: the 'governmentalization' (Nyhart 2009: 201) of museums and the mutation of natural history museums into 'centres for gathering, dispensing and exchanging biological information' (Nyhart 2009: 240).

Nyhart's account situates the Museum für Naturkunde Berlin at the intersection of aesthetic, scientific and political formations that have gained novel traction amid its recent digitisation and data efforts. Specifically, the enmeshments of the museum's governmental and informational functions have intensified. The unprecedented investment of €660 million as well as large-scale projects to integrate natural history collections across Germany and the European Union attest to the political valence of data held in museums. Similarly, with exhibitions such as *Artefacts* (2018–19), co-produced with the European Commission's Joint Research Centre, the Berlin museum has positioned itself as a distributor of independent, fact-based evidence, seeking to produce well-informed subjects. The political valence is thus manifold, covering both economic rationales (bioeconomy, automation, application labs) and the production of data-literate and scientifically informed citizens. For instance, the nightingale project combines 'scientific' and 'socio-cultural' dimensions that connect the birds across complex interactions of people, stories, histories, technologies and infrastructures. But just as the textual practices and infrastructures of natural history introduced with Linnaean nomenclature and taxonomy contributed to the making of particular versions of diversity, so do the practices of data-based biodiversity. Indeed, we argue that the production and process of digital data construct a different notion diversity. Like Margareta von Oswald (see her essay in this volume), we contend that (digital) data practices and their infrastructures perform specific versions of bio/diversity.

Nightingales in data

On a summer's night in 2018, a group of 17 people gathered at the southern entrance of Berlin's Volkspark Friedrichshain, one of Berlin's largest parks, to participate in a 'nightingale tour'. The tour leader, a biologist and staff member at the Natural History Museum, welcomed the group and introduced the project. Participants learned that Berlin is the nightingale capital of the world, and that it offers an ideal environment to carry out research into the birds' different songs, or 'dialects'. She instructed them on how to use the Naturblick app to record bird songs before providing additional information about *Luscinia megarhynchos* on laminated A4 sheets. The sheets bore images of a small, brown bird, chicks in a nest, diagrams, numbers and maps. People clustered around the tour leader as she started moving through the park. The group congealed into a sensing organism, mobile phones ready, and headed into the silent dark.

> A nightingale starts to sing. The tour guide smiles and points her finger up in the air. The nightingale's vocalizations travel through the leaves and the chill night air down to our ears; the group momentarily becomes silent. The father and his child move closer to the tree from which the song just reached us. Torchlights are dancing here and there trying to spot the bird among the green leaves. Screens are touched to activate the digital recording.
> (Tour guide—Fieldnotes)

The bird songs were picked up by the mobile phone's microphone and converted into a stream of discrete numbers by an analogue-to-digital converter on the phone's logic board before being saved as an mp4 file. The Naturblick app then generated an image of audio signal frequencies and amplitude change over time, which served as the species' representative signature. The file was also sent directly to the server of the Naturblick team at the Museum für Naturkunde Berlin, where members of the nightingale project could access them.

Aside from recording bird songs, the participants were invited to join two (open) workshops at the museum to learn about bioacoustics analysis. They were shown how to use software (Avisoft-SASLab Pro) for analysing the recorded bird songs. Participants learned how scientists visualise, describe and use the nightingale songs.[3] Avisoft runs on Windows, its graphical user interface is sparse and technical: grey background, a mixture of familiar icons and obscure buttons for generating different statistical reports and manipulating variables (e.g. threshold, group time, hysteresis).

As Chiara Garbellotto sat in one of the newly built and fairly nondescript education rooms at the museum, the standard screens and grey and white office-style tables provided a stark contrast to the park. A sense of place vanished as nightingale songs turned into spectrograms (also called sonograms). The spectrograms in Avisoft are set within a diagrammatic space, showing black audio waves on a white background running along an x-axis (time) and a y-axis (frequency). Using spectrogram samples, a team member explained the categories for quantitative analysis: size of repertoire, category of song, song rate, duration, stereotypy (repeated utterance), frequency, number of elements. These variables are used to compare the song's elements and correlate them with additional data, such as the location and date of the recording. One team member, a PhD student, then compiled a list of all the different song elements identified in the analysed recordings into a catalogue. The instructor urged participants to select 'good data' for the group exercise, which in this case meant choosing spectrograms that were distinct and easy to label, such as trills, which were recognisable by bold, black, sharp traces on the spectrograms.

Participants were informed that Avisoft was used to 'clean' the recordings prior to analysis, that is, it removed any 'ambient' sound in order to isolate the single nightingale's song. While seemingly sensible, this type of 'data cleaning' reveals the tension that inheres in classification systems. On the one hand, the Avisoft interface assumes the abstract ideal of stable and unique classificatory principles and mutually exclusive categories (Bowker and Star 2000: 11). On the other, as with any classification system, objects have to be standardised in order to be processed across media and languages. And there are always moments when birds and their songs don't quite fit.

Recording and analysing digital bird songs showed the constructedness of our notions of data and species. The data were both abstract—the bits and bytes travelling from mobile phone microphones to servers, softwares and databases—and material (phones, laptops, the print-outs of sonograms). It took a good deal of work to create a functionable data set—standardisation, cleaning, quantification, visualisation—work that occurred beyond the sight of the participants. And it required a sequence of decisions, big and small, setting the type of protocols, formats and research questions. The same was true for the nightingales as they moved from living beings to a set of diagrammatic representations on a computer screen, classified by Linnaean nomenclature, data points on the map of the project homepage. According to Staffan Müller-Wille, Linnaean taxonomy, introduced in the late 18th century, 'enhanced flows of data' and established 'a system of relations and equivalence, rather than difference' (2017: 126). Taxonomy and nomenclature turn nightingale into *Liscinia megarhyncho* and into a member of the Old World flycatcher family. For Müller-Wille, name and classification function as 'containers' that can be added to or divided and that have no value in and of themselves aside from facilitating human communication, exchange and ordering. Rising concurrently with the establishment of natural history collections—the Berlin museum's collection dates back to 1805—the Linnaean system turned animals and plants turned into units that could be managed, reorganised and exchanged within and between institutions (Müller-Wille 2017). In this sense, the Linnaean taxonomy had long ago made animals into data creatures.

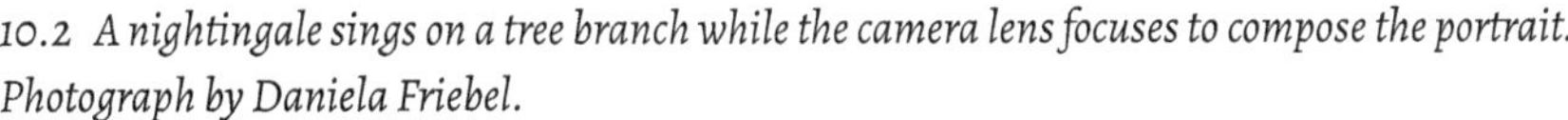

10.2 A nightingale sings on a tree branch while the camera lens focuses to compose the portrait. Photograph by Daniela Friebel.

Modern digital tools preserved the Linnaean system —the Naturblick app provides the Latin binomial for each taxa—but they also brought novel paradigms. One such novel paradigm is 'interoperability', a property allowing data to flow across different systems, products and infrastructures. The paradigm is crucial because communication and exchange occur between humans, machines and computers. It requires shared terminologies, institutional and disciplinary domains and semantic metadata. This entails a host of new data, standards, infrastructures, etc. Interoperability, next to time and space, is a vector for ordering. As such, it is associated with another paradigmatic change, which Geoffrey Bowker (2000) has identified in biodiversity sciences: the transformation of data and databases into ends in themselves. Vincent Devictor and Bernadette Bensaude-Vincent (2016) argue that 'global biodiversity' is an artefact of data infrastructures and that the concept 'is, above all, a policy-making platform' (2016: 13). The collection of occurrence data together with the massive digitisation of natural history collections—a potential area for citizen science—works to legitimise a particular research style (Devictor and Bensaude-Vincent 2016: 13). Nyhart's 'biological perspective' has become datafied with biodiversity science and ecology, and rendered into technoscience.

As a data creature, the nightingale is an aggregate of different data points that circulate from park to mobile phone to museum to global database to policy reports and biodiversity assessments. According to Müller-Wille, those data points can be expanded indefinitely. There will always be another occurrence, another song to record. But what his diagnosis of natural history misses is that the form of data compels some logics and not others. The discovery and management of biodiversity require standardisation to produce generalizable knowledge. 'No science', Lorraine Daston and Peter Galison write, 'can do without such standardised working objects, for unrefined natural objects are too quirkily particular to cooperate in generalizations and comparisons' (1992: 85). In other words, the nightingale as data creature is an object of science composed of standard protocols and international classification systems. Through their ability to standardise, nomenclature and taxonomy carry prescriptive power. But who decides what counts as a standard and whom or what does this decision serve?

Citizens in data

The 'citizen' in citizen science is difficult to pin down. In the considerable literature on citizen science, the citizen is imagined as a non-descript person positioned outside of science proper who is distinguished, primarily, by his or her activity. Citizens are described as 'people who actively observe, report, collect, analyse and disseminate information via text, audio, or video messages' (Sheth 2009). In a similar vein, the EU report 'Using New Data Sources for Policymaking' (Schade et al. 2017) states that citizen scientists engage with policy, interact with scientists and politicians and contribute to scientific information and knowledge. They are variously presented as distinct from 'stakeholders' and as representing 'one particular stakeholder group'. Once enrolled in citizen science projects, they become 'participants'. On the nightingale project website, citizen science is described as scientific projects undertaken by 'interested lay people and amateurs'. So while the 'citizen' appears prominently in project descriptions and citizen science discourse, the term remains a 'floating signifier' (Lévi-Strauss 1987), a signifier with a vague or unspecifiable signified. These diverse designations all assume that citizens—whatever they are—come into being performatively through practices of interacting or engaging with science. Rather than focusing on what citizenship is, a semiotic understanding of diversity turns our attention to how 'citizenship' is done.

A central concern of the nightingale project, and a key practice through which citizenship is enacted, is 'language'. The study of bird songs and learning behaviour gained popularity in the 1950s with the spread of sonogram technology. This turned the practices of amateur naturalists in the birding community into a scientific method (Marler and Slabbekoorn 2004: 11). The study of single-species song repertoires navigates a complex terrain between variability (due to 'dialects' and improvisation) and universalism at the species level (Devictor and Bensaude-Vincent 2016: 13). Moreover, it brings together concepts of phonotypical and genetic evolution, sexual selection and social learning (Devictor and Bensaude-Vincent 2016: 25) to address intraspecies behaviours within the (acoustic) environment individual birds occupy. One of the main applications of research on vocal learning is determining the biological substrate of human language evolution. Language is not only a 'mystery' for evolutionary theory, it is a key biological and sociological unit for establishing bio/diversity. Reardon notes that the lead scientist at the Human Genome Diversity Project, a controversial effort begun in the 1990s at Stanford University to gather genetic material from interesting 'populations', proposed collecting samples 'from 50 individuals from 200 isolated "aboriginal tribes" defined according to language' (2001: 363). Here, language is identified as a stable classifier by which to assemble a particular social group—'aboriginal tribes'—and distinguish them from other groups. At the same time, the choice of the term 'aboriginal tribe' makes evident the social and political values that persist in the doing of biological sciences and that stand in stark contrast to the relational and process-based approach to culture in the social and cultural sciences. A third conception of language appears through the data-based infrastructures that subtend the project in the form of 'semantic metadata', i.e. the 'metadata that describes the "meaning" of data' (Melton and Buxton 2006: 75). Given the 'fundamental relationship between the speaking subject and the citizen subject' (Isin and Ruppert 2015: 52), the data-based engagements prompted by the app suggest two important problematisations of this relationship. First, the introduction of apps to facilitate or, at times, enable civic duties add a novel range of utterances to the speech of the citizen subject, from clicking consent boxes to allowing the extraction of data streams from devices. Second, this type of speech is no longer entirely readable by humans and as such is incongruent with conventional practices of accountability.

Biological sciences have long incorporated sociological categories and, as the passage from Reardon shows, have used them to explicate orders in the natural world. Here, human language, a complex and continuously changing socio-cultural phenomenon, becomes representative of and for a particular genetic make-up. Much of feminist science studies is dedicated to unpacking the problems that arise when contested terminology is elided in favour of a narrowly defined scientificity. Messy and complex histories inhere in the term 'citizen'. There is of course no requirement to prove national citizenship status in order to participate in citizen science, although the nightingale's project's second component did specifically enrol 'new citizens'. For the third component, the collection of bird song data, participants needed to use the Naturblick app, which is available on iOS and Android accounts. The smart phone, its operating system and the app thus become material expressions or correlates of 'citizenship'. For some users, then, citizenship depends on being in possession of a Google account or being registered at the Google App Store. Given the well-documented malpractices of Google and its parent company Alphabet, such prerequisites are not trivial.[4] The app download and sign-in procedure show that the project not only collects data on nightingales but, through its infrastructures, also collects data on its participants. The invisible data traffic suggests that even while users might be able to read some of the data-based utterances, they might not have the literacy required for understanding their consequences. To put it bluntly, while many app-based citizen science projects intend to create scientifically literate citizens, they might also entrench illiteracy of data privacy issues.

Here emerges another prominent figuration of the citizen, the 'user'. Upon opening the Naturblick app on a smartphone, the catchy logo of a stylised eye with a quill for a pupil (a visual nod to the app's name, which translates as 'nature's gaze') hovers above an extravagantly coloured bird wing. Throughout the app, eye-catching buttons bearing simple logos or photographs of animals let users easily navigate and interact with the app. When first opening the app, a pop-up window informs the user about the new data protection guidelines. It spells out the terms regarding the authorship of image, sound recordings and their automatically issued geo-coordinates. Users have to agree that all recordings will fall under the CC BY SA 4.0 licence. The agreement form notes that where names are made known, they will be identified as authors. If no name is provided, the default author will be the museum's Naturblick app. It also informs users that they can share their recordings with project partners such as the nightingale project and other publicly funded citizen science projects. The section on the collection of usage data states that all data will be collected for purely scientific purposes. Should they no longer be needed, they will be deleted. The app collects device ID and 'user interaction data'. The audio files recorded are saved on the Museum's Naturblick server and available on the user's device in a folder called Naturblick, which the app automatically creates. From there, any user is able to access or reproduce them on other devices. They are also available online as part of the map on the nightingale project's website, from which they are downloadable.

10.3 An online map that locates the verified recordings shared by the App users at the end of the second season of the nightingale project. Reproduced courtesy of the Forschungsfall Nachtigall team at the Museum für Naturkunde Berlin.

The scientific institutions of Western modernity have also been dedicated to registering humans in addition to non-human animals. Such registering and counting always require classifications and categorisations: who to count is a central question for state-sponsored efforts targeting the arithmetrics of population. Writing about the technology of census-taking, Theodore Porter argues that 'any actual count depends on the specification and political acceptance of a whole array of conventions' (1994: 391). The first hurdles are 'definitional problems', that is, the question of who to count and the constitution of the 'who'. In other words, who to count is tied to the question of who counts prior to the study design. In critical citizenship studies, attention has focused on how conceptions of citizenship, which traditionally focus on rights, obligations, expectations and nation-state membership, have changed with the rise of supranational (and subnational) institutions such as the European Union, introducing a notion of citizenship that is 'performed in relation to sociotechnical arrangements' (Isin and Ruppert 2015: 4) and based on specific norms, values and technologies. Critical data studies expand on these sociotechnical arrangements by examining the ways in which governments and state agencies define citizenship in contradistinction to 'foreignness' through the logic of data-based surveillance regimes (e.g. Browne 2015).

On the nightingale project's website, participants are addressed simultaneously as 'laymen and amateurs' and invited to become 'citizen researchers'. Participation is described as a 'dialogue between science and society', with the museum as mediator. This enrolment of the project's participants in the museum's mission returns us to Nyhart's argument about the governmental function of museums. A crucial component of this function is the creation of narratives of participation to legitimise the institution. The coexistence of 'citizen science' in the museum with other professional terminology and related practices such as 'knowledge transfer', 'participation' and 'open science' is part of a professionalization and standardization of participatory technologies (Chilvers and Kearnes 2016: 44). These take the form of data-gathering efforts at various scales, and are part of a data-driven 'biological perspective' that relies on the binary opposition of science/society. One technology that appears to have been particularly generative in the case of the nightingale project was the creation of imagined participant categories for funding schemes and accounting procedures. The need to identify target publics for both the project's initial proposal and the final evaluation required defining a list of subjects—'citizens', 'clubs', 'new citizens', 'school and kindergarten students', 'scientific team', and 'cooperation partners, collaborators, input providers'. Moreover, under the umbrella of 'citizen science', the explicit separation of the scientific activities from educational and cultural activities re-produce divisions at the epistemological and ontological levels. Citizens emerge as data-literate 'researchers' who record nightingales and produce data; students, who lack conservationist knowledge, learn how to identify nightingales; new Berliners as representatives of their country of origin provide memories of their 'previous life' where nightingales figure as cultural symbols. The clear delineation of these identities is a response to the formal requirements of projects within European and state funding schemes. At the same time, such categorisations might render invisible the partial or undisciplined connections between participants and between research objects and subjects (see also the contributions to this volume by Gerbich, Puzon and Tinius).

In sociology, anthropology and political theory, 'citizen' and 'citizenship' are highly contested concepts in both theory and practice. Nowadays, citizenship depends on being informed. We see this in test requirements for citizenship candidates as well as in the enormous amounts of information we must process if we are to make use of our rights as citizens, consumers, students, employees etc. In the nightingale project, data and participants are co-produced. As participants gather and collect data via their smartphones, they generate actionable data for science, the museum, the German government, European funders and a host of other entities not readily identifiable, or, not yet assembled given the rapid developments in the current data economy. At the same time, data production turns citizens into participants and scientists. But the exact remit of these designations, the political consequences and efficacies and historical meanings of these subject positions remain obscure. The history of statistics has demonstrated how populations and individuals have been rendered visible and governable through data. A future history of museums might demonstrate how data have been rendered visible and valent through participation.

Conclusion

> CS [citizen science] is definitively needed, but also not all the scientific projects can be turned into CS, though some can. For biodiversity monitoring, CS is the future. It helps raise awareness of conservation issues: if people know how to look, they can also care. Species conservation is an issue.
> (Tour guide, private conversation)

In this chapter we focused on the ambiguous nature of bio/diversity on the basis of a citizen science project conceived and run by the Naturkunde Museum für Berlin and dedicated to recording and mapping nightingale songs. In particular, we attended to the data practices of the project—from recording and collecting to analysing—in order to capture how different versions of citizens and species are made in and with data. On the basis of this, we put forward the notion of the 'data creature' to understand the ways in which nightingales and 'citizens' are brought into being.

Our key argument was that doing diversity moves between biological and social registers and that data are novel mediators for terms and practices to criss-cross these domains. Data practices have also extended the 'biological perspective' that is associated with the move from a taxonomy-oriented natural history to an ecology-oriented biology. Natural history museums have been instrumental in construing and disseminating this perspective and, by doing so, have assumed both informational and political functions. These functions have only intensified as data-based efforts to capture, collect and communicate biodiversity have increased. And we can see a reintroduction of taxonomy-oriented logics and formalisms in the ways in which standards and protocols are structuring the capture of biodiversity. One of the problems this poses is the intransparency of data and their digital infrastructures. If the aim of citizen science is the production of scientifically literate people and their participation in scientific practices, then it is crucial to help participants develop a 'critical data consciousness' (Nadim 2018) and to explore the possibility of making scientific epistemology—its historicity and its social and political constructedness—an object of collaboration among scientists and non-scientists as well. This would also help integrate citizen science and civic participation. In fact, for citizen science to work, it requires civic participation.

The form of problems posed by diversity in natural history and citizenship discourse share a similar tension between universalism and particularism. Like the citizen, the species is a 'historical and geographic figure' (Isin and Ruppert 2015: 19) whose form and substance is tied to ideas, practices and institutions such as natural history museums. Questions as to the unit of analysis (how to measure/diagnose diversity?), scale (is diversity a trait of individuals or groups?) and mode of ordering (population, culture, flock, participants, etc.) connect practices and categories across biological and socio-political discourses. Importantly, the 'liberal subject form' (Brown 2006), which shapes the ontological foundation of Western concepts of citizenship, is deeply connected to the history and scientific understanding of (human) bodies. The history of this understanding is also a history of data practices.

An important application of the research serves the monitoring of species within the urban environment, especially through the production of occurrence maps. This data is directly relevant to the development of conservation and protection policies in connection to urban planning. Nightingales are particularly interesting in this regard because of their preferred habitat: 'bushes with branches close to the ground (as food and reproduction areas), tree/shrub over-holders (as singing and warning stations) and high perennial vegetation (as food areas)' (Witt 1996: 13). Berlin is nowadays considered 'the capital of nightingales' because of its particular urban conditions, which themselves are the result of its multiple reconstructions and divisions. For Witt, bush pruning and the 'cleaning' of public spaces were to blame for the decrease in nightingale species populations as part of clean-up works conducted in the eastern neighbourhoods of the city in the years after German reunification. Human activity shapes nature just as nature and environmental changes shape human activities. Losing social diversity—in the form of public spaces and mixed-used housing—leads to the loss of biodiversity. The data creatures produced in the project will live on, in databases, project reports, friendships, scientific papers, mobile phones and other unlikely places. They are ready to inform urban planning and make the city more liveable for humans and nightingales alike.

Acknowledgements

Chiara Garbellotto's doctoral research has been funded by the Alexander von Humboldt Foundation as part of the research award for Sharon Macdonald's Alexander von Humboldt Professorship (2017–2020). She thanks the colleagues at the Centre for Anthropological Research on Museums and Heritage (CARMAH) for the inspiring discussions and the support received, especially by her cohort companion doctoral researcher Nazlı Cabadağ. We would like to give special thanks to the *Forschungsfall Nachtigall* team at the Museum für Naturkunde and all the project's participants for the curiosity and availability. We are particularly grateful to Silke Voigt-Heucke and Sarah Darwin for their comments on an earlier draft of the paper.

Notes

1 On the role of lists in the production of natural orders, see Müller-Wille and Charmantier (2012) and Pugliano (2012); on note-taking and double-entry bookkeeping, see te Heesen (2005a; (2005b); on the role of description as a type of technology in early natural history, see Ogilvie (2008).

2 With reference to the performativity of technologies and language, we suggest that how we account for biodiversity also shapes how we relate to it. See, for example Asdal (2008) and Höhler and Ziegler (2010). This accounting entails a range of objects and narratives through which diversity becomes enacted differently. By way of, say, remote-sensing data and global environmental monitoring networks, biodiversity is turned into a set of variables that allow the calculation of global biodiversity trends. These are subsequently ameniable to and necessitate specific neoliberal forms of governance, what Turnhout et al. (2014) have termed 'measurementality', that reify diversity as a marketable value for cost-benefit analyses.

3 Avisoft is made by a German software developer and since its release in the mid-1990s has become a central tool for 'investigating acoustic communication in various animal species including birds, mammals, rodents, frogs, fish and insects' (Avisoft website). It is used by researchers worldwide and currently costs 2,400 euros (1,800 euros for additional licences).

4 Most recent accusations focus on racism (Barmann 2022), sexism (Glaser and Adams 2021), labour relations (Robitzski 2021), algorithmic bias (Wong 2020), censorship (Roth 2021), data privacy and the facilitation of misinformation and 'fake news' (Ohlheiser 2017).

References

Asdal, K. 2008. 'Enacting things through numbers: Taking nature into account/ing', *Geoforum*, 39(1): 123–132.

Barmann, J. 2022. 'Alphabet hit with racial discrimination. Lawsuit by former diversity recruiter for Google', 22 March 2022, *SFist* https://sfist.com/2022/03/22/alphabet-hit-with-racial-discrimination-lawsuit-by-former-diversity-recruiter-for-google/ (accessed 4 April 2022).

Bowker, G. C. 2000. 'Biodiversity Datadiversity', *Social Studies of Science*, 30(5): 643–83.

Bowker, G. C., and S. L. Star. 2000. *Sorting Things Out*. Cambridge, MA: MIT Press.

Brown, W. 2006. 'American nightmare: Neoliberalism, neoconservatism, and de-democratization', *Political Theory*, 34(6): 690–714.

Browne, S. 2015. *Dark Matters: On the Surveillance of Blackness*. Durham: Duke University Press.

Chilvers, J., and M. Kearnes (eds). 2016. *Remaking Participation: Science, Environment and Emergent Publics*. London: Routledge.

Daston, L., and P. Galison. 1992 'The image of objectivity', *Representations*, (40): 81–128.

Devictor, V., and B. Bensaude-Vincent. 2016. 'From ecological records to Big Data: The invention of global biodiversity', *History and Philosophy of the Life Sciences*, 38(4).

Federal Government Position Paper. 2017. *Guidelines for the New EU Framework Programme for Research and Innovation*. https://www.bmbf.de/files/Federal_government_FP9_guidelines_September_2017.pdf (accessed 4 April 2022).

Franklin, S., C. Lury, and J. Stacey. 2000. *Global Nature, Global Culture*. London: SAGE Publications.

Gabrys, J. 2017. 'The becoming environmental of computation from citizen sensing to planetary computerization', *Italian Journal of Science & Technology Studies*, 8(1): 5–21.

Glaser, A., and C. Adams. 2021. 'Google advised mental health care when workers complained about racism and sexism', 7 March 2021, *NBCNews*. https://www.nbcnews.com/tech/tech-news/google-advised-mental-health-care-when-workers-complained-about-racism-n1259728 (accessed 4 April 2022).

Haraway, D. 2018. *Modest_Witness@Second_Millennium. FemaleMan_Meets_OncoMouse: Feminism and Technoscience*. New York: Routledge.

Heesen, A. te. 2005a. 'The notebook: A paper technology', in B. Latour, and P. Weibel (eds), *Making Things Public. Atmospheres of Democracy*, 582–89. Cambridge, MA: MIT Press.

Heesen, A. te. 2005b. 'Accounting for the natural world: Double-entry bookkeeping in the field', in L. Schiebinger, and C. Swan (eds), *Colonial Botany: Science, Commerce, and Politics in the Early Modern World*, 237–251. Philadelphia: University Pennsylvania Press.

Höhler, S. and R. Ziegler 2010. 'Nature's accountability: Stocks and stories', Science as Culture 19(4): 417–430.

Isin, E. F., and E. Ruppert 2015. *Being Digital Citizens*. London: Rowman & Littlefield.

Kimura, A. H., and A. Kinchy. 2016. 'Citizen science: Probing the virtues and contexts of participatory research', *Engaging Science, Technology, and Society*, 2: 331–361.

Kohler, R. 2002. *Landscapes & Labscapes: Exploring the Lab-Field Border in Biology*. Chicago: University of Chicago Press.

Kohler, R. 2006. *All Creatures: Naturalists, Collectors, and Biodiversity, 1850–1950*. Princeton University Press.

Lévi-Strauss, C. 1987. *Introduction to the Work of Marcel Mauss*. London: Routledge.

Marler, P., and H. W. Slabbekoorn (eds). 2004. *Nature's Music: The Science of Birdsong*. Amsterdam: Elsevier Academic.

McGhie, H. 2019. 'Museum collections and biodiversity conservation', *Curating Tomorrow*. https://curatingtomorrow236646048.files.wordpress.com/2019/08/museum-collections-and-biodiversity-conservation-2019.pdf (accessed 4 April 2022).

Melton, J., and S. Buxton. 2006. 'Metadata—An overview', in J. Melton, and S. Buxton (eds), *Querying XML*, 67–84. Burlington: Morgan Kaufmann.

Müller-Wille, S. 2017. 'Names and numbers: "Data" in classical natural history, 1758–1859', *Osiris*, 32(1): 109–128.

Müller-Wille, S., and I. Charmantier. 2012. 'Lists as research technologies', *Isis*, 103(4): 743–752.

Nadim, T. 2018. 'c u soon humans need to sleep now so many conversations today thx', in T. Nadim, and N. Wagner (eds), *The Influencing Machine*, 72–81. Berlin: nGbK.

Nadim, T. 2022. 'All the data creatures', in E. J. Gonzalez-Polledo, and S. Posocco (eds), *Bioinformation Worlds and Futures*, 20–35. London: Routledge.

Nyhart, L. N. 2009. *Modern Nature: The Rise of the Biological Perspective in Germany*. Chicago: University of Chicago Press.

Ohlheiser, A. 2017. 'How far-right trolls named the wrong man as the Las Vegas shooter, 2 October 2017, *The Washington Post*. https://www.washingtonpost.com/news/the-intersect/wp/2017/10/02/how-far-right-trolls-named-the-wrong-man-as-the-las-vegas-shooter/ (accessed 4 April 2022).

Ogilvie, B. W. 2008. *The Science of Describing: Natural History in Renaissance Europe*. Chicago: University of Chicago Press.

Porter, T. M. 1994. 'Making things quantitative', *Science in Context*, 7(3): 389–407.

Pugliano, V. 2012. 'Specimen lists: Artisanal writing or natural historical paperwork?', *Isis*, 103(4): 716–26.

Reardon, J. 2001. 'The human genome diversity project: A case study in coproduction', *Social Studies of Science*, 31(3): 357–388.

Robitzski, D. 2021 April 27. 'Google investors condemn company for punishing whistleblowers', 27 April 2021, *Futurism*.

https://futurism.com/the-byte/google-investors-condemn-punishing-whistleblowers (accessed 4 April 2022).

Roth, A. 2021. 'This article is more than 6 months old Apple and Google accused of 'political censorship' over Alexei Navalny app', 17 September 2021, *The Guardian*. https://www.theguardian.com/world/2021/sep/17/apple-and-google-accused-of-political-censorship-over-alexei-navalny-app (accessed 4 April 2022).

Schade, S., M. Manzoni-Brusati, C. Tsinaraki, et al. 2017. *Using New Data Sources for Policymaking, JRC Technical Reports*. Luxembourg: Publications Office of the European Union.

Sheth, A. 2009. 'Citizen sensing, social signals, and enriching human experience', *IEEE Internet Computing*, 13(4): 87–92.

Strasser, B. J., L. Baudry, D. Mahr, G. Sanchez, and E. Tancoigne. 2019. '"Citizen Science"? Rethinking science and public participation', *Science & Technology Studies*: 52–76.

Subramaniam, B. 2014. *Ghost Stories for Darwin: The Science of Variation and the Politics of Diversity*. Urbana: University of Illinois.

Turnhout, E., K. Neves, and E. de Lijster 2014. '"Measurementality" in biodiversity governance: Knowledge, transparency, and the Intergovernmental Science-Policy Platform on Biodiversity and Ecosystem Services (Ipbes)', *Environment and Planning A: Economy and Space*, 46(3): 581–597.

Witt, K. 1996. *Bestand der Nachtigall (Luscinia Megarhynchos) in Berlin in den Jahren 1993–95*. Berl. Ornithol. Ber. 6: 3 22.

Wong, J. C. 2020. 'More than 1,200 Google workers condemn firing of AI scientist Timnit Gebru', 4 December 2020, *The Guardian*. https://www.theguardian.com/technology/2020/dec/04/timnit-gebru-google-ai-fired-diversity-ethics (accessed 4 April 2022).

Exploring the Futurabilities of Museums
Making differences with the *Museum Divan* at the Museum for Islamic Art in Berlin

Christine Gerbich

The main argument of this chapter is that organisational learning is key to enhancing the futurabilities of museums. Unlike organisations in the economic sector, where organisational learning is a tool to increase productivity, organisational learning in the context of museums aims to foster democratisation through participation. (See, for example, Brown & Peers 2003, Dahlgren & Hermes 2015, Lynch 2011, Macdonald 1998, Meijer-van Mensch 2012, Mörsch 2009, Runnel & Pruulmann-Vengerfeldt 2014, Sternfeld 2013, Witcomb 2003.)

The chapter draws on an understanding of museum organisations and heritage as relational and co-produced, as dynamic and complex, as assemblages of people, materialities, practices and ideas (Harrison 2013, Macdonald 2013, Macdonald et al. 2018, Waterton & Dittmer 2014). Knowledge in organisations is not static, and learning is not unidirectional or dependent on fixed structures. Rather, learning is a situated process that encompasses emotional, physical and cognitive elements and includes the performance of knowledge as 'knowing' (Cook & Brown 1999). As situated practices, learning and knowing are constrained by material, social, emotional, imaginary and political factors. Those need not be formal boundaries, such as departments or disciplines. They can also be communities of practice—groups of people who share a common domain of interest, collectively accumulate knowledge and classify it into new or existing categories (Argyris & Schön 1978, Gherardi 2000, Gherardi et al. 1998, Gherardi 2011, Lave & Wenger 1991, Levitt & March 1988, Pallett & Chilvers 2015, Wenger 2000, Yanow & Ybema 2009)

The heterogenous practices at play in museums are shaped by various temporal structures and ways of referencing between present, past and future. This draws on a praxeological understanding of time that refrains from a rationalist idea of the future. This means that the future is understood neither as a linear process that can be fully controlled or planned in the present, nor as a social category shared by all individuals and groups in a museum (Appadurai 2013, Berardi 2017, Bryant and Knight 2017, Reckwitz 2016, Schatzki 2010, Pink et al. 2017, Harrison et al. 2020).

The following analysis reflects on museums as mindful institutions (Janes 2010) and explores four abilities that I believe are key to fostering the futurabilities of museums: *recognising* museums as political agents to counteract social or political injustices; *allowing* dialogue about the future potential of the museum through participatory projects; *investigating* the possibilities and challenges of democratic future-making through participation; and *nourishing* ideas, practices, routines and structures that promote the envisioning of new, democratic futures.[1]

I show that the implementation of the new practice not only reveals the heterogeneous views of the future within the curatorial team, but also highlights how moving away from 'pragmatic' time regimes can promote democratic learning within a museum. This includes devoting time to unlearning, that is, to understanding one's privilege as 'one's loss' (Spivak et al. 1996: 4) and reflecting on how people may be encouraged to 'speak back' (Castro Varela, María do Mar 2017, Sternfeld 2016).

These explorations draw on ethnography as a tool for 'trying to see and experience life-worlds from the point of view of those who live them and within the context of which they are part' (Macdonald 2013: 9). As co-initiator and co-organiser of the Museum Divan, I consider the results of evaluations and autoethnographic field notes (Karra and Phillips 2007). In doing so, I use my own 'becoming-with' (Gherardi 2019: 741) as a white German academic as an epistemic strategy to understand the museum's futurabilities. This includes taking 'the terror out of error' (Mörsch 2011b) and reflecting on my own struggles and failures as valuable sources for (un)learning. Being able to do so signals trust and a deep commitment to learning. In this spirit, I wish to express my gratitude to all the participants, especially those who took the time to participate in the Museum Divan, my colleagues from the Museum for Islamic Art and the researchers involved in the TOPOI-funded exhibition The Heritage of the Old Kings: Ctesiphon and the Persian Sources of Islamic Art.

Recognising the museum's social agency

The Museum for Islamic Art belongs to the Prussian Cultural Heritage Foundation's State Museums and is housed in the Pergamon Museum on Berlin's Museum Island. Founded in 1904, most of its collections were acquired at archaeological excavations or purchased on the art market (Kröger and Heiden 2004). The museum presents itself as occupying 'an unrivalled position in Germany—no other institution contains such a systematic and comprehensive collection of masterpieces of art and applied arts and objects of material culture stemming from Islamic societies as well as the Christian and Jewish communities living among them'.[2]

The museum's founders, directors and curatorial staff have played a vital role in the emergence of Islamic art history as a discipline. When I joined the museum in 2009 as part of a third-party funded project,[3] I quickly noticed staff members' alignment with the intellectual heritage and curatorial approaches of the institution's past. This included interpreting the material heritage of regions with Muslim-majority populations as 'art'. One rationale for that approach was that it valued Muslim-majority populations as a 'denominator for global achievements'. Another explanation was the partial lack of knowledge about the symbolic meanings of objects from these eras and regions. Adding other layers of knowledge could lead to an 'overinterpretation' of objects (Gonnella 2013: 147–148).

Object specialists at the museum regarded themselves as 'cultural experts' (Carpentier 2014: 117) with knowledge accredited by academic degrees. Their task was to nurture, contribute and share the knowledge produced by the institution. Education and outreach were neither part of curation nor embedded in the museum itself. Rather, it was provided by a single representative from Visitor Services, a centralised department formally attached to the State Museum's General Directorate. The 'services' were geared towards complementing curatorial work through educational programmes, guided tours and pedagogical material (Schmidl and Nolte 2008). Opportunities for exchange and learning across professional communities were rare, and overarching debates, such as the lively discussions about 'participation' in the field of education, did not find their way into the museum (Jaschke and Nora Sternfeld 2012, Kazeem et al. 2009, Mörsch 2009, 2011a, Gesser et al. 2012, Muttenthaler and Wonisch 2007).

Seen through the lens of theories about learning in organisations, the community of curators at the museum was 'sticky' (Wenger et al. 2002: 153). They were members of a prestigious group of experts, and as such had felt no need to expand their professional boundaries or to reimagine traditional ways of interpreting objects.

Change came in 2009 with the appointment of a new director, Stefan Weber, who was entrusted with revamping the museum. He formulated a new vision early on in his tenure with 'New Spaces for Old Treasures' (Weber 2013b). Colleagues inside and outside the Berlin State Museums believed that his view represented a 'new era' and 'a fresh wind' (field note, 3 February 2009).

Amid increasing anti-Muslim racism in Europe and an overall negative portrayal of Islam and Muslims in public debates, researchers at the time reflected critically on representations of 'Islam' in museums (Kamel 2004, Shalem 2012, Shaw 2012, Shatanawi 2012). Drawing on postcolonial theories, most prominently Edward Said's critique of orientalism (1995), they pointed to the intellectual appropriation of 'Islamic' cultures into a Western canon of art history, and criticised the neglect of the symbolic meanings attached to and the practices associated with objects in their regions of origin (Necipoğlu 2013, Rabbat 2013). Despite critical debates over art historical methods, the museum's main actors had always 'defined the qualitative otherness of the subject, since in most cases there was no one to look back, thus no agency on the other side to be counted into the equation' (Troelenberg 2015: 228).

Acknowledging the debates on the historical traditions that shaped Islamic art history, Stefan Weber suggested displaying objects not only as art but as material culture in order to make 'the many layers of meanings of an object accessible' (Weber 2013a: 39). Unlike his predecessors, Weber recognised the controversial debates on Islam and Muslims (Weber 2015) and envisioned the expansion of the museum's role as an educational space to help counteract essentialising perspectives. The museum would present contemporary perspectives on the diversity of Islam and its global entanglements in the past and present.

The emergence of 'messy' diversity: the Museum Divan concept

The new director, eager to put his visions into practice, was acutely aware of the lack of resources for education and outreach. Discussing the situation during a planning meeting for the new permanent exhibition, he said: 'We know a lot about art history, but when it comes to communicating with our visitors, we have to learn a lot, we are clueless') (field note October 2010). To enhance the Museum's educational potential, he co-initiated several third-party funded projects.[4]

It was at this particular moment in time that I began to conceive the Museum Divan. It was meant to respond critically to the Western epistemological traditions that had shaped Islamic art history and to give voice to Berlin's diverse urban society in order to foster learning among museum professionals.

Since research on museum users and exhibition evaluations are not carried out on a regular basis at the Berlin State Museums, in-depth knowledge about people's perspectives and behaviours in the galleries was lacking. The director and I agreed that implementing evaluative practices was a useful tool for learning. As I have argued elsewhere (Gerbich 2014), such evaluations are a means for democratisation. The idea was to foster dialogue concerning the uses of the museum in the lives of Berliners—including their motivations for visiting the galleries, their experiences in the museum, their ideas about what the future role of the Museum could be—and thus incorporate alternative perspectives on the collections. Overall, the approach aimed to challenge preconceived notions about the 'the general public' or 'the visitor'. The approach drew on an understanding of publics as performed and emergent (Barnett et al. 2010). It sought to bring together groups of people that would develop reflexive qualities in the process of working together (Chilvers and Kearnes 2016). Rather than approaching people as members of neatly defined 'target groups', the Museum Divan understands diversity as 'messy', a tangle 'of cross-cutting and intersecting diversities – of, say, gender, sexuality, ableness and religion' (Macdonald 2018).

'Doing diversity' in this way was about avoid framing 'migrants' or 'Muslims' as homogenous groups.[5] Drawing on research revealing significant differences between 'migrants' with regard to their socio-economic status, cultural lifestyles (Haug et al. 2008, Sinus Sociovision 2007) and beliefs, we abandoned the concept of the 'migrant community'. The Museum Divan recognises the diversity of a 'postmigrant' society (Foroutan 2015a; Foroutan 2015b) and pays attention to the heterogeneity and intersecting inequalities within 'communities' (Crooke 2010, see, e.g. Watson 2007).

We thus decided to contact people with gatekeeper roles through which the museum's networks could be expanded. Given the regional focus of the museum and the need to build new networks, we mainly approached stakeholders with migrant experiences from Turkey, Iraq, Syria, Iran and other Muslim-majority countries. To understand the perspectives and questions of novices, we also approached people who had never been to any of these regions.

Investigating processes of learning through participation

To investigate the learning potential that the Museum Divan offered, I use data collected during the making of the exhibition The Heritage of the Old Kings: Ctesiphon and the Persian Sources of Islamic Art.[6]

Funded by the TOPOI Excellence Cluster,[7] this exhibition was organised to showcase the work of nine researchers from the Museum for Islamic Art[8] and various universities in Berlin. It addressed cultural entanglements and dynamics during pre-Islamic times in the Mediterranean and their influence on cultural production after Islamic conquerors took power. The focus of the exhibition was a set of objects excavated in the late 1920s and early 30s from the ancient ruins of Ctesiphon, the capital of the Sasanian Empire (224–651AD). My colleagues—trained in archaeology, architecture, art history and restoration—were interested in the city's architecture, among them the ruins of Tāq Kasrā (Arch of King Chosrau) and an īwān (or vaulted hall). They described the objects as 'iconic', featuring as they do on postcards, stamps, and 'in every school-book and in all good history books' (workshop transcript, C3, 10.06.2014). The exhibition aimed to experiment with new practices of curating and to include a 'mediator' in the process. A Ph.D. scholarship student in the TOPOI programme, I took over this role and suggested to my colleagues to organise a Museum Divan.

'This is not museum reality'.

Future-making does not happen overnight. It is a process shaped by a constant renegotiation of ideas and a refinement of practices (Gherardi 2012: 217). In the process of implementing the Museum Divan, I became aware of their conflicting notions of 'knowledge' and 'learning', of the different ideas of museum users, of the role attributed to Museum Divan participants and of the lack of knowledge regarding evaluative practices.

During one of our first team meetings, the director described my role as being 'to prove whether our messages come across in the end' (field note, SW 5 May 2014). Another colleague, citing a survey I had conducted several years earlier, remarked with consternation: 'But, there have *already* been evaluations, and they already have a huge influence on what we are doing. We *always* ask ourselves now how our displays affect people and whom we are addressing' (field note, C1, 5 May 2014). I realised that my colleagues did not understand the difference between summative evaluations (carried out at the end of an exhibition project), and the process-oriented evaluations I had in mind. I explained to the team the idea of learning as participation, and how members' contributions and criticisms could be used as a tool for reflecting on our messages and their epistemic assumptions.

My approach was meant to break with the existing understanding of curators as cultural experts. From the reactions of the colleagues, it became clear that they had different ideas about the future.[9] Some understood the future as a space to anticipate new possibilities. Among these were the director, who pledged his support to join meetings. Another colleague self-critically reflected on an encounter that made him aware of the different meanings that archaeologists and local people attached to a certain monument: 'It was a shock. I think one should definitely go and ask lay people. Talk to them. The earlier the better. So that they can connect. Wherever they come from. Because we are very much professionally entangled. And this, I think, is not always a useful filter' (C2, 5.11.2015).

Other colleagues formulated their expectations against the background of existing experiences. They were critical about the necessity of adding additional voices, emphasising that the focus of the exhibition had already been decided: 'It was very clear that this [the exhibition] would be a stage for TOPOI to present its work, to transmit the research to the public. *This* is what we do' (C1, 5.11.2015) On another occasion, one member of the museum staff argued that implementing the Museum Divan was too ambitious: 'This is not museum reality!' Working together with citizens was thought to be 'too time consuming', a source of stress that would add to the overall workload that the museum staff faced.

Indeed, changing curatorial practice was a complex and difficult undertaking. Soon after implementing the Museum Divan approach, I became aware of the rhythms that shaped our practices. At the beginning of the project, specialists shared their knowledge about the objects and their ideas about what the exhibition should communicate. Decisions about which objects to display and what kinds of information to provide on the labels were usually made in the final stages of exhibition preparations. But I wanted the specialist to communicate their knowledge and make their ideas explicit earlier. That way, I would be able to discuss objects with Museum Divan members ahead of time. But making their ideas explicit was time-intensive and interrupted their workflow.

Learning about and renegotiating the different time routines that shaped our daily work was important but the process was often impeded by the many other concurrent projects at the museum. Tight schedules and the fact that the team worked from separate locations in Berlin made regular conversations difficult. Minor tasks, such as compiling lists of objects for focus groups, took way more time than expected.

Time was not only a crucial resource. It was also a constant source of struggle in the work of putting the Museum Divan into practice. Specialists felt that they had devoted more time than they would have otherwise to such a small project. I felt up against an established and powerful time regime that stood at odds with the new practices that we had agreed on. One of the most important lessons to arise from the Museum Divan learned was the politics of time (Osborne 1995). As I show in the next section, taking time and spending it generously instead of sticking to pragmatic time regimes are key for democratic future-making.

Taking time for relationship-building

Together with Jana Braun, an experienced museologist who supported me in organising the Museum Divan, I approached Berliners who might be interested in longer-term collaboration due to their personal or professional interests in the region. Noting the challenges we faced, Jana ironically remarked: 'It's not exactly that people have been waiting for us' (J., field note 10 September 2015).

Among those who decided against participating were members of a network of social workers in a district of Berlin where the *Alternative für Deutschland*, a nationalist party promoting anti-Muslim racism, had gained many votes. The network of social workers provided creative after-school programmes for socially disadvantaged youth. After contacting them several times, they finally allowed me to attend a meeting. There I presented the Museum Divan as an opportunity to learn about Islam and Islamic regions, to voice criticisms and to formulate new visions. The social workers showed little interest in joining, however. The network coordinator later explained their reluctance: 'Well, their [the social workers'] first obstacle is always: "It doesn't fit into my... I don't care. Islamic art, well, what will I see there?" They've never been to the museum before, but they associate it with a certain kind of detachment.... Another obstacle is "art". Whenever you use the word "art", they tend to hesitate' (J. interview, 5.11.2015).

Participation is a voluntary act that requires those who become involved to share an interest and develop a common understanding of a theme or problem (Botkin et al. 1998 (1979): 30). As my example reveals, one of the challenges faced by the museum was its privileged position as an authority and its reputation as an elitist institution.

Like the social workers, many of the people we approached had never been to the museum before and were much in doubt about their ability as 'lay persons' to contribute to the knowledge of 'specialists'. Most of them had never heard about the Sasanians, and could not relate to the exhibition's subject matter. Moreover, some wondered why a museum for Islamic art would deal with objects from the pre-Islamic era, and why an 'art' museum would engage in archaeological research? The entire process—finding potential partners, introducing the Museum for Islamic Art, presenting researchers' complex ideas in comprehensive language and negotiating their potential role—was therefore incredibly time-consuming.

Such difficulties aside, Jana and I managed to assemble a diverse group of people in terms of age, gender, social and educational background, migrant experience, religious identity and location. Among them were professionals from other parts of Berlin's cultural sector interested in talking about the art and regions of Muslim-majority regions. These included the co-initiator of the Arabic film festival, a stage designer working for a post-migrant theatre and an artist from Iraq. There were also two people with a professional interest in the regions, two archaeologist and two journalists. Others were also interested in forging relationships with the institution: JUMA (Jung, Muslimisch, Aktiv – Young, Muslim, Active)—a network of young Muslim activists—two employees of Berlin's cultural administration and a social worker providing cultural activities in the Eastern part of the city. One person had participated in a previous Museum Divan event and expressed an interest in joining again to break up her usual routine. As compensation, the participants were made honorary Friends of the Museum for one year, which provided them with free admission to all Berlin State Museums.

Taking time for listening out

Judging by the evaluations from another exhibition project, I knew that the staged grandeur of the Museum's galleries could produce uncomfortable feelings in participants. Therefore, Jana and I took the time to reflect on our own positions as white, academic representatives of a powerful institution. We were familiar with the quotidian practices that are needed to stage and preserve a museum's grandeur, and we have acquired social and cultural capital (Bourdieu 1984, Bourdieu et al. 1990), such as knowing dress codes that allow us to move through the museum's galleries with confidence.

From those reflections, we decided to 'hack' (Spivak 2004: 559) ritual practices of professional performance—and bend our own time budgets. For example, when first meeting people, we travelled to locations of their choosing, asked them to address us by our first names (uncommon in Germany) and scheduled in ample time for initial chats. We told them that our knowledge about the collections was restricted, talked about the Museum Divan's aims and explained what their potential roles could be. We encouraged them to be 'honest' and critical, and explained that sharing even trivial-seeming comments, thoughts or experiences could help. We also made clear that our own powers were limited, and that we were not in full control of how their contributions would feed back into the future exhibition. We embraced listening as a political act to disrupt power and privilege (Bassel 2017). Such 'listening out', as Kate Lacey has argued (2013: 8), means being attentive and responsive to differences between ourselves and our partners (Connolly 1995). As the following example reveals, listening out was crucial for learning about alternative perspectives on Ctesiphon.

In November 2015, Jana and I met a potential participant. It was freezing cold that day, but in the first minutes of our encounter, our partner started sweating, and talking fast. He said that he felt honoured but also 'all in a dither' to meet people from 'one of these big museums on Museum Island'. He came 'from a neighbourhood where ordinary people live, mostly migrants from Turkey, or Iraq. Many immigrants have fears. Everybody who is blond, who looks German, reminds them of the public authorities.' Jana offered refreshments and I opened the window and took the time to listen before we explained what the Museum Divan was all about. The participant began to tell us about his art, the inspiration he took from his migration to Germany from Iraq in the 1980s and his experiences with loss, such as the collection of photos he burned before fleeing his country. After first contacting him on the phone, Jana mentioned that he was unfamiliar with the Sasanians and their capital. Now it turned out that the opposite was the case. Among the photos he had left behind were many from Tāq Kasrā, where he had worked as a photographer for tourists. His accounts revealed much about the meanings that locals attached to the site, which later shaped our exhibition. At the end of a long and lively conversation we explained our plans. 'The Divan is about an exchange of thoughts and ideas. And you might have noticed, Jana and I don't know much about the place. You are the expert.' He thanked us: 'It was nice meeting you, and it really took away my fears. Now I know what to expect' (field note and interview, 11 November 2015).

Taking time for joint learning

In gauging people's response to future exhibition objects and collecting ideas about how to engage them, Jana and I organised two workshops to revisit the collections.[10] To stimulate conversation, we prepared a mock-up exhibition using cardboard dummies of five objects that curators were planning to put on display in the future. Each was 'displayed' on a table, and participants were asked to suggest which information and additional materials would be useful. Every participant was asked to choose an object and to write down their thoughts, guided by a set of questions prepared in advance (see Figure 11.1).

The first workshop had eight participants, including Stefan Weber, the Museum's director. After the others left, he stayed to talk with Jana and me. In the previous workshops I organised, people had actively discussed the objects and contributed many new ideas and suggestions. This one was different. The participants were slow to choose an object and had difficulties relating them to their own lives. The themes that the exhibition sought to address—such as the development of stylistic features from pre-Islamic to Islamic times—did not seem to interest them. Stefan begged to differ, however. He sensed that the people had been enthusiastic about the topic, and suggested we provide more context to make it easier for them. We also discussed whether the time spent organising such a workshop justified the output it provided.

11.1 Museum Divan participants Cathrin Schaer, Fadi Abdelnour, Dani Mansour and Farzad Akvahan engaging with object replicas during a revisiting collections workshop, November 2015. Photograph by Jana Braun.

Taking the time to talk through such issues was, I submit, most valuable for our joint learning. And taking the time to participate in the workshop allowed us to share information about the needed resources and to discuss issues of interpretation for specific examples. The context-bound understanding of people's reactions, hesitations and questions was used on several occasions as we developed labels and interactive spaces. We also took into account the significance that the participants attached to Sasanian objects. Consider the following response: 'I remember the stories about the Sassanians. I like the exhibition, because you can walk through the history of the region where I come from. This is brilliant. The Sassanians were so powerful, but few people here know about them.' Such voices had hitherto been neglected at the Museum for Islamic Art.

Taking time for unlearning through affective engagement

There are ways of knowing that are difficult to communicate through brief evaluations, and which hence may be easily discounted or dismissed (Yanow 2004: 11). These include the affects and emotions that people feel at an exhibition.

One of the methods Jana and I employed to collect people's perspectives on the museum's galleries was photo elicitation. We asked Museum Divan participants to photograph everything in the museum that they found interesting, or worth remarking on. After their tours, they sent us the images, which then structured the interviews that followed (Collier 1996: 281). Among the participants were people trained in archaeology, Islamic art history and Islamic studies, as well as a group of young Muslim activists with migrant experiences from the JUMA network.

During our conversations, the participants' ambivalent feelings regarding the museum's representational strategies became apparent. Many of their accounts were shaped by enthusiasm for the aesthetic qualities of objects and their ability to counteract the negative ways in which 'Islam' and Islamic regions were depicted in the media. They imagined the museum as a space enabling people to learn about the cultural, social and religious diversity of regions with Muslim-majority populations and their global entanglements. Some described the galleries as a space that allowed them to wonder and dream, to travel through time and space, to reimagine their social position, as a spiritual space in which objects serve as a means to experience the divine and to connect believers across time and space.

At the same time, they expressed dissatisfaction and critique. They questioned whether the museum staff was willing to talk with novices in Islamic art history. Some pointed to details that they perceived as indicating a 'careless' attitude to gallery visitors. Many noted the 'sterile', 'loveless', 'dreary' and 'cold' atmosphere of the displays, which they said were unable to show the affective dimensions of Islam and Islamic regions. They wanted the museum to do a better job recognising the symbolic and spiritual meanings of the objects by, say, introducing other forms of artistic expression. Without referring explicitly to postcolonial debates, they criticised Eurocentric perspectives on the arts and cultures of Islamic regions (field notes, November 2015).

The conversations with the participants were not only time-intensive but also emotionally charged. It confronted us with our privileges (white, German citizenship, formal degree in higher education, etc.). And it forced us to reflect on the effects of long-standing curatorial traditions that had preferred objects over people, their cultures and their beliefs.

Nurturing change means curbing pragmatism

This chapter has explored the futurabilities of the Museum for Islamic Art—the institution's ability to grasp its potential for democratic future-making along with the obstacles that lie in the way. The means for understanding those futurabilities was the Museum Divan, a participatory approach geared to a 'messy' diversity. The programme was initiated in response to increasing anti-Muslim sentiment and in recognition of the museum's responsibility to counteract stereotypes about Islam and Muslim-majority populations.

11.2 Interactive space with images of Museum Divan participations and comment board in the exhibition The Heritage of the Old Kings. Ctesiphon and the Persian Sources of Islamic Art, November 2016. Photograph by John-Paul Sumner.

The work of the Museum Divan has shown that the curatorial team has different visions of the museum's future, and different reasons for engaging in new practices. Moreover, it has highlighted the importance of abandoning 'pragmatic' approaches to time. Taking the time to build relationships, listen, learn with others and unlearn old patterns is crucial for bringing about real change. Many obstacles to change needed uncovering: an insufficient theoretical understanding of the problems, stubborn attitudes to participatory practices in museums, the museum's status as an authority and the failure to see the interests, needs and feelings of exhibition users.

For all the diversity of the participants, they shared some views: the sense that they cannot compete with museum experts, and a tendency to see the museum as a world different from their own, but also as a source of inspiration to learn, reflect, rethink stereotypical ideas and hope for more democratic futures.

What is the best way to nurture such futures? The generous funding provided by TOPOI and the trust that the museum's leadership placed in its organisers have been vital for exploring future possibilities and leaving our familiar comfort zones. The work may not lead to a complete reconsideration of existing practices or an abandonment of all past knowledge. But slipping into the role of 'amateurs' in a Saidian sense (Said 1994) can facilitate zones for utopian future-making and help us better understand epistemic traditions and their alternatives. Openness to these sorts of negotiations offers unexpected perspectives on the collections and on oneself.

Unlearning is a strenuous process, and it demands a deliberate rejection of pragmatism, which tends to reaffirm the way things are. The Museum for Islamic Art has made several steps towards a new future by focusing more on relationship-building and initiating processes of systematic reflection. Museum Divan participants' perspectives were presented in an interactive space where people could leave their comments and questions on the exhibition (Figure 11.2). During my time at the museum, the number of people working in public engagement has increased vastly and with them the efforts of the museum to interconnect with society. As the share of people shaped by migration has increased, and the Museum Divan project has been repeated many times over, debates on the decolonisation of Islamic art history and museum practices have begun in earnest. It is because of and not in spite of these struggles that a more hopeful future stands before us.

Acknowledgements

This research was completed with funding from Sharon Macdonald's Alexander von Humboldt Professorship as part of the project *Making Differences: Transforming Museums and Heritage in the Twenty-First Century*. The Excellence Cluster TOPOI provided generous funding for the exhibition project and for the first phase of my doctoral research. I am very grateful to all Museum Divan participants and my colleagues from the exhibition's curatorial team, in particular Stefan Weber, Ute Franke, Karin Schmidl, John-Paul Sumner and Jana Braun for their kind support and critical feedback during the process. Finally, many thanks to my colleagues from CARMAH – Nazlı Cabadağ, Larissa Förster, Chiara Garbellotto, Duane Jethro, Harriet Merrow, Sharon Macdonald, Tahani Nadim, Margareta von Oswald, Katarzyna Puzon and Jonas Tinius for their thought-provoking comments.

Notes

1 This was inspired by a mindfulness approach taught by Tara Brach (2019).

2 See http://www.smb.museum/en/museums-institutions/museum-fuer-islamische-kunst/about-us/profile.html (accessed 27 November 2017).

3 Museum Laboratory: A Project on Mediating the Histories of Islamic Art and Cultures was initiated by Susan Kamel, Susanne Lanwerd and the author, and funded from 2009 until 2014 by VolkswagenStiftung. See Kamel & Gerbich (2014).

4 For an overview, see www.smb.museum/en/museums-institutions/museum-fuer-islamische-kunst/collection-research/research-cooperation/ (accessed 27 February 2021).

5 In her essay '*Refugees* sind keine Zielgruppe' ('Refugees are not a target-group'), Carmen Mörsch (2016) argues that using marginalised social positionalities as a category for defining 'target' groups may be a gesture at equality, but it also helps ascribe fixed qualities to a group. As an alternative, she proposes reconsidering the aims of cultural education by taking clear positions against discriminating practices.

6 The exhibition ran from 15 November 2016 to 23 April 2017.

7 See www.topoi.org/project/c-3-1/ (accessed 6 February 2021).

8 https://www.smb.museum/en/museums-institutions/museum-fuer-islamische-kunst/collection-research/research-cooperation/ctesiphon.html (accessed 22 November 2019).

9 For more on the topic, see Bryant & Knight 2017.

10 The methodology was developed in 2005 by Museums, Libraries, Archives (MLA) London and Collections Trust. See: https://326gtd123dbk1xdkdm489u1q-wpengine.netdna-ssl.com/wp-content/uploads/2016/10/Revisiting-Museum-Collections-toolkit.pdf. Last accessed 21 November 2019.

References

Appadurai, A. 2013. *The Future as Cultural Fact. Essays on the Global Condition.* London: Verso.

Argyris, C., and D.A. Schön. 1978. *Organizational Learning. A Theory of Action Perspective. Reading,* Mass.: Addison-Wesley.

Barnett, C., J. Newman, and N. Mahony (eds). 2010. *Rethinking the Public. Innovations in Research, Theory and Politics.* Bristol: Policy Press.

Bassel, L. 2017. *The Politics of Listening. Possibilities and Challenges for Democratic Life.* London: Palgrave Macmillan UK.

Berardi, F. 2017. *Futurability. The Age of Impotence and the Horizon of Possibility*. London, New York: Verso.

Boast, R. 2011. 'Neocolonial Collaboration: Museum as Contact Zone Revisited', *Museum Anthropology,* 34(1): 56–70.

Botkin, J.W., M. Elmanjra, and M. Malitza. 1998 (1979). *No Limits to Learning. Bridging the Human Gap.* A Report to the Club of Rome. Oxford, New York: Pergamon Press.

Bourdieu, P. 1984. *Distinction. A Social Critique of the Judgement of Taste.* London: Routledge and Kegan Paul.

Bourdieu, P., A. Darbel, and D. Schnapper. 1990. *The Love of Art. European Art Museums and their Public.* Stanford, California: Stanford University Press.

Brach, T. 2019. *Radical compassion. Learning to love yourself and your world with the practice of RAIN.* New York: Viking.

Bryant, R., D.M. Knight. 2017. *The Anthropology of the Future.* Cambridge: Cambridge University Press.

Brown, A.K., and L. L. Peers. 2003. *Museums and Source Communities*. A Routledge reader. London, New York: Routledge.

Carpentier, N. 2014. 'Facing the death of the author. Cultural professionals' identity work and the fantasies of control', in P. Runnel, P. Pruulmann-Vengerfeldt (eds), *Democratising the Museum. Reflections on Participatory Technologies*, 111–30. Frankfurt a.M: Peter Lang GmbH Internationaler Verlag der Wissenschaften.

Castro Varela, M. d. M. 2017. '(Un-)Wissen. Verlernen als komplexer Lernprozess', migrazine – Online Magazin von Migrantinnen für alle, 1. http://www.migrazine.at/artikel/un-wissen-verlernen-als-komplexer-lernprozess (accessed 7 March 2022).

Chilvers J., and M. Kearnes. 2016. 'Participation in the Making: Rethinking Public Engagement in Co-productionist Terms', in J. Chilvers, and M. Kearnes (eds), *Remaking Participation. Science, Environment and Emergent Publics*, 31–63. London, New York: Routledge.

Clifford, J. 1997. *Routes, Travel and Translation in the late Twentieth Century*. Cambridge: Harvard University Press.

Collier, J. 1996. 'Visual anthropology', in J. Wagner, and H. S. Becker (eds), *Images of Information. Still Photography in the Social Sciences*, 271–81. Ann Arbor, Mich.: UMI Books on demand. Facsimile, Sage. 1979

Connolly, W.E. 1995. *The Ethos of Pluralization*. Minneapolis: University of Minnesota Press.

Cook, S. D. N., and J. S. Brown. 1999. 'Bridging Epistemologies: The Generative Dance Between Organizational Knowledge and Organizational Knowing', *Organization Science*, 10(4):381–400.

Crooke, E. 2010. 'Museums and Community', in S. Macdonald (ed.), *A Companion to Museum Studies*, 170–85. Chichester, UK: Wiley.

Dahlgren, P., and J. Hermes. 2015. 'The Democratic Horizons of the Museum: Citizenship and Culture', in S. Macdonald, and H. R. Leahy (eds), *The International Handbooks of Museum Studies*, 117–38. Chichester, UK: Wiley.

Foroutan, N. 2015a. *Berlin postmigrantisch. Einstellungen der Berliner Bevölkerung zu Musliminnen und Muslimen in Deutschland: Länderstudie Berlin*. Berlin: Berliner Institut für empirische Integrations- und Migrationsforschung.

Foroutan, N. 2015b. *Deutschland postmigrantisch. 1. Gesellschaft, Religion, Identität. Erste Ergebnisse*. Berlin: Berliner Institut für empirische Integrations- und Migrationsforschung der Humboldt-Universität zu Berlin.

Gerbich, C. 2014. 'Partizipieren und evaluieren', in S. Kamel, and C. Gerbich (eds), *Experimentierfeld Museum. Internationale Perspektiven auf Museum, Islam und Inklusion*. Bielefeld: transcript.

Gesser, S., M. Handschin, A. Janelli, S. Lichtensteiger (eds). 2012. *Das partizipative Museum: Zwischen Teilhabe und User Generated Content. Neue Anforderungen an kulturhistorische Ausstellungen*. Bielefeld: transcript.

Gherardi, S. 2000. 'Practice-Based Theorizing on Learning and Knowing in Organizations', *Organization*, 7(2):211–23.

Gherardi, S. 2011. 'Organizational Learning: The Sociology of Practice', in M. Easterby-Smith (ed.), *Handbook of Organizational Learning and Knowledge Management*, 2nd ed., 43–66. Chichester, UK: Wiley.

Gherardi, S. 2012. 'Why Do Practices Change and Why Do They Persist? Models of Explanations', in P. Hager, A. Lee, and A. Reich (eds), *Practice, Learning and Change. Practice-Theory Perspectives on Professional Learning,* 217–31. Dordrecht: Springer Netherlands.

Gherardi, S. 2019. 'Theorizing affective ethnography for organization studies', *Organization,* 26(6): 741–60.

Gherardi, S., D. Nicolini, F. Odella. 1998. 'Toward a Social Understanding of How People Learn in Organizations: The Notion of Situated Curriculum', *Management Learning,* 29(3): 273–97.

Gonnella, J. 2013. 'Islamic Art Versus Material Culture: Museum of Islamic Art or Museum of Islamic Culture?', in B. Junod, G. Khalil, and S. Weber (eds), *'Islamic Art and the Museum'. Discussions on scientific and museological approaches to art and archaeology of the Muslim world,* 144–50. London, San Fransisco, Beirut: Saqi Books.

Hanberger, A. 2006. 'Evaluation of and for Democracy', *Evaluation,* 12(1): 17–37.

Harrison, R. 2013. 'Reassembling ethnographic museum collections', in R. Harrison, S. Byrne, and A. Clarke (eds), *Reassembling the Collection. Ethnographic Museums and Indigenous Agency,* 3–38. Santa Fe: School for Advanced Research Press (SAR Press).

Harrison, R. et al. 2020. *Heritage Futures: Comparative Approaches to Natural and Cultural Heritage Practices*. London: UCL Press.

Haug, S., S. Müssig, and A. Stichs. 2008. *Muslimisches Leben in Deutschland. Im Auftrag der Deutschen Islam Konferenz,* Berlin.

House, E.R., and K. R. R. Howe. 1999. *Values in Evaluation and Social Research.* Thousand Oaks: Sage.

Janes, R. R. 2010. 'The mindful museum', *Curator,* 53(3): 325–338.

Jaschke, B., and N. Sternfeld. 2012. *Educational Turn. Handlungsräume der Kunst- und Kulturvermittlung.* Wien: Turia + Kant.

Kamel, S. 2004. *Wege zur Vermittlung von Religionen in Berliner Museen: Black Kaaba meets White Cube.* Wiesbaden: VS Verlag für Sozialwissenschaften.

Kamel, S., and C. Gerbich (eds). 2014. *Experimentierfeld Museum. Internationale Perspektiven auf Museum, Islam und Inklusion.* Bielefeld: transcript.

Karra, N., and N. Phillips. 2007. 'Researching "Back Home": International Management Research as Autoethnography', *Organizational Research Methods,* 11(3): 541–561.

Kazeem, B., C. Martinz-Turek, N. Sternfeld. 2009. *Das Unbehagen im Museum. Postkoloniale Museologien.* Wien: Turia + Kant.

Kröger, J., and D. Heiden (eds). 2004. *Islamische Kunst in Berliner Sammlungen: 100 Jahre Museum für Islamische Kunst in Berlin.* Berlin: Parthas.

Lacey, K. 2013. *Listening Publics. The Politics and Experience of Listening in the Media Age.* Cambridge: Polity Press.

Lave, J., and E. Wenger. 1991. *Situated Learning. Legitimate Peripheral Participation.* Cambridge: Cambridge University Press.

Levitt, B., and J.G. March. 1988. 'Organizational Learning', *Annual Review of Sociology,* 14(1):319–38.

Lynch, B. 2011. *Whose cake is it anyway? A collaborative investigation into engagement and participation in 12 museums and galleries in the UK.* https://www.phf.org.uk/wp-content/uploads/2014/10/Whose-cake-is-it-anyway.pdf (accessed 7 March 2022).

Macdonald, S. 1998. 'Exhibitions of power and power of exhibitions', in S. Macdonald (ed.), *The Politics of Display. Museums, Science, Culture.* London, New York: Routledge.

Macdonald, S. 2013. *Memorylands. Heritage and identity in Europe today.* Oxon, New York: Routledge.

Macdonald, S. 2018. Diverse Museum Diversities. https://www.zflprojekte.de/zfl-blog/2018/10/20/sharon-macdonald-diverse-museum-diversities/ (accessed 7 March 2022).

Macdonald, S., C. Gerbich, and M. von Oswald. 2018. 'No museum is an island: Ethnography beyond methodological containerism', *Museum and Society,* 16(2): 138–156.

Meijer-van Mensch, L. 2012. 'Von Zielgruppen zu Communities. Ein Plädoyer für das Museum als Agora einer vielschichtigen Constituent Community', in S. Gesser, M. Handschin, A. Jannelli, and S. Lichtensteiger (eds), *Das partizipative Museum. Zwischen Teilhabe und User Generated Content. Neue Anforderungen an kulturhistorische Ausstellungen,* 86–94. Bielefeld: transcript.

Mörsch, C. 2009. 'Am Kreuzpunkt von vier Diskursen: Die documenta 12 Vermittlung zwischen Affirmation, Reporduktion, Dekonstruktion und Transformation', in C. Mörsch (ed.), *Kunstvermittlung 2. Zwischen kritischer Praxis und Dienstleistung auf der Documenta 12.* Ergebnisse eines Forschungsprojektes, 9–33. Berlin, Zürich: Diaphanes.

Mörsch, C. 2011a. 'Mehr Werte umverteilen. Über Macht-sensiblen Umgang mit Partizipation im Museum', *Die Schweizer Museumszeitschrift / La revue suisse des musées / la revista svizzera die musei,* 6:13–17.

Mörsch, C. 2011b. 'Take the Terror out of Error', in F. Allen (ed.), *Education.* London, Cambridge, MA: Whitechapel Gallery; MIT Press.

Mörsch, C. 2016. 'Refugees sind keine Zielgruppe', in M. Ziese, C. Gritschke (eds), *Geflüchtete und Kulturelle Bildung,* 67–74. Bielefeld: transcript.

Muttenthaler, R., and R. Wonisch. 2007. *Gesten des Zeigens. Zur Repräsentation von Gender und Race in Ausstellungen.* Bielefeld: transcript.

Necipoğlu, G. 2013. 'The concept of Islamic Art: inherited discourses and new approaches', in B. Junod, G. Khalil, and S. Weber (eds), *'Islamic Art and the Museum'. Discussions on scientific and museological approaches to art and archaeology of the Muslim world,* 57–75. London, San Fransisco, Beirut: Saqi Books.

Osborne, P. 1995. *The Politics of Time.* London: Verso.

Oswald, M. von, and J. Tinius (eds). 2020. *Across Anthropology: Troubling Colonial Legacies, Museums, and the Curatorial.* Leuven: Leuven University Press. https://acrossanthropologie.online (accessed 7 March 2022).

Pallett, H., J. Chilvers. 2015. 'Organizations in the making: Learning and intervening at the science-policy interface', *Progress in Human Geography,* 39(2):146–66.

Pink, S., J. Sjöberg, A. Irving, and J. F. Salazar (eds). 2017. *Anthropologies and Futures: Researching Emerging and Uncertain Worlds.* London: Bloomsbury.

Pratt, M. L. 1992. *Imperial Eyes: Travel Writing and Transculturation.* London: Routledge.

Rabbat, N. 2013. 'Islamic Art at a crossroads?', in B. Junod, G. Khalil, and S. Weber (eds), *'Islamic Art and the Museum'. Discussions on scientific and museological approaches to art and archaeology of the Muslim world,* 76–83. London, San Fransisco, Beirut: Saqi Books.

Reckwitz, A. 2016. *Zukunftspraktiken: Die Zeitlichkeit des sozialen und die Krise der modernen Rationalisierung der Zukunft*. Bielefeld: transcript.

Runnel, P., P. Pruulmann-Vengerfeldt (eds). 2014. *Democratising the Museum. Reflections on Participatory Technologies*. Frankfurt a.M: Peter Lang GmbH Internationaler Verlag der Wissenschaften.

Said, E. W. 1994. *Representations of the intellectual: the 1993 Reith lectures / Edward W. Said*. New York: Pantheon Books.

Said, E. W. 1995. *Orientalism. Western conceptions of the Orient*, Repr. with a new afterword. London: Penguin Books.

Schatzki, T. R. 2010. *The Timespace of Human Activity: On Performance, Society, and History as Indeterminate Teleological Events*. Lanham, MD: Lexington Books.

Schmidl, K., and A. Nolte. 2008. *Paul und die Weltreligionen. Islam*. München: Prestel.

Shalem, A. 2012. 'What do we mean when we say 'Islamic art'? A plea for a critical rewriting of the history of the arts of Islam', *Journal of Art Historiography*, 6:6-AS/1.

Shatanawi, M. 2012. 'Curating against Dissent: Museums and the Public Debate on Islam', in C. G. Flood (ed.), *Political and Cultural Representations of Muslims: Islam in the Plural*, Muslim minorities 11, 177–192. Leiden: Brill.

Shaw, W. 2012. 'The Islam in Islamic art history: secularism and public discours', in M. Carey, and M. S. Graves (eds), *Islamic Art Historiography*, 6.

Sinus Sociovision. 2007. Die Milieus der Menschen mit Migrationshintergrund in Deutschland. Eine qualitative Untersuchung von Sinus Sociovision.

Spivak, G. C. 2004. 'Righting Wrongs', *The South Atlantic Quarterly*, 103(2/3): 523–81. https://blogs.commons.georgetown.edu/engl-218-fall2010/files/Righting-Wrongs.pdf (accessed 7 March 2022).

Spivak G. C., D. Landry, and G. M. MacLean. 1996. *The Spivak reader. Selected works of Gayatri Chakravorty Spivak*. New York: Routledge.

Sternfeld, N. 2013. Playing by the rules of the game: Participation in the postrepresentative Museum. https://cummastudies.files.wordpress.com/2013/08/cummapapers1_sternfeld.pdf (accessed 7 March 2022).

Sternfeld, N. 2016. Learning Unlearning. https://cummastudies.files.wordpress.com/2016/09/cumma-papers-20.pdf (accessed 7 March 2022).

Troelenberg, E.-M. 2015. 'Arabesques, Unicorns, and Invisible Masters: The Art Historian's Gaze as Symptomatic Action?', *Muqarnas Online*, 32: 213 – 232.

Waterton, E., and J. Dittmer. 2014. 'The museum as assemblage: bringing forth affect at the Australian War Memorial', *Museum Management and Curatorship*, 29(2): 122–39.

Watson, S. 2007. 'Museums and their communities', in S. Watson (ed.), *Museums and their Communities*, 1–23. London: Routledge.

Weber, S. 2013a. 'A concert of things: Thoughts on objects of Islamic art in the museum context', in B. Junod, G. Khalil, and S. Weber (eds), *'Islamic Art and the Museum'. Discussions on scientific and museological approaches to art and archaeology of the Muslim world*, 28–53. London, San Fransisco, Beirut: Saqi Books.

Weber, S. 2013b. 'New spaces for old treasures. Plans for the new Museum of Islamic Art at the Pergamon Museum', in B. Junod, G. Khalil, and S. Weber (eds), *'Islamic Art and the Museum'. Discussions on scientific and museological approaches to art and archaeology of the Muslim world*, 293–320. London, San Fransisco, Beirut: Saqi Books.

Weber, S. 2015. 'Kulturelle Bildung in der Islamdebatte', in D. Molthagen (ed.), *Handlungsempfehlungen zur Auseinandersetzung mit islamischem Extremismus und Islamfeindlichkeit,* 261–74. Berlin: Friedrich-Ebert-Stiftung, Forum Berlin.

Wenger, E. 2000. 'Communities of Practice and Social Learning Systems', *Organization,* 7(2): 225–46.

Wenger, E., R. A. McDermott, and W. Snyder. 2002. *Cultivating Communities of Practice. A Guide to Managing Knowledge.* Boston, Mass.: Harvard Business School Press.

Witcomb, A. 2003. *Re-imagining the Museum. Beyond the Mausoleum.* London: Routledge.

Yanow, D. 2004. 'Translating Local Knowledge at Organizational Peripheries', *British Journal of Management,* 15(S1): 9–25.

Yanow, D., and S. Ybema. 2009. 'Interpretivism in Organizational Research: On Elephants and Blind Researchers', in D. A. Buchanan, and A. Bryman (eds), *The SAGE Handbook of Organizational Research Methods,* 39–60. Los Angeles: Sage.

Willkommen im Museum
Making and Unmaking Refugees in the Multaka Project

Rikke Gram

Outside the German Historical Museum, I met up with Sawsan,[1] a 25-year-old Syrian who had lived for almost two years in Berlin. Since late 2015 Sawsan had been part of the Multaka team, which offered Arabic-language tours in four museums in central Berlin, the German Historical Museum being one of them. Sawsan explained why she had chosen to work as a guide in this museum. For her, Multaka aims to support 'refugees and newcomers' and help them integrate into German society. The educational museum tours are 'about building this cultural bridge between the refugees and the country they are moving into'. She believes that the German Historical Museum can help them feel a sense of belonging:

> [F]or example, when the people see what Germany has been through after the Second World War, they are going to feel themselves less foreign....So they're not going to feel excluded from this community, because this community has suffered exactly the same as what they are suffering right now.

Sawan was referring to a museum installation in which two films showing aerial views and close-ups of bombed-out German cities at the end of the Second World War play on a continuous loop.

In this chapter, I show how the Multaka project has made museums in Berlin relevant for Arabic speakers, and how this has helped challenge those national institutions as places focusing exclusively on German history and memory and refashion them into places of migration, relatable to people with contemporary transnational lives. I will unpack the ways in which Multaka makes and unmakes differences, project participants refuse or accept the 'refugee' label, and the museums' objects and installations come to represent not only the German past but also the Arab present. I argue that Multaka makes museums into 'contact zones' (Clifford 1997) by inviting marginalised people to provide their own perspectives and expert knowledge and by showing that German and Arabic speakers share material cultures and memories. James Clifford applies the notion of contact zones to museums that work with subaltern groups and use objects to provide an opening for conversation across differences. In contact zones, people from the periphery join those from the centre, and the '*collection* becomes an ongoing historical, political, moral *relationship*' (ibid.: 192, original italics) in which social ties are the critical outcome.

Multaka was founded in late 2015 to train Arabic-speaking migrants as guides at four large, centrally-located museums in Berlin: the German Historical Museum, the Bode Museum, the Museum of the Ancient Near East and the Museum of Islamic Art (the latter two are situated within the Pergamon Museum). The project was a response to the 2015 'Summer of Migration', which saw the influx of migrants and refugees from the Middle East and Africa across the borders of Europe (Kasparek and Speer 2015). For Multaka's founders, museums are 'meeting points" or 'crossroads'—this is the translation of *multaka* from Arabic—bringing together museum objects and people. Amid the forced migration of the mid-2010s, the Multaka project was an expression of *Willkommenskultur*, part of an effort to welcome people forced to flee to Germany initiated by mainstream German society, including private individuals, public institutions and corporate companies (Karakayali 2019) and atone for Germany's past national crimes by protecting those fleeing persecution and war (Bock and Macdonald 2019). *Willkommenskultur* seeks to turn immigrants from social outsiders to active participants, ones who have rights and opportunities and who contribute to cultural diversity (Hamann and Karakayali 2016; Heckmann 2012). Below I show how Multaka gave individuals the chance to work in museums and reduce differences across languages, nationalities and pasts. After exploring the nuances of the term 'refugee', I discuss the guides' use of objects acquired from the home regions of Arabic-speaking migrants. The chapter ends with a section exploring how objects exhibited to represent Germany's past conflicts take on new meanings when linked to memories of people who have recently fled their homelands.

The founding of Multaka

The idea for a project in which guides offer tours in Arabic came from members of the Syrian Heritage Archive, a project affiliated with the Museum of Islamic Art, and was first presented to the museum's director in the late summer of 2015. The initial idea was to provide work for some of the many newcomers who approached the archive seeking employment. Museum staff had already been thinking about how to respond to the sharp rise in asylum seekers fleeing war in the Middle East and how to take action against growing Islamophobia. The museum's director embraced the idea of engaging Arabic speakers as guides in the museum. Shortly thereafter, he met with the Federal Ministry of Family Affairs, Senior Citizens, Women and Youth (BMFSFJ), which agreed to fund the project. The director then approached the head of the Museum of the Ancient Near East. Like the Museum of Islamic Art, it also houses collections from the former Ottoman Empire, which includes present-day Syria and Iraq, where many migrants were from. Multaka was based on the idea that museums can serve as gathering places for diasporic communities, as hubs connecting the migration histories of objects with those of people (Basu 2011). The head of the Prussian Cultural Heritage Foundation (Stiftung Preussicher Kulturbesitz), the foundation governing Berlin's state museums, urged the director of the Museum of Islamic Art to include the Bode Museum in the project because its Byzantine collection covers the Christian Middle East. The BMFSFJ funding came from the federal program *Demokratie Leben*, a key part of the government's strategy for preventing extremism, Islamic radicalisation, hostility towards Muslims and Islam, antisemitism, antiziganism, and discrimination based on sexuality and gender (BMFSFJ 2016). A central element in the funding was a historical reckoning with National Socialism and the socialist regime of the German Democratic Republic. The importance of engaging with Germany's past national crimes led the project founders to invite the German Historical Museum to be its fourth institutional member.

Multaka was, then, realised as an endeavour across four museums, consisting of guided tours in Arabic. It was founded by the heads of the museums and placed outside the established educational programs at a remarkable speed. Two freelance project managers were hired, as were 19 Syrian and Iraqi guides. (Later that number was increased to 25.) Each guide was paid for the tours they gave. The guides varied with regard to age, education, professional experience, religious affiliation, residence status, reasons for coming to Germany and length of time spent outside their home countries. All had university degrees or were studying at a university in the city. The first tours in Arabic took place at the end of 2015; since then, Arabic-language tours have taken place twice a week in all four museums. Many other related events and workshops have occurred in English and German. I conducted an ethnographic study of the work inside and outside the museums between spring 2016 and spring 2017.

A diversity of 'refugees'

On 21 May 2016, the UNESCO World Day for Cultural Diversity for Dialogue and Development, the German Historical Museum held an award ceremony for the initiative *Kultur öffnet Welten*, during which the Federal Commissioner for Culture and Media, Monika Grütters, awarded three projects for their work with 'refugees'. Multaka was one of ten projects nominated for an award. In her speech, Grütters stressed the crucial role of cultural institutions in representing Germany's openness towards the rest of the world and their social responsibility to integrate people fleeing crisis regions. She thanked the German Historical Museum for hosting the event, and for exhibiting a history that itself was shaped by migration. In awarding the final prize to Multaka, Grütters praised the director of the Museum of Islamic Art for initiating the project and lauded its use of refugees as tour guides. She herself had participated in a tour.

Multaka's official homepage states that it offers 'Refugees as Guides in Berlin's Museums',[2] and many media outlets, museums, and members of the team refer to Multaka as a project 'by, with and for refugees' (field note 4.4.2016). But this is, strictly speaking, inaccurate. According to the United Nations High Commissioner for Refugees, 'refugees' have been defined under international law since the 1951 Refugee Convention, which outlines their basic rights and secure protection and grants them access to assistance from states and international organisations.[3] Most (though not all) of the Multaka guides do not have the official status as 'refugee'. Rather, they are students or have German work permits; one guide even had European citizenship. Multaka was granted funding for 'refugees', but the project participants were concerned with newcomers from Syria and Iraq more generally. Indeed, the emphasis on 'refugees' was not something that everyone in the Multaka project agreed with. Below I take a closer look at the term's usage and implications.

From the café in the Bode Museum, one has a view down the grand staircase to the equestrian statue of the Great Elector Friedrich Wilhelm von Brandenburg (1620–1688). The Elector invited Jews and Huguenots to live under his jurisdiction, opening up Brandenburg and Berlin to religious refugees (Beuys 2012). I was meeting with Mahoor, a Multaka guide in the Bode Museum, who, before coming to Germany, worked with restoration in the Homs Museum in Syria. She is one of the founding members of Multaka. She also worked in the Syrian Heritage Archive and was present when they devised the idea for the project. After she showed me around the museum, we sat for a coffee in the café. One question was burning in my head. At a team meeting a while back, she had objected to the use of the term 'refugees' to describe tour attendees. I asked her to explain her concerns. 'Naming and labelling people', she replied, is not helpful. 'They are just normal people, they are newly coming here. They just came here recently because of a certain, you know, uncontrollable situation. They didn't choose it.' Indeed, she found the term problematic in the context not only of Multaka but of any of the many projects aimed at newcomers. 'Most of the time...it was kind of using them because of the media, everyone was like, you know...taking photos with refugees, labelling something with a refugee, it´s just benefiting from the situation in a way'. Mahoor was not denying that people want to do good; she just wanted the diversity of the newcomers to be acknowledged rather reducing them to their recent experience of fleeing their homeland.

Mahoor's concerns are similar to those of others in cultural education who have criticised institutions for not recognising the diverse identities of migrants and for reducing them to mere beneficiaries instead of enabling them as active participants (Mörsch 2016; Landkammer 2017; Lynch 2017). In this way, they have argued, cultural projects may risk amplifying inequalities by pre-defining refugees as a 'target group' and categorising them solely in terms of migration and flight. This logic tends to be especially pronounced in the language of project funding (Mörsch 2016).

In 1943, Hannah Arendt also objected to the use of the term 'refugee' to describe immigrants. 'In the first place, we don't like to be called 'refugees'' (Arendt 1996: 110), she observed, arguing that insistence on the term disregards their efforts to belong and overcome violent pasts. Members of Multaka rarely use the term 'refugee' as a marker for self-identification, and, even though the funding of Multaka was earmarked for 'refugees', it did not preclude the involvement of people who fell outside that category. As one guide with whom I spoke put it, 'I'm not a refugee. I didn't flee'. She always wanted to move to Germany, where her sister had settled long before the war. Nevertheless, some guides, Mahoor among them, argued for preserving the term but using it in a wider sense: 'We´re all refugees. I have a different status, but I´m a refugee, I´m not in my home, so I´m a refugee.' Another guide explained that if one understands refugees as people who cannot return to their home country, he also counts as a refugee. This, he felt, was the definition of refugee that Multaka preferred.

A more expansive sense of who counts as a refugee is one way for the guides to escape the confines of the term. But they also want to demonstrate that their lived experiences of migration goes beyond legal status and so to reimagine the idea of the refugee in much the same way that they have sought to do with museums themselves.

Gearing the tours to refugees in this broader sense affects who participates. As an episode I observed shows, participants need not always be Arabic speakers. On a very hot day in late August of 2016, a crowd assembled in the Aleppo room of the Museum of Islamic Art for a tour. Within moments, the inadequacy of the museum's air conditioning became uncomfortably apparent. The guide had to simultaneously translate from Arabic into German for the group's German-speaking escorts but many in the group spoke neither Arabic nor German. I was told that they were part of a project in Brandenburg preparing refugees for the job market. Several in the group spoke Farsi, so one participant volunteered to translate. But she spoke English, a language in which the guide was not fluent, so a Syrian man offered to translate from Arabic into English. After they figured out who was doing the interpreting—from Arabic to English to Farsi—the tour could finally commence, and we could leave the unbearably hot Aleppo room. As I followed the group around in the museum, one man seemed especially inattentive and detached. I asked him if there was anything he found interesting on the tour. He shrugged and told me in broken English that he was from Pakistan and spoke only Urdu.

There is another recurrent category of visitors that I encountered on the tours: Arabic speakers who are not refugees but from countries like Israel, Egypt or Canada. They take part because they are Arabic native speakers and because the tours are for free. These different types of visitors are well known among Multaka organizers and guides, and they have prompted discussions about whether the program should be open for people with language skills other than Arabic, and whether Multaka should attract *all* Arabic speakers in Berlin, no matter their legal status. The composition of the participants made clear that interest in the project went well beyond its original target audience, suggesting that demand for Arabic-language information in museums was greater than previously assumed.

Old museums in new use

The Multaka guides have professional backgrounds in law, engineering, architecture and other areas. Although some are trained in archaeology or Islamic studies, few of them had much experience working in museums before joining the project. This was not seen as a disadvantage because the tours emphasise dialogic interpretation, in which guides focus less on providing art historical context for the objects than on acting as mediators between the objects and the visitors (Lielich-Wolf and Avenarius 2008). In the following I show how the museums in the Multaka project centre on objects and their entangled histories in times of transnational identity-making (Macdonald 2003).

The strategies used in museums to connect with participants vary from institution to institution, but they all seek to link objects to visitors' lived experience, and in this way facilitate their entry into German society. By granting Arabic-language access to the museums and by showing how cultures from the Middle East are represented and valued, the Multaka guides aims at helping the newcomers belong and feel included.

12.1 Multaka tour in the Bode Museum. Photograph by Milena Schlösser. Reproduced courtesy of Museum für Islamische Kunst, Staatliche Museen zu Berlin.

While I was accompanying Mahnoor on a tour, she stopped in front of one of the museum's most popular attractions—a golden mosaic apse from Ravenna depicting a young Christ. She asked the visitors to relate the mosaic to a building in their home country or city. Some said that mosaics like that exist on numerous churches and villas in their town of Idlib, a place that flourished during the Byzantine Empire. Mahnoor pointed out the similarities to the Umayyad Mosque, the great mosque of Damascus, with its golden façade and nature ornaments. I asked her why it was important for her to connect the museum in Berlin with the previous experiences of the participants on her tours. 'I think it´s about creating a stronger way to connect to here, to the object itself and to the place' she told me. 'When they feel there is a connection, not only with the object itself, they have something similar, they have something they feel is like home'. Mahnoor uses the objects that are from the participants' home countries (or that are similar) to help them feel less foreign in Germany and offer them a way of belonging in Berlin.

Another Multaka guide I met is Farah, who works at the Museum of Islamic Art. An architect, she sees the museum as the material outcome of the meeting between Islam and the local communities in which Islam has come to play a central role. She believes that the exhibition of objects can show the diversity of the regions that the museum represents, a diversity that dates back to pre-Islamic times. In the museum, visitors can experience art from the Alhambra palace made of local Spanish cedar wood next to a niche from a Jewish home in Damascus. For her, the locality of the objects is crucial; she argues that many of the objects in the exhibition have little or no connection to Islam. Instead, Farah presents the objects not as objects of Islamic art, which is foreign to the lives of many Muslims today, but as objects that, like them, have crossed borders on their journey to Berlin.

According to the anthropologist Talal Asad, to understand Islam in Europe we have to understand how Europe is constructed by Europeans in a way that misrepresents Muslims, who are 'included within and excluded from Europe at one and the same time' (Asad 2013: 11). Europe today is considered primarily Christian, and as such is defined, implicitly or explicitly, in opposition to Islam. Museums can mirror these broader societal representations. As the curator Mirjam Shatanawi argues, museums of Islamic Art tend to place 'the greatness of the Muslim world in the past' (Shatanawi 2012: 179) by emphasising their 'origins in (colonial) collecting practices of the 18th and 19th century' (ibid.: 178) and privileging objects made before 1800. This is the case for the permanent exhibition of the Museum of Islamic Art in Berlin. To make the museum more interesting for contemporary newcomers, Farah and the other guides downplay its focus on art and instead emphasise the religious diversity of the communities and regions where Islam was the dominant religion. Farah argues that Islam is inextricably linked with migration—the Islamic calendar begins in the year that the prophet Muhammad migrated from Mecca to Medina. At the beginning of every tour, she asks visitors where they come from and lets their answers determine her choice of objects. When she has visitors from Iraq, she makes sure to talk about Samarra, as she knows that it will pique their interest. She'll say, 'Let´s go to Aleppo, or let´s go to Spain'. She tells visitors that they, like her, 'are immigrants'. She wants to drive home the message that 'it´s not only a good chance for Syrians to come here; it´s a good chance for Germany...Just as all these ideas migrated from one place to another...we did too.' The past movements of people, ideas, and skills across the Muslim world created the wealth of beautiful objects on display in the museum. For the Multaka project, the movement of people from the Middle East to Germany today stands to be no less enriching.

But understanding museums as contact zones assumes a centre and a periphery, an opposition between the places where objects are kept and the places where they are collected (Clifford 1997). And when people from areas where objects were once collected interact with collections, their interpretations can come into conflict with the official stance of museums.

On one tour I accompanied in the Museum of the Ancient Near East, Farah made her first stop in front of the Ishtar Gate. She usually starts here because she has to pass by the gate on the first floor to reach the Islamic art collection on the second floor of the Pergamon Museum's southern wing. The 14-meter-tall gate stood at the entrance to the ancient city of Babylon. Built in the 6th century BCE, it was excavated in the early 20th century by German archaeologists and later brought to Berlin. The excavation site is shown on a map next to the gate in the museum. Farah told me how some visitors react when they enter the museum: 'If they are from Iraq... first they are very happy, sometimes just to see the map. And then they ask how [the Ishtar Gate] ended up here.... And sometimes they ask very concrete questions such as; on whose authority was it acquired? You know, these types of questions, and it leads to big discussions'.

12.2 Multaka tour in the Museum of the Ancient Near East. Photograph by Wesam Muhammed. Reproduced courtesy of Museum für Islamische Kunst, Staatliche Museen zu Berlin.

According to the Multaka guides, issues of ownership are on the minds of many visitors. Farah stressed this point several times. She led me to the upstairs hall of the Museum of Islamic Art and gestured at the Mschatta Facade: 'When I say it's a gift, they start to laugh'. The idea that the facade, part of a 6th-century Sasanian palace, was a gift from the Sultan of the Ottoman Empire Abdul Hamid II to the German Kaiser Wilhelm II causes much amusement among the attendees of her tour. Evidently, their understanding of history diverges from the version told by the museum.

The participants and guides regard the objects as part of archaeology's long history of entanglement with Western colonial and neo-colonial interventions in the Middle East. The objects from the Ottoman Empire precipitate conversations about whether the museums have the right to keep them, how they came to acquire them, and where they originated. Moreover, many immigrants and refugees arrived in Germany with memories of the recent destruction of their heritage. They witnessed the detonation of the Baalshamin temple in Palmyra in 2015, amid other acts of destruction receiving global media attention (De Cesari 2015). Off the back of these experiences, they want to talk about the security situation in the Middle East and the illicit trade in antiquities that helps fund conflicts in the region. Even though the guides clearly state that the museums are not involved in current illegal activities, the visitors want them to acknowledge the consequences of past practices and want Western museums to engage with the dark elements of their history.

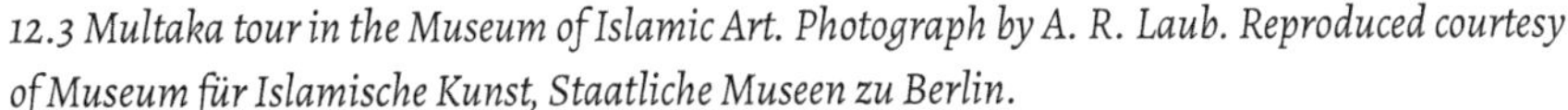
12.3 Multaka tour in the Museum of Islamic Art. Photograph by A. R. Laub. Reproduced courtesy of Museum für Islamische Kunst, Staatliche Museen zu Berlin.

Multidirectional memory

Relating the migration of objects to the migration of visitors and guides is one way that Multaka has made the museums meaningful to people from the Middle East. Another way is by identifying commonalities between German history and the experiences of tour participants. Multaka guides connect museum objects with their own stories and those of the visitors, with pasts shaped by migration and conflict, with memories of Syria and Iraq and visits to local mosques. The aim is to generate a kind of knowledge that is different from that produced by curators, something more personal and less reliant on expertise.

While meeting with Sawsan at the German Historical Museum, I saw an example of how this could work. She showed me two 19th-century paintings of ships caught in storms, which she uses to 'open a whole new level of discussion' in her tour groups:

> It always starts with the same joke: What do you think that is? What do you think is happening? And then they always, always answer the same way: *ha ha* Syrian refugees, *ha ha* refugees going through from Izmir...This is the pram, the small boat they use. And the funny thing is that the refugees are not from Syria or Iraq but from Germany.

For Sawsan and her tour groups, humour turns the traumatic lived experiences of refugees into a lens through which to understand the German past and to relate personal memories to German history.

12.4 Multaka tour in the German Historical Museum. Photograph by Milena Schlösser. Reproduced courtesy of Museum für Islamische Kunst, Staatliche Museen zu Berlin.

The sociologist Maurice Halbwachs (Halbwachs 1967) has argued that memory, because it recalls a lived past, is a collective endeavour that fosters belonging. Memory may be stored consciously or subconsciously, but its telling is only possible when the collective means to reconstruct it are at hand. For this reason, shared memory is a social act that builds collective solidarity. A cultural memory consisting of texts, images and rituals that are collectively maintained and shared creates a sense of belonging to a certain society or culture (Assmann 1988). Museums are places where cultural memory is made, preserved, and remade, not only over time but also across nationalities and geographical borders (Cesari and Rigney 2014). The task of Multaka's tours is to take shared memories and link them to museums and thus give the latter new relevance for broader publics. The guides acknowledge the importance of the national frameworks in which the museums exist, but they also recognise that many of the memories in the Multaka project arose in another framework altogether.

Museums and their collections are places where meaning is collectively constituted (Crane 2010) and belonging is shaped through shared recollection. As literary scholars Michael Rothberg and Yasemin Yildiz argue, '[M]igration is never a one-way process of integration: migrants have brought memories of their own—sometimes traumatic—national and transnational histories into German space...' (Rothberg and Yildiz 2011: 37). In this regard, Multaka encourages belonging through acts of memory: connecting to a 'German' history means actively engaging with a collective memory. Rothberg and Yildiz argue that performing memory is a way of creating belonging and widening the boundaries of collectives.

Sawsan stressed to me that Germany's history in the 1930s and 40s was particularly applicable to the current situation in Syria. 'The interesting thing', she observed, as we stood in front of a wall of photos and posters from the German elections of 1933,

> is that you can see armed soldiers holding pictures of Hindenburg and Hitler, which gives you an insight that maybe the elections weren´t as free as they were presented as. Because, of course, weapons are scary, yeah? And we suffered from that in Syria every time there was an election. We hadn´t had elections before but in the most recent election, actually the first presidential election, there were people, they were actually secret service people standing at each box, and they were actually looking at what people, at who people were voting for. So you don´t want to die, you´re going to pick Bashar al-Assad. Yeah? It´s just this idea of soldiers with pictures being present. Because it should be a democratic process, there shouldn´t be any soldiers or arms involved in the voting, which is really personal. I find this very interesting, and people say: 'Ahh just like us, just like us, just like us'. They always have the same comment: 'it´s just like us'. And this actually gives people a chance to understand the German community more, because the German community 50 or 80 years ago actually suffered from the same political repression that we suffered from, and they are actually feeling this connection, which makes them feel less foreign in the country.

Drawing on memories of the participants to make sense of photos taken in Germany in 1933 is a form of 'multidirectional memory', in which recollections of the past are 'subject to ongoing negotiation, cross-referencing, and borrowing; as productive and not privative' (Rothberg 2014: 176). Rothberg argues that memory need not be understood as competitive—a zero-sum struggle between the histories and victimisations of different social groups. Memory, he maintains, is not exclusive to any particular group and cannot be claimed as such; rather, historical events can be used to articulate and give meaning to other events, past or present. In other words, we are shaped not only by our own lived past but also by how we connect our past with histories that we do not consider our own. This makes the public sphere into a discursive space where 'both the subjects and spaces of the public are open to continual reconstruction' (Rothberg 2009: 5). But connecting memories across time and space without making them redundant is a difficult balancing act.

At the end of a tour in the German Historical Museum, I found myself in front of a series of aerial photographs showing the destroyed cities of Nuremberg and Dresden. Standing next to me was a tour participant. I asked him if the images give him hope that Syria could be rebuilt and one day become like Germany, an economically powerful country that people flee to and no longer from. The young man shrugged and said he found the idea encouraging, but believed there was little hope for Syria.

Conclusion

Multaka challenges the idea that the term refugees refer entirely to displaced persons and asylum seekers and that permanent exhibitions at national museums must represent an enduring national identity. The project guides make transnational connections by emphasising the similarities between the trajectories of the objects and the tour participants while pointing out the commonalities between the cultural heritage in the Middle East and that cherished in Berlin. For them, political history is multidirectional, capable of linking memories across time and space. Multaka aims at making Arabic-speaking newcomers in Germany feel welcome by removing the language barrier and making museums more accessible. The tours alert them to the similarities between the German past and the Syrian or Iraqi present, but they also point out the differences and the lessons that can be drawn from them. The connections between archaeological objects and current conflicts in the Middle East also make visitors aware of the museums' past. Of course, the interconnected perspective fostered by the tours, where the centre and the periphery merge, is not reflected in the museums' permanent exhibitions, which limits what the guides can do. Nevertheless, stressing shared ties to archaeological objects can decrease the sense of difference between Germans and new arrivals from Syria and Iraq and help them feel at home. Understanding the shared heritage can help newcomers feel that they too belong in Berlin.

Acknowledgements

This research was carried out as part of the Master's degree program in European Ethnology and in connection with the *Making Differences* project at the Humboldt University of Berlin. I would like to thank Sharon Macdonald, Katarzyna Puzon and Christine Gerbich for their support. Especially, I want to thank Multaka for agreeing to participate in my research and allowing me to observe their work.

Notes

1 For the sake of privacy, all names have been changed by the author.
2 Multaka – Concept and Content. https://multaka.de/en/concept/ (accessed 5 August 2021).
3 UNHCR Viewpoint: 'Refugee' or 'migrant' – Which is right? https://www.unhcr.org/news/latest/2016/7/55df0e556/unhcr-viewpoint-refugee-migrant-right.html (accessed 5 August 2021).

References

Arendt, H. 1996. 'We Refugees', in M. Robinson (ed.), *Altogether Elsewhere. Writers on Exile*, 110–119. San Diego: Harcourt Brace.

Asad, T. 2013. 'Muslims and European Identity: can Europe represent Islam', in E. Hallam and B. Street (eds), *Cultural Encounters: Representing Otherness*, 11–28. New York: Taylor & Francis.

Assmann, J. 1988. 'Kollektives Gedächtnis und kulturelle Identität', in J. Assmann, and T. Hölscher (eds), *Kultur und Gedächtnis*, 9–19. Frankfurt am Main: Suhrkamp.

Basu, P. 2011. 'Object Diasporas, Resourcing Communities. Sierra Leonean Collections in the Global Museumscape', *Museum Anthropology*, 34(1): 28–42.

Beuys, B. 2012. *Der Große Kurfürst. Friedrich Wilhelm von Brandenburg, der Mann, der Preußen schuf.* München: Dt. Taschenbuch-Verl.

Bock, J., and S. Macdonald. 2019. 'Introduction. Making, Experiencing and Managing Difference in a Changing Germany', in J. Bock, and S. Macdonald (eds), *Refugees Welcome? Difference and Diversity in a Changing Germany*, 1–40. New York: Berghahn Books.

Bundesministerium für Familie, Senioren, Frauen und Jugend (BMFSFJ) 2016. *Strategie der Bundesregierung zur Extremismusprävention und Demokratieförderung*. Berlin: BMFSFJ.

Cesari, C. De, and A. Rigney. 2014. 'Introduction', in C. De Cesari, and A. Rigney (eds), *Transnational Memory. Circulation, Articulation, Scales*, 1–28. Berlin: De Gruyter.

Cesari, C. 2015. 'Post-Colonial Ruins. Archaeologies of Political Violence and IS', *Anthropology Today*, 31(6): 22–26.

Clifford, J. 1997. 'Museums as Contact Zones', in J. Clifford (ed.), *Routes. Travel and Translation in the late Twentieth Century*, 188–219. Cambridge: Harvard University Press.

Crane, S. 2000. 'Introduction: Of Museums and Memory', in S. Crane (ed.), *Museums and Memory*, 1–16. Stanford: Stanford University Press.

Halbwachs, M. 1967. *Das kollektive Gedächtnis*. Stuttgart: Enke.

Hamann, U., and S. Karakayali. 2016. 'Practicing Willkommenskultur: Migration and Solidarity in Germany', *Intersections. East European Journal of Society and Politics*, 2(4): 69–86.

Heckmann, F. 2012. *Was bedeutet 'Willkommenskultur'? Eröffnungsvortrag zur Auftaktveranstaltung des Programms 'Vielfalt gefällt' der Baden-Württemberg Stiftung und des Ministeriums für Integration*. Stuttgart: Europäisches Forum für Migrationsstudien.

Karakayali, S. 2019. 'Solidarity with Refugees: Negotiations of Proximity and Memory', in J. Bock, and S. Macdonald (eds), *Refugees Welcome? Difference and Diversity in a Changing Germany*, 191–213. New York: Berghahn Books.

Kasparek, B., and M. Speer. 2015. *Of Hope. Hungary and the long Summer of Migration*. http://bordermonitoring.eu/ungarn/2015/09/of-hope-en/ (accessed 5 August 2021).

Landkammer, N. 2017. 'Visitors or Community? Collaborative Museology and the Role of Education and Outreach in Ethnographic Museums', in C. Mörsch, A. Sachs, and T. Sieber (eds), *Contemporary Curating and Museum Education*, 269–280. Bielefeld: transcript.

Lielich-Wolf, A., and G. Avenarius. 2008. 'Der Dialog als Methode in der Kunstvermittlung', *Standbein Spielbein*, 80: 50–54.

Lynch, B. 2017. '"Good for You, But I Don't Care!". Critical Museum Pedagogy in Educational and Curatorial Practice', in C. Mörsch, A. Sachs, and T. Sieber (eds), *Contemporary Curating and Museum Education*, 255–268. Bielefeld: transcript.

Macdonald, S. 2003. 'Museums, National, Postnational and Transcultural Identities', *Museum and Society* 1(1): 1–16.

Macdonald, S. 2013. *Memorylands. Heritage and Identity in Europe Today*, New York: Routledge.

Mörsch, C. 2016. 'Refugees sind keine Zielgruppe', in C. Gritschke, and M. Ziese (eds), *Geflüchtete und kulturelle Bildung. Formate und Konzepte für ein neues Praxisfeld*, 67–74. Bielefeld: transcript.

Rothberg, M. 2009. *Multidirectional memory. Remembering the Holocaust in the Age of Decolonization*. Stanford : Stanford University Press.

Rothberg, M. 2014. 'Multidirectional memory', *Témoigner. Entre histoire et mémoire. Revue pluridisciplinaire de la Fondation Auschwitz*, (119): 176.

Rothberg, M., and Y. Yildiz. 2011. 'Memory Citizenship. Migrant Archives of Holocaust Remembrance in Contemporary Germany', *Parallax*, 17 (4): 32–48.

Shatanawi, M. 2012. 'Curating against Dissent: Museums and the Public Debate on Islam', in C. Flood, S. Hutchings, G. Miazhevich, and H. Nickels (eds), *Political and Cultural Representations of Muslims. Islam in the Plural*, 177–192. Boston: Brill.

i,Slam. Belonging and Difference on Stage in Berlin[1]

Katarzyna Puzon

'Islam belongs to Germany'. With these words, a young woman concluded forcefully her performance on the stage as part of the i,Slam Finale, an event held to celebrate the seventh anniversary of i,Slam, a collective of young Muslims, most of whom are slam poets. The jubilee took place in the Bärensaal (Bear Hall) of Berlin's Old City Hall in December 2018. Placed on a high plinth, the bronze sculpture of the bear, Berlin's symbol, overlooked the hall in which the audience gathered to listen to slam poets' recitations. i,Slam often chooses prominent locations for their large public events to amplify their visibility and presence in the city. This was the case with their fifth jubilee, too, during which the i,Slam Kunstpreis (i,Slam Art Prize) was awarded in 2016.[2] The ceremony attended by around 500 people took place in a convention centre in Berlin's Pariser Platz, just at the foot of the Brandenburg Gate. Belonging was also one of the themes addressed in the artists' works presented that evening, as evidenced by the video titled 'Heimkehr' ('Homecoming'), the prize winner. It shows a young Muslim woman hastening through a forest, against a soundtrack of recordings from rallies of the anti-Islam Pegida movement (Patriotic Europeans against the Islamisation of the Occident; in German: *Patriotische Europäer gegen die Islamisierung des Abendlandes*). At some point, she asks into the camera: 'How can it be that this country, the country of my father, my family, my friends, the country that is my home, that this country is betraying me? And with whom?'[3]

This chapter discusses how young Muslim slam poets negotiate their belonging through explicit and implicit references to Islam. Situating their practices in the current German context, it examines how they can contribute towards a notion of heritage that disrupts the binary of 'here' and 'there' – and, to some degree, of 'now' and 'then' – and that highlights perpetuation over preservation (Shaw 2021), as well as disrupting categories and making connections (Puzon, Macdonald and Shatanawi 2021). I reflect on how i,Slam poets grapple with the dilemma of wanting to be seen as German, on the one hand, and holding on to their 'Muslimness', on the other hand. To this end, I probe into their activity as constitutive of the young Muslim poets' understandings of belonging in Germany and analyse how this is articulated in their slam poetry and the practices in which it is embedded and embodied. In addition, I draw attention to the ways in which Islam is put on stage – literally in the case of i,Slam's events but also more broadly – and what comes into play when this happens. The idea of onstage is especially salient here because poetry slam involves a contest in which young spoken word artists perform self-written lyrics in public.[4]

As I show below, i'Slam poets deploy certain characteristics of 'Islamic heritage', which can be defined as intangible, and combine them with a contemporary format of poetry performance. This practice exemplifies an embodied form of heritage-making that results in doing a new heritage as a new belonging. Before elaborating on this doing, I first delve into recent political debates on Islam in Germany in order to contextualise i,Slam's activities.

Belonging and recognition

The phrase 'Islam belongs to Germany' has a contested public history. It has been voiced on various occasions, especially by politicians. President Christian Wulff (2010–2012), for instance, famously pronounced that 'now Islam also belongs to Germany' in his 2010 speech delivered during the celebrations of '20 Years of German Unity' (Hildebrandt 2015). In 2015, Chancellor Angela Merkel asserted that Islam 'belonged to' Germany at a press conference after the meeting with Turkey's Prime Minister Ahmet Davutoglu (2014–2016) in Berlin. Wulff's successor Joachim Gauck (2012–2017) broadly agreed, though with some reservations. He spoke about Islam followers, and not Islam, while declaring in a 2012 interview for the weekly newspaper *Die Zeit* that 'Muslims who live here belong to Germany' (Hildebrandt and di Lorenzo 2012). Gauck explained his claim by stating that anyone 'who came here and does not only pay taxes but also likes being here, also because here he has rights and freedoms which he does not have there where he comes from, is one of us as long as he obeys the fundamental principles'. He added: 'I can also understand those who ask: Where did Islam shape this Europe, did it experience the Enlightenment, even a Reformation? I understand this as long as such questions do not carry a racist undertone' (ibid.). His references to the European Enlightenment and Reformation confirm the common presumption, at least in Germany, that Islam cannot 'fully' belong to the modern secular world[5] and therefore, cannot constitute a part of its heritage.

Public debates on Islam reached another level, so to speak, during the 'refugee crisis' of 2015 and 2016, when Islam became an even more contentious subject. In 2018, Horst Seehofer, the newly appointed Minister of the Interior and a stark opponent of Angela Merkel's open-door refugee policy, sparked controversy when he stated: 'Islam does not belong to Germany'. He further clarified a couple of months later at the German Islam Conference (*Deutsche Islam Konferenz*) – a forum for dialogue between the German State and Muslims living Germany[6] – when he said that Muslims residing in Germany belonged in that country. In these ongoing deliberations on belonging, the distinction is made between 'Islam' and 'Muslims'. Namely, discussions revolve around whether the former is or only the latter are part of German society, as well as around disputes over the incommensurability of Islam with a German *Leitkultur* (guiding or dominant culture). This is especially reflected in public statements of the nationalist Alternative for Germany (AfD) party, as in the claim of the party's deputy leader, Beatrix von Storch, that 'Islam is a political ideology incompatible with the German Basic Law' ('Von Storch: "Islam nicht mit Grundgesetz vereinbar"', 2016).

A doing–undoing dynamic is a crucial aspect of these and other debates on belonging, as well as of the politics of recognition or the politics of difference. As Judith Butler notes, 'if the schemes of recognition that are available to us are those that "undo" the person by conferring recognition, or "undo" the person by withholding recognition, then recognition becomes a site of power by which the human is differentially produced' (2004: 2). Drawing on Patchen Markell, Schirin Amir-Moazami's (2018) analysis of recognition and Islam in a liberal secular context illuminates how the marking of some groups and individuals is embedded in these schemes. She discusses the problematic dichotomy reproduced of an 'unmarked We' – the majority – and the marked minority and demonstrates how it has operated in Germany in relation to Muslims. This has played out along, though not exclusively, religious lines, casting Muslims as the religious Other, with either a Turk or an Arab standing as the predominant representation of the Muslim. Otherness, and the Other for that matter, is not merely perceived in terms of difference – and potentially as part of a valued diversity – but also positioned as culturally inferior (cf. Argyrou 2000) or as a kind of deviation from the norm (e.g. Fernando 2019). Amir-Moazami posits that a politics of recognition is predicated upon the marked–unmarked dyad as well as the inclusion exclusion dynamic (see e.g. Asad 2003). To make the point, she refers to Joachim Gauck's talk at the newly established Centre for Islamic Theology at Münster University in 2013. He then stated:

> And now Islam is also becoming one of the academic disciplines at our universities. Behind this is a reciprocal act of recognition: our society is changing, because it includes an increasing number of Muslims – just as Islam for its part is developing in contact with our society. This entails demands being imposed on both sides – that is all part of it. Admittedly, some people who are resistant to change try to make mileage out of it. But the majority knows that we can only live in fruitful coexistence if we treat each other with respect and come together in a spirit of openness. The foundations for this is *our* basic rights and freedoms, *our* history and language [emphasis added by S. A.-M.]. (2018: 434)

Gauck's speech[7] raises at least two interesting – yet quite problematic – issues that merit attention. Firstly, by not mentioning the established position of *Islamwissenschaft* (Islamic studies) in Germany, especially given that his talk was held in the context of the recent foundation of institutes of Islamic theology, Gauck ignores over a century-long presence of this academic discipline in Germany (see, e.g. Gräf, Krawietz and Moazami 2018). Secondly, and perhaps more importantly, despite his assertion that recognition comes from 'both sides', that is, the majority and the minority, the quote, and especially the last sentence, clearly signals that the rights and history of the majority – the unmarked '*our*' – determine the nature of the recognition of the minority by the majority.

Elaborating on the politics of minorities making a claim for religious freedom in a liberal secular context, Saba Mahmood (2016) attends to the tension implicated in the concept of minority. She propounds that 'on the one hand, a minority is supposed to be an equal partner with the majority in the building of the nation; on the other hand, its difference (religious, racial, ethnic) poses an incipient threat to the identity of the nation that is grounded in the religious, linguistic, and cultural norms of the majority' (ibid.: 32). As a result, the majority versus minority distinction fixes the role of 'both sides', that is, the non-Muslim majority and the Muslim minority, as well as who recognises whom. In addition, it reinforces the 'us' and 'them' dichotomy by picturing 'the majority' and 'the minority' in somewhat oppositional terms and grouping both separately as part of a collective sameness (Handler 1988). In what follows, I discuss how i,Slam poets challenge this binary logic in a German context by means of embodied heritage-making.

Muslim heritage on stage in Berlin

In 2011, i,Slam started its activity as an explicit response to the controversial book '*Deutschland schafft sich ab: Wie wir unser Land aufs Spiel setzen*' (translated into the English as 'Germany Abolishes Itself: How We Are Putting Our Country at Risk'). Authored by Thilo Sarrazin, former senator of finance for the State of Berlin, the monograph came out in 2010 and was widely criticised as racist and Islamophobic, though it was also positively received by some.[8] Shortly after its publication, many public debates about Muslim youth were held, but 'nobody talked to them', Youssef, i,Slam's co-founder, said disapprovingly. This prompted him to think about poetry slam, with which he had already experimented, as a space where young Muslims could speak for themselves.

The birth of poetry slam dates back to the mid-1980s when Marc Smith, a writer based in Chicago, initiated a more vibrant and engaging alternative to the format of open mic and other then current modes of poetry performance in the local Green Mill bar. Fairly quickly, this new form of cultural expression appealed to many, especially to minorities and marginalised groups and individuals.

i,Slam poets, mostly aged between 20 and 30 years, are from various ethnic backgrounds. The majority can be denoted as belonging to the Arab or Turkish diaspora, that is, to one or other of the two largest Muslim communities in Germany. i,Slam was the first group self-identifying openly as a Muslim collective on the German slam poetry scene. When I asked Youssef what characterised their activity as Islamic, rather than referring to Islam as a religion, he talked about different forms of discrimination towards minorities. Poems performed by i,Slam are not solely – or even primarily – concerned with Islam or multiple ways of being Muslim.[9] In their texts, the slam poets not only deal with discrimination against Muslims but also are critical of social injustice and 'global racism' more broadly.

Creating a 'stage' on which to present different ideas and views, i,Slam established a public platform through which to speak for themselves. Their Five Pillars of i,Slam, inspired by the concept of the five pillars of Islam (*arkan al-Islam*), reflect the general tenets of poetry slam. These pillars are: respect the poet (every poet gets his or her recognition regardless of their performance); own construction (every poet must ensure that the poems are their own texts – no intellectual theft); no aids (the poet is not allowed to use props such as costumes or musical instruments); time limit (the poet must not exceed the time limit of six minutes, otherwise they lose points); no verbalism (verbal attacks of any kind are prohibited – the Islamic framework must be respected here). Some of these rules resonate with what Jeanette Jouili (2012) terms '*halal* arts' (permissible arts), which, as she explains,'includes, for instance, the avoidance of vulgarity and insulting speech, and respect for Islamic modesty requirements (the interpretation of these forms may, of course, vary). Often, however, the contents involve topics that reflect a political consciousness and a commitment to social justice' (ibid.: 402).

i,Slam crafted their self-image by drawing on the prominence of oral traditions in Islam. Their idea of slam poetry evokes public recitations, including *qira'at* (Qur'anic recitations), pointing to a well-established practice in Islam, also cultivated by i,Slam, as some of their events open with a recitation of the Qur'an.

Delineating i,Slam's beginnings, Youssef highlighted that the group established a 'symbiosis between their heritage [*Heritage* – he used an English word], legacy (*Vermächtnis*), ancestors (*Vorfahren*) and a modern form of poetry'. This symbiosis plays out in manifold ways. Their catchy name 'i,Slam' not only references Islam but also has the double entendre of 'I slam', which works in German (*Ich slamme*), too. Derived from the verb *qara'a*, which translates as 'read' or 'recite', the Arabic word *iqra'* (recite!) is believed to have been revealed to the Prophet Muhammad, marking the beginnings of Islam.Youssef links this revelation to the way in which i,Slam was conceived when he had a Eureka moment and came up with the name *Ich slamme*, subsequently transformed into the neatly anglicised i,Slam. Therefore, the collective's official statement *Alles began mit einem Wort* (It all began with a word), which also features on their T-shirts, refers to both *Ich slamme* and *iqra'*.

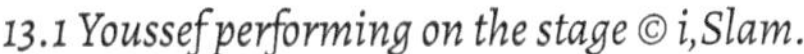

13.1 Youssef performing on the stage © i,Slam.

Favouring speech over writing, the format foregrounds the salience of auditory experience and listening in Islam[10] (see, e.g. Hirschkind 2006; Kapchan 2016; McMurray 2021). Moreover, it alludes to storytelling considered an art form in, albeit not only, Middle Eastern cultures. For a *hakawati* (storyteller in Arabic), a story is important, yet a particular emphasis is placed on its delivery.

In her seminal ethnography, *Veiled Sentiments. Honour and Poetry in a Bedouin Society*, Lila Abu-Lughod (1986) mentions 'the social context of *performed* poetry' as vital for oral tradition. In the case of i,Slam, this concerns, among other things, audience participation, which is integral to a live performance. Lauren Osborne's (2016) description of Qur'anic recitations as an 'emergent phenomenon', when the performer and the audience enter into a sort of interaction, also resonates with poetry slam that, as Susan Somers-Willett (2009: 8) notes, is 'best understood by what it means to achieve or effect: a more intimate and authentic connection to its audience'.

Despite appearing improvised, slams are meticulously prepared shows. Drawing on performance art and rooted in oral traditions, they combine several elements, such as writing, performance, competition and audience participation. The last characteristic is crucial for the format of poetry slam because the audience actively participates by giving each poem a score, and is thus engaged in developments on the stage and reacts to them, which entails applauding or booing those who perform. The principles on which i,Slam relies specify that anyone can act as a judge (Somers-Willett, 2009). During one of their events, for example, a stand-up performer left the stage after some audience members had interrupted his guest show because they had disapproved of his remarks about the headscarf. Although the format is known for its open-door policy which stipulates that everyone is welcome to participate or perform, i,Slam's events are mostly attended by members of Muslim communities.

Founded in Berlin, the collective has now grown into a network of about 300 performers in Germany, Austria and Switzerland (its German-speaking part).[11] In Germany, their activity is not limited to Berlin, as local groups operate in several cities, for instance, in Cologne, Mainz, Hamburg, Munich and Stuttgart. In Europe, and more globally due to i,Slam's connections with groups in Tunisia, Egypt, Malaysia and Singapore, the collective became part of what Annelies Moors and Jeanette Jouili have named 'Islamically inspired artistic scene' (2014; see also, e.g. Herding 2013; Jouili 2019). Other genres are represented too, such as rap and hip-hop which influenced the popularity of spoken word and slam poetry in those circles.

Through the genre of slam poetry, intentionally unsettling of stereotypes, i,Slam engages in 'undoing' Islamophobic myths, as well as striving to challenge those about gender, race, nationality, ethnicity and religion. By means of parody, they disrupt simplistic depictions of Islam in Germany and play on fears of Muslims and other Others (on parody in slam poetry, see, e.g. Hoffman 2001).

Somers-Willett (2009: 8) describes poetry slams as 'laboratories for identity expression and performance'. In this respect, i,Slam's activity emerges as a practice which transpires in the immediate context of performing poems and represents an embodied form of heritage-making that favours perpetuation over preservation (Shaw 2021). Wendy Shaw distinguishes between 'objective heritage preservation' and 'embodied heritage perpetuation'. The former, which applies to any religion or culture, suggests that Islam can be identified by means of certain categories, norms and sets of elements, whereas the latter deals with Islam as perpetually producing its identity by reconstructing the past and looking towards the future. The past–future connection is well encapsulated in Youssef's ensuing declaration about i,Slam: 'we do it for what comes after us and what came before us'. In order to understand better the role of belonging in this, I reflect below further how i,Slam's practices challenge not only the us-versus-them logic but also the binary of 'here' and 'there'.

'It is always good to see *Heimat*'

'It is always good to see *Heimat*', Youssef said to me after casting a glance at the Aleppo Room and the display of the legacy of the Umayyad Caliphate at the Museum of Islamic Art. Both the Room, with inscriptions of poetry on its wood panels ('*ajami*), and the Umayyads, the Muslim dynasty (661–749) established in Damascus, made him think of *Heimat*, by which he meant Syria, and in particular Aleppo where he was born. He was heading towards the room where the panel discussion 'Art as an escape from a faulty system?' was held. The event was organised by i,Slam as part of the Muslim Cultural Days in order to converse about the meaning of art in practices of marginalised groups in the current political climate.[12]

13.2 Panel discussion during the 2019 Muslim Cultural Days at the Museum of Islamic Art. Photograph by Katarzyna Puzon. Reproduced courtesy of Staatliche Museen Berlin and i,Slam.

The German word *Heimat* has no equivalent in English and roughly means home, homeland or a sense of belonging. Youssef considers the city of Aleppo his first home (*Heimat*), his place of origin and a foundational part of his identity. In 2002, he moved with his family to Germany, and 2 years later, when he turned 12, he started writing poems to 'have better access to the German language'. Berlin became his second home but, as he emphasised, not his *Heimat*. He told me: 'I have Arabic culture and there is lot of German culture in me'. 'Too much of it', he added laughingly. 'But when', he carried on, 'this Germany tells me that I am not German, I do not feel German'. He experiences this not only when he hears public pronouncements, such as those of certain politicians, but also when he, for example, receives threatening letters, as well as in everyday situations. For this reason, he associates *Heimat* first with Syria, and then partly with Germany, because 'such feelings depend on one's surroundings'.

The term *Heimat* is negatively tainted due to its connotations with Germany's Nazi era and is regarded as an exclusionary construct (Bausinger 1986). As a way of reclaiming it, some propose the use of *Heimaten*, the plural of *Heimat*, and others study *Heimat* as a process or *Beheimatung* (homing), a 'feeling at home' embracing belonging and being at home not limited to the place of origin (Binder 2010; Göb 2019; Greverus 1979; Römhild 2018).

To Youssef, *Heimat* is not a problematic word. 'I have nothing to do with the Nazis', he remarked. His place of origin plays a crucial role in his self-identification, including in his interpretation of heritage, which to him denotes much more than just his *Herkunft* (origins). Youssef refers to it as *Vermächtnis* (legacy) that he inherited from past generations and views as empowering. He therefore makes a distinction between heritage as a place, which he identifies more in terms of *Herkunft*, that is, his place of origin, and heritage that builds on his ancestors' legacy and constitutes a kind of resource, which underpins his current activity.

Understanding heritage as composed of multiple parts, he looks at this legacy as something that he embodies and that is 'the result' of various components and of 'socialising which I have enjoyed and which my father enjoyed'. Youssef's conception of heritage is a positive one, that sees it not as a constraining 'cultural *baggage*' (Jouili 2019) but as having liberating potential to express oneself. By mixing up different heritages, he crafts his own one that affords him creativity. This partly resonates with what Sharon Macdonald calls 'transcultural heritage' wherein 'transcultural', approached as assemblage, entails 'bringing together elements from different cultures and fusing these in what becomes a new form, though it may retain identifiable elements of previous assemblages' (2013: 163; see also Macdonald 2014). The mixing and fusion of cultures – or differences – may take multifarious forms and generate different constellations, as i,Slam's practices aptly illustrate, and is perceptible in other art forms which they promote. Calligraffiti, with which i,Slam's office in Berlin's Wedding district is embellished, constitutes one example. It merges modern graffiti styles with classical Arabic calligraphy, which is used to convey ideas and as decoration and is in fact associated with different faiths in the MENA region. Calligraffiti references Islamic heritage due to the fundamental role of Arabic calligraphy in Islam – and Islamic art for that matter.

Building upon the notion of transcultural processes of heritage-making, the next section is concerned with forms of belonging – and non-belonging – addressed in i,Slam's poetry and with some of the themes it invokes.

Being German and being Muslim

Poems performed by Leila, an i,Slam member born in Germany, do not primarily attend to Islam or her religiosity as a Muslim woman, but centre on what it means to be German, or a Muslim German in particular. In one of her poems, she says: 'She calls me a foreigner, she calls me a migrant, she calls me a person with migration background, and now I am a New German'. The term 'migration background' (*Migrationshintergrund*), which she mentions, is officially used to identify those who were not born as German citizens or who have at least one parent who was not born a German citizen. 'New German', or 'New Berliner' for that matter, is a name applied by some to those who arrived seeking refuge in Germany during the 'refugee crisis' of 2015 and 2016 (see e.g. Bock & Macdonald 2019). Leila's poems bring to focus the distinction made between those who are seen as German and those who are considered conditionally German. She is concerned not just with the fixed categorisation of Muslims but also with the constant relabelling of those deemed not 'fully' belonging in Germany.

In his study on citizenship and exclusion, anthropologist Damani Partridge notes that 'the process of "foreign" incorporation is not one of normalisation, but one of differentiation' (2012: 18). This mechanism plays out along the lines of what he calls 'a politics of exclusionary incorporation', which suggests that despite being formally (German) citizens, some cannot exercise their citizenship fully. Practices of naming and renaming fall within these 'technologies of exclusion' (ibid.: 19) and serve as conventional ways of managing the difference of Islam – or Muslimness. They are tantamount to practices of integration that represent a perpetual process of 'becoming' German, a sort of never-ending gestation period, or what Abdelmalek Sayad has termed an 'indefinite temporariness' (1999; see also Fadil 2019). The tedious process of 'becoming' German is well captured in the following excerpt from Leila's poem:

> But when I tell you that I would just like to be German, I mean that I would like to be unconditionally German, without a footnote, without an exception, without scandal and without patriotism. But with the same rights, standards and brands.

The excerpt raises a number of questions pertinent to what it means to be identified repeatedly as a non-German or not fully German. It draws attention to various ways of marking those who do not belong and shows how this operates through 'extra' descriptors, such as a 'footnote' or an 'exception', which classify someone as 'different'. Although especially the excerpt's last sentence partly invokes the notion of 'the right to have rights' (Arendt 1973), the text implies a 'call for equality', which, I suggest, corresponds with Hegel's *Gleichgültigkeit*, translated as indifference or equivalence. Its literal meaning conveys the idea of equal validity or equality. It is this equal validity, I contend, that Leila addresses in her poem.

This resonates with the issues voiced by anthropologist Mayanthi Fernando's French interlocutors. She points outs that 'Muslim French argue that they are not "different", but French. Moreover, they argue that the demands they make are claims to equal citizenship and justice rather than to difference, claims made by citizens with as equal a right to France as any other citizen' (Fernando, 2019: 266). A similar 'call for equality' is discernible in i,Slam poets' practices and is conveyed in their reflections on Heimat and belonging, as mentioned above in the 'Heimkehr' video, for example. Their 'call for equality' epitomises a call for being a German citizen 'without a footnote', as Leila notes in her poem, and thus someone who does not need to earn belonging more than others. Like Fernando's French interlocutors, i,Slam poets challenge the image of Muslims as non-German and consider their Muslimness as already German.

Making connections

Slam poetry remains the chief form of i,Slam's cultural expression. They also support and collaborate with those who are involved in other kinds of creative work and artistic production through which various cultural, political and social issues are addressed (see, e.g. Puzon 2016). For example, in the case of the i,Slam Kunstpreis, a contest for socially engaged art, artists were awarded in seven categories: singing/hip-hop, music, photography, literature, poetry, design and film. In addition, i,Slam experimented with various formats, for instance when they held a series of flash mobs called i,Slam for Justice in four German cities in 2013.

The 2012 i,Slam – we,Slam event provides an example of broader collaborative endeavours and making connections, in that case among young poets representing three Abrahamic religions: Islam, Judaism and Christianity. The rationale behind this was to create a stage on which they could speak together openly about their beliefs. A key idea of i,Slam is that 'being on the stage' will encourage young people to raise questions that are vital to them and will, therefore, empower them. The stage 'is for those who have something to say', as Youssef put it. His statement did not just point to self-expression but also to the group's credo 'we don't want any superstars in i,Slam'.

Organised under the slogan '*Ver-Bindungen schaffen*' (Making Bonds and Connections), the 2019 Muslim Cultural Days constituted their attempt to collaborate with others. The event covered different parts of Berlin, and meetings and performances took place across the city over 4 days. The aim was to showcase the diversity of Muslim communities and reach out to those who might not be familiar with Islam, as well as reflecting on past developments and future possibilities of forming alliances. Flagging up 'connections' as a leading theme of the Muslim Culture Days, the focus was on Berlin's Muslims, with the intent to 'invite all non-Muslim citizens to learn about the Muslim life and cultural diversity'.[13]

The launch event was dedicated to possible cooperation between organisations representing marginalised groups in Germany. The following ones were invited as speakers: the Initiative Black People in Germany, the Academy of the Jewish Museum Berlin (JMB), the Archiv RomaniPhen, a feminist association of Sinti and Roma women, and GLADT – an organisation of black and PoC lesbians, gays, bisexuals, trans*[14], inter* and queer people. The subject of alliances was the focal point of the meeting. One speaker called for the need to adopt a multilayered approach, along with an intersectional one, and highlighted that marginalised groups do not embody one community. A former representative of the JMB brought attention to the problem of *Hierarchisierung* (creating hierarchies) that often hampers collaborative efforts because some groups are given more consideration, especially those deemed more important historically and thus more relevant in the German context. She meant the Jewish community, and drew on her experience as a leader of the Migration and Diversity Programme and the Jewish-Islamic Forum at the JMB's Academy.

In their endeavour of making connections, i,Slam deals with the Othering of Muslims and strives to bring about a change. This necessitates altering the focus – orientation – by drawing attention to what is not instantly visible[15] and fostering diverse connections, as well as looking at Muslim heritage as not just belonging elsewhere but also as part of the past, present and future in Germany.

Conclusion

In German, there is a distinction between the following two words indicating belonging: *Zugehörigkeit* (belonging to) and *Zusammengehörigkeit* (belonging with, in the sense of togetherness) (see also Pfaff-Czarnecka 2011). This distinction resembles the divergence between differences brought together to embody a fixed category and differences that are constantly negotiated. In the former case, rather than maintaining heterogeneity, differences are often turned into a sameness. The category of 'the Muslim' epitomises this tendency, as the debates on Islam belonging or not belonging discussed here illustrate. The process of granting equal validity to Muslims or those with a 'migration background' resembles 'conditional belonging' with respect to becoming a German citizen; in this case, a German Muslim who never seems to belong enough.

By situating the question of belonging in the current German context, the primary purpose of this chapter was that of examining i,Slam's practices and the ways in which young Muslims negotiate differences by claiming their place in Berlin – and in Germany more generally. i,Slam poets' identification as Muslims is no different than their self-positioning as Germans. This is manifest in their call for recognition as Muslims, as well as recognition as Turkish or Arabic, for example, all as part of being German citizens without footnotes.

As I have shown, i,Slam poets do not necessarily conform to a certain 'bridge of understanding' (Winegar 2008) with which the 'majority' could feel comfortable. In so doing, they do not eschew their religion to make themselves more relatable or to fit the image of the 'good Muslim' – one that is 'westernised' and secular (Mamdani 2005). Rather, their practices, representing an embodied form of heritage-making, offer a lens through which one can rethink the relationship between Islam and heritage in Germany. By virtue of this, i,Slam poets question what it means to be German – and a Muslim German in particular. Combining oral traditions of 'Islamic heritage' with a contemporary format of poetry performance, this model of heritage heightens translocal elements (Puzon 2019) and accentuates connections. i,Slam's practices thus reveal doing a new heritage as a new belonging which attends to diverse articulations of Islam not only in Germany but also across Europe and beyond.

Acknowledgements

This research was funded by the Alexander von Humboldt Foundation as part of Sharon Macdonald's Alexander von Humboldt Professorship. I would like to thank i,Slam as well as colleagues at CARMAH, especially those who were part of the *Making Differences* project.

Notes

1 This chapter is an adaptation of the chapter 'Germans without Footnotes: Islam, Belonging and Poetry Slam' published in Islam and Heritage in Europe: Pasts, Presents and Future Possibilities (Routledge, 2021).

2 The prize was funded by the German Federal Ministry for Family, Seniors, Women, and Youth as part of the Living Democracy programme.

3 Unless otherwise indicated, all translations are my own.

4 Despite sharing many qualities, the two forms of poetry, slam and spoken word, differ mainly in this way that unlike the latter, the former is staged as a competition which involves audience participation.

5 The 'framework of the "West"', as Wendy Shaw (2020) shrewdly argues, 'is less the recognition of a secular cultural geography than a legacy of the universalisation of Protestant values through the occlusion of religion as a visible agent. Such ghosts may be the most difficult of all agents to battle, as they can always claim that they were never there'.

6 http://www.deutsche-islam-konferenz.de. For a critical account of the Conference, see Bayat (2016).

7 For a full text of Gauck's speech, see http://www.bundespraesident.de/SharedDocs/ Downloads/DE/Reden/2013/11/131128-Themenbesuch-Islam.pdf;jsessionid=FD02305F80AD576C432C050A167AFA8C.1_cid362? blob=publicationFile

8 It even became a bestseller in the category of non-fiction literature (Sachbuch) and enjoyed this status from mid-September 2010 to early February 2011 (see Stein, 2012).

9 For more on different ways of being Muslim, see Osella and Soares (2010); Fadil & Fernando (2015); Özyürek (2015).

10 For example, Kristina Nelson points out that 'the Qur'an is not the Qur'an unless it is heard' (2001: xiv), which positions oral and auditory qualities of the Qur'an as being of primary importance.

11 The Berlin-based group runs a Youtube channel called Erklaeriker. See their website https://www.i-slam.de/erklaeriker/

12 Apart from organising slams, workshops and other public events, i,Slam poets have performed in museums. In Berlin, this was, for instance, the case with the Neukölln Museum's Festival für Demokratie und Vielfalt (Festival for Democracy and Diversity) that accompanied their 2017 exhibition Die Sache mit der Religion (The Case of Religion). The collective has also been involved in the project TAMAM – Das Bildungsprojekt von Moscheegemeinden mit dem Museum für Islamische

Kunst (TAMAM – The Mosque Communities' Education Project with the Museum of Islamic Art) run by the Museum of Islamic Art in cooperation with the Institute of Islamic Theology in Osnabrück.

13 https://muslimische-kulturtage.de/programm-2019/

14 An asterisk after 'trans' or 'inter' indicates an umbrella word that encompasses a wide range of gender variations. See also, for example, Stryker (2008).

15 The 2019–20 exhibition Re:Orient – The Invention of the Muslim Other at the GRASSI Museum of Ethnology in Leipzig addressed this subject. Its aim was to 'reorient visitors towards what is all too often left unseen when they look at "the others"'. See https://grassi-voelkerkunde.skd.museum/en/exhibitions/reorient/

References

Abu-Lughod, L. 1986. *Veiled sentiments: Honor and poetry in a Bedouin society*. Berkeley, CA: University of California Press.

Amir-Moazami, S. 2018. 'Recognition and its traps in liberal secular conditions: The case of Muslims in Europe', in B. Gräf, B. Krawietz, and S. Amir-Moazami (eds), *Ways of knowing Muslim cultures and societies. Studies in honour of Gudrun Krämer* (Social, Economic and Political Studies of the Middle East and Asia, 122), 427–440. Leiden: Brill.

Arendt, H. 1973. *The origins of totalitarianism*. New York: Harcourt Brace Jovanovich.

Argyrou, V. 2000. 'Self-accountability, ethics and the problem of meaning', in M. Strathern (ed.), *Audit cultures:Anthropological studies in accountability, ethics and the academy*, 196–211. London: Routledge.

Asad, T. 2003. *Formations of the secular: Christianity, Islam, modernity*. Stanford: Stanford University Press.

Bausinger, H. 1986. 'Heimat in einer offenen Gesellschaft. Begriffsgeschichte als Problemgeschichte', in J. Kelter (ed.), *Die Ohnmacht der Gefühle. Heimat zwischen Wunsch und Wirklichkeit*, 76–90. Weingarten: Drumlin-Verlag.

Bayat, M. 2016. *Die politische und mediale Repräsentation in Deutschland lebender Muslime: Eine Studie am Beispiel der Deutschen Islam Konferenz*. Wiesbaden: Springer VS.

Binder, B. 2010. 'Beheimatung statt Heimat: Translokale Perspektiven auf Räume der Zugehörigkeit', in M. Seifert (ed.), *Zwischen Emotion und Kalkül.'Heimat' als Argument im Prozess der Moderne*, 189–204. Dresden: Leipziger Uni-Vlg.

Bock, J.-J., and S. Macdonald (eds). 2019. *Refugees welcome? Difference and diversity in a changing Germany*. Oxford: Berghahn.

Butler, J. 2004. *Undoing gender*. New York & Abingdon: Routledge.

Fadil, N. 2019. 'The anthropology of Islam in Europe: A double epistemological impasse', *Annual Review of Anthropology*, 48: 117–132.

Fadil, N., and M. Fernando. 2015. 'Rediscovering the 'everyday' Muslim. Notes on an anthropological divide', *HAU: Journal of Ethnographic Theory*, 5(2): 59–88.

Fernando, M. 2019. 'State sovereignty and the politics of indifference', *Public Culture*, 31(2): 261–273.

Göb, A. 2019. 'Heimat im Subrubanen? Zur Lebenswelt von Subrubaniten', in M. Hülz, O. Kühne, and F. Weber (eds), *Heimat: Ein vielfältiges Konstrukt*, 245–258. Wiesbaden: Springer VS.

Gräf, B., B. Krawietz, and S. Amir-Moazami (eds). 2018. *Ways of knowing Muslim cultures and societies. Studies in honour of Gudrun Krämer* (Social, Economic and Political Studies of the Middle East and Asia, 122). Leiden: Brill.

Greverus, I.-M. 1979. *Auf der Suche nach Heimat*. München: Beck.

Handler, R. 1988. *Nationalism and the politics of culture in Quebec*. Madison, Wisconsin: University of Wisconsin Press.

Herding, M. 2013. *Inventing the Muslim cool. Islamic youth culture in Western Europe*. Bielefeld: transcript.

Hildebrandt, T. 'Christian Wulff: "Der Islam gehört zu Deutschland"', *Die Zeit*. 12 March 2015. https://www.zeit.de/2015/09/christian-wullf-angela-merkel-islam- deutschland (accessed 8 March 2022).

Hildebrandt,T., and G. di Lorenzo, G. Joachim Gauck:'Meine Seele hat Narben', *Die Zeit*. 31 May 2012. https://www.zeit.de/2012/23/Interview-Gauck (accessed 8 March 2022).

Hirschkind, C. 2006. *The ethical soundscapes: Cassette sermon and Islamic counterpublics*. New York: Columbia University Press.

Hoffman, T. 2001. 'Treacherous laughter: The poetry slam, slam poetry and the politics of resistance', *Studies in American Humor*, 3(8): 49–64.

Jouili, J. 2012. 'Halal arts: What's in a concept?', *Material Religion: The Journal of Objects, Art and Belief*, 8(3): 402–403.

Jouili, J. S. 2019. 'Islam and culture: Dis/junctures in a modern conceptual terrain', *Comparative Studies in Society and History*, 61(1): 207–237.

Kapchan, D. 2016. 'Listening acts, secular and sacred: Sound knowledge among Sufi Muslims in secular France', in K. van Nieuwkerk, M. Levine, and M. Stokes (eds), *Islam and popular culture*, 23–40. Austin, TX: University of Texas Press.

Macdonald S. 2013. *Memorylands: Heritage and identity in Europe today*. London: Rouledge.

Macdonald, S. 2014. 'Migrating heritage, networks and networking: Europe and Islamic heritage', in P. Innocenti (ed.), *Migrating heritage. Experiences of cultural networks and cultural dialogue in Europe*, 53–64. Surrey: Ashgate.

Mahmood, S. 2016. *Religious difference in a secular age: A minority report*. Princeton, NJ: Princeton University Press.

Mamdani, M. 2005. *Good Muslim, bad Muslim: America, the cold war and the roots of terror*. New York: Three Leaves Press.

McMurray, P. 2021. 'Cemetery poetics: The sonic life of cemeteries in Muslim Europe', in K. Puzon, S. Macdonald, and M. Shatanawi (eds), *Islam and heritage in Europe: Pasts, presents and future possibilities*, 51–67. London & New York: Routledge.

Moors, A., and J. Jouili. 2014. 'Introduction: Islamic sounds and the politics of listening', *Anthropological Quarterly*, 87(4): 977–988.

Nelson, K. 2001. *The art of reciting the Qur'an*. Cairo: American University in Cairo Press.

Osborne, L. 2016. 'The experience of the recited Qur'an', *International Journal of Middle East Studies*, 48: 124–128.

Osella, F., and B. Soares, B. 2010. 'Islam, politics, anthropology', in B. Soares, and F. Osella (eds), *Islam, politics and anthropology*, 1–22. Oxford: Wiley-Blackwell.

Özyürek, E. 2015. *Being German, becoming Muslim. Race, religion and conversion in the New Europe*. Princeton, NJ: Princeton University Press.

Partridge, D. 2012. *Hypersexuality and headscarves: Race, sex and citizenship in the New Germany*. Bloomington, IN: Indiana University Press.

Pfaff-Czarnecka, J. 2011. *From 'identity' to 'belonging' in social research: Plurality, social boundaries and the politics of the self.* (Working Papers in Development Sociology and Social Anthropology, 368). Bielefeld: Universität Bielefeld.

Puzon, K. 2016. 'Memory and artistic production in a post-war Arab city', in D. O'Rawe, and M. Phelan (eds), *Post-conflict performance, film and visual arts: Cities of memory*, 265–283. London: Palgrave Macmillan.

Puzon, K. 2019. 'Participatory matters: Access, migration and heritage in Berlin museums', in H. Oevermann, and E. Gantner (eds), *Securing urban heritage: Agents, access and securitization*, 31–46. London & New York: Routledge.

Puzon, K., S. Macdonald, and M. Shatanawi (eds). 2021. *Islam and heritage in Europe: Pasts, presents and future possibilities*. London & New York: Routledge.

Römhild, R. 2018. 'Global *Heimat*. (Post)Migrant productions of transnational space', *Anthropological Journal of European Cultures*, 21(1): 27–39.

Sayad, A. 1999. *La double absence. Des illusions de l'émigré aux souffrances de l'immigré*. Paris: Le Seuil.

Shaw, W. M. K. 2021. 'From postcoloniality to decoloniality, from heritage to perpetuation: The Islamic at the museum', in K. Puzon, S. Macdonald, and M. Shatanawi (eds), *Islam and heritage in Europe: Pasts, presents and future possibilities*, 31–50. London & New York: Routledge.

Shaw, W. M. K. 'Reenchantment: From the facts of Orientalism to the suste- nance of storytelling', *TRAFO – Blog for Transregional Research*. 7 May 2020. https:// trafo.hypotheses.org/23643 (accessed 8 March 2022).

Somers-Willett, S. 2009. *The cultural politics of slam poetry. Race, identity and the performance of popular verse in America*. Ann Arbor, MI: The University of Michigan Press.

Stein, C. 2012. *Die Sprache der Sarrazin-Debatte: Eine diskurslinguistische Analyse*. Marburg: Tectum Verlag.

Storch, B. von. 2016. 'Islam nicht mit Grundgesetz vereinbar', *Frankfurter Allgemeine*. 17 April 2016. https://www.faz.net/aktuell/politik/inland/von-storch-islam-nicht-mit-grundgesetz-vereinbar-14182472.html (accessed 8 March 2022).

Stryker, S. 2008. *Transgender history*. Berkeley, CA: Seal Press.

Winegar, J. 2008. 'The humanity game: Art, Islam and the war on terror', *Anthropological Quarterly*, 81(3): 651–681.

Transnational Entanglements of Queer Solidarity
Berlin Walks with Istanbul Pride March

Nazlı Cabadağ

It is the 1st of July 2018, a warm summer day in Berlin. I pass through pedestrians as I walk towards the public square where a crowd is slowly gathering. Turkish pop song lyrics rise from the amplifiers. In a few minutes, the Istanbul LGBTI+ march will start despite the ban by the Governor's office of Istanbul.[1] This year, for the first time, the organising committee rescheduled the march from the last Sunday of June (to commemorate the Stonewall Riots of 1969) to avoid overlapping with the Ramadan holiday of Turkey's Muslim majority. As I pass the last crosswalk before mingling with the crowd, I notice the big pink banner that I helped to prepare. The glittery letters of ISTANBUL PRIDE gleam in the sunlight. We are at Hermannplatz, the vibrant square of Berlin's Neukölln borough. The destination of the Walk is Oranienplatz, a square in the famous migrant district of Kreuzberg, also known as Little Istanbul.

Over the following few hours, small groups disperse and meet with each other in alleys and corners in the Beyoğlu district of Istanbul, just like they have done since 2015, in order to outsmart the police. In Berlin, in the meantime, we walk along the artery connecting the two districts, accompanied by the big banner, a van with amplifiers blasting out Turkish and Kurdish songs and by German police officers who loosely encircle the demonstration. This is the event *Berlin Walks with Istanbul Pride March*.

Approximately 1000 people are shouting slogans and carrying placards and banners, using words from the queer slang *lubunca* and humour with which I am familiar from the LGBTI+ activist repertoire in Turkey.[2] Placards merge various languages and references: 'Lubunya Gücü! Queer Power!', 'Queer & Muslimisch ist KEIN Widerspruch!' ('Queer & Muslim is NOT contradiction!') or 'Yasak ne Ayol!' ('What is ban Ayol!') and more.[3] The popular slogan of *lubun* circles echo on the streets of Berlin: 'Nerdesin Aşkım?' ('Where are you my love?') someone asks. 'Burdayım Aşkım!' ('Here I am my love!') the crowd shouts back. Happy selfies are taken and posted online with the hashtag *lubunPrideBerlin*. Celebratory captions accompany the pictures on social media.

14.1 The poster of the Berlin Walks with Istanbul Pride combining symbolic architectures of two cities: the Galata Tower, the Brandenburger Tor and the plate of Hermannplatz subway station. Retrieved from the Facebook event page.

During and after the Walk, I collected various comments on how *BWIP* had 'brought Istanbul to Berlin'. Such comments implied that the event blurred the distance between locations, enacting an experience close to the carnivalesque atmosphere of Istanbul Pride before 2016. On the one hand, the approximation was talked about as an example of a much-needed act, especially in this particular time of history, when transnational queer solidarity has come under threat in conservative authoritarian states ruled by anti-gender governments, such as those of Turkey, Poland and Hungary. On the other hand, some of the Turkey-based activists said they did not find the event empowering, and pointed out the differences between the historical and political contexts of Berlin and Istanbul, and the material realities of those inhabiting them. Shouting the same slogans, carrying the same banners, dancing to the same songs at the same time had surfaced the unequal vulnerability of the bodies that appear on the streets in Berlin and Istanbul.

The responses intrigued me both as one of the organisers of the event in Berlin and as an anthropologist who thinks about the translocal entanglements of queer conditions and activisms. Therefore, in considering the example of the Berlin Solidarity Walk, I explore the uneasiness of transnational queer solidarity across differences configured by borders. In the first section of the chapter, I situate the Walk against the backdrop of new wave migration from Turkey to Germany. Then I address the ambivalent position of Turkish and Kurdish queer migrants at the intersection of privilege and racialised otherness. In the second section, I argue that the transnational attachments of Berlin-based *lubuns* to Turkey's queer movements complicate the experience of geographical distance and neatly bounded locales. In the example of the Berlin Solidarity Walk, I suggest that *restlessness* surfaced as a diasporic affective force and sparked the Solidarity Walk, which then took a collective form in recontextualising the transnational heritage of LGBT pride in Berlin against the crackdown on queer lives in Turkey.

In addition to my participation and interviews, the discussions and arguments of this paper arise from my engagement with Turkey's queer movements and my affective situatedness in the field. In other words, I depart from my own restlessness across the blurry boundaries of the researched and the researcher. I begin by unpacking the background of the recent political dynamics that require international and diasporic queer solidarity – a pressing matter for Turkey's LGBTI+ movements.

We disperse to Berlin

'This is the last warning! Disperse! And, let life go back to its normal course!' the Turkish police announced, as they typically do right before unleashing tear gas and rubber bullets on demonstrators. This time the addressees were the participants of the 7th Istanbul Trans Pride March in 2016.

In the following week the organising committee of Istanbul LGBTI+ Pride Week responded to the ban by playing with the wording of the police announcement:

> On Sunday, 26 June we will disperse to every single corner of Istiklal Avenue, we are reuniting with each other on every street and avenue in Beyoğlu. Instead of living a life that is imposed on, a life that normalises violence, oppression and denial; we are living the life we chose, the life in which we exist with pride and honour and we are 'Letting life go back to its "normal" course' by:
>
> DISPERSING, DISPERSING, DISPERSING
> (LGBTI News Turkey, 2016)

All-day long, crowds dispersed and assembled in the side streets of Beyoğlu, in small squares and on the ferry, as well as on Instagram live streams and Twitter hashtags. The committee press release was read over and over again wherever possible, and its videos were shared online. The slogan *dağılıyoruz* ('We disperse') echoed throughout the streets of the historically renowned queer centre Taksim-Beyoğlu (Biricik 2010; Çetin 2016) and beyond. Articulated by 'a group whose solidarity rests on a common and forcible exclusion from public space', the slogan 'We disperse' signified fluidity and spontaneity in response to the police and historical continuity by alluding to the restricted spatial mobility of queers. The appearance and disappearance of queer bodies in multiple places at the same time defined a new queer activist practice and emerged as an innovative 'form that freedom of assembly might take when it is explicitly denied as a right' (Butler, 2015). What the movement did was neither simple compliance nor 'straight' refusal, but a playful subversion of the police order into a novel example of dissent and solidarity in the face of state violence.

The authoritarian crackdown on dissidence had been increasing since the summer of 2013, when the nationwide anti-government *Gezi* protests challenged the sovereignty of the governing Justice and Development Party (AKP) and the single-handed leadership of Recep Tayyip Erdoğan. Regarded as the largest anti-government mobilisation in the history of the Republic, *Gezi* was a turning point for the LGBTI+ movement in Turkey. During the occupation of Gezi Park, which initially protested against the reconstruction of an Ottoman-era artillery barrack and the planned demolishment of one of the last green areas in Istanbul, *LGBT Blok* (LGBT Block) took an active role in organising everyday life in the occupied area. The block built up alliances with several groups such as anti-capitalist Muslims and football hooligans, which were uncommon encounters and allies for queer circles in the public imaginary. Due to these unusual alliances and the plurality of its components, *Gezi* itself was argued to be 'a queer becoming in togetherness that transgressed self-castigating sensations of anxiety and fear in the face of state violence' (Zengin 2013). In 2013 and then again in 2014, LGBTI+ pride marches were partially experienced as an extension of *Gezi* when they unprecedentedly gathered thousands of people in the Istiklal Avenue even though Taksim Square and Istiklal Avenue were removed from the list of places for protest and assembly.

The authoritarianism of the AKP peaked in 2016 with the state of emergency that was declared after the failed coup attempt of 15 July. Many people fled the country to avoid incarceration; others left to pursue futures elsewhere, where they hoped to avoid social and political repression. Due to its secular character amid future anxiety, this migration has been called a *bunaltı göçü* – the migration of the suffocated (Ağır and Karcı 2017). The communities that emerged in the aftermath of this migration in the cities of destination are occasionally referred to as the Gezi Diaspora because the ideals they espouse were assumed to be formed during the Gezi uprisings and because their feeling of suffocation was partially due to their experience of Gezi as a space of freedom and possibility, which now seems out of reach.[4]

Most of those who left Turkey during this wave of migration moved to European countries. Germany, particularly Berlin, was a primary destination due to the bonds with the already existing Turkish and Kurdish diasporas there. Germany has been a site of dispersal since it signed a the 'Recruitment and Procurement of Foreign Workers' treaty with Turkey in 1961 (Mandel 2008; Yurdakul 2009; Abadan-Unat 2011; Berger and Mohr 2010). Although economic pull factors played a role in early migration (and continue to today), Germany also became the main destination for political exiles after the military coup in 1980 and during the war that erupted between the Kurdistan's Workers Party (Partîya Karkerên Kurdistanê) and the Turkish Army in the 1990s. What makes the current migration distinct from the previous waves is that Turkey regards it as a brain drain. Compared with the labour migrants of the previous mass migration, 'it's the other side of the population now leaving in ever-greater numbers: the liberals, the intellectuals and the well-to-do' (Lowen 2017). These newcomers are argued to be 'the new face of the Turkish migrant' and their diasporic encounters are often associated with the phrase 'but you don't look like Turkish' (Türkmen 2019); they are seen, that is, as having a privileged life relative to previous waves of migrants, the majority of whom came from lower socio-economic backgrounds.[5]

However, privilege in this case is less clear cut: it intersects with marginality in the experience of new migrants, especially those in need of solidarity. To understand the ambiguity, consider the Academics for Peace, an association of 1128 academics who publicly condemned the violence committed by the Turkish Army in the Kurdish provinces in 2016. Many were subsequently accused of terrorism and dozens were dismissed, detained or arrested. Those who landed in Germany belong to the high-skilled migrants, yet they mostly receive temporary and precarious positions supported by fellowships and networks, some of which such as the 'Adopt a Scholar' programme (Özdemir et.al 2019) are explicitly paternalistic. Their experiences exemplify how solidarity among unequals can take vertical forms, in the liberal projects that turn people into objects of pity (Partridge 2019).

Solidarity and privilege

The criticism and disappointment expressed by Turkey-based activists about the Berlin Walk implies a similar type of verticality. To those who are in need of support, it was perceived as a gesture of the privileged. Lara, a member of the Istanbul Pride Committee I interview, called the event a failure. 'It feels weird. It is like "Oh, you cannot walk in the Middle East, so we are walking in Europe for you". And that is unlovely. People do not feel like in solidarity then.' Three months after the walk, I was one of the speakers in the panel 'Nieder mit eurer Moral! Die LGBTI+ Bewegung und ihre Kampfstrategien' organised by the Rosa Luxemburg Foundation. I talked about the flourishing scene of diasporic queer activists and mentioned the Berlin Walk as an example. A Turkey-based audience member observed that it was not empowering to see that it was possible to walk happily and safely in Berlin while they were under police attack in Istanbul. 'Do we all have to move to Berlin to be able to enjoy the Pride now?' they asked. The question haunted me for days afterward. The unequal distribution of vulnerability across locations was palpable in the uncomfortable emotions and self-questioning of several *lubuns* based in Berlin. Throughout my observant participation and interviews, reconsideration of post-migrant vulnerability was a recurring theme among my interlocutors. Everyday life was mostly described as safer and easier for a queer person in Berlin than for one in Turkey. For instance, when asked about the situation for queers in Turkey, Evrim—a queer activist refugee from Turkey—refused to answer the question. He thought it should be answered by those who are still at risk living in Turkey. The experience of migration raised the question of whether *lubuns* can still 'have a say' in Turkey's queer movements while living in Berlin.

When the banner *Istanbul Pride* appeared in the middle of Berlin, it depicted the walk as a re-enactment of the Istanbul March. But the re-enactment missed taking an ethical stance: refusing to occupy the subject position of the ones who are at risk. It was perceived as an act of speaking on behalf of those who cannot in Turkey. Heartbreakingly, as Lara stated in the interview, it neglected the unequal vulnerability of the bodies in the two geographically distant events. Before I discuss the affective attachments of *lubuns* that blur this geographical distance, I take the heartbreak as a call to revisit the slogan 'No Borders for Queers!'. However, I want to shift the focus from the material differences between Istanbul and Berlin to the differences generated by the intricate realities of migration, ethnicity and sexuality in the German context. In that way, we can see that the slogan 'No Borders for Queers!' does not only risk concealing the material conditions that rendered walking possible in one location while making it a site of oppression in another. It also suggests an imaginary transnational queer community, which risks concealing the situatedness of LGBT subjects. After all, borders exist not only between national territories but also between subject categories that are included, aligned and expelled differently by regulatory regimes in national and local contexts.

Borders and dispersal of *pride*

Annual pride parades that commemorate the Stonewall Rebellion of 1969 have undergone a process of normalisation of LGBT subjectivities developed under the hegemony of liberal paradigms of identity and visibility.[6] Within this paradigm, coming-out and 'being proud' emerged as the normative indicators of the global 'gay' culture and politics, which led to the commodification and domestication of gay culture in mainstream Euro-American contexts (Manalansan 1995; Duggan 2002). Thus, annual pride parades went from being events that radically challenged the heterosexualisation of public spaces to opportunities for a neoliberal form of sexual citizenship like that epitomised by Berlin's Christopher Street Day.

The incorporation of LGBT politics into the liberal rights-based agendas of Western governments and institutions also played a crucial role in their regulation of borders and migration (El-Tayeb 2011; Haritaworn 2015). Jasbir Puar coined the term *homonationalism* to analyse the ways in which LGBT subjects achieve national belonging and consumer- citizenship at the expense of racialised others (2007). In explaining the racialisation of queerphobia in Western European contexts, scholars interrogated the invention of queer-friendliness as a Western value that generated white queer subjects worthy of protection at the expense of 'homophobic migrants' (Bacchetta et.al. 2015; Haritaworn 2008; Haritaworn et.al 2008). For instance, mainstream LGBT politics in Germany adhere to a notion of a 'hateful other' in the figure of the Muslim migrant. Turks and Arabs are singled out as people who embody 'Muslim homophobia' and the 'moral panic' around them leads to gendering and sexualising the debates surrounding integration (Yılmaz-Günay and Wolter 2013; Haritaworn 2015; Kosnick 2015).

Solidarity discourse occasionally masks the homo-colonial motivations of anti-migrant and anti-Muslim racism of mainstream LGBT groups and NGOs (Haritaworn 2008, 2012). The billboard campaign 'Love Deserves Respect' by LSVD was one contentious example in Berlin. Displayed mainly in migrant-populated districts such as Neukölln and Kreuzberg, the trilingual posters in German, Turkish and Arabic used in the campaign depicted same-sex-looking couples kissing. Aimed at Turkish and Arabic residents, the campaign ascribes homophobia to minority groups racialised as Muslim and marks certain districts of Berlin as homophobic and transphobic, which in turn plays a role in legitimising the gentrification of these districts (Kosnick 2015).

It is this context in which queer solidarity suggests itself as a slippery ground for queers of colour, for queer migrants and for queer diasporas constituted by uncomfortable emotions and the need to acknowledge and reflect on differences between them.

The Berlin solidarity walk did not only crystallise the unequal vulnerability of bodies in Istanbul and Berlin. It also embodied the ambivalent position of *lubuns* as racialised queer migrants at the intersection of privilege and marginalisation. Adopting an intersectional lens can, therefore, multiply the borders indicated in the slogan 'No Borders for Queers!' Such a lens can also complicate the privilege ascribed to new migrants. In the example of *lubuns*, narratives of privilege resonate with the normative understanding of a queer migration expected to move from the location of oppression to the location of liberation (Luibhéid 2008; Manalansan 2006; Halberstam 2005; Fortier 2001). The flat itinerary of the queer migrant erases the racialised subject position of *lubuns* in the anti-migrant complicity of Germany's mainstream LGBT movements. The political implications of appearing on the streets of Berlin as a racialised queer can be understood only within this context.

14.2 Istanbul Pride Solidarity Demo, 2018, Hermannplatz, Berlin. Photograph by C.Suthorn / CC-BY-SA.05 / commons.wikimedia.org.

This liberation story, with its neatly bounded subjects and locations, overlooks the multilocality of the affective and political connectivities in migrant experience. Hence, in the next section I discuss the *restlessness* that emerged as 'the force of encounter' in migrant *lubun* belongings (Gregg and Seigworth 2010) and that sparked the organisation of the Berlin Solidarity Walk as a translocal act.

Berlin Walks with Istanbul Pride March

While waiting for a screening at the Berlin Kuir Fest 2018,[7] a group of *lubuns*, including me, talked about the Istanbul LGBTI+ Pride March, which was scheduled to take place in two weeks. Many questions, speculations, opinions and feelings flew around. Would it be possible to walk on Istiklal Avenue in Taksim this year? Would the Istanbul Pride Committee agree to use the 'legal' demonstration site in Bakırköy instead of Taksim, to which many political and historical meanings were attached? What about more police attacks? Most of us agreed that it was very difficult to stay home alone in Berlin that day. And that was when the idea to organise a Berlin walk to coincide with Istanbul Pride arose. Why not also walk along with those in Istanbul instead of following social media on tenterhooks? Everyone was thrilled. We would do the walk not merely for those in Istanbul, after all. It was also for us here in Berlin; otherwise we would spend an entire restless day jumping from one live stream to another. The restlessness that bonded us with 'there' was also bonding us together 'here'. It *messed up* the neat boundaries between locations and identities.[8]

Intersectionality was one of the concepts I pitched as a corrective to the flat accounts of queer migration, which define fixed locations of departure and arrival and associate them with certain values such as oppression and privilege. Some have pointed out how the term intersectionality has been re-appropriated by the neoliberal multiculturalist diversity politics of today's Europe (Bilge 2013) and have shown how, much like the language of diversity, the language of intersectionality has largely replaced intersectional analysis itself (Puar 2012, Cho et.al 2013). Cho, Crenshaw and McCall emphasise the potential of the term to foreground the 'social dynamics and relations that constitute subjects' rather than to reify identities (2013: 798). They suggest that relying on diversity and the inclusion of as many marginalised identity categories as possible may have limited transformative potential. (See Macdonald's chapter in this volume.)

This limitation was hinted at when the collective pronoun *We* posed itself as an impasse to the organising group *Kuir+Lubun Berlin,* which had made its first public appearance in the Solidarity Walk. Back then it was a newly formed group that had emerged out of the need to build a network of Turkish-speaking LGBTI+ new Berliners. Also present, though fewer in number, were older Berliners consisting of second- and third-generation queers with a migration history in their family.[9] As one of the founding members, I experienced how the efforts of inclusivity troubled the group when defining the *We* in textual form. Whenever a Facebook description or an event call had to be written, the question 'Who are we?' required too many descriptions and keywords. Often, activists turned this question into a joke by articulating it with a particular intonation that signalled the difficulty of finding an answer—and sometimes to its dullness and pointlessness.

One year after the solidarity walk, the group came together to organise *Kuir+Lubun Berlin Pride March.* The aim was to highlight the 'local' experience and define *who* was walking. Juggling words such as *Türkiyeli* (being from Turkey), Turkish-speaking, migrant, people of colour and non-white in different combinations, the group held some tense discussions in its efforts to frame its intersectional perspective. Another identity category was added to the definition every other day; often we worried whether we could find an inclusive enough definition. This was not only because of the ballooning number of categories for describing sexual orientations and gender minorities, but also because of Berlin's 'migratory setting', which is 'thickened' by histories of migration from Turkey to Germany (Aydemir and Rotas 2008). As a consequence of this 60-year-long migration history, there were and remain different migrant subjectivities and experiences. After long negotiations, the organisers of *Kuir+Lubun Berlin* adopted a long list of identities, which caused some confusion about the the walk's causes and allies. The event was perceived as a space for people of colour only. In the message group of the organisers, there was more than one question about whether 'whites' were also welcomed to the demonstration or not. The absurdly long list of identities had turned into one of those paralysing and dull moments that 'still and quell the perpetual motion' of assemblages (Puar 2012: 213). A year later, the restlessness that had motivated the solidarity walk was mired in questions of identity.

In arguing for the queer potential that lies in the restlessness that exceeded, or more precisely, troubled, the representational strategies of the activist group, I follow Puar's suggestion that intersectionality be re-read as an assemblage by taking power relations and situated subjectivities into consideration. Interrogating the solidarity walk as an assemblage that brings together multiple forces, matters, locations, temporalities, bodies and affects can map out its local, translocal and transnational implications. Such a perspective can identify the conflicting, ambivalent and unpredictable arrangements that can emerge and mess with the established accounts of identity, migration and activism. The Berlin solidarity walk, I argue, was a temporary assemblage that inhabited the restlessness of the transnational *lubun* bonds and provided solidarity for queers across borders. More precisely, the walk reclaimed and recontextualised the heritage of New York's Stonewall uprisings to protest against the conservative crackdown in Turkey. Moreover, it embodied an alternative pride march to the 'über-normalisation' of white gay visibility, company sponsorships and state institutions such as police forces and the German army (Çetin 2018).[10]

Restless solidarities

In her meditations on the queer diaspora, Anne-Marie Fortier suggests that the shift to diaspora away from ethnicity or nation marks a turning point in thinking about a community that is not defined by commonality, but, rather, by 'difference, dispersal, (dis)connection, diversity, and multilocality' (2002: 193). She defines a spacious terrain that brings queer conditions together with their multiplicities, contradictions, maybe even with their 'impossibilities', which Gopinath traces as a queer diasporic potential (2005).

Feeling restless on the day of the Istanbul Pride March was a diasporic affect that was shaped at once by attachment and movement (Ahmed 1999, Fortier 2002). Sharing the anxiety, fear and hope of those who are dispersed in Turkey had mobilised the groups in Berlin. It was not only their sense responsibility by way of vertical solidarity. It was also their emotional need to stand by those who share the attachment. The walk, therefore, was related to the idea of a shared home—a site of belonging, becoming and regrounding (Ahmed et.al 2003). But even though Turkey functioned as the geographical home of the organisers' restlessness, the walk included a wider range of 'community', one unified under the imaginary global community of queers encompassed by the heritage of *pride*. Hence, though sparked by *lubun* restlessness, the walk was also a queer solidarity performance that embodied another form of diaspora 'away from nation and ethnicity' (Fortier

2002). The Berlin walk was meant to raise a voice against the violent crackdown of the Turkish government but it also became a demand for a mythical transnational 'home', free of heterosexist violence.

The walk assembled a multitude of others and unchosen allies and founded a theretofore undefined *we*. It was unpredictable *who* else would join them in protest against the ban on Istanbul Pride. In a context where homonationalist LGBTI discourse was going mainstream, the unpredictability added to the uneasiness of solidarity. Butler contends that the political opening of solidarity emerges from such unpredictability rather than from deliberate agreements (2015), however. In this regard, she follows Muñoz's idea of the queer horizon's open 'not-yet' (2009).

Despite the uneasiness and the multiple attachments, bodies *aligned* with others 'against other others' in the moment of solidarity (Ahmed 2014: 28). An ephemeral community without identitarian shared values emerged in the plurality of those who walked. Solidarity had temporarily surmounted the impasse of the identity lists. The queer potential occurred in the togetherness of *walking*, which extended the diasporic spaciousness of the event to make room for difference, conflict and the unknown. In this example, solidarity took the form of intersectional queer politics, positioning the event against multiple regulatory regimes, local and transnational. Even though the discursive focus of the walk was Istanbul Pride and Turkey's crackdown on queer lives, taking to the streets in Berlin had political implications. The walk was a queer-of-colour take on *pride* that momentarily anchored a transnational political heritage in Berlin through a link to Istanbul.

Anti-fascist and queer-of-colour activism in Berlin have organised an alternative event as a political critique against the commercial and predominantly white Christopher Street Day (CSD) (Çetin 2018). The *Transgenialen Christopher Street Day* parade took place between 1997 and 2013 in the historically left and migrant space of Kreuzberg while the CSD parade was held in Mitte. The Berlin Solidarity Walk and TCSD followed similar urban strategies by appearing in historically left and migrant districts. But the timing of TCSD to coincide with CDS turned the event into a political critique against the mainstream parade.

By contrast, the simultaneity of the Solidarity Walk and Istanbul Pride was a crystallised moment in the simultaneity of migrant lives, which both stem from and foster transnational attachments (Levitt & Schiller 2004). A burgeoning scholarship on the digitally mediated co-presence of migrant lives (Diminescu 2008, Madianou and Miller 2012, Madianou 2016) and the 'emotional affordances' of digital media (Bareither 2019) have thrown light on the live streaming of new media technologies and the simultaneity of migrant lives. These real-time broadcasting captures many details 'on site' and thus amplifies the experience of 'thereness'. At the same time, the augmented thereness strengthens the sense of 'hereness' and intensifies the feeling of being 'away'. Diminescu contends that the immediacy of digital connectivity affords 'co-presence' across geographies and the experience of presence 'becomes less physical, less "topological" and more active and affective (Diminescu 2008: 572). I agree that digital affordances intensify affective transnational attachments, yet the geographical and physical role of presence and absence appears significant in my examination of cross-border queer solidarities. One of my interlocutors once described live streams to be 'like a gas pump', supplying a fuel he could get only by going to Turkey. In short, live streams sharpen the co-presence of geographically distant lives as well as the restlessness of those who are 'away' but affectively and politically connected. That is why, in the chat that led to the planning of the Solidarity Walk, livestream was an uncomfortable topic, for it once again pointed to the ambivalence of a migrant experience shaped simultaneously by hereness and thereness.

My question is not whether restlessness can evolve into enduring political commitments. I argue, rather, that the Berlin Solidarity Walk was a moment that crystallised and collectivised the affective attachment of *lubuns*. The conflicting concepts—assembly and dispersal, privilege and marginalisation, attachment and movement, here and there—temporarily overlapped in the act of walking in solidarity with Istanbul Pride.

Concluding remarks

The restlessness that motivated the event *Berlin Walks with Istanbul Pride March* is confined neither to the *lubun* scene nor the diasporic community. People can feel restless, anxious, tense, antsy and fidgety whenever they mobilise politically. In that sense, the restlessness I described here is not very different from the force that mobilised the masses during the Gezi uprising in 2013. I have nevertheless argued for the particularity of this restlessness by exploring what it *did* in the context of the Berlin Solidarity Walk. Merging the local, translocal and transnational dynamics, the Walk signified the tensions and entanglements of LGBT politics across borders and the difficult politics of solidarity across differences. I was intrigued by the critiques that regarded the walk as a *failure* because it neglected the differences in the material conditions and physical vulnerability between Istanbul and Berlin.

I suggested that restlessness could explain the 'failed' recognition of material differences across Istanbul and Berlin and argued that the affective entanglements of *here* and *there* in the migrant experiences made reflective forms of solidarity difficult. But restlessness also reflected the queer potential for cross-border solidarity, located as it was at the site of belonging rather than identity. In this sense, the walk can be read as a reflexive outcome of a restlessness that resists description in the language of identity yet nevertheless embodies the moment of solidarity.

Difference and dispersal—the constitutive elements of queer (Warner 1991) and diasporic (Clifford 1994, Fortier 2002) collectivities—render the ground of solidarity uneasy, not only in the relationships between diasporas and 'home', but also where LGBT politics are complicit in nationalist anti-migrant discourses. This uneasiness can also be productive insofar as it encourages us to reflect on solidarity practices, which when built on dialogue, criticism and accountability can be an important part of a political project (Dean 1998). Committing to the slogan 'No borders for queers!' in a world where borders make material and affective differences in our lives requires recognition and constant negotiation around those differences. It is important that activists espouse this uneasy slogan as they work to acknowledge the power imbalances and the situatedness of slogans, actions and people and to redraw the borders of activism, commonality and belonging. After all, as Lesbians and Gays Support Migrants organisation poignantly reminds us, 'Solidarity is not an intention; it is an action, and it must keep being done'.[11]

Acknowledgements

This research was completed with funding from Sharon Macdonald's Alexander von Humboldt Professorship as part of the project *Making Differences: Transforming Museums and Heritage*. I would like to thank all the *lubuns* who shared their thoughts, comments and feelings with me in Berlin and İstanbul. I feel grateful to be surrounded by you. I especially thank Sharon, Deniz, Tunay, Hannes and Christine who shared their valuable feedback on this paper.

Notes

1 Throughout the paper, I use LGBTI+ to refer to the (queer) movement(s) in Turkey. It is the abbreviation most Turkey-based groups use.

2 Lubunca is a slang developed and used by queer circles in Turkey. Although it was historically used by mainly gay men and trans women to disguise the content of their conversations in public, the slang gradually became popular in various LGBTI+ circles. For more, see Nicholas Kontovas's unpublished dissertation *Lubunca: The Historical Development of İstanbul's Queer Slang and A Social-Functional Approach to Diachronic Processes in Language*. In the diasporic context of Berlin, the word *lubun* was reappropriated to signify the intersectional subject position of someone who is queer and from Turkey or has a bond with Turkey. Throughout the paper, I occasionally use it to refer to my research participants.

3 *Ayol* is a colloquial expression in Turkish associated with an effeminate way of talking.

4 For more on the dynamics and narratives of the recent wave of migration, see 'Affective Digital Media of New Migration from Turkey: Feelings, Affinities, and Politics' (Savaş 2019), 'Bu Ülkeden Gitmek: Yeni Türkiye'nin Göç İklimini Buradakiler ve Oradakiler Anlatıyor' (Kazaz & Mavituna 2018); 'Yeni Ülke Yeni Hayat' (Çuhadar 2019); and 'Gezi Generation' Fleeing Turkey' (Gürsel 2018).

5 The term 'new wave' has been employed by media outlets and by some migrants themselves. For instance, it appears in the name of a Facebook group 'New Wave in Berlin', which has over 3,000 members. This video by Deutsche Welle also uses the term: https://www.dw.com/tr/almanyan%C4%B1n-yeni-dalga-g%C3%B6%C3%A7menleri/av-52244931 (accessed 14 March 2022).

6 The mainstream histories about the 1969 *Stonewall* riots have systematically white-washed events over the course of decades by erasing the role of Black and Latinx trans women in the three-day long resistance against the police and by presenting the heroic subject to be a white cis gay man. For more on the intersectional roots of queer politics, see Roderick A. Ferguson' 'One Dimensional Queer' (2018).

7 The first and only queer film festival *Pembe Hayat KuirFest* was banned in Turkey as part of the city-wide ban on all LGBTI+ events. *Kuir Fest Berlin* took place in Berlin in 2018 and in 2019 as part of the growing transnational solidarity in response to the ban, as the festival director stated in an interview (Clements 2019). See http://daddy.land/stories/crushin-on-kuirfest (accessed 14 March 2022).

8 Martin Manalansan theorises mess as constitutive of queerness and queer immigrants. He regards mess as 'a productive orientation toward bodies, objects, and ideas that do not toe the line of hygiene, "practicality" or functionality, value, and proper space/time coordination' (2014: 98).

9 For the sake of clarity, I use the term generation even though it predominantly connotes a heterosexual family lineage and national belonging that exclude queer kin-making practices. For a detailed account of queer time, which is argued to be 'out of sync' with linear time frames, see Halberstam (2005).

10 Christopher Street in New York is where the Stonewall Inn is located. Berlin's Christopher Street Day has taken place since 1979. In 2010, the organisers of the event announced that they would bestow Judith Butler with a civil courage award for her work. But she rejected the award. Instead, she called out the 'racist complicity' of the host organisations and offered the prize to local organisations for queers of colour.

11 Retrieved from https://era-magazine.com/2020/07/21/queer-solidarity-smashes-borders-a-history-of-lgbt-solidarity-activism/

References

Abadan-Unat, N. 2011. *Turks in Europe: From Guest Worker to Transnational Citizen.* New York, Oxford: Berghahn Books.

Ahmed, S. 1999. 'Home and Away: Narratives of migration and estrangement', *International Journal of Cultural Studies,* 2(3): 329–347.

Ahmed, S., C. Castada, A. M. Fortier, and M. Sheller (eds). 2003. *Uprootings/regroundings: Questions of Home and Migration.* Oxford: Berg.

Ahmed, S. 2014. *Cultural Politics of Emotion.* Edinburgh: Edinburgh University Press.

Ağır, V., and İ Karcı. 2017. 'Germany: Immigration of the suffocated', Bianet. https://bianet.org/english/insan-haklari/185233-germany-immigration-of-the-suffocated (accessed 14 March 2022).

Aydemir, M., and A. Rotas (eds). 2008. *Migratory Settings.* Amsterdam: Rodopi.

Bacchetta, P., F. El-Tayeb, and J. Haritaworn. 2015. 'Queer of colour formations and translocal spaces in Europe', *Environment and Planning D: Society and Space,* 33(5): 769–778.

Bareither, C. 2019. 'Doing Emotion through Digital Media: An Ethnographic Perspective on Media Practices and Emotional Affordances', *Ethnologia Europaea,* 49(1).

Berger, J., and J. Mohr. 2010. *A Seventh Man. A Book of Images and Words about the Experience of Migrant Workers in Europe.* London: Verso.

Bilge, S. 2013. 'Intersectionality Undone: Saving intersectionality from feminist intersectionality studies', *Du Bois Review: Social Science Research on Race,* 10(2): 405–424.

Biricik, A. 2010. 'Öteki'nin ürettiği Mekanlar ve Toplumsal Cinsiyet Kurguları [Places Produced by Others and Fictions of Gender/Sexuality]', *Dosya,* 19: 81–85.

Butler, J. 2015. *Notes Toward a Performative Theory of Assembly.* Cambridge, MA: Harvard University Press.

Cho, S., K. W. Crenshaw and L. McCall. 2013. 'Toward a field of intersectionality studies: Theory, applications, and praxis', *Signs: Journal of Women in Culture and Society*, 38(4): 785–810.

Clifford, J. 1994. 'Diasporas', *Cultural Anthropology*, 9(3): 302–338.

Çetin, Z. 2016. *The Dynamics of the Queer Movement in Turkey Before and During the Conservative AKP Government.* Berlin: SWB.

Çetin, Z. 2018. 'The Dynamics of Queer Politics and Gentrification in Berlin', in C. Sweetapple (ed.), *The Queer Intersectional in Contemporary Germany: Essays on Racism, Capitalism and Sexual Politics.* Gießen: Psychosozial-Verlag.

Çuhadar, B. 2019. *Yeni Ülke Yeni Hayat.* İstanbul: Artemis Yayınları.

Dean, J. 1998. 'Feminist solidarity, reflective solidarity: Theorizing connections after identity politics', *Women & Politics*, 18(4): 1–26.

Diminescu, D. 2008. 'The connected migrant: an epistemological manifesto', *Social Science Information*, 47(4): 565–579.

Duggan, L. 2002 'The new homonormativity: the sexual politics of neoliberalism', in R. Castronovo, and D. Nelson (eds), *Materializing Democracy: Toward a Revitalized Cultural Politics*, 175–194. Durham, NC: Duke University Press.

El-Tayeb, F. 2011. *European others: queering ethnicity in postnational Europe.* MN: University of Minnesota Press.

Fortier, A. 2002. 'Queer Diaspora', in D. Richardson and S. Seidman (eds), *Handbook of Lesbian & Gay Studies*, 183–197. London: Sage.

Fortier, A. M. 2001. 'Coming home: queer migrations and multiple evocations of home', *European Journal of Cultural Studies* 4(4): 405– 424.

Gopinath, G. 2005. *Impossible desires: Queer diasporas and South Asian public cultures.* Durham, NC: Duke University Press.

Gregg, M., and Seigworth, G. J. 2010. *The affect theory reader.* Durham, NC: Duke University Press.

Halberstam, J. 2005. *In a queer time and place: Transgender bodies, subcultural lives.* New York: New York University Press.

Haritaworn, J. 2008. 'Loyal repetitions of the nation: gay assimilation and the "war on terror"', *Dark Matter*, 3.

Haritaworn, J., T. Tauqir, and E. Erdem. 2008. 'Gay imperialism: Gender and sexuality discourse in the "war on terror"', in A. Kunstman, and E. Miyake (eds), *Out of place: Interrogating silences in queerness/raciality*, 71–95. York: Raw Nerve Books.

Haritaworn, J. 2012. 'Women's rights, gay rights and anti-Muslim racism in Europe: Introduction', *European journal of women's studies*, 19(1): 73–78.

Haritaworn, J. 2015. *Queer lovers and hateful others: Regenerating violent times and places.* London: Pluto Press.

Kazaz G., and İ. H. Mavituna. 2018. *Bu Ülkeden Gitmek: Yeni Türkiye'nin Göç İklimini Buradakiler ve Oradakiler Anlatıyor.* İstanbul: Metropolis Yayıncılık.

Kontovas, N. 2012. *Lubunca: The Historical Development of İstanbul's Queer Slang and a Social-Functional Approach to Diachronic Processes in Language.* PhD thesis. Indiana University.

Kosnick, K. 2015. 'A clash of subcultures? Questioning Queer–Muslim antagonisms in the neoliberal city', *International Journal of Urban and Regional Research*, 39(4): 687–703.

Levitt, P., and N. G. Schiller. 2004. 'Transnational perspectives on migration: conceptualizing simultaneity', *International Migration Review,* 38(3): 1002–1039.

LGBTI News Turkey. 2016. 'Istanbul LGBTI+ Pride Committee Statement: We are Dispersing!', 24 June 2016. https://lgbtinewsturkey.com/2016/06/24/Istanbul-lgbti-pride-committee-statement-we-are-dispersing/ (accessed 14 March 2022).

Lowen, M. 2017. December 28). Turkey brain drain: Crackdown pushes intellectuals out. BBC News, 28 December 2017. https://www.bbc.co.uk/news/world-europe-42433668 (accessed 14 March 2022).

Luibhéid, E. 2008. 'Queer/migration: An unruly body of scholarship', *GLQ: A Journal of Lesbian and Gay Studies,* 14(2): 169–190.

Madianou, M., and D. Miller. 2012. *Migration and new media: Transnational families and polymedia.* London: Routledge.

Madianou, M. 2016, 'Ambient co-presence: Transnational family practices in polymedia environment', *Global Networks,* 16(2): 183–201.

Manalansan, M. F. 1995. 'In the shadows of Stonewall: Examining gay transnational politics and the diasporic dilemma', *GLQ: A Journal of Lesbian and Gay Studies,* 2(4): 425–438.

Manalansan, M. F. 2006. 'Queer intersections: Sexuality and gender in migration studies', *International Migration Review,* 40(1): 224–249.

Manalansan, M. F. 2014. 'The "stuff" of archives: Mess, migration, and queer lives', *Radical History Review,* 2014(120): 94–107.

Mandel, R. 2008. *Cosmopolitan anxieties: Turkish challenges to citizenship and belonging in Germany.* Durham and London: Duke University Press.

Muñoz, J. E. 2009. *Cruising Utopia: The Then and There of Queer Futurity.* New York: NYU Press.

Özdemir, S. S., N. Mutluer, and E. Özyürek. 2019. 'Exile and Plurality in Neoliberal Times: Turkey's Academics for Peace', *Public Culture,* 31(2): 235–259.

Partridge, D. J. 2019. 'Articulating a Noncitizen Politics: Nation-State Pity vs. Democratic Inclusion', in J. J. Bock, and S. Macdonald (eds), *Refugees welcome?: difference and diversity in a changing Germany,* 265–287. New York, Oxford: Berghahn Books.

Puar, J. K. 2007. *Terrorist assemblages: Homonationalism in queer times.* Durham and London: Duke University Press.

Puar, Jasbir K. 2012. '"I would rather be a cyborg than a goddess": Becoming-Intersectional in Assemblage Theory', *Philosophia* 2.1: 49–66.

Savaş, Ö. 2019. 'Affective Digital Media of New Migration From Turkey: Feelings, Affinities, and Politics', *International Journal of Communication,* 13: 5405–5426.

Türkmen, G. 2019. '"But you don't look Turkish!": The changing face of Turkish immigration to Germany', ResetDoc. https://www.resetdoc.org/story/dont-look-turkish-changing-faceturkish-immigration-germany/ (accessed 14 March 2022).

Warner M. 1991. 'Fear of a queer planet', *Social Text* 9(14): 3–17.

Yılmaz-Günay, K., and S. A. Wolter. 2013. 'Pink washing Germany? Der deutsche Homonationalismus und die "jüdische Karte"', in D. Gürsel, Z. Çetin, and Allmende e.V. (eds), *Wer macht Demo_kratie. Kritische Migrationsforschung.* Münster: Edition Assemblage.

Yurdakul, G. 2009. *From guest workers into Muslims: The transformation of Turkish immigrant associations in Germany.* Newcastle: Cambridge Scholars Publishing.

Zengin, A. 2013. '"What is queer about Gezi?", Fieldsights—Hot Spots', Cultural Anthropology Online, 31 October 2013. https://culanth.org/fieldsights/what-is-queer-about-gezi (accessed 20 July 2021).

Difficult Heritage and Digital Media

'Selfie culture' and Emotional Practices at the Memorial to the Murdered Jews of Europe

Christoph Bareither

15.1 Christine's smile (used with permission).

Christine's picture would appear completely mundane at most touristic places in Berlin. Christine, a young woman, with a camera around her neck and a backpack over her shoulders, is resting at a place mentioned in probably every travel guide to the city. As she turns her face towards the camera, she performs a warm and friendly smile. Later, she uploads this picture (next to two others) on *Instagram*, one of the largest and currently most popular social media platforms, where she adds several hashtags, such as: '#memorialtothemurderedjewsofeurope #berlin #jewish #history #neverforget #lchaim #tolife #tolove'.

As these hashtags already indicate, the place at which this picture is taken is the 'Memorial to the Murdered Jews of Europe', colloquially referred to as the 'Holocaust Memorial' (the name which I will use in the following). Designed by architect Peter Eisenman, the memorial is a field of 2711 concrete blocks, covering 19,000 square metres in total, located in the very heart of the German capital, right next to the Brandenburg Gate and many other touristic hotspots. Below the memorial, visitors can enter an 'information centre' with its permanent exhibition on the history of the Holocaust. While the exhibition 'documents the persecution and extermination of the Jews of Europe and the historical sites of the crimes',[1] the memorial above ground is designed to afford a different kind of experience. As Barbara Kirshenblatt-Gimblett has prominently argued regarding the making of heritage, the 'production of hereness in the absence of actualities depends increasingly on virtualities.' (Kirshenblatt-Gimblett 1998: 169) In the case of the Berlin memorial, at which the actualities of the Holocaust are absent, Eisenman created a material space that affords such virtualities in the form of intense emotional experience. As he puts it, the 'space is created for loss and contemplation, for elements of memory'.[2] However, Eisenman did not want to determine how visitors feel at the place. In fact, he was very much aware that: 'People are going to picnic in the field. Children will play tag in the field. There will be fashion models modeling there and films will be shot there. I can easily imagine some spy shoot 'em ups ending in the field. What can I say? It's not a sacred place.'[3]

The openness and accessibility of the memorial, which visitors can enter without going through any kind of entrance or gate, is certainly one of the reasons why it became one of the most visited Holocaust memorials in the world and one of the most frequented heritage sites in Berlin. Its particular architecture, which affords the taking of aesthetically complex pictures, has also made the memorial extremely popular on social media. One can find tens of thousands of pictures taken here and then publicly shared online on *Instagram* and *Facebook* – including the picture of Christine.

Considering the context of the picture, Christine's smile seems highly ambivalent. Is it appropriate to take a picture of oneself at the Holocaust memorial; a picture that clearly puts the aesthetic representation of one's own body into the centre? Christine is very much aware of where she is. She even emphasizes her awareness of the memorial's context through hashtags such as #jewish or #neverforget. These hashtags indicate that remembering the Holocaust matters emotionally to her. Her happy smile and posture, however, suggest an emotional indifference towards the past or even, as some would say (see section 2), disrespect of Holocaust victims.

Digital self-representations, taken at the memorial and shared online, frequently materialize this very ambivalence through social media. Such pictures have repeatedly sparked conflict in not only public debates in Germany but also similar debates connected to the Auschwitz memorial in Poland or the 9/11 memorial in New York. At the heart of such conflicts lies the question of whether digital self-representations when produced at sites of difficult heritage are always practices of articulating emotional indifference towards these places and, therefore, disrespect the commemoration of a troubling past.

This chapter, therefore, takes a closer look at digital self-representations taken at the Holocaust memorial Berlin and uploaded on social media. I apply a notion of 'digital self-representation' which not only refers to the particular format of the 'selfie' as a 'photograph that one has taken of oneself' (Eckel, Ruchatz, and Wirth 2018: 4), although the selfie will play a crucial role in the following. The term 'digital self-representations' in this chapter refers to pictures in which a) a particular person (or group of people) is clearly at the centre of the picture; b) this person is attentive of the fact that he or she is being photographed (often facing the camera directly) and performs accordingly through a variety of facial expressions, gestures, postures, etc.; or c) the person being portrayed (and not the person taking the picture) is uploading the picture on social media in order to represent his- or herself in a particular context.

The first section of this chapter outlines the basic approach of my analysis, starting with the methods of digital ethnography, which I apply here in the context of difficult heritage and tourism to explore emotional practices that are enacted through digital self-representations and social media. The second section sets the empirical scene by describing the so-called 'Yolocaust' project and the surrounding conflict that emerged in public debates regarding 'selfie culture' at the Holocaust Memorial. I show why many observers and visitors are critical about digital self-representations and how their criticism connects to questions of emotional indifference in the context of Holocaust remembrance; however, I will also argue that the sweeping condemnation of digital self-representations remains simplistic and does not account for the complexity of these practices. Instead, as the third section shows, many visitors explore and enact potential emotional relationships to the pasts that sites of difficult heritage represent through digital self-representations. This leads towards the conclusion, in which I discuss how this kind of doing emotion constitutes different but not necessarily indifferent ways of presencing the past. These different ways of past presencing, I will argue, deviate from established practices of remembrance but are, nonetheless, meaningful for the actors involved. They unfold a particular potential especially for visitors of younger generations – the so-called 'digital natives' – in that they allow the exploration of *personal* connections to sites of difficult heritage and new forms of social exchange about shared relationships to difficult pasts.

Methods

My analysis draws upon a digital ethnography of visitors' media practices at the Holocaust memorial both offline and online, including participant observation at the memorial, 17 face-to-face interviews with 41 visitors at the site and 24 chat interviews with users of *Instagram* and *Facebook* who had been contacted shortly (most often one or several days) after they visited the memorial and posted pictures online. The fieldnotes and interviews were triangulated with a qualitative computer-assisted analysis of 800 social media posts (again on *Instagram* and *Facebook*), about 390 of which were digital self-representations. Additionally, the qualitative analysis included 200 comments to a particular social media debate in the context of the 'Yolocaust' project (see below). My selection of interviewees and the selection of the 800 social media posts built upon an inductive process of identifying particular media practices, which I followed throughout my research both offline and online. This resulted in a sample of interviewees with an equal gender balance, visitors aged between 12 and 77 years (most of them between 20 and 40 years), and from 29 different countries (visitors' names in this article are fully anonymised).

My research was guided by the principles of digital and Internet ethnography (Hine 2015; Pink et al. 2016), followed ethical principles of care in Internet research (Boellstorff et al. 2012: 129) and applied a rigorous digital coding procedure (using the software MAXQDA) which is based on Grounded Theory Methodology (Strauss and Corbin 1994), but also develops a more ethnography-oriented coding style (Emerson, Fretz, and Shaw 2011: 177–200; Breidenstein et al. 2015: 124–139) more relatable to general practice theories and other concepts that were operationalized in my research.

Difficult heritage

The research field in which I apply this approach can be usefully framed with the notion of 'difficult heritage'. Sites of 'difficult heritage' are material reminders of 'a past that is recognised as meaningful in the present but that is also contested and awkward for public reconciliation with a positive, self-affirming contemporary identity' (Macdonald 2009: 1). In other words: difficult heritage is troubling. As Sharon Macdonald (2009, 2015) has pointed out, Germany has been particularly invested in making such difficult heritage publicly visible, especially regarding WW2 and the history of the Holocaust. The Holocaust Memorial, located in the centre of the German capital, is part of this process and was the anchor point of controversial debates about German memory cultures for several years. During its planning phase, Jürgen Habermas (1999) tellingly called it the memorial 'that shall remain a thorn' (my translation). Its existence is an acknowledgement of the fact that 'apologising for past wrongs also requires a bringing of those wrongs into view' (Macdonald 2015: 16).

It is worth asking here what this 'bringing into view' entails. One dimension of the visibility of difficult heritage is usually constituted through the curated dissemination of historical information. Museums and heritage sites *inform* about particular pasts by allowing visitors to engage, for example, with texts, pictures, videos and audio guides, to learn about historical facts. The second, equally important dimension of this visibility, which is always intrinsically connected to the first, is emotional. Museums and heritage sites do not only provide information, but they constitute a material basis for the unfolding of *emotions* in relation to specific pasts. They do not only offer particular ways of knowing, they also offer ways of feeling the past. Accordingly, as Laurajane Smith and Gary Campbell (2015) argue, it is crucial to consider the emotional and affective dimension of visitors' experiences:

> If we accept that heritage is political, that it is a political resource used in conflicts over the understanding of the past and its relevance for the present, then understanding how the interplay of emotions, imagination and the process of remembering and commemoration are informed by people's culturally and socially diverse affective responses must become a growing area of focus for the field. (Smith and Campbell 2015: 455)

Emotional practices and emotional affordances

Sharing this intention, a growing body of literature has emerged throughout the last few years that takes the emotional or affective dimension of heritage and museums into account (e.g. Witcomb 2007, 2012; Macdonald 2013; Gregory 2014; Golańska 2015; Smith and Campbell 2015; Waterton and Watson 2015; Tschofen 2016; Campbell, Smith, and Wetherell 2017; Tolia-Kelly, Waterton, and Watson 2017; Smith, Wetherell, and Campbell 2018), including works with a focus on difficult heritage (Sather-Wagstaff 2017) and the Berlin Holocaust memorial in particular (Knudsen 2008; Dekel 2013; Witcomb 2013; Bareither 2019). This kind of research follows an understanding of emotions or affects as entangled with everyday practices embedded in particular social and cultural contexts especially when conducted from an ethnographic perspective. It goes beyond a simplistic distinction between 'knowing' and 'feeling' that reproduces the Cartesian dualism of mind and body. Instead, it suggests 'that recognizing reason/cognition, affect/emotion and memory as being mutually constitutive and reinforcing of each other is a positive step for anyone interested in understanding and researching the contemporary significance of the past' (Smith and Campbell 2015: 452). The cultural anthropologist Bernhard Tschofen has proposed considering the 'emotional knowledge of the historical' ('Gefühlswissen des Historischen', Tschofen 2016: 144) as a conceptual frame for this perspective. How we feel about the past is always intrinsically related to our implicit knowledge of it, and vice versa, we come to know the past through our bodies and feelings.

This points us to the importance of emotional engagement with difficult heritage. Here, I draw upon the concept of 'emotional practices' by Monique Scheer (2012, 2016) and the concept of 'affective practices' by Margaret Wetherell (2013; Wetherell, Smith, and Campbell 2018), which can be productively brought together with other ethnographic or qualitative approaches to the study of emotions in everyday life (e.g. Abu-Lughod and Lutz 1990; Hochschild 2003; Ahmed 2014; Reckwitz 2017). Generally speaking, both concepts apply the notion of practice, in the sense carved out by practice theories (and in close relation to the work of Pierre Bourdieu), to understand emotions or affects as part of routinized doings in everyday life. As Scheer puts it, emotions are not something we *have*, emotions are something we *do* in social and cultural encounters (Scheer 2016: 16). Neither concept follows a conceptual distinction between emotions, affects and feelings, as is made in some studies of emotions. Praxeological or praxeographic approaches tend to treat these terms in close relation to each other and often interchangeably. Respectively, what I label emotional practices in the following could also be called affective practices. The two variations certainly have different heuristic advantages and disadvantages, but both achieve the same analytical goal here. They allow one to analyse and describe with ethnographic methods how emotions (or affects) are *enacted* in relation to difficult heritage.

This chapter focuses on emotional practices enacted through digital self-representations and the sharing of these pictures as well as the adding of captions and comments (including hashtags and emojis) on social media. These practices build upon the particular emotional affordances of digital cameras, smartphones and social media platforms, such as *Instagram* and *Facebook*. As I have argued elsewhere, 'emotional affordances' can be understood as capacities to enable, prompt and restrict the enactment of specific emotional experiences unfolding in between media technologies (or material environments) and an actor's practical sense of their use (Bareither 2019: 15). This means that it is crucial for my ethnographic analysis of digital self-representations to account for how the particular functions of smartphones and other digital cameras, as well as social media platforms, enable and restrict specific ways of articulating, mobilizing and sharing emotions.

Digital self-representations and social media in touristic contexts

Visitors who use digital media to engage emotionally with memorial sites are usually tourists and follow particular touristic routines. Thus, the particularities of tourist photography 'as a socially consumptive and constructive practice that performatively produces and uses visual, communicative culture' come into play (Sather-Wagstaff 2008: 97). As Jonas Larsen has pointed out, such practices do not only include the moment of taking a picture. Instead, they include 'looking for, framing and taking photographs, posing for cameras and choreographing posing bodies', followed by 'editing, displaying and circulating photographs' as well as their movements through 'wires, databases, emails, screens, photo albums and potentially many other places' (Larsen 2008: 143; also see Larsen 2014).

All of these practices can be related to what John Urry famously called the 'tourist gaze' (Urry and Larsen 2011; in relation to the Holocaust memorial, also see Knudsen 2008). This is a form of touristic looking through which the landscapes, scenes, people or objects encountered by tourists are visually consumed. Photography plays a crucial role in this process as it allows tourists 'to make fleeting gazes last longer' (Urry and Larsen 2011: 156) and, therefore, '[m]uch tourism becomes [...] a search for the photogenic' (178).

While the notion of the 'tourist gaze' contributes to understanding the aesthetic and emotional dimension of tourist photography, my own empirical research demonstrates that tourist photography can be much more than a form of pleasurable visual consumption. Visitors do not only *consume* the place through digital photography at the Holocaust Memorial, but they also emotionally *engage* with the place and the past it represents.

Similar observations have been made by other scholars regarding tourist photography at sites of difficult heritage or traumatic memory (e.g. Sather-Wagstaff 2008; Hilmar 2016; Douglas 2017). Looking at the practices of 'picturing experience' at the 9/11 memorial in New York, Joy Sather-Wagstaff argues that photographs 'are devices for the performance of subjectivities, for the making of various social relationships and cultural realities, and most importantly, for memory, recalling the past in service to the present' (Sather-Wagstaff 2008: 80). In a similar vein, Till Hilmar observes at the Auschwitz memorial site that with 'their pictures, visitors not only seek to emphasize and materialize certain details about the past, but also to express modes of encountering and experiencing the past on site' (Hilmar 2016: 457).

In the following, I build upon these previous studies to ask in greater detail about the role of visitors' digital self-representations as emotional practices in relation to difficult heritage while acknowledging the particular role of social media in this process. The function of digital photography as a form of emotional engagement comes to light especially when visitors share their pictures on social media; pictures are often contextualized with captions, comments, hashtags and emojis, emphasizing how the person taking the picture (or being represented in it) *relates* to the past that the memorial represents. Since these practices are an integral part of the memory experiences of millions of visitors, it seems crucial to pay particular attention to their specific implications.

'Yolocaust' and 'selfie culture'

Before I go on to describe various kinds of digital self-representations and their contextualization in detail, this section sets the empirical scene by describing the public negotiation of 'selfie culture' and the heated criticism of digital self-representations in relation to difficult heritage. In early 2017, the frequently posted digital self-representations taken at the Holocaust Memorial were noticed by Jewish-German satirist Shahak Shapira, who responded to them with the infamous 'Yolocaust' project. The project title is a combination of 'Holocaust' and the term 'Yolo', commonly known as an abbreviation for the saying 'you only live once' and usually associated with a young 'Hipster' generation. For this project, Shapira edited digital self-representations which were taken at the memorial and put historical footage from concentration camps, including dead bodies of victims, into the background. After he published these remixes on a website, the visitors who took the original pictures were supposed to write him a message and ask to be 'undouched' by him if they want the pictures to be taken offline again. All the self-representations he used were publicly accessible at the time. Some of them were pictures with people simply smiling into the camera while taking a selfie. Others showed acrobatic moves that visitors performed between the blocks. One picture was particularly extreme, as it showed two young men jumping on the blocks with the caption 'Jumping on Dead Jews @ Holocaust Memorial', which received 87 Likes before Shapira discovered, altered and re-posted it.

By using these examples and manipulating them with new background pictures showing Holocaust victims, Shahak Shapira suggests a very specific interpretation of the memorial. He suggests that the place should be experienced as a direct link to the horrors of the Holocaust and, accordingly, it should serve as a source of inspiration for solemn reflection and collective remembrance. His project 'Yolocaust' went viral on social media and was recognized widely by the German and international press. Shapira claims that he received overwhelmingly supportive e-mails not only from many viewers, but also from an international research institute and even the Yad Vashem Holocaust

Remembrance Center in Jerusalem. There were also critical voices among them, including the Memorial's architect, Peter Eisenman.[4] Despite these critical voices, however, a lot of the feedback to the 'Yolocaust' project in both the German and international press was positive. As Shapira explained later, shortly after the project went online, 2.5 million people visited the website and all of the portrayed visitors contacted Shapira to apologize and asked to be 'undouched' by him. As promised, he took the pictures off the website and left only a written documentation of the project online.

Needless to say, the pictures had already been copied and distributed countless times and are still easily publicly accessible through various websites. The most popular documentation of the project, including the original pictures, is a video summary produced by the Facebook page AJ+, which clearly takes a positive stance towards the position of Shapira and speaks out against what it refers to as 'selfie culture'.[5] This video received more than 79 million views, about 23,000 'Facebook reactions' (mostly 'likes', but also 'angry' and 'sad' emojis), was shared more than 20,000 times and publicly commented on more than 2,300 times.

Shaming the 'selfie monsters'

Although some of these comments take the video as a starting point for lengthy explanations of conspiracy theories (Holocaust denial included) or discussing other political issues, such as the Israeli-Palestinian conflict, several hundred of them take a particular stance towards the 'Yolocaust' project. A qualitative computer-assisted analysis of a random sample of 200 of these last kind of comments shows that most of them (about three-quarters) are supportive of Shapira's intention. One viewer writes: 'Kudos to the creator -- these selfie monsters have lost all humanity and respect for sanctity of memorials, temples, -- it's good they get shamed in public. Need more such righteous "warriors" online.' Another one comments more diplomatically: 'The generation of selfie needed a lesson learnt – to be less self-centred of what you want to do but rather how others might be affected by what you do. The memorial belongs to those who died tragically and not a backdrop for those who want to show off on FB [Facebook, C.B.] they've been there.'

Terms such as 'selfie monsters' and 'the generation of selfie' are frequently reappearing, being prompted by the video itself, which, at one point, posits the threat: 'But selfie culture beware –', before showing Shapira again who states he will do this again in two weeks if visitors don't stop doing 'stupid sh*t'. Here, the term 'selfie culture' does not only refer to the particular routine of self-photography (the 'selfie'). Instead, the term functions as an idiom to denote a culture in which the aesthetic representation of oneself is apparently valued higher than engaging in 'appropriate' practices of remembrance. Tellingly, the terms most frequently appearing in the comments to the video documentation are 'respect' and 'disrespect', which are used to describe the inappropriateness of these 'acts of millennialism', as another viewer frames them. Comparisons are made to similar practices that viewers have personally observed at other memorial sites, for example, the memorial and museum at Auschwitz-Birkenau or the 9/11 memorial in New York.

From the perspective of emotional practice theory, these practices of public shaming function as *regulating* emotional practices, sanctioning specific kinds of emotions that are considered wrong or inappropriate by a particular group of actors. In doing so, they also attempt to establish a clear-cut dichotomy between 'respect' and 'disrespect', 'appropriate' vs. 'inappropriate', 'righteous warriors' vs. 'selfie monsters'. These seemingly clear-cut dichotomies are not only emerging in the context of the 'Yolocaust' conflict. They appear quite regularly at the site as well, for example, when tour guides tell visitors about the inappropriateness of photographic self-representation at the site, or when visitors told me in interviews how they were 'shocked' by other people taking selfies. The reason for this 'shock' – both offline and online – is that, to many observers, selfies and other forms of digital self-representation seem to demonstrate, enact and propagate an *emotional indifference* towards the Holocaust.

Indifference in Holocaust commemoration

Why this kind of indifference matters is probably best reflected through the speech 'The Perils of Indifference' that Eli Wiesel, Holocaust survivor, Nobel laureate and historian, gave at the White House on 12 April 12 1999, in the presence of Bill and Hillary Clinton.[6] 'What is indifference?', Wiesel asks. 'Etymologically, the word means "no difference". A strange and unnatural state in which the lines blur between light and darkness, dusk and dawn, crime and punishment, cruelty and compassion, good and evil.' He continues to describe the role of indifference for the Holocaust with poetic accuracy: 'It is, after all, awkward, troublesome, to be involved in another person's pain and despair. Yet, for the person who is indifferent, his or her neighbor are of no consequence. And, therefore, their lives are meaningless. Their hidden or even visible anguish is of no interest. Indifference reduces the other to an abstraction.' And he observes: 'In a way, to be indifferent to that suffering is what makes the human being inhuman.'

Here, the question of emotional indifference is far more than a question of attitude; being indifferent towards the Holocaust becomes a constitutive moment of being *not* human. From this perspective, it is only logical that the public portrayal of emotional indifference through digital self-representations appears problematic to many observers. After all, a rationalized mass genocide on the scale of the Holocaust may, indeed, happen *again*. 'It happened, therefore it can happen again: that is the core of what we have to say' (Levi 2017: 186). This phrase by Holocaust survivor Primo Levi is quoted above the entrance to the Information Centre below the Holocaust Memorial and, thus, serves as a guiding principle for the memorial as a whole. In a world in which right-wing populism is on the rise on a global scale, this fear seems more justified than ever since the end of WW2.

In a chat-interview with Adam, a young man from New York, who was at the time writing a screenplay and sent me detailed, almost poetic reflections on his experiences at the Holocaust memorial, picks up on this point. His elaborate description is worth quoting in detail:

> In the age of social media and the total ubiquity of mobile phones, many people seem unable to experience anything *directly* anymore, instead filtering their daily interactions through the lens of their phone screen (or laptop screen). And when you live that way, removed from true 'first-hand' experience, things just don't have the same gravity. A memorial is then just a place you 'see', rather than a place you go to *feel*. That's what it is, isn't it? People visit a place like the Holocaust Memorial or Auschwitz-Birkenau, and they are unable (or perhaps, on a subconscious level, unwilling) to have an experience of *feeling*. The mass extermination of millions of Jews (as well as homosexuals and other groups) should affect us all on a very deep level, disturb us, break our hearts and make us vigilant in working to ensure nothing like this could ever happen again. But I'm afraid it actually *could*, in some way, happen again, because so much of the population has become desensitized to such a degree that they can't tell when bad things are on the horizon.

Adam directly relates his observation that more and more people seem to be emotionally indifferent towards the Holocaust to 'the age of social media and the total ubiquity of mobile phones'. The project 'Yolocaust' aims in the same direction, although it takes much more extreme measures and publicly shames those who appear to portray their emotional indifference towards the memorial.

The question remains whether digital self-representations do indeed perform emotional indifference; and, if they do, is that all that they do? Is every kind of digital self-representation the same? Does a picture in which a person is aesthetically highlighted in front of the Holocaust memorial *automatically* disrespect Holocaust victims and the culture of their remembrance?

Digital self-representations and emotional practices

An ethnographic analysis of the variety of digital self-representations and related practices both offline and online clearly demonstrates that this is not the case. Considering Adam's critical reflection quoted above, it might be surprising that he, in fact, took a selfie at the Holocaust memorial himself and shared it on social media.

As already described above, you will find countless digital self-representations on *Instagram* and *Facebook* taken at the memorial, often selfies, some of them taken with a selfie-stick. First and foremost, this raises the question why one would take a picture of oneself in front of a memorial in the first place. As Anja Dinhopl and Ulrike Gretzel point out: 'While tourist photography and the tourist gaze shape each other, tourist photography is also a performance of the self in tourism' (Dinhopl and Gretzel 2016: 132). They use particularly the example of tourist selfies to argue that the space or scene of the tourist gaze fades gradually into the background in much contemporary tourist photography, and '[a]s the tourist destination becomes the distant backdrop or prompt or completely disappears from the photo, the self becomes elevated as a touristic product—it is what tourists are there to consume' (134).

15.2 Adam's selfie (used with permission).

This argument relates to the notion of the 'tourist gaze' (see above) and observes a process of touristic consumption regarding one's own bodily presence at a particular touristic site. By translating this observation into the language of emotional practice theory, I argue that digital self-representations in the context of tourism enact pleasurable experiences as they perform and materialize an aesthetic visual artefact which allows for good feelings regarding one's own body and its presence within a 'remarkable' environment.

However, the fact that a digital self-representation allows one to mobilize good feelings about oneself and/or about one's own presence at a particular site does not exclude the possibility that it constitutes, simultaneously, a practice of emotional engagement with the memorial. Adam already articulates this through the caption in his social media post, where he states that: 'I found it to be the most meaningful and impactful monument—of any kind—that I've ever visited.' Considering that Adam is very critical about smartphones and social media, this might make us wonder why he would choose the particular format of the selfie (next to two other pictures) to articulate this experience. In our interview, Adam explains: 'In taking my photo [the selfie, C.B.], my intention was to say, in an earnest, honest and straightforward way, "I was here. I *witnessed* this, and I'm sharing it on social media because this was a powerful experience for me, an important and humbling experience that I want to share with friends and loved ones".'

Putting oneself into the picture

Adam's case demonstrates a simple fact: digital self-representations can be a form of aesthetic self-representation *and*, at the same time, a practice of emotional engagement. Kate Douglas observes in her analysis of the format of the selfie at trauma memorial sites that 'selfies have the ability to be acts of witness: as engaged responses, as demonstrations of affect and as admissions of complicity and/or communion' (Douglas 2017: 13). If we acknowledge this fact, the analytical perspective shifts to the question *how* visitors emotionally engage with the memorial through such pictures (not only selfies but all digital self-representations). Similar to Adam, many visitors use digital pictures to articulate commemoration and compassion with Holocaust victims, but they do so in very different ways.

Benedikt, for example, decided to share a selfie on which he cried while visiting the memorial. His social media post is contextualised with the caption: 'You can't do much…just stop and ask yourself «What have we done?!»' The caption is followed by several hashtags, one of which is '#cry'. In our chat interview he explains: 'It was just an honest moment. Not pretending to be fake with all filters […] I just wanted to be very honest about my visit there. That place touched me deeply and that's what I felt in the moment. […] I felt just sadness … Just that actually.'

15.3 Benedikt's selfie (used with permission).

Such pictures, in which the visitors look directly into the camera, are not the only kind of digital self-representations relevant here. Pictures in which visitors are portrayed (often through pictures taken by friends and family) in a situation in which they interact with the memorial are equally important. These pictures might include portraits of people who touch the memorial or who are wandering in-between the blocks while appearing to be lost in their thoughts. Visitors often ask their friends or family to take a picture of them while they sit on one of the blocks and look into the far.

15.4 Katarina and Haasim looking into the distance (used with permission).

Katarina and Haasim, for example, took this kind of picture in almost exactly the same position in front of almost exactly the same background (on different days) and both uploaded it on *Instagram*. Katarina contextualised her self-representation with the caption 'Walking through the passageways of history in #Berlin 🇩🇪', already pointing her followers (who appreciated the post with more than 140 likes) towards her emotional experience of commemorating the past. When I ask about the picture in our chat interview, Katarina explains that she is, in fact, critical about the 'many people posting smiling happy photos there', which is why she tried 'to capture the place but still keep a serious note to it'. After I tell her about the 'Yolocaust' project and after she views the video documentation of it online, she states that she completely supports the artist in his critique and that she now feels 'conflicted' about her own self-representation, since 'we are in a way shifting attention from the memorial to ourselves'. On the other hand, this seems necessary to her in order to communicate what she feels, 'in a way to draw attention to the place and what it stands for'.

Haasim is even more explicit regarding this point. While visiting the memorial, he took great care in posing for the picture, directing his friend to the right angle, and later curating it through colour adjustment and filters to have the right aesthetic expression. His posture is strategic, as he explains in our chat interview: 'I also took a thoughtful concerned look not directly into the objective, to invite the viewer to think with me about what happened [...].' After I point out that some viewers still might consider this picture 'superficial' and 'inappropriate' because it puts him as the person in the centre, he continues:

> I hesitated before posing for the pics; if those were real tombs [the concrete blocks, C.B.], I wouldn't have accepted. But I also see the memorial as a piece of art. So, I wanted to convey feelings through my pics and mark my presence there. I come from Lebanon, and most of my followers are Lebanese. Many of them hate Jews. So, the purpose of my pic was also provocative. So, I might agree with people who see it as superficial when the pics are randomly taken. But in my case, it meant more for me.

These examples demonstrate that, for many visitors, the function of digital self-representations at the Holocaust Memorial is not limited to the purpose of aesthetic self-representation. They can constitute practices of conveying sadness, anger, compassion, commemoration and more; they can serve to grasp the attention of others or even to explicitly provoke discussion. Digital self-representations are not necessarily playing into emotional indifference. Instead, by literally putting themselves into the picture, visitors use them to engage in cultures of remembrance.

Happy remembrance?

While all the visitors interviewed quoted above created digital self-representations, they still insist that their own representations are different from the 'smiling happy photos' taken by countless others. In doing so, they implicitly or explicitly suggest that the portrayal of happiness is the actually 'inappropriate' practice in the context of the memorial that articulates an emotional indifference towards the past. On the one hand, this critique of 'happy pictures' might be justified considering the fact that many visitors, as my ethnographic study also confirms, simply follow the tourist routines of smiling for pictures at 'remarkable' sites without reflecting much about the implications of their smile – and this is also true for the Holocaust Memorial. Even among the visitors smiling for pictures, however, there are many who do *not* consider their own smile to be an articulation of emotional indifference. On the contrary, they consider their smile to be a different but meaningful practice of remembrance. As Lina, a 28-year-old tourist from Belgium, puts it: 'I think that even if you smile you can still have respect for the things that the memorial stands for, which happened here. I don't think a smile is in contrast to respecting it.' Tara, a young woman from Washington D.C., emphasizes the same point as she explains to me what kind of pictures she took:

> Um, we smiled, and we kinda just had our hands crossed, like joined behind our backs. I think something like this is powerful, but it's also really unifying, so I don't think there is a problem smiling. I think that, you know, the struggle of people's past has been able to cultivate what we have today. So I don't wanna say: 'Why not

> enjoy the site?', but: 'Why not show that you were there and that you were happy with the experience that you had?'
>
> As Tara and Lina explain, a smile can be a form of commemoration as well. This brings me back to the introductory example: Christine's warm and friendly smile, contextualized by hashtags such as '#jewish #history #neverforget #lchaim #tolife #tolove'.

In our chat interview, Christine tells me about her family history, about how her grandfather had to flee from Poland to Germany by foot and how she got interested in the history of WW2 and the Holocaust. Although she is not Jewish, she always wears a necklace with the Hebrew symbol 'L'Chaim' ('to life') around her neck, which also inspired her choice of hashtags. In our interview she reflects upon her smiling pictures (my translation):

> I've been thinking about posting the pictures for a long time. ... because of the smile; actually, it's a serious topic behind the memorial. But then I thought to myself, this history belongs to us, we have to accept it. I accepted it and try to do everything differently in my life than was done then. I just don't have the right words right now 🤭 [Emoji 'Face with Hand Over Mouth', C.B.]. I am very cosmopolitan, take an interest in other cultures [...]. I am very interested in Israel and the Jewish culture and then I just thought, because I am somehow at 'peace' with all this, I can smile on my pictures at the memorial.

Just as in the cases described above, Christine's smile is not simply an articulation of happiness that demonstrates her emotional indifference, let alone disrespect, towards the Holocaust. On the contrary, Christine's smile is enacted as part of her ongoing interest in the history of the Holocaust and, from her point of view, an emotionally meaningful practice of remembrance and commemoration. As such, her 'happy picture' fulfils a similar function as the other digital self-representations with a more 'serious' tone that I have described above, and it even goes one step further: for Christine, her picture becomes part of a process of figuring out her personal way of commemorating the past. In her case, this is achieved through a smile as an emotional practice that acknowledges the horrors of the Holocaust while still expressing confidence and even happiness about how the world unified against the crimes of the past.

Conclusion

The ethnographic examples in this article demonstrate that digital self-representations at sites of difficult heritage can constitute complex practices of emotional engagement with the past. If memorials to atrocities serve as a reminder of particular pasts that affect us through our knowing and feeling bodies, then digital technologies can become media for relating to the past through one's own body and making these particular relationships publicly visible.

While many of these practices of digital self-representation are not entirely new and photographic portraits in front of memorials have been a part of tourists' photographic routines for decades, new digital technologies still enhance the ubiquity, frequency and style (e.g. selfies) of mediated self-representations at such sites. Even more crucially, they allow visitors to digitally share these representations with their friends and the global public. While also the sharing of and talking about such representations is not a genuinely new phenomenon, digital infrastructures and especially social media platforms afford a dynamic renegotiation of self-representation related to the Holocaust. However, the significant transformations of memory practices that we are currently witnessing in relation to digital media are not simply an effect of technological change. They go hand in hand with broader socio-cultural transformations. Not only the technologies of self-representation change, also the cultures of self-representation do.

While the critics of 'selfie culture' make a valid point in criticising emotional indifference towards the Holocaust, we need to look more closely at these practices in order to see whether they are, indeed, articulating emotional indifference. As I have shown, many of these practices do the exact opposite. This argument is not supposed to prevent a critique of emotional indifference towards the Holocaust. In fact, considering the current rise of populist truth-making in public debates, this critique seems more crucial than ever. The Holocaust Memorial has already been questioned concerning its legitimacy by right-wing politicians, most prominently by Björn Höcke, who called it the 'memorial of shame' ('Denkmal der Schande') and asked for a '180 degree turn in memory politics'.[7] Careful analytical attention to how difficult heritage is experienced, how visitors *feel* about it and how the *digital* transformations of memory cultures shape these emotional relationships is of particular value in the light of such developments.

It might be tempting to see a direct connection between the digital transformations of memory cultures and a supposed growth in emotional indifference towards the past. Indeed, there might be some truth in my interviewee Adam's observation that many people are 'filtering their daily interactions through the lens of their phone screen' and are, thus, 'removed from true "first-hand" experience', which results in experiences in which 'things just don't have the same gravity' (see full quote above). At the same time, however, blaming 'selfie culture' and equating digital media practices with 'superficial' remembrance is much too simplistic, as Adam demonstrates himself through his social media post. Digital devices can become powerful media of personal emotional engagements in their own right.

This argument resonates with broader discussions in the field of museums and heritage regarding the transformations of contemporary cultures of remembrance. Juliane Brauer and Aleida Assmann (2011) suggest considering the process of historical imagination and presencing of the past ('Vergegenwärtigung') when looking at the entanglements of media and commemoration in Holocaust remembrance. Brauer and Assmann's case is different from my own, since they studied video projects conducted by German school students working with video interviews with Holocaust survivors and witnesses. The researchers' observations about the historical imagination, however, are relevant for my case as well. They argue that practices of presencing the past through media entail far more than subjective emotional immersion into this past. Instead, they are about connecting to the past in order to make this past a meaningful part of one's own *present* (Brauer and Assmann 2011: 80).

This argument also corresponds with what Thomas Thiemeyer (2018) has suggested regarding current transformations of Holocaust commemoration in both Germany and Israel. Together with Jackie Feldman, Tanja Seider and students from universities in both countries, they explored contemporary practices of remembrance (also touching upon the 'Yolocaust' debate and digital media), leading Thiemeyer to observe an ongoing transition towards a 'performative culture of remembrance' ('performative Erinnerungskultur', Thiemeyer 2018: 18). The growing performative aspect of Holocaust remembrance, he suggests, is anchored in how visitors *individually* appropriate the past, how they come to make it their own and meaningful for their present (18).

This observation of a growing tendency towards *individual* appropriation in Holocaust remembrance does not suggest that memory practices become entirely fragmented. Instead, it points us to the growing importance of *personal* connections to the past for a generation of young people who are increasingly estranged from the shared historical experience of WW2. My own ethnographic analysis supports these observations, and it highlights the crucial role that digital media can play for visitors in their practices of personally relating to the past through emotional practices and, thus, of making the past part of each visitor's own present.

Looking at social media, we also see that for many visitors, performing and experiencing their personal relationship to the past is not the end of the story. Instead, they are often *shared*. The personal experiences of individuals in contemporary digital cultures of remembrance have high socio-cultural value and can contribute to the constitution of and exchange within 'emotional communities' (Gregory 2014). Consequently, when emotional relationships to the past are shared on platforms such as *Instagram* and *Facebook*, this is where an emerging both performative and digital culture of Holocaust remembrance constitutes its particular social impact.

That is to say, if we follow Eli Wiesel in acknowledging that 'it can happen again', this does not call for a general condemnation of digital media practices at sites of difficult heritage. On the contrary, as we grow into a society without witnesses of that time and weaker personal connections to it, even digital self-representations – or maybe *especially* digital self-representations – can play an important role in the making and sharing of personal experiences. To the critics, these practices might seem mundane, shallow and inappropriate articulations of emotional indifference towards the Holocaust – the term 'selfie culture' is representing this perspective. For many visitors, however, these practices can become different yet meaningful ways of relating to the past.

Acknowledgements

I want to express my gratitude to all visitors and interviewees involved in this project for sharing their experience of the memorial and for their trust in giving me permission to use their pictures as part of an ethnographic text. I am also thankful to the Foundation Memorial to the Murdered Jews of Europe for providing the space to conduct interviews and getting in touch with visitors; to several student assistants (Antje Hoffmann, Wesley Merkes, Christian Hörner, Alexander Köpke) for their work; and to the members of the Centre for Anthropological Research on Museums and Heritage (CARMAH) and its director Sharon Macdonald for their invaluable support. The research was carried out in the context of Christoph Bareither's membership at the Centre for Anthropological research on Museums and Heritage (CARMAH) in Berlin, funded by the Alexander von Humboldt Foundation as part of the research award for Sharon Macdonald's Alexander von Humboldt Professorship.

Notes

1 https://www.stiftung-denkmal.de/memorials/memorial-to-the-murdered-jews-of-europe/?lang=en (accessed 1 May 2020).
2 https://www.stiftung-denkmal.de/memorials/memorial-to-the-murdered-jews-of-europe/?lang=en (accessed 1 May 2020). See section "Peter Eisenman about the Memorial".
3 https://www.spiegel.de/international/spiegel-interview-with-holocaust-monument-architect-peter-eisenman-how-long-does-one-feel-guilty-a-355252.html (accessed 1 May 2020).
4 https://www.bbc.com/news/world-europe-38675835 (accessed 1 May 2020).
5 https://www.facebook.com/ajplusenglish/videos/holocaust-selfie-culture-yolocaust/914675568673951/ (accessed 1 May 2020).
6 http://www.historyplace.com/speeches/wiesel.htm (accessed 1 May 2020).
7 https://www.sueddeutsche.de/politik/parteien-die-hoecke-rede-von-dresden-in-wortlaut-auszuegen-dpa.urn-newsml-dpa-com-20090101-170118-99-928143, translated by the author (accessed 1 May 2020).

References

Abu-Lughod, L. and C. Lutz (eds). 1990. *Language and the Politics of Emotion.* Cambridge, UK, New York, Paris: Cambridge University Press.

Ahmed, S. 2014. *The Cultural Politics of Emotion,* 2nd ed. Edinburgh: Edinburgh University Press.

Bareither, C. 2019. 'Doing emotion through digital media: an ethnographic perspective on media practices and emotional affordances', *Ethnologia Europaea,* 49(1): 7–23.

Boellstorff, T., B. Nardi, C. Pearce, and T. L. Taylor. 2012. *Ethnography and Virtual Worlds: A Handbook of Method.* Princeton: Princeton University Press.

Brauer, J., and A. Assmann. 2011. 'Bilder, Gefühle, Erwartungen: über die emotionale Dimension von Gedenkstätten und den Umgang von Jugendlichen mit dem Holocaust', *Geschichte und Gesellschaft,* 37(1): 72–103.

Breidenstein, G., S. Hirschauer, H. Kalthoff, and B. Nieswand. 2015. *Ethnografie: die Praxis der Feldforschung,* 2nd ed. Constance, Munich: UVK.

Campbell, G., L. Smith, and M. Wetherell. 2017. 'Nostalgia and heritage: potentials, mobilisations and effects', *International Journal of Heritage Studies*, 23(7): 609–611.

Dekel, I. 2013. *Mediation at the Holocaust Memorial in Berlin*. New York: Palgrave Macmillan.

Dinhopl, A. and U. Gretzel. 2016. 'Selfie-taking as touristic looking', *Annals of Tourism Research* 57 (January): 126–139.

Douglas, K. 2017. 'Youth, trauma and memorialisation: the selfie as witnessing', *Memory Studies*: 1–16.

Eckel, J., J. Ruchatz, and S. Wirth. 2018. 'The selfie as image (and) practice: approaching digital Self-Photography', in J. Eckel, J. Ruchatz, and S. Wirth (eds), *Exploring the Selfie: Historical, Theoretical and Analytical Approaches to Digital Self-Photography*, 1–23. London, New York, Shanghai: Palgrave Macmillan.

Emerson, R. M., R. I. Fretz, and L. L. Shaw. 2011. *Writing Ethnographic Fieldnotes*, 2nd ed. Chicago; London: The University of Chicago Press.

Glaser, B. G., and A. L. Strauss. 2006 (1967). *The Discovery of Grounded Theory: Strategies of Qualitative Research*. New Brunswick, London: Aldine Transaction.

Golańska, D. 2015. 'Affective spaces, sensuous engagements: in quest of a synaesthetic approach to "dark memorials"', *International Journal of Heritage Studies*, 21(8): 773–790.

Gregory, J. 2014. 'Connecting with the past through social media: the "beautiful buildings and cool places Perth has lost" Facebook Group', *International Journal of Heritage Studies*, 21(1): 22–45.

Habermas, J. 1999. 'Der Zeigefinger: die Deutschen und ihr Denkmal', *DIE ZEIT*. https://www.zeit.de/1999/14/199914.denkmal.2_.xml/komplettansicht (accessed 1st February 2020).

Hilmar, T. 2016. 'Storyboards of remembrance: representations of the past in visitors photography at Auschwitz', *Memory Studies*, 9(4): 455–470.

Hine, C. 2015. *Ethnography for the Internet: Embedded, Embodied and Everyday*. London: Bloomsbury.

Hochschild, A. R. 2003. *The Managed Heart: Commercialization of Human Feeling*. Berkeley: University of California Press.

Kirshenblatt-Gimblett, B. 1998. *Destination Culture: Tourism, Museums, and Heritage*. Berkeley: University of California Press.

Knudsen, B. T. 2008. 'Emotional geography: authenticity, embodiment and cultural heritage' *Ethnologia Europaea*, 36(2): 5–15.

Larsen, J. 2008. 'Practices and flows of digital photography: an ethnographic framework', *Mobilities*, 3(1): 141–160.

Larsen, J. 2014. 'The (im)mobile life of digital photographs: the case of tourist photography', in J. Larsen, and M. Sandbye (eds), *Digital Snaps: The New Face of Photography*, 25–46. London: Tauris.

Levi, P. 2017. *The Drowned and the Saved*. New York: Simon & Schuster.

Macdonald, S. 2009. *Difficult Heritage: Negotiating the Nazi Past in Nuremberg and Beyond*. London, New York: Routledge.

Macdonald, S. 2013. *Memorylands: Heritage and Identity in Europe Today*. London, New York: Routledge.

Macdonald, S. 2015. 'Is "difficult heritage" still "difficult"?', *Museum*, 67(1-4): 6–22.

Pink, S., H. A. Horst, J. Postill, L. Hjorth, T. Lewis, and J. Tacchi. 2016. *Digital Ethnography: Principles and Practice.* Los Angeles: Sage.

Reckwitz, A. 2017. 'Practices and their affects', in A. Hui, E. Shove, and T. R. Schatzki (eds), *The Nexus of Practices: Connections, Constellations, Practitioners*, 114–125. London, New York: Routledge.

Sather-Wagstaff, J. 2008. 'Picturing experience: a tourist-centered perspective on commemorative historical sites', *Tourist Studies,* 8(1): 77–103.

Sather-Wagstaff, J. 2017. 'Making polysense of the world: affect, memory, heritage', in D. P. Tolia-Kelly, E. Waterton, and S. Watson (eds), *Heritage, Affect and Emotion: Politics, Practices and Infrastructures*, 12–29. London, New York: Routledge.

Scheer, M. 2012. 'Are emotions a kind of practice (and is that what makes them have a history)? A bourdieuian approach to understanding emotion', *History and Theory,* 51: 193–220.

Scheer, M. 2016. 'Emotionspraktiken: Wie man über das Tun an die Gefühle herankommt', in M. Beitl and I. Schneider (eds), *Emotional Turn?! Europäisch ethnologische Zugänge zu Gefühlen & Gefühlswelten: Beiträge der 27. Österreichischen Volkskundetagung in Dornbirn vom 29. Mai – 1. Juni 2013*, 15–36. Wien: Selbstverlag des Vereins für Volkskunde.

Smith, L. and G. Campbell. 2015. 'The elephant in the room: heritage, affect and emotion', in W. Logan, M. Nic Craith, and U. Kockel (eds), *A Companion to Heritage Studies*, 443–460. Oxford: Wiley-Blackwell.

Smith, L., M. Wetherell, and G. Campbell (eds). 2018. *Emotion, Affective Practices, and the Past in the Present.* Milton: Routledge.

Strauss, A. L., and J. Corbin. 1994. 'Grounded theory methodology: an overview', in N. K. Denzin and Y. S. Lincoln (eds), *Handbook of Qualitative Research*, 273–285. London, New York: SAGE.

Thiemeyer, T. 2018. 'Erinnerungspraxis und Erinnerungskultur', in T. Thiemeyer, J. Feldman, and T. Seider (eds), *Erinnerungspraxis zwischen gestern und morgen: Wie wir uns heute an NS-Zeit und Shoah erinnern: Ein deutsch-israelisches Studienprojekt*, 7–20. Tübingen: Tübinger Vereinigung für Volkskunde.

Tolia-Kelly, D. P., E. Waterton, and S. Watson (eds). 2017. *Heritage, Affect and Emotion: Politics, Practices and Infrastructures.* London, New York: Routledge.

Tschofen, B. 2016. ',„Eingeatmete Geschichtsträchtigkeit": Konzepte des Erlebens in der Geschichtskultur', in S. Willner, G. Koch, and S. Samida (eds), *Doing History: Performative Praktiken in der Geschichtskultur*, 137–150. Münster, New York: Waxmann.

Urry, J., and J. Larsen. 2011. *The Tourist Gaze 3.0*, 3rd ed. London: Sage.

Waterton, E. and S. Watson. 2015. 'A war long forgotten: feeling the past in an English country village', *Angelaki*, 20(3): 89–103.

Wetherell, M. 2013. 'Feeling rules, atmospheres and affective practice: some reflections on the analysis of emotional episodes', in C. Maxwell and P. Aggleton (eds), *Privilege, Agency and Affect,* 35, 221–239. London: Palgrave Macmillan UK.

Wetherell, M., L. Smith, and G. Campbell. 2018. 'Introduction: affective heritage practices', in L. Smith, M. Wetherell, and G. Campbell (eds), *Emotion, Affective Practices, and the Past in the Present*, 1–21. Milton: Routledge.

Witcomb, A. 2007. 'Beyond nostalgia: the role of affect in generating historical understanding at heritage sites', in S. E. R. Watson, S. Macleod, and S. J. Knell (eds), *Museum Revolutions: Museums and Change*, 263–275. London: Routledge.

Witcomb, A. 2012. 'On memory, affect and atonement: the Long Tan Memorial Cross(es)', *Historic Environment*, 24(3): 35–42.

Witcomb, A. 2013. 'Using immersive and interactive approaches to interpreting traumatic experiences for tourists: potentials and limitations', in R. Staiff (ed.), *Heritage and Tourism: Place, Encounter, Engagement*, 152–170. London: Routledge.

Making Differences to Doing Diversity in Museums and Heritage. An Afterword

Sharon Macdonald

This book has presented a diverse range of attempts to make differences – and to engage more diversity – in museums and heritage. Our focus is on Berlin but similar developments and initiatives are underway elsewhere in Germany and beyond. Not only representing greater social and cultural diversity in museum and heritage contents but also engaging a greater range of participants in the doing of museums and heritage themselves are hallmarks of processes that are ongoing in many parts of the world.

The forms that diversity and diversification take, however, themselves vary and the direction of travel is not simply towards more of both. Which differences and which ways of doing diversity are given prominence may differ not only from one heritage organization to the next but also between countries, and newer emphases – such as on global South and North disparities – may displace ones that were given more attention previously, such as class. Moreover, museums and heritage continue to be used as powerful tools for performing homogeneous, usually national, narratives, and there are even retroactive moves to reinforce this, as well as instances of attempts to wipe out heritage that speaks to other histories and experiences, as Russia is perpetrating in Ukraine.

Evident in our Berlin ethnography – *Making Differences* – is that the drive towards increasing diversity in museums and heritage comes from a wide range of actors. In the case of Berlin, the State – in the form both of the national and city-level governments – has espoused the expansion of diversity as a goal and supported it through certain funding streams. In setting up their own diversity initiatives, civil institutions, such as museums and heritage sites, may respond to and make use of these but the impetus is certainly not only from the State and is usually multiple. It is often driven by particular members of staff, such as directors or curators, but these do not operate alone but are inspired (or deterred) by what they see happening elsewhere, including internationally. Freelance staff, who are not so embedded in existing structures, are sometimes especially able to make significant differences. All are likely to be influenced too by other players, such as specific interest groups and activists that mobilise around heritage, as well as by wider discourse and commentary, of which academic contributions are part. Yet, as our wide range of cases is able to show, not all heritage developments are channelled through established heritage organizations. The push to do heritage differently – as we see, for example, in the case of street-renaming and Pride marches – can and does also come directly from those who feel personally moved, usually by their specific subject-positions but also through forms of solidarity across difference, to make change. Engaging ethnographically with such a range of cases as we have done in the *Making Differences* project and in this book makes this multiplicity of impulse evident, as well as the fact that actors may occupy multiple positions and that they and their ideas may flow between organizations. Acknowledging this is itself important as it means that difference-making is likely to be more effective if it engages with a broader range of actors. That effective diversification works best with a diversity of participants might sound self-evident but that is certainly not what always happens in practice. As such, it is worth stating explicitly as one ingredient for doing diversity not just more but better.

Another consequence of the multiple, mixed and entangled impulses involved in doing diversity is that their politics are not necessarily clear-cut. The same development might be equally motivated by a sense of social justice or cynical opportunism, and, equally, it might lead to multiple and even contradictory results. Highlighting such ambivalences and complexities – and the specificities and context-dependencies of practice – is what ethnography typically does, and is sometimes accused of *only* doing. Chapters here look in detail at specific cases and they often highlight complexities – and this is important not least because what goes on 'in real life' is generally more mixed-up and multiple than in abstracted and theoretical accounts. But in doing so, ethnographers – including those writing in this volume – also seek to show where generalizations and simplifications are inadequate, how existing theorizations or concepts need nuancing, and where process does not lead straightforwardly to expected outcomes. Ethnography contributes an attuning sensibility – a highlighting of more usually taken-for-granted assumptions and ways of thinking or doing, and thus of possible pitfalls and potholes along the road to making differences.

Ethnography propels its practitioners into contexts that exceed their research design – even where the ethnographer plays a major role in shaping the initiative that they are studying (as is the case in several chapters here). In the *Making Differences* project this meant into contexts in which the questions and concepts with which we were working and grappling, were being worked with and through or even against by those who we sought to understand. We were, therefore, also being attuned by our encounters and interlocutors. As such, those reflections and ideas that we might call our own were indelibly shaped not just by analysis of what those in our field took for granted but by an extraordinarily rich and self-reflective field of debate and practice. The fact that there is so much great thought and action out there – sometimes in unexpected places – underlines how worthwhile it is to expand the range of those involved in any diversity initiatives, which means going beyond those who already see themselves as diversity experts.

At the risk of overlooking richness and complexity and/or of stating the obvious, two lists follow: the first is of some of the problems or hurdles involved in doing diversity in museums and heritage that can be found in the preceding chapters; and the second is of some of the ways in which these can be addressed. Rather than spell out in which chapters and in relation to which particular examples or details they occur, the statements are here presented baldly. While this may make them seem cruder than they would otherwise be, hopefully this strategy can help enlist the reader – you – in thinking back or, indeed, going on to search through further, perhaps in finding contradictions as well as substantiation. As the lists are far from exhaustive, they should also be regarded as open-ended – for you to add to as you wish and not only with examples from this book.

Challenges for doing diversity in museums and heritage

1. Terms and concepts – certain words offend or mobilise and they can carry inflections that are not evident to all who encounter them. Their effects – especially deleterious ones – may only start showing up as processes develop. Classifications can constrain more than participants realise. Translations are often especially tricky.
2. Categories and assumptions from the past are easily carried forward invisibly and by stealth. This can happen within infrastructures such as databases and/or through organizational structures, images and language.
3. What 'diversity' means – and the models of diversity in operation – vary, with participants easily being unaware of this or of the assumptions that certain models carry (e.g. that cultures are neatly distinct, or that there is a fixed set of differences).
4. Polarization and binarization are ever-present tendencies, especially in debates about contentious heritage (and perhaps especially in Germany). This can overlook connections and reduce positions in ways that hinder productive debate and developments.
5. Reflecting on problematic categories and processes can face a risk of reproducing the language or terms used (in chapters here referred to as the 'diversity double-bind' and the 'double presence of difference').
6. Undertaking diversity work in an 'additive mode' – 'more diversity please!' – without addressing how diversity is being conceptualised may lead to implicit hierarchies or unintended equivalences being instated or to a depoliticization of difference.
7. Practice is never just the implementation of conscious decision-making – it also involves accidents, emotions, obstinate objects, obstinate people, media affordances, time-constraints and much more. The devil – where different outcomes to those wanted result – is often in the detail.

What can be done

1. Increase the diversity of participants, including beyond usual suspects and categories. Mix things and people up. Embrace expertises but don't let them silence other inputs.
2. Develop formats that allow people to come together in open-ended ways, with enough time for addressing premisses, changing parameters and reshaping directions.
3. Pay attention to language and categories, drawing among other things on existing studies and guides.

4. Co-critically examine which notions and models of diversity and difference – and structuring of questions and debates – are being mobilised, and consider whether to do otherwise.
5. Explicitly address what might need to be unlearned – especially established and taken-for-granted ways of doing things.
6. Draw on as many sources as possible – including from other cases and informal discussion (especially of where things have not worked out) – to become attuned to potential obstinacies and devils.
7. Harness the insights of ethnographers – including those in this book.

Notes on Contributors

Christoph Bareither is Professor of Historical and Cultural Anthropology at the Ludwig Uhland Institute (LUI) at the University of Tübingen. Between 2017 and 2021, he was Junior Professor for Media Anthropology at CARMAH (the Centre for Anthropological Research on Museums and Heritage) at the Humboldt-Universität zu Berlin. His research is concerned with the transformations of everyday practices and experiences enabled by digital technologies. He is especially interested in the fields of media and digital anthropology, museum and heritage studies, popular culture and game studies, digital methods, ethnographic data analysis, and the ethnography of emotions.

Magdalena Buchczyk is a Junior Professor for Social Anthropology and Cultural Expressions at CARMAH (the Centre for Anthropological Research on Museums and Heritage) and in the Institute for European Ethnology, Humboldt-Universität zu Berlin. Her research focuses on the ethnographic exploration of material culture, museums, heritage and craft, with fieldwork in Germany, Poland, Romania and the UK. She is also Senior Research Fellow at the University of Bristol and has previously worked at Goldsmiths and UCL and has co-curated exhibitions at the Horniman Museum, Pilsudski Institute and Constance Howard Gallery in London as well as Coexist Gallery in Bristol. Her publications include articles in *Museum Anthropology*, *Journal of Museum Ethnography*, *Oxford Review of Education* and *Journal of American Folklore*. Magdalena Buchczyk's monograph, *Weaving Europe, Crafting the Museum*, based on her research on the collections of the Museum of European Cultures, will appear in 2023.

Nazlı Cabadağ is a doctoral researcher who worked on the Making Differences project between 2017 and 2021. She has studied modes of solidarity with Turkish-speaking queer communities based in Berlin and has an MA in Cultural Studies from Sabancı University in Istanbul. She has co-authored an article in the book *Doing Tolerance: Urban Interventions and Forms of Participation* (2020).

Larissa Förster is a research associate at CARMAH. Between 2016 and 2019, she was a postdoctoral researcher working on the Making Differences project. She is now head of the Department for Cultural Goods and Collections from Colonial Contexts of the German Lost Art Foundation. She has co-edited *Provenienzforschung in ethnografischen Sammlungen der Kolonialzeit* (2018) and *Museumsethnologie – Eine Einführung: Theorien, Debatten, Praktiken* (2019).

Chiara Garbellotto is a doctoral researcher based at the Institute of European Ethnology, Humboldt-Universität zu Berlin and at the Humanities of Nature department of the Museum für Naturkunde Berlin. She worked on the *Making Differences* project at CARMAH (the Centre for Anthropological Research on Museums and Heritage) between 2017 and 2020. With a background in cultural anthropology and museum studies, her research and work focus on ecologies of public engagement and collaborative practices in between (natural) sciences and the arts. Moving from feminist STS sensibilities, she explores more-than-human worlds co-designing workshops and events and tinkering with non-linear storytelling and speculative fiction.

Christine Gerbich is a doctoral researcher who between 2016 and 2021 worked on the *Making Differences* project at CARMAH (the Centre for Anthropological Research on Museums and Heritage), Humboldt-Universität zu Berlin. She conducted research in the Museum for Islamic Art in the Pergamon Museum in Berlin. She previously completed an MA at University of Mannheim. She is co-editor (with Susan Kamel) of *Experimentierfeld Museum. Internationale Perspektiven auf Museum, Islam und Inklusion* (2014), and has also published in *Museum and Society*, and in *Islam and Heritage in Europe. Pasts, Presents and Future Possibilities* (eds Puzon, Macdonald and Shatanawi, 2021).

Rikke Gram is a junior curator at the Museum Pankow, Berlin. Between 2015–2018 she was a Masters student of European Ethnology working on the *Making Differences* project at CARMAH (the Centre for Anthropological Research on Museums and Heritage), Humboldt-Universität zu Berlin. From 2019–2021 she was a research fellow at the Institute for Migration Research and Intercultural Studies at the University of Osnabrück. Previously she completed a Masters degree in History and International Development at Roskilde University. She has published *Berliner Blätter* and in *Islam and Heritage in Europe. Pasts, Presents and Future Possibilities* (eds Puzon, Macdonald and Shatanawi, 2021).

Duane Jethro is a Junior Research Fellow at the Centre for Curating the Archive at the University of Cape Town. He thinks and works with notions of archive in its manifold forms. He has held a postdoctoral position at CARMAH (Centre for Anthropological Research on Museums and Heritage) at the Humboldt-Universität zu Berlin, and the Archive and Public Culture Research Initiative, at the University of Cape Town. His published work includes the 2020 book *Heritage Formation and the Senses in Post-Apartheid South Africa: Aesthetics of Power*. He has published in the journals *Material Religion*, the *International Journal of Heritage Studies* and *Tourist Studies*.

Sharon Macdonald is Director of CARMAH (the Centre for Anthropological Research on Museums and Heritage), which she established within the remit of her Alexander von Humboldt Professorship in Social Anthropology at the Humboldt-Universität zu Berlin.

Recent publications include *Heritage Futures* (as co-author, 2020), *Refugees Welcome? Difference and Diversity in a Changing Germany* (as co-editor, 2019), and *Islam and Heritage in Europe: Pasts, Presents and Future Possibilities* (as co-editor, 2021).

Harriet Merrow is a junior curator at the Museum Neukölln in Berlin. She worked on the Making Differences project from 2017 to 2020 and conducted visitor research in museums in Austria and the United States. Previously she completed an MA in European Ethnology at the Humboldt University of Berlin.

Tahani Nadim is Junior Professor for Socio-Cultural Anthropology in a joint appointment between the Museum für Naturkunde Berlin and the Institute of European Ethnology, Humboldt-Universität zu Berlin and a researcher at CARMAH (the Centre for Anthropological Research on Museums and Heritage). She co-heads the interdisciplinary research centre Humanities of Nature at the Museum für Naturkunde Berlin and runs the experimental research unit Bureau for Troubles in which she collaborates with artists and curators. Her work focuses on the datafication of nature and the politics of museum collections and digitization.

Nnenna Onuoha is a doctoral researcher in Anthropology with Critical Media Practice at Harvard University. Between 2018 and 2020, she worked as a visual anthropologist on the *Making Differences* project at CARMAH (the Centre for Anthropological Research on Museums and Heritage) at the Humboldt-Universität zu Berlin.

Margareta von Oswald is an anthropologist, curator and post-doctoral researcher at CARMAH. She worked as a doctoral fellow in the *Making Differences* project from 2016 to 2021. Her forthcoming book, *Working through Colonial Collections: An Ethnography of the Ethnological Museum in Berlin* is based on ethnographic and archival research she conducted between 2013 and 2015. Recent publications include *Across Anthropology: Troubling Colonial Legacies, Museums, and the Curatorial* (edited with Jonas Tinius, 2020).

Katarzyna Puzon is an anthropologist and Research Associate at CARMAH (the Centre for Anthropological Research on Museums and Heritage), Humboldt-Universität zu Berlin. She worked as a postdoctoral researcher on the *Making Differences* project between 2016 and 2020. Her publications include, as co-editor, *Islam and Heritage in Europe: Pasts, Presents and Future Possibilities* (2021). She is currently completing a book on temporality, heritage and loss in Beirut, which is based on her long-term research in Lebanon.

Jonas Tinius is an associate member of the Centre for Anthropological Research on Museums and Heritage at the Humboldt University of Berlin and scientific coordinator of the ERC Consolidator Grant project Minor Universality: Narrative World Productions After Western Universalism. He is the editor of *Across Anthropology: Troubling Colonial Legacies, Museums, and the Curatorial* (with Margareta von Oswald, 2020). His *State of the Arts. An Anthropology of German Theatre* is in press with Cambridge University Press.

Museum

Viviane Mörmann

The Corporate Art Index

Twenty-One Ways to Work With Art

2020, 224 p., pb.
35,00 € (DE), 978-3-8376-5650-3
E-Book:
PDF: 34,99 € (DE), ISBN 978-3-8394-5650-7

Insa Müller

The Local Museum in the Global Village

Rethinking Ideas, Functions, and Practices of Local History Museums in Rapidly Changing Diverse Communities

2020, 260 p., pb., ill.
40,00 € (DE), 978-3-8376-5191-1
E-Book:
PDF: 39,99 € (DE), ISBN 978-3-8394-5191-5

Constance DeVereaux, Steffen Höhne, Martin Tröndle, Marjo Mäenpää (eds.)

Journal of Cultural Management and Cultural Policy/ Zeitschrift für Kulturmanagement und Kulturpolitik

Vol. 7, Issue 1: Digital Arts and Culture – Transformation or Transgression?

2021, 210 p., pb., ill.
44,99 € (DE), 978-3-8376-5389-2
E-Book:
PDF: 44,99 € (DE), ISBN 978-3-8394-5389-6

CPSIA information can be obtained
at www.ICGtesting.com
Printed in the USA
JSHW051455230223
38141JS00004B/24

9 783837 664096